A BASIC MUSIC
LIBRARY

A BASIC MUSIC LIBRARY

Essential Scores and Sound Recordings

FOURTH EDITION

COMPILED BY THE MUSIC LIBRARY ASSOCIATION

DANIEL F. BOOMHOWER, *Editor*

VOLUME 2: WORLD MUSIC

Edited by

LIZA VICK

AMERICAN LIBRARY ASSOCIATION

CHICAGO   2018

While extensive effort has gone into ensuring the reliability of the information in this book, the publisher makes no warranty, express or implied, with respect to the material contained herein.

ISBN: 978-0-8389-1530-1 (print)

Library of Congress Cataloging-in-Publication Data

Names: Boomhower, Daniel F., 1976– | Komara, Edward M., 1966– | Maple, Amanda, 1956– | Vick, Liza. | Music Library Association.

Title: A basic music library : essential scores and sound recordings / compiled by the Music Library Association ; Daniel F. Boomhower, editor ; Edward Komara, Amanda Maple, and Liza Vick, associate editors.

Description: Fourth edition. | Chicago : American Library Association, 2018. | Includes bibliographical references and index.

Identifiers: LCCN 2013020223 | ISBN 9780838910399 (v. 1 ; alk. paper) | ISBN 9780838915301 (v. 2 ; alk. paper) | ISBN 9780838915318 (v. 3 ; alk. paper)

Subjects: LCSH: Music—Bibliography. | Music libraries—Collection development.

Classification: LCC ML113 .B3 2017 | DDC 016.78—dc23 LC record available at https:// lccn.loc.gov/2013020223

Composition by Dianne M. Rooney in Charis SIL typeface.

⊗ This paper meets the requirements of ANSI/NISO Z39.48-1992 (Permanence of Paper)

Printed in the United States of America

22 21 20 19 18   5 4 3 2 1

CONTENTS

GENERAL INTRODUCTION

by DANIEL F. BOOMHOWER

This volume is intended to offer suggestions for anyone, regardless of musical training or experience, who is seeking to develop music collections in libraries of all kinds. While containing the thoughtful advice of librarians and scholars, these suggestions must be matched to real-world circumstances. It seems entirely unlikely that a library would need to include in its collection every item listed in this volume. Only some of the lists in this volume may be useful for one library; other institutions may need much more in a particular area than could possibly be included in this publication.

The fluid nature of the market of music materials, especially sound recordings, will make it unlikely that every item in the volume or even in a single list could be acquired at any given time. Likewise, important new publications will continue to appear that find their way into library collections through routine collection development processes. Through the listing of individual items here, the contributors and editors of this volume have strived to offer *representative* lists that might provide an indication of the nature of the various kinds of music available. Additionally, we have provided introductory information that gives an overview of particular concepts and issues relevant to the various styles of

music treated here. Through these introductions, it is hoped that the reader will become confident in extending the scope of his collection-building efforts to include content not cited here.

Library collections must serve a specific community. Identifying and acquiring the materials that are most useful to that community should remain the focus of library collecting. This volume offers generalized guidance. A "basic" music collection is not a "perfect" music collection. Indeed, the "perfect" music collection may emerge from helpful suggestions, but it is something that has to be carefully developed to be useful to real readers and listeners. With that in mind, I hope this volume is useful, and that it also serves as a point of departure.

A Basic Music Library, published in three previous editions (1978, 1983, and 1997), was originally conceived to offer collecting guidance to library selectors without a music background who often worked in public libraries and smaller academic libraries. However, with the dramatic expansion in the amount of music available and the amount of music sought by patrons in libraries of all kinds, the audience for *A Basic Music Library* may now be considered to be much larger. This would include a greater number of library selectors with training in some musical tradition, but with unequal command of all styles of music.

Reflecting the changing nature of available music and the diversity of patron interests that libraries seek to serve, *A Basic Music Library* has evolved with each successive edition. Initially, the focus was on printed materials: books and scores. In the third edition, books were no longer included and sound recordings became a dominant component of the publication. In all three of these editions, the better portion of the publication treated music in the Western art music tradition, or what is typically called "classical music." The shift from books to sound recordings in the third edition reflected both the changing nature of libraries' needs and the appearance of publications that provided suitable guidance for developing collections of music books.

This fourth edition has also adapted to changing circumstances in libraries, whether a given library seeks to sustain existing collections or to establish new music collections. Most significantly, the fourth edition will comprise three separate volumes that treat "popular music," "world music," and "classical music," respectively. This flexible format will enable users of *A Basic Music Library* to focus attention on the materials of greatest interest. To meet changing library needs, the fourth edition also incorporates:

■ expanded coverage of world music, including CDs and DVDs;

■ updated coverage of popular music, including CDs, DVDs, and songbooks;

■ integrated coverage of classical music, combining printed music with CDs and DVDs; and

■ citations that have been carefully balanced in order to offer a culturally, geographically, and stylistically diverse representation of music throughout the world.

Library collecting is the process of employing limited resources to bring together the best materials, drawn from a variety of available sources, that will serve the needs of library users at a particular time and place. The present volume was compiled in exactly the same way. There is not sufficient space to include items some may consider "basic," and some may imagine the nature of the lists included here as greatly expanding the notion of "basic." A fine line must be tread. On the one hand, too short a list begins to assume a prescriptive nature. On the other hand, too long a list can obscure what is of greatest importance. Similarly, the perception of what it might cost to build an appropriate collection in a particular musical area greatly depends on the number of items that seem necessary. The goal of the lists in this publication is to offer a representative snapshot of the scope of music from different regions of the world, in different genres, and for different instruments. From these lists, and with the guidance of the introductory essays, it should become possible to determine what is most suitable for meeting the needs of one's library and community.

Bringing this volume to completion involved significant effort on the part of many individuals and institutions. First and foremost, the contributors whose work fills these pages deserve the greatest thanks. Without their time and expertise this volume would not have been possible. Likewise, the associate editors gave enormously of their time to organize the contributions and to see that each contribution reached the page in the best and clearest form, reflective of the high standards evident in each chapter. As work on this fourth edition got underway, the editors sought counsel from a range of authorities on the nature of musical canons, and their thoughts were published in the Music Library Association's journal *Notes,* volume 64, no. 2, pages 209–247. These essays served as a counterpoise to the nitty-gritty work of defining a core selection of titles that represents as much of the world's music as possible. We are also deeply indebted to the contributors and editors of the previous editions of *A Basic Music Library,* upon whose excellent work this edition is grounded. In particular, William E. Anderson provided a significant amount of material that served as the basis of revisions for many popular and world music chapters.

VOLUME

WORLD MUSIC

2

Introduction by **LIZA VICK**

World music is difficult to categorize and document adequately, so editorial tasks for volume 2 were fraught with many difficulties and rewards. The geographic arrangement of the recommendations acts only as a framework, and not a rigid categorization. The balance between traditional and folk, popular and classical citations varies from area to area. This may indicate, for example, that classical or "art" music is more relevant in some areas than in others, but this often reflects differences in publishing output and availability rates.

Western European classical music is covered in volume 3 of this volume, so it is largely omitted here. Some small amount of duplication exists between regional sections, and certain groups are represented in more than one area (e.g., Jewish, Islamic). This reflects the true nature of world music, which is increasingly difficult to define by geographic means. It is especially difficult to separate diaspora from country-specific recordings, especially in the popular music realm (where styles fuse and evolve constantly).

In today's globalized music market, traditional and popular music are difficult to separate. The practical decision not to divide the strands for many geographic areas reflects the organic development of forms and their

degrees of interconnection. However, large geographic areas have been broken down in this way as logic dictated and to make the sections more easily navigable. These sections are North America, portions of Africa and East Asia, Indonesia, India, and the Caribbean. The divisions are undoubtedly imperfect. Recordings designated as traditional/folk are usually field recordings (sometimes compiled by an ethnomusicologist) or predominantly of a traditional music nature. Popular recordings are those generally geared toward the "world beat" market or that consist of popular genres.

Diaspora is increasingly important in world music collecting. A few areas are featured in their own sections (Jewish, sub-Saharan African, and Caribbean), while others are integrated throughout anthologies and regional areas (Islamic music, for example, is covered under "International Anthologies"; "Middle East, North Africa, Central Asia"; "Sub-Saharan Africa"; "Europe"; and others). Necessarily, not every musical diaspora is covered. It is the editor's hope that future editions will expand and augment this area as well as emerging fields of ethnomusicology that may impact recording output.

Sections are arranged by region, and into anthologies (country and regional), and individual artists and groups, with citations grouped by format (sound recordings, videos, occasional scores). The vast majority are sound recordings. General anthologies appear at the end of respective regional sections unless they span many areas of the globe or are not geographically oriented (see "International Anthologies" for additional diaspora as well as devotional works). In each chapter, up to 10 percent of the listed items have a star (★) indicating a high priority for library acquisitions.

The citations listed are intended to be representative of major cultural areas, artists, genres, and styles. They are not intended to be used in isolation but only as an informed starting point in conjunction with other expert sources. Canonicity is a tricky concept, at best, in any musical genre, and especially so in world music; so the fluidity of these listings cannot be stressed enough.

World music recordings emerged from many places, including from early ethnomusicologists in the field during the first half of the twentieth century, such as E. M. von Hornbostel (Berlin Phonogramm-Archiv), Helen Myers, and others. The second half of that century brought on the scene collector-scholars, such as Alan Lomax (Smithsonian Folkways) and Hugh Tracey (International Library of African Music). These recordings are available in their original formats in archives, and many have been preserved and released and reissued commercially. Also included here are recordings of theater and art music within largely-traditional cultures, some influenced by Western styles (for example, from China, Japan, and Korea). There are many types of music not represented on widely available recordings, not recorded at all, or available only in archives. These include music for rituals and ceremonies, religious rites considered private and sacred by the cultures they emerge from. Ethnomusicologists and librarians ideally respect these ethical dilemmas.

Citation details, including name order, name and title wording, diacritics, and spelling are largely taken from OCLC and Library of Congress authority records or from physical recordings. Limitations on space and time prevented listing every performer for anthologies, and instruments performed are omitted. Directors, producers, compilers, and editors are only included sparingly. Dates listed refer to original releases and reissues. Major series are included following the item title, and alternate languages are given selectively. Geographic sources consulted in the preparation of volume 2 include the *CIA World Factbook,* the *Getty Thesaurus of Geographic Names,* and *Nationmaster.* Citations considered essential are flagged.

Out-of-print items are included because a significant number of recordings are reissued and availability via digital media will likely change. Some titles are and will be increasingly available as MP3 downloads from free websites or online music stores like iTunes; others are available via streaming services such as Smithsonian Global Sound and Contemporary World Music (Alexander Street Press, http://alexanderstreet.com/products/music.htm). It is also important to note that Smithsonian Folkways releases originally LP material on custom CD and generally reissues back catalog materials on demand in emerging formats (such as DRM-free digital downloads). These citations are noted as CD on demand or custom CD series (www.folkways.si.edu). In addition, world music abounds on the Internet, on fee-based and free sources such as Rhapsody, Pandora, Last.fm, and Mondomix and Calabash (www.mondomix.com), as well as on YouTube (with the usual copyright caveats).

The JVC Video Anthology of World Music and Dance is a must-have set for world music libraries and is now available on DVD. Insight Media (www.insight-media.com) sells sets by area; vendors such as Lyrichord (www.lyrichord.com) and Multicultural Media (www.multiculturalmedia.com) offer them individually, in sets, and as a complete collection.

Although limitations of space and time make this volume inadequate as a sole source for collection building, it can serve as a basis for collecting when used in conjunction with other resources. The following additional (though highly selective) resources will be useful for librarians constructing a basic world music collection or familiarizing themselves with genres.

The associate editor for world music would like to thank several people without whom this section would never have reached fruition. First and foremost, the contributors and Drew Beisswenger, assistant editor, for all of their hard work, invaluable expertise, and patience. William E. Anderson (co-editor for Sound Recordings, 3rd edition) contributed legacy data and discography lists he updated during the intervening years. Virginia Danielson (former Richard F. French Librarian, Loeb Music Library, Harvard University) provided financial support for the work and much editorial advice. Beth Iseminger (former music cataloger, Harvard University) provided frequent feedback from a cataloging and world music perspective. Donne Guerra (former curatorial assistant in the Archive of World Music, Harvard University) provided information about acquisitions techniques and vendors. Yingzhen Zhang, student worker (at Harvard University), provided months of editorial assistance.

SELECTIVE LIST OF REFERENCE SOURCES

AllMusic (www.allmusic.com)

BBC Radio 3—World Music (www.bbc.co.uk/radio3/ worldmusic)

Garland Encyclopedia of World Music, Vols. 1–10 (New York: Routledge Press, 1997–2001; http://glnd .alexanderstreet.com)

Garland Handbook of . . . series (includes Latin American, Southeast Asian, African music). (New York: Routledge Press)

National Geographic Music (www.nationalgeographic .com)

World Music: The Rough Guides, Vols. 1 and 2 (London: Rough Guides, 1999–2000)

ACQUISITIONS GATEWAY WEBSITES

Ethnomusicology Research Guide, by Maureen Russell, Ethnomusicology Archive, UCLA

> http://guides.library.ucla.edu/ethno

Internet Collection and Acquisition Resources, by Michael Fling (and revised by Keith Cochran), Lilly Music Library, Indiana University (see disclaimers):

> World Music, General CDs and Videos: https://libraries.indiana.edu/internet -collection-acquisition-resources-music -library#world

Consult label directories and new acquisitions lists for libraries with strong ethnomusicology collections.

RECORDING LABELS AND DISTRIBUTORS

These labels carry a variety of recordings covering different regions and are useful for basic collecting. Label and review information courtesy of Virginia Danielson and Donna Guerra.

Archives Internationales de Musique Populaire (AIMP) (www.ville-ge.ch/meg/phonotheque.php)

Arhoolie (www.arhoolie.com)

Bear Family Records (www.bear-family.de)

Buda Musique (www.budamusique.com)

CDRoots (www.cdroots.com)

Le Chant du Monde (www.lechantdumonde.com)

Harmonia Mundi Distributors (www.harmoniamundi .com; distributes Network Medien, Ocora, Le Chant du Monde, Long Distance, among others)

Long Distance (www.longdistance.fr)

Network Medien (www.networkmedien.de/en.html)

Pan Records (www.panrecords.nl)

Rounder (www.rounder.com; carries *Alan Lomax Collection* series)

Smithsonian Folkways (www.folkways.si.edu; *Custom CD* series and many more; world music staple)

Yazoo Records (www.yazoorecords.com; released field recordings)

REVIEW SOURCES

CD Hotlist: New Releases for Libraries (http://cdhotlist .com)

Ethnomusicology, Recording Reviews and Discographies section (www.ethnomusicology.org/?OG _CurrentDisco; journal published by the Society for Ethnomusicology)

RootsWorld Recording Reviews (www.rootsworld .com/rw/)

Yearbook for Traditional Music (http://ictmusic.org/ publications/yearbook-for-traditional-music)

Consult academic and trade publications devoted to popular music, which will cover some global pop artists.

1

Folk and Traditional Music of North America

Compiled by ANDREW JUSTICE *and* MARK MCKNIGHT

Collecting folk and traditional music is perhaps more challenging than it first might seem. Defining exactly what is "folk" can be problematic, and "traditional" likewise can be an imprecise and ill-fitting term. Nonetheless, the recordings in this section fall primarily within the realm of music from North America (Canada and the United States) that derives directly or at least in part from oral tradition or that is inspired by such music. Thus many examples can be found here from myriad field recordings made by pioneer folklorist and ethnomusicologist Alan Lomax, reissued by Rounder as the *Alan Lomax Collection*, as well as music that came out of the folk-revival movement of the 1950s and 1960s (Pete Seeger; Peter, Paul, and Mary; Bob Dylan; Joan Baez; Judy Collins; and Woody Guthrie, and others), to contemporary folk and singer-songwriters (such as Iris Dement, Nanci Griffith, Leo Kottke, Bruce Cockburn, Christine Lavin, and Leonard Cohen, and others).

In many ways, this trajectory reflects the growth and development of field recording technology and the early years of the discipline of ethnomusicology, which included the pioneering efforts of musicologist Charles Seeger in the 1930s. As part of President Franklin D. Roosevelt's Works Progress Administration (WPA). The WPA included a number of initiatives to collect, record, and preserve folk and traditional music across the country that was in danger of soon being lost. Together with Alan Lomax, Alan's father John, and members of Seeger's own family—his wife Ruth and children Pete, Mike, and Peggy—as well as others who recognized the importance of preserving America's musical heritage, Seeger played a vital role in educating Americans about the significance of such music and of ensuring its availability to future generations. Also important in this endeavor were Moses Asch and Marian Distler, who in 1948 founded Folkways Records. Folkways focused not only on North American traditions but also on music from around the world and helped promote an interest in folk music that greatly influenced the American folk music revival discussed above. The Smithsonian Institution Center for Folklife and Cultural Heritage acquired Folkways in 1986 to ensure that the recordings in the catalog would remain in print. These recordings, issued as part of the Smithsonian Folkways recording project, are available on demand as custom CDs, custom cassettes, or digital downloads (www.folkways.si.edu). Among other more recent initiatives is the Rough Guide series, which began in the 1980s as a series of travel guides and has since expanded to include collections of music from virtually every geographical area and a vast array of musical styles from around the world (for example, *Rough Guide to the Music of Canada*), reflecting the concomitant rise in popularity of

world music. Among other similar independent labels, Massachusetts-based Rounder Records has specialized in American roots music, focusing on blues, bluegrass, folk, soul, Cajun, and Celtic music, and many Rounder recordings are found in these lists.

The United States is populated largely by immigrants—the same, of course, can be said of Canada. Various immigrant diasporas arrived in the New World, each with its own musical traditions and repertoire, and there will obviously be an overlap with the corresponding sections of each group's respective place of origin. In other words, some of the same tunes found here on the three-volume set *Irish Music from Cleveland* might also be found in the section of traditional Irish music in chapter 6, "Traditional and Popular Music of Europe." But it is also important to keep in mind that the processes of assimilation and cross-fertilization also are evident, and perhaps even paramount—witness, for example, Louisiana zydeco, with its elements of African, Anglo-American, French, German, and Latin American music, all of which combine to make a richly distinctive genre that is much more than any of its parts. The same can be said for Texas-Czech polka bands or the many varieties of Celtic music found across Canada, as well as the array of Latin American popular styles from the Caribbean and Central and South America that have migrated northward. In addition, it is important to consider the diversity of musical traditions within the vast array of North American aboriginal communities (Native Americans of the United States or, in Canada, First Nations, Inuit, and Métis peoples), as well as the changes reflecting assimilation and political and stylistic evolution that have occurred within these communities over time. This section includes everything from reissues of historic field recordings of Navajo songs by pioneer ethnographer Laura Boulton in the 1930s to contemporary recordings of intertribal powwows and newly composed works that combine modern and traditional sensibilities and styles in fresh and innovative ways (for example, Robert Mirabal and Rare Tribal Mob's *Music from a Painted Cave*).

It should also be noted that any discussion of non-native folk and traditional music in Canada and the United States will include, to a large degree, the music from the British Isles and from Africa. These two traditions serve as the foundation not only for much of the music in this chapter but also for many of the musical styles and genres found elsewhere in the book: country, bluegrass, rock, pop, blues, rhythm and blues, hip-hop, gospel, and other contemporary American popular genres. This fact demonstrates the reality that music does not always fit neatly into predefined labels or categories. While maintaining an emphasis on Anglo-American and African American music, we have attempted to provide a representative sample of many other diasporic traditions, while realizing that the diversity of immigrant traditions within our borders may simply be too vast and complex to be reflected adequately in a "basic" music collection. The *Garland Encyclopedia of World Music, Volume 3: United States and Canada* is an excellent source for further information on music of the multitude of immigrant groups that have settled in these two countries.

Although we might generally think of folk and traditional music in North America as being rooted in music of past generations, it is in fact dynamic and ever-changing. New styles, based on these various roots, constantly emerge, evolve, and develop in new and always interesting ways that reflect the reality of global interactions in the twenty-first century.

This chapter is divided into two main sections—Canada (French and British) and the United States—with the latter comprising six major subsections: African American (Folk), Anglo-American (Traditional and Modern Folk), French (Cajun and Zydeco), Hawaiian, Native American, and Immigrant Diasporas (Hispanic music in the United States is covered in the section "Mexico and Southwestern United States" in chapter 2; for Jewish music in North America, see chapter 7.) We have attempted to include anthologies of various performers that provide general overviews of particular styles or traditions, as well as representative recordings of individual artists. This chapter was completed with the invaluable help of students Katie Buehner, Leah Cole, Anna Perkins Griner, and James Wintle.

CANADA
FRENCH AND BRITISH

INDIVIDUAL ARTISTS AND GROUPS

1   Baillargeon, Hélène, and Alan Mills. *Chansons d'Acadie* [Folk Songs of Acadia]. Custom Compact Disc Series. Smithsonian Folkways: FW 6923. 1956, 2000s. CD.

2   Bottine Souriante. *Anthologie.* Productions Mille-Pattes: 675270204122. 2001. CD.

3   Cockburn, Bruce. *Life Short Call Now.* Rounder: 11661-3244-2. 2006. CD.

4   Cormier, Joseph. *Joseph Cormier and Friends: Old Time Wedding Reels and Other Favorite Scottish Fiddle Tunes* (Connie MacGillivray, Edmond Boudreau, Lonnie Cormier, and Jim Spellman). Rounder: CD 7013. 1992. CD.

5   Hemsworth, Wade. *Folk Songs of the Canadian North Woods.* Smithsonian Folkways: FW 6821. 1955, 1990s. CD.

6   Holmes, Fraser, and the North Shore Singers. *Songs from Cape Breton Island.* Custom Compact Disc Series. Smithsonian Folkways: FE 4450. 1955, 2001. CD.

7   LeBlanc, Suzie. *Tout passé: chants d'Acadie.* Atma Classique: ACD 2 2522. 2007. CD.

8   Lightfoot, Gordon. *The Very Best of Gordon Lightfoot, Vols. 1 and 2.* BGO Records: BGOCD 703. 1975, 2006. CD.

9   MacMaster, Natalie. *Yours Truly.* Rounder: 1166170652. 2006. CD.

10 McGarrigle, Kate, and Anna McGarrigle
    10.1 *French Record: Entre la jeunesse et la tendresse.* La Tribu Canada: 7217. 1981, 2003. CD.
    10.2 *Love Over and Over.* Hannibal: D 31807. 1983, 1997. CD.
    10.3 *Tell My Sister.* Nonesuch: 2-527267. 1976, 2011. 3 CDs.

11 Sainte-Marie, Buffy. *The Best of Buffy Sainte-Marie.* Vanguard Twofer. Vanguard: VCD-3/4. 1970, 1986. CD.

12 Tremblay, Lucie Blue. *Lucie Blue Tremblay.* Maggie and Shanti Musique: MSMCD 1001. 1986, 1998. CD.

13 Tyson, Ian
    13.1 *And Stood There Amazed.* Vanguard: VCD 79471. 1991. CD.
    13.2 *Songs from the Gravel Road.* Vanguard: 79787-2. 2005. CD.

14 Wailin' Jennys. *Firecracker.* Red House: RHR CD 195. 2006. CD.

ANTHOLOGIES

15 *Alberta: Wild Roses, Northern Lights.* Smithsonian Folkways: SFW CD 40538. 1900s, 2006. CD.

16 *Classic Canadian Songs* (Brenda Dalen, compiler). Smithsonian Folkways: SFW CD 40539. 1953, 2006. CD.

17 *The Doukhobors of British Columbia.* Custom Compact Disc Series. Smithsonian Folkways: FR 8972. 1962, 2001. CD.

18 *Folk Music from Nova Scotia.* Smithsonian Folkways: FM 4006. 1956, 2001. CD.

19 *Folksongs of Saskatchewan.* Custom Compact Disc Series. Smithsonian Folkways: FE 4312. 1963, 2000. CD.

20 *The Heart of Cape Breton: Fiddle Music Recorded Live along the Ceilidh Trail.* Smithsonian Folkways: SFW CD 40491. 2000, 2002. CD.

21 ★*Masters of French Canadian Dances, Vol. 1* (Joseph Allard). Custom Compact Disc Series. Smithsonian Folkways: RF 110. 1979, 2000s. CD.

22 ★*Masters of French Canadian Music, Vol. 2* (Alfred Montmarquette). Custom Compact Disc Series. Smithsonian Folkways: RF 111. 1980, 2000s. CD.

23 ★*Masters of French Canadian Music, Vol. 3* (Gabriel Labbé and Philippe Bruneau). Custom Compact Disc Series. Smithsonian Folkways: RBF 114. 1980, 1999. CD.

24 ★*Masters of French Canadian Music, Vol. 4* (Henri Lacroix, Théodore Duguay, Joseph Plante, and Joseph Guilmette). Custom Compact Disc Series. Smithsonian Folkways: RF 115. 1982, 2001. CD.

25 *Rough Guide to the Music of Canada.* Rough Guide. World Music Network: RGNET 1125 CD. 2005. CD.

26 ★*35 Years of Stony Plain.* Stony Plain: SPCD 1354. 2011. 2 CDs, DVD.

27 *Traditional Music from Cape Breton Island.* Nimbus: NI 5383. 1993. CD.

UNITED STATES
AFRICAN AMERICAN FOLK

INDIVIDUAL ARTISTS AND GROUPS

28 Belleville A Cappella Choir (Alan Lomax, compiler). *Southern Journey, Vol. 11: Honor the Lamb.* Alan Lomax Collection. Rounder: CD 1711. 1961, 1998. CD.

29 Carolina Chocolate Drops. *Dona Got a Ramblin' Mind.* Music Maker: MMCD 76. 2006. CD.

30 Cotten, Elizabeth. *Freight Train and Other North Carolina Folk Songs.* Smithsonian Folkways: CD SF 40009. 1958, 1989. CD.

31 Havens, Richie. *Nobody Left to Crown.* Verve Forecast: B0011631-02. 2008. CD.

32 Jackson, John. *Rappahannock Blues.* Smithsonian Folkways: SFW 40181. 1970, 2010. CD.

33 Jenkins, Ella
  33.1 *African American Folk Rhythms* (Goodwill Spiritual Choir of Monumental Baptist Church). Smithsonian Folkways: SFW CD 45003. 1960, 1998. CD.
  33.2 *A Life of Song.* Smithsonian Folkways: SFW 45067. 2011. CD. Juvenile.

34 ★Johnson, Robert. *The Centennial Collection.* Columbia; Legacy: 88697 85907 2. 1936, 2011. 2 CDs.

35 Jones, Bessie. *Put Your Hand on Your Hip, and Let Your Backbone Slip: Songs and Games from the Georgia Sea Islands.* Rounder: 11587-2. 2001. CD.

36 Leadbelly
  36.1 *Absolutely the Best.* Fuel: 302 061 080 2. 1939, 2000. CD.
  36.2 ★*Gwine Dig a Hole and Put the Devil In.* Library of Congress Recordings, Vol. 2. Rounder: CD 1045. 1991. CD.
  36.3 ★*Lead Belly: The Smithsonian Folkways Collection.* Smithsonian Folkways: SFW 40201. 2015. 5 CDs, booklet.
  36.4 ★*Let It Shine on Me.* Library of Congress Recordings, Vol. 3. Rounder: CD 1046. 1940, 1991. CD.
  36.5 ★*Midnight Special.* Library of Congress Recordings, Vol. 1. Rounder: CD 1044. 1934, 1991. CD.
  36.6 ★*Nobody Knows the Trouble I've Seen.* Library of Congress Recordings, Vol. 5. Rounder: CD 1098. 1994. CD.

37 ★Leadbelly and Woody Guthrie. *Folkways: The Original Vision.* Smithsonian Folkways: CD SF 40001. 1940, 1989. CD.

38 McIntosh County Shouters. *Slave Shout Songs from the Coast of Georgia.* Smithsonian Folkways: FE 4344. 1984, 2006. CD.

39 Moving Star Hall Singers. *Sea Island Folk Festival.* Smithsonian Folkways: F-3841. 1964, 2004. CD

40 Odetta. *Looking for a Home: Thanks to Leadbelly.* MC Records: MC0044. 2001. CD.

41 Odetta and Bill Lee. *Odetta at Town Hall.* Vanguard: VMD 2109. 1963, 1991. CD.

42 Staples, Mavis. *You Are Not Alone* (Jeff Tweedy). Anti: ANTI-87076-2. 2010. CD.

43 Sweet Honey in the Rock
   43.1 *Breaths.* Flying Fish: FF 70105. 1988. CD.
   43.2 *Live at Carnegie Hall.* Flying Fish: FF 70106. 1988. CD.
   43.3 *Still the Same Me.* Rounder: 11661-8100-2. 2000. CD.

ANTHOLOGIES

44 ★*Alligator Records 40th Anniversary Collection.* Alligator: ALCD 125/26. 2011. 2 CDs.

45 *Been in the Storm So Long: A Collection of Spirituals, Folk Tales, and Children's Games from John's Island, South Carolina.* Smithsonian Folkways: CD SF 40031. 1963, 1990. CD.

46 *Black Banjo Songsters.* Smithsonian Folkways: SF 40079. 1974, 1998. CD.

47 ★*Classic Sounds of New Orleans from Smithsonian Folkways.* Smithsonian Folkways: SFW 40183. 2010. CD.

48 *Freedom Songs: Selma Alabama.* Smithsonian Folkways: FH 5594. 1965, 2004. CD.

49 *Negro Work Songs and Calls.* Rounder Select: CD 1517. 1943, 1999. CD. Library of Congress Archive of Folk Culture.

50 *New Orleans Brass Bands: Through the Streets of the City.* Smithsonian Folkways: SFW CD 40212. 2014. CD.

51 ★*Prison Songs* (Alan Lomax, compiler). Alan Lomax Collection. Rounder: CD 1714-CD 1715. 1947, 1997. 2 CDs.

52 *Recording Black Culture* (John Work, III, compiler). Spring Fed Records: SFR-104. 2007. CD.

53 *Southern Journey, Vol. 6: Sheep, Sheep, Don'tcha Know the Road? Southern Music, Sacred and Sinful* (Alan Lomax, compiler). Alan Lomax Collection. Rounder: CD 1706. 1959, 1997. CD.

54 *Southern Journey, Vol. 8: Velvet Voices: Eastern Shores Choirs, Quartets, and Colonial Era Music* (Alan Lomax, compiler). Alan Lomax Collection. Rounder: CD 1708. 1961, 1997. CD.

55 *Southern Journey, Vol. 12: Georgia Sea Islands: Biblical Songs and Spirituals* (Alan Lomax, compiler). Alan Lomax Collection. Rounder: CD 1712. 1959, 1998. CD.

56 *Southern Journey, Vol. 13: Earliest Times: Georgia Sea Island Songs for Everyday Living* (Alan Lomax, compiler). Alan Lomax Collection. Rounder: CD 1713. 1959, 1998. CD.

57 ★*Voices of the Civil Rights Movement: Black American Freedom Songs, 1960–1966.* Smithsonian Folkways: SF 40084. 1980, 1997. 2 CDs.

ANGLO-AMERICAN FOLK

Traditional Folk

INDIVIDUAL ARTISTS AND GROUPS

58 Boggs, Dock. *Dock Boggs, His Folkways Years, 1963–1968* (Mike Seeger, compiler). Smithsonian Folkways: SFW 40108. 1998. 2 CDs.

59 Doc Watson Family. *The Doc Watson Family.* Smithsonian Folkways: 44493110. 1963, 1990. CD.

60 Guthrie, Woody
   60.1 *The Live Wire: Woody Guthrie in Performance, 1949.* Rounder: 11661-1167-2. 1949, 2010. CD.
   60.2 ★*Woody at 100: The Woody Guthrie Centennial Collection.* Smithsonian Folkways: SFW 40200. 2012. 3 CDs.

61 Jarrell, Tommy. *The Legacy of Tommy Jarrell, Vol. 1: Sail Away Ladies.* County Records: CO-CD-2724. 1999. CD.

62 Milner, Dan, David Coffin, and Jeff Davis. *Civil War Naval Songs.* Smithsonian Folkways: SFW 40189. 2011. CD.

63 Proffitt, Frank. *Frank Proffitt Sings Folk Songs.* Custom Compact Disc Series. Smithsonian Folkways: FW02360. 1962, 2000s. CD.

64 Reed, Ola Belle. *Rising Sun Melodies.* Smithsonian Folkways: SFW 40202. 1976, 2010. CD.

65 Ritchie, Jean
   65.1 *Ballads from Her Appalachian Family Tradition.* Smithsonian Folkways: SFW CD 40145. 1961, 2003. CD.
   65.2 *Jean Ritchie and Doc Watson at Folk City.* Smithsonian Folkways: CD SF 40005. 1963, 1990. CD.

66 Seeger, Mike, and Peggy Seeger. *Fly Down Little Bird.* Appleseed: APR CD 1125. 2004, 2011. CD.

67 ★Seeger, Pete
   67.1 *The Complete Bowdoin College Concert, 1960.* Smithsonian Folkways: SFW 40184. 1960, 2012. 2 CDs.

67.2 *Tomorrow's Children*. Appleseed: APR CD 1123. 2010. CD.

68 Thomasson, Benny. *Legendary Texas Fiddler: Recordings from 1966–1969*. County Records: CO-CD 2737. 2005. CD.

69 Watson, Doc
69.1 *The Essential Doc Watson*. Vanguard: VCD-45/46. 1973, 1986. CD.
69.2 *Legacy* (David Holt and Richard Watson). High Windy Audio: HW1258. 2002. 3 CDs.
69.3 *The Original Folkways Recordings of Doc Watson and Clarence Ashley, 1960–1962*. Smithsonian Folkways: CD SF 40029. 1960, 1994. 2 CDs.
69.4 *The Vanguard Years*. Vanguard: 155/58-2. 1967, 1995. 4 CDs.

ANTHOLOGIES

70 *American Fiddle Tunes* (Alan Jabbour, compiler). Rounder: 18964-1518-2. 1971, 2000. CD.

71 *American Roots Music*. Palm Pictures: PALMDVD-3039-2. 2001. 2 DVDs.

72 ★*Anthology of American Folk Music* (Harry Everett Smith, compiler). Smithsonian Folkways: SFW 40090. 1927, 1997. 6 CDs.

73 *The Art of Traditional Fiddle*. North American Traditions Series. Rounder: 1166-11592-2. 2001. CD.

74 *Awake, My Soul: The Story of the Sacred Harp*. Awake Productions: AP-002. 2008. 2 DVDs. Special edition.

75 *Back in the Saddle Again*. New World: 80314. 1983. 2 CDs.

76 *Ballads and Songs of the Blue Ridge Mountains: Persistence and Change*. Custom Compact Disc Series. Smithsonian Folkways: FS 3831. 1968, 2000s. CD.

77 *Bloody War Songs, 1924–1939*. Tompkins Square: TSQ 2479. 2010. CD.

78 *Choose Your Partners: Contra Dance & Square Dance Music of New Hampshire*. Smithsonian Folkways: SFW CD 40126. 1999. CD.

79 *Classic American Ballads from Smithsonian Folkways*. Smithsonian Folkways: SFW CD 40215. 2015. DC.

80 ★*Classic Appalachian Blues from Smithsonian Folkways*. Smithsonian Folkways: SFW 40198. 1971, 2010. CD.

81 *Classic Banjo from Smithsonian Folkways*. Smithsonian Folkways: SFW CD 40209. 2013. CD.

82 ★*Classic Folk Music from Smithsonian Folkways*. Smithsonian Folkways: SFW CD 40110. 1955, 2001. CD.

83 ★*Classic Labor Songs from Smithsonian Folkways*. Smithsonian Folkways: SFW CD 40166. 1937, 2006. CD.

84 *Classic Maritime Music from Smithsonian Folkways*. Smithsonian Folkways: SFW CD 40053. 1951, 2004. CD.

85 ★*Classic Mountain Songs from Smithsonian Folkways*. Smithsonian Folkways: SFW CD 40094. 1958, 2002. CD.

86 *Classic Old-Time Fiddle from Smithsonian Folkways*. Smithsonian Folkways: SFW CD 40193. 1951, 2007. CD.

87 ★*Classic Old-Time Music from Smithsonian Folkways*. Smithsonian Folkways: SFW CD 40093. 1962, 2003. CD.

88 ★*Classic Railroad Songs from Smithsonian Folkways*. Smithsonian Folkways: SFW CD 40192. 1952, 2006. CD.

89 *Cowboy Songs, Ballads, and Cattle Calls from Texas*. Rounder: CD 1512. 1941, 1999. CD. Library of Congress Archive of Folk Culture.

90 ★*Cowboy Songs of the Old West* (Alan Lomax and Ed McCurdy, compilers and performers). Legacy: CD 392. 1994. CD.

91 *Cowboy Songs on Folkways* (Guy William Logsdon, compiler). Smithsonian Folkways: SF 40043. 1944, 1991. CD.

92 *Dark Holler: Old Love Songs and Ballads* (John Cohen, compiler). Smithsonian Folkways: SFW CD 40159. 1964, 2005. CD.

93 *Early Mandolin Classics, Vol. 1*. Rounder: CD 1050. 1989. CD.

94 *Georgia Folk: A Sampler of Traditional Sounds*. Global Village: CD 03. 1985. CD.

95 Hammons Family. *The Hammons Family: The Traditions of a West Virginia Family and their Friends*. Rounder: CD 1504/05. 1973, 1998. 2 CDs.

96 ★*Harry Smith's Anthology of American Folk Music, Vol. 4.* (Harry Everett Smith, compiler). Revenant: RVN 211. 1928, 2000. 2 CDs.

97 *I'm on My Journey Home: Vocal Styles and Resources in Folk Music.* New World: 80223-2. 1978, 2002. CD.

98 ★*The JVC/Smithsonian Folkways Video Anthology of Music and Dance in the Americas.* JVC, Victor Co. of Japan; dist. by Multicultural Media: JVCAIIVOL01–JVCAIIVOL06. 1995, 2005. 6 DVDs, 6 booklets.

99 *Mountain Music of Kentucky.* Smithsonian Folkways: SF 40077. 1959, 1996. 2 CDs.

100 ★*Oh My Little Darling: Folk Song Types.* New World: 80245-2. 1977, 2002. CD.

101 *People Take Warning: Murder Ballads and Disaster Songs, 1913–1938.* Tompkins Square: TSQ 2509. 2010. 3 CDs.

102 *Roots Music: An American Journey.* Rounder: 11661-0501-2, 11661-0502-2, 11661-0503-2, 11661-0504-2, 11661-0505-2. 1976, 2001. 4 CDs, booklet.

103 *Southern Journey, Vol. 2: Ballads and Breakdowns* (Alan Lomax, compiler). Alan Lomax Collection. Rounder: CD 1702. 1959, 1997. CD.

104 *Southern Journey, Vol. 4: Brethren, We Meet Again: Southern White Spirituals* (Alan Lomax, compiler). Alan Lomax Collection. Rounder: CD 1704. 1959, 1997. CD.

105 *Southern Journey, Vol. 5: Bad Man Ballads* (Alan Lomax, compiler). Alan Lomax Collection. Rounder: CD 1705. 1959, 1997. CD.

106 *Southern Journey, Vol. 7: Ozark Frontier* (Alan Lomax, compiler). Alan Lomax Collection. Rounder: CD 1707. 1961, 1997. CD.

107 *Traditional Music from Grayson and Carroll Counties, Virginia.* Custom Compact Disc Series. Smithsonian Folkways: FS 3811. 1962, 2000. CD.

Modern Folk

INDIVIDUAL ARTISTS AND GROUPS

108 Almanac Singers
108.1 *The Original Talking Union with the Almanac Singers* (Pete Seeger). Custom Compact Disc Series. Smithsonian Folkways: FH 5285. 1955, 2001. CD.
108.2 *Which Side Are You On? The Best of the Almanac Singers.* Rev-Ola: RVLA182. 2007. CD.

109 Alvin, Dave. *Public Domain: Songs from the Wild Land* (Guilty Men). Hightone: HCD 8122. 2000. CD.

110 Baez, Joan
110.1 *Diamonds and Rust.* A&M: CD 3233. 1975, 1988. CD.
110.2 *The First 10 Years.* Vanguard: VCD-113/14. 1988. CD.
110.3 *Joan Baez.* A&M: 069 490 418-2. 1999. CD.

111 Blake, Norman. *The Norman and Nancy Blake Compact Disc* (Nancy Blake). Rounder: CD 11505. 1986. CD.

112 Block, Rory. *Best Blues and Originals.* Rounder: CD 11525. 1981, 1987. CD.

113 Bok, Gordon. *North Wind's Clearing: Songs of the Maine Coast.* Folk-Legacy: CD-1005. 1995. CD.

114 Bromberg, David. *Try Me One More Time.* Appleseed: APR CD 1099. 2007. CD.

115 Brothers Four. *Greatest Hits.* SBME Special Markets: 724139. 1962, 2008. CD.

116 Cassidy, Eva
116.1 *American Tune.* Blix Street: G2-10079. 1989, 2003. CD.
116.2 *Imagine.* Blix Street: G2-10075. 1987, 2002. CD.

117 Cockburn, Bruce. *Anything, Anytime, Anywhere: Singles 1979–2002.* Rounder: 11661-3180-2. 2002. CD.

118 Cohen, Leonard. *Songs of Leonard Cohen.* Columbia: CK 9533. 1968, 2007. CD.

119 Collins, Judy. *The Very Best of Judy Collins.* Elektra Traditions; Rhino: R2 74374. 1964, 2001. CD.

120 Cooder, Ry. *My Name Is Buddy.* Nonesuch: 79961-2. 2007. CD.

121 DeMent, Iris. *Infamous Angel.* Warner Bros.: 9 45238-2. 1992. CD.

122 Duser, Guy Van. *American Finger Style Guitar.* Rounder: CD 111533. 1977, 1987. CD.

123 Dylan, Bob
123.1 *Another Side of Bob Dylan.* Columbia: CK 8993. 1964. CD.
123.2 *Bob Dylan's Greatest Hits.* Columbia: CK 9463. 1967, 1985. CD.
123.3 *Bob Dylan's Greatest Hits, Vol. 2.* Columbia: C2K 65976. 1999. 2 CDs.

123.4   *The Essential Bob Dylan*. Columbia: C2K 85168, CK 85169–CK 85170. 1963, 2000. 2 CDs.

123.5   *The Other Side of the Mirror: Bob Dylan Live at the Newport Folk Festival 1963–1965*. Sony: 88697. 1963, 2007. DVD.

123.6   *The Times They Are a-Changin'*. Columbia: CK 94240. 2005. CD.

123.7   *The Witmark Demos, 1962–1964* (Colin Escott, ed.; Jeff Rosen and Steve Berkowitz, prods.). Bootleg Series, Vol. 9. Columbia: 88697 76179 2. 2010. 2 CDs.

124   Elliott, Jack. *I Stand Alone*. Anti-: 86814-2. 2006. CD.

125   Enslow, Anne, and Ridley Enslow. *Music of the American Colonies*. Enslow Pub.: EPI-CD 1614. 2000. CD, teacher curriculum guide sheet.

126   Erbsen, Wayne. *Railroad Fever*. Native Ground Music: NG-CD-930. 1998. CD.

127   Erbsen, Wayne, and Laura Boosinger. *Log Cabin Songs*. Native Ground Music: NG-CD-115. 2001. CD.

128   Garcia, Jerry. *The Pizza Tapes* (David Grisman and Tony Rice). Acoustic Disc: ACD-41; 91041-2. 1993, 2000. CD.

129   Gilkyson, Eliza. *Land of Milk and Honey* (Mary Chapin Carpenter, Iris DeMent, Slaid Cleaves, and Patty Griffin). Red House: RHR CD 174. 2004. CD.

130   Glazer, Tom. *A Treasury of Civil War Songs Sung by Tom Glazer*. Smithsonian Folkways: SFW 40187. 1973, 2011. CD.

131   Gorka, John. *I Know*. Red House: RHR CD18. 1988. CD.

132   Grisman, David. *The David Grisman Quintet*. Kaleidoscope. 1986. CD.

133   Guthrie, Arlo. *The Best of Arlo Guthrie*. Warner Bros.: 3117-2. 1972, 1989. CD.

134   Guthrie, Woody

134.1   ★*The Asch Recordings, Vols. 1–4* (Jeffrey Place, Guy William Logsdon, Cisco Houston, and others). Smithsonian Folkways: SF CD 40100–40102; SFW CD 40103; SFW CD 40112. 1944, 1999. 4 CDs.

134.2   *The Columbia River Collection*. Rounder: CD 1036. 1987. CD.

134.3   *The Greatest Songs of Woody Guthrie*. Vanguard: VCD-35/36. 1972, 1991. CD.

135   Hardin, Tim. *The Best of Tim Hardin*. 20th Century Masters—The Millennium Collection. Polydor: 440 016 405-2. 2002. CD.

136   Highwaymen. *The Folk Hits Collection*. Varese Sarabande: 302 066 847 2. 2007. CD.

137   Hollow Trees. *The Hollow Trees*. Water Music: 302 060 819-2. 2005. CD.

138   Houston, Cisco. *The Folkways Years, 1944–1961*. Smithsonian Folkways: SF CD 40059. 1944, 1994. CD.

139   Hurley, Michael. *Have Moicy!* (Jeffrey Frederick). Rounder: CD 3010. 1991. CD.

140   Ian and Sylvia. *Greatest Hits*. Vanguard: VCD-5/6. 1986. CD.

141   Indigo Girls. *Indigo Girls*. Epic: EK 45044. 1989. CD.

142   Ives, Burl

142.1   *The Best of Burl Ives*. 20th Century Masters—The Millennium Collection. MCA: 088 112 656-2. 2001. CD.

142.2   *Return of the Wayfaring Stranger*. Collectables: COL-CD-6662. 1950, 2000. CD.

143   Kahn, Si. *I'll Be There: Songs for Jobs with Justice* (Trapezoid). Flying Fish: FF 70509. 1989. CD.

144   Kaplansky, Lucy. *Over the Hills*. Red House: RHR CD 200. 2007. CD.

145   Kingston Trio

145.1   *The Essential Kingston Trio*. Shout! Factory: 826663-10183. 1958, 2006. 2 CDs.

145.2   *The Kingston Trio*. Capitol: CDP 7 92710 2. 1990. CD.

146   Kottke, Leo

146.1   *One Guitar, No Vocals*. Private Music: 01005-82171-2. 1999. CD.

146.2   *6- and 12-String Guitar*. Rhino: R2 71612. 1969, 1994. CD.

147   Kweskin, Jim

147.1   *Garden of Joy; Jim Kweskin's America* (Geoff and Maria Muldaur). Collectables: COL-CD-7668. 1967, 2005. CD.

147.2   *Greatest Hits* (Jug band). Vanguard: VCD-13/14. 1988. CD.

148   Langstaff, John. *John Langstaff Sings the Water Is Wide: American and British Ballads and Folksongs*. Revels: CD 2202. 2002. CD.

149   Lavin, Christine. *Attainable Love*. Philo: CD PH 1132. 1990. CD.

150 Limeliters. *Two Classic Albums from the Limeliters: The Slightly Fabulous Limeliters and Sing Out!* Collector's Choice: 24. 1961, 1996. CD.

151 McCutcheon, John. *Water from Another Time: A Retrospective.* Rounder: CD 11555. 1989. CD.

152 McGuinn, Roger. *Treasures from the Folk Den.* Appleseed: APR CD 1046. 2001. CD.

153 Michael, Walt. *Hammered Dulcimer: Retrospective.* Flying Fish: SDA 92741. 1980s, 1998. CD.

154 Mitchell, Elizabeth. *Sunny Day* (Daniel Littleton, Storey Littleton, Levon Helm, Dan Zanes, Jon Langford, Chris Wood, and Children of Agape Choir). Smithsonian Folkways: SFW 45064. 2010. CD. Juvenile.

155 Moore, Wayne. *A Treasury of American Railroad Songs and Ballads, Vol. 2.* Shiloh: SCD4098. 2001. CD.

156 Morrissey, Bill. *North.* Philo: CD PH 1106. 1986. CD.

157 Mothersbaugh, Mark. *The Royal Tenenbaums: Original Soundtrack.* Hollywood: 2061-623472. 2001. CD.

158 Near, Holly
   158.1 *And Still We Sing: The Outspoken Collection.* Calico Tracks: CTM0005. 2002. CD.
   158.2 *Show Up.* Calico Tracks: CTM0007. 2006. CD.

159 New Lost City Ramblers. *The Early Years, 1958–1962.* Smithsonian Folkways: CD SF 40036. 1958, 1991. CD.

160 O'Brien, Tim. *Cornbread Nation.* Howdie Skies Records, Sugar Hill: SUG-CD-4005. 2005. CD.

161 Ochs, Phil
   161.1 *I Ain't Marching Anymore.* Hannibal: HNCD 4422. 1965, 1986. CD.
   161.2 *There but for Fortune.* Elektra: 60832-2. 1964, 1989. CD.

162 Ostroushko, Peter. *Slüz Düz Music: Original American Dance Tunes with an Old World Flavor.* Rounder: CD 0204. 1985, 1995. CD.

163 Paxton, Tom. *The Very Best of Tom Paxton.* Flying Fish: FF 70519. 1986, 1988. CD.

164 Peter, Paul, and Mary
   164.1 *In Concert.* Warner Bros.: 1555-2. 1964, 1989. 2 CDs.
   164.2 *In These Times.* Rhino: R2 73957. 2003. CD.
   164.3 *Ten Years Together: The Best of Peter, Paul and Mary.* Rhino, WEA: 512215. 1970, 2008. CD.

165 Phillips, Utah
   165.1 *Good Though!* Philo: CD PH 1004. 1997. CD.
   165.2 *The Telling Takes Me Home.* Philo: CD PH 1210. 1975, 1997. CD.

166 Plant, Robert. *Raising Sand* (Alison Krauss). Rounder: 11661-9075-2. 2007. CD.

167 Polansky, Larry, composer. *Lonesome Road: The Crawford Variations.* New World: 80566-2. 1998, 2001. CD. Recorded Anthology of American Music.

168 Prine, John. *Prime Prine: The Best of John Prine.* Atlantic: 18202-2. 1972, 1989. CD.

169 Prine, John, and Mac Wiseman. *Standard Songs for Average People.* Oh Boy: OBR-038. 2007. CD.

170 Red Clay Ramblers. *Twisted Laurel; Merchant's Lunch.* Flying Fish: FF70055. 1967, 1991. CD.

171 Rodriguez, Daniel. *The Spirit of America.* Manhattan: 7243 5 37564 2 0. 2002. CD.

172 Ronstadt, Linda, and Ann Allen Savoy. *Adieu False Heart.* Vanguard: 79808-2. 2006. CD.

173 Rooftop Singers. *The Rooftop Singers.* Vanguard: 73158. 2007. CD.

174 Rosenthal, Phil. *This Land Is Your Land: Favorite American Folk Songs.* American Melody: AM-CD-5118. 1999. CD.

175 Rowan, Peter. *Quartet* (Tony Rice, Bryn Davies and Sharon Gilchrist). Rounder: 11661-0579-2. 2007. CD.

176 Rusby, Kate. *Underneath the Stars.* Compass: 7 4370 2. 2003, 2004. CD.

177 Rzewski, Frederic, composer. *The People United Will Never Be Defeated! North American Ballads; Down by the Riverside; Winnsboro Cotton Mill Blues* (Marc Andre Hamelin, Sergio Ortega). Hyperion: CDA67077. 1998, 1999. CD. Variations (classical tradition) on a folk theme.

178 Sabatella, Matthew. *Ballad of America, Vol. 1: Over a Wide and Fruitful Land.* Slipstream: SLP 0006. 2004. CD.

179 Seeger, Mike
    179.1 *American Folksongs for Children: Ninety-Four Songs* (Peggy Seeger). Rounder: CD 8001. 1996. 2 CDs.
    179.2 *Early Southern Guitar Sounds.* Smithsonian Folkways: SFW CD 40157. 2007. CD.
    179.3 *Solo Oldtime Music.* Rounder: CD 0278. 1991. CD.

180 Seeger, Peggy
    180.1 *Bring Me Home.* Appleseed: APR CD 1106. 2008. CD.
    180.2 *The Folkways Years, 1955–1992: Songs of Love and Politics.* Smithsonian Folkways: CD SF 40048. 1955, 1992. CD.

181 Seeger, Pete
    181.1 ★*American Favorite Ballads, Vol. 1.* Smithsonian Folkways: SFW CD 40150. 1954, 2002. CD.
    181.2 ★*American Favorite Ballads, Vol. 2.* Smithsonian Folkways: SFW CD 40151. 1954, 2003. CD.
    181.3 ★*American Favorite Ballads, Vol. 3.* Smithsonian Folkways: SFW CD 40152. 1953, 2004. CD.
    181.4 ★*American Favorite Ballads, Vol. 4.* Smithsonian Folkways: SFW CD 40153. 1950, 2006. CD.
    181.5 ★*American Favorite Ballads, Vol. 5.* Smithsonian Folkways: SFW CD 40154. 1954, 2007. CD.
    181.6 ★*American Industrial Ballads.* Smithsonian Folkways: CD SF 40058. 1957, 1992. CD.
    181.7 ★*The Essential Pete Seeger.* Sony: 92835. 1941, 2005. CD.
    181.8 ★*If I Had a Hammer: Songs of Hope and Struggle.* Smithsonian Folkways. CD 40096. 1955, 1998. CD.
    181.9 ★*We Shall Overcome: The Complete Carnegie Hall Concert.* Columbia: C2K 45312. 1963, 1989. 2 CDs.

182 Seekers. *The Very Best of the Seekers.* EMI: 7243 8 57411 2 8. 1964, 1997. CD.

183 Simon and Garfunkel
    183.1 *Parsley, Sage, Rosemary and Thyme.* Columbia Legacy: CK 66001. 1966, 2001. CD.
    183.2 *Sounds of Silence.* Columbia: CK 65998. 1964, 2001. CD.

184 Slosberg, Daniel. *Pierre Cruzatte: A Musical Journey along the Lewis and Clark Trail with Daniel Slosberg.* Native Ground Music: NG-CD-940. 2002. CD.

185 Sordill, Willie, and others. *Walls to Roses: Songs of Changing Men.* Custom Compact Disc Series. Smithsonian Folkways: FTS 37587. 1978, 2000s. CD.

186 Sorrels, Rosalie
    186.1 *The Long Memory* (Utah Phillips). Red House: RHR CD 83. 1996. CD.
    186.2 *Strangers in Another Country: The Songs of Bruce "Utah" Phillips.* Red House: RHR CD 214. 2008. CD.

187 Springsteen, Bruce
    187.1 *Live in Dublin.* Columbia: 88697 09582 2. 2007. 2 CDs.
    187.2 *We Shall Overcome: The Seeger Sessions* (Pete Seeger). Columbia: 82876 82867 2. 1998, 2006. CD, DVD.

188 Staines, Bill. *The First Million Miles.* Rounder: CD 11560. 1989. CD.

189 Uncle Earl. *Waterloo, Tennessee.* Rounder: 11661-0577-2. 2007. CD.

190 Ungar, Jay, and Molly Mason. *Harvest Home.* Angel: 7243 5 56720 2 5. 1999. CD.

191 Van Ronk, Dave
    191.1 *And the Tin Pan Bended, and the Story Ended.* Smithsonian Folkways: SFW CD 40156. 2001, 2004. CD.
    191.2 *The Folkways Years, 1959–1961.* Smithsonian Folkways: CD SF 40041. 1959, 1991. CD.

192 Van Zandt, Townes. *Live at the Old Quarter, Houston, Texas.* Tomato Music: TOM-3011. 1973, 2002. CD.

193 Varner, Tom. *The Window up Above: American Songs 1770–1998.* New World: 80552-2. 1998. CD.

194 Watson, Doc, and Merle Watson. *Columbus Stockade Blues: The Best of the 70s.* Raven: RVCD-319. 2010. CD.

195 Weavers
    195.1 *The Weavers at Carnegie Hall.* Vanguard: VMD-73101. 1955, 1998. CD.
    195.2 *The Weavers Greatest Hits.* Vanguard: VCD-15/16. 1971, 1986. CD.

196 Williams, Robin, and Linda Williams. *Back 40.* Red House Records: RHR CD 274. 2013. CD.

197 Winchester, Jesse. *The Best of Jesse Winchester.* Rhino, Bearsville: R2 70085. 1971, 1989. CD.

198 Wolf, Kate. *Gold in California: A Retrospective of Recordings, 1975–1985.* Rhino: R2 71485. 1986. 2 CDs.

199 Zanes, Dan. *Catch That Train!* Festival Five: FFR009. 2006. CD.

200 Zanes, Dan, and Carl Sandburg. *Parades and Panoramas: 25 Songs Collected by Carl Sandburg for the American Songbag.* Festival Five: FFR-007. 2004. CD.

ANTHOLOGIES

201 *American Fogies, Vol. 1.* Rounder: CD 0379. 1996. CD.

202 *American Fogies, Vol. 2.* Rounder: CD 0389. 1996. CD.

203 *Appalachian Journey* (Yo-Yo Ma, Edgar Meyer, Mark O'Connor, and others). Sony Classical: SK 66782. 2000. CD.

204 *Back Roads to Cold Mountain.* Smithsonian Folkways: SFW CD 40149. 1927, 2004. CD.

205 *The Best of Broadside 1962–1988: Anthems of the American Underground from the Pages of Broadside Magazine* (Jeffrey Place and Ronald D. Cohen, compilers). Smithsonian Folkways: SFW CD 40130. 2000. 5 CDs, text.

206 *The Best of Hootenanny* (Jack Linkletter, host). Shout! Factory: 826663-10220. 1963, 2007. 3 DVDs.

207 *Brave Boys: New England Traditions in Folk Music.* New World: 80239-2. 1977, 1995. CD.

208 *Dark and Light in Spanish New Mexico.* New World: 80292-2. 1978, 1995. CD.

209 *Don't Mourn—Organize! Songs of Labor Songwriter Joe Hill.* Smithsonian Folkways: CD SF 40026. 1941, 1990. CD.

210 *Down from the Mountain: A Film Celebrating the Music from the Movie "O Brother, Where Art Thou?"* Artisan Home Entertainment: 12324. 2000. DVD.

211 *The Evening Concerts: The Newport Folk Festival 1963* (Sam Hinton, Mississippi John Hurt, Jack Elliott, Joan Baez, and Bob Dylan). Vanguard: VCD 77002. 1964, 1990s. CD.

212 *Family Folk Festival: A Multicultural Sing Along.* Music for Little People: 9 42506-2. 2001. CD.

213 *Feeding the Flame: Songs by Men to End AIDS.* Flying Fish: FF 70541. 1990. CD.

214 *Friends of Old-Time Music: The Folk Arrival, 1961–1965.* Smithsonian Folkways: SFW CD 40160. 196?, 2006. 3 CDs.

215 *Greatest Folk Singers of the Sixties.* Vanguard: VCD-17/18. 1987. CD.

216 *Happy Land: Musical Tributes to Laura Ingalls Wilder.* Pa's Fiddle: SAR 1259. 1923, 2005. CD.

217 *Haywire Mac* (Harry McClintock and Sam Eskin). Custom Compact Disc Series. Smithsonian Folkways: FW 05272. 1972, 2001. CD.

218 *If You Ain't Got the Do-Re-Mi: Songs of Rags to Riches.* Smithsonian Folkways: SFW CD 40195. 1954, 2007. CD.

219 *In Country: Folk Songs of Americans in the Vietnam War.* Flying Fish: FF 70552. 1991. CD.

220 *Mermaid Avenue* (Billy Bragg and others). Elektra: 62204-2. 1998. CD.

221 *Mermaid Avenue, Vol. 2* (Billy Bragg and Wilco and others). Elektra: 62522-2. 2000. CD.

222 *A Mighty Wind: The Album.* DMZ, Columbia, Sony Music Soundtrax: CK 89222. 2003. CD.

223 *Music from the Miramax Motion Picture Cold Mountain.* Columbia: CK 86843. 2003. CD.

224 *New Golden Ring. Five Days Singing, Vol. 1.* Folk-Legacy Records: CD-41. 1971, 1996. CD.

225 *A Nod to Bob: An Artists' Tribute to Bob Dylan on His Sixtieth Birthday.* Red House: RHR CD 154. 2001. CD.

226 *O Brother, Where Art Thou?* Lost Highway; Mercury: 088 170 069-2. 2000. CD.

227 *Putumayo Presents Americana.* Putumayo World Music: PUT 266-2. 2007. CD.

228 *Rounder Banjo.* Rounder: CD 11542. 1987. CD.

229 *Rounder Bluegrass Guitar.* Rounder: CD 11576. 1996. CD.

230 *Rounder Fiddle.* Rounder: CD 11565. 1990. CD.

231 *Rounder Guitar.* Rounder: CD 11541. 1987. CD.

232 *Rounder Old Time Music* (Snuffy Jenkins, Norman Blake, Hazel Dickens, Ricky Skaggs, Ola Belle Reed, and Bashful Brother Oswald). Rounder: CD 11510. 1952, 1988. CD.

233 *Sandburg Out Loud.* August House Publishers. 2002. CD.

234 *Song of America.* 31 Tigers: 120654-6. 2007. 3 CDs, booklet.

235 *Songs of the Mormons and Songs of the West* (Duncan Emrich, ed.). Rounder: 18964-1520-2. 1952, 2002. CD. Library of Congress Archive of Folk Culture.

236 *Til We Outnumber 'Em (Woody Guthrie Tribute).* Righteous Babe: RBR019-D. 1996, 2000. CD.

237 *An Untamed Sense of Control* (Roscoe Holcomb, John Cohen, Carter Stanley, Barbecue Bob, Frank Hutchison, and A. P. Carter). Smithsonian Folkways: SFW CD 40144. 1953, 2003. CD.

FRENCH (CAJUN AND ZYDECO)

Cajun

INDIVIDUAL ARTISTS AND GROUPS

238 Abshire, Nathan. *French Blues* (Pine Grove Boys). Arhoolie: CD 373. 1972, 1992. CD.

239 Balfa, Dewey. *Under a Green Oak Tree (En Bas d'un Chêne Vert)* (Marc Savoy, D. L. Menard). Arhoolie: CD 312. 1989. CD.

240 Balfa Brothers. *The Balfa Brothers Play Traditional Cajun Music, Vols. 1 and 2.* Swallow: CD 6011. 1990. CD.

241 Beausoleil. *Allons à Lafayette and More with Canray Fontenot* (Michael Doucet and Canray Fontenot). Arhoolie: CD 308. 1981, 1989. CD.

242 Choates, Harry. *The Fiddle King of Cajun Swing.* Arhoolie: CD 380. 1946, 1993. CD.

243 Doucet, Michael. *From Now On.* Smithsonian Folkways: SFW CD 40177. 2008. CD.

244 Doucet, Michael, and Beausoleil. *Bayou Deluxe: The Best of Michael Doucet & Beausoleil.* Rhino Records: R2 71169. 1993. CD.

245 Hackberry Ramblers. *Early Recordings 1935–1950* (Luderin Darbone and Hackberry Ramblers). Arhoolie: CD 7050. 1935, 2003. CD.

246 Kershaw, Doug. *The Best of Doug Kershaw.* Warner Bros.: 25964-2. 1972, 1989. CD.

247 LeJeune, Iry. *Iry LeJeune, Cajun's Greatest* (Eddie Shuler). Ace: CDCHD 428. 1948, 1992. CD.

248 Lost Bayou Ramblers. *Live à la Blue Moon* (Louis Michot, Andre Michot, Chris Courville, Alan LaFleur, Cavan Carruth, and Whitney Broussard). Swallow: SW-6205. 2007. CD.

249 Menard, D. L. *No Matter Where You At, There You Are* (Eddie LeJeune, Ken Smith, and Blackie Forestier). Rounder: 6021. 1988. CD.

250 Racines. *Racines* (Steve Riley, Kevin Wimmer, Mitch Reed, and Chris Stafford). Swallow: SW-6197. 2006. CD.

251 Red Stick Ramblers. *Made in the Shade.* Sugarhill: SUG-CD-4038. 2007. CD.

252 Riley, Steve, and the Mamou Playboys
  252.1 *Best of Steve Riley and the Mamou Playboys.* Rounder: 6117. 2 CDs.
  252.2 *Steve Riley and the Mamou Playboys.* Rounder: 6038. 1990. CD.

253 Savoy Family Band. *Turn Loose but Don't Let Go.* Arhoolie: CD 525. 2008. CD.

254 Sonnier, Jo-el. *Cajun Life.* Rounder: 3049. 1988. CD.

ANTHOLOGIES

255 *Cajun Honky Tonk: The Khoury Recordings: The Early 1950s.* Arhoolie: CD 427. 1995. CD.

256 ★*Cajun Music: The Essential Collection.* Rounder Heritage; Essential Cajun. Rounder: 1166-11604-2. 2002. CD.

257 *Cajun Social Music.* Smithsonian Folkways: SF 40006. 1990. CD.

258 *Folksongs of the Louisiana Acadians.* Arhoolie: CD 359. 1994. CD.

259 *Louisiana Cajun French Music from the Southwest Prairies, Vols. 1 and 2.* Rounder: 6001, 6002. 1964, 1989. 2 CDs.

260 *Louisiana Cajun Music Special: Bon Temps Rouler.* Swallow: CD-103. 1988. CD.

Cajun and Zydeco

ANTHOLOGIES

261 *Another Saturday Night: Classic Recordings from the Louisiana Bayous.* Ace: CDCH 288. 1990. CD.

262 ★*Cajun and Creole Music, 1934–1937: The Classic Louisiana Recordings.* Alan Lomax Collection. Rounder: 11661-1842-2. 1999. CD.

263 *Cajun and Creole Music II, 1934–1937: The Classic Louisiana Recordings.* Alan Lomax Collection. Rounder: 11661-1843-2. 1999. CD.

264 *Cajun Champs.* Arhoolie: CD 327. 1988, 2004. CD.

265 *Cajun Music and Zydeco.* Rounder: 11572. 1992, 1997. CD.

266 *J'ai été au Bal (I Went to the Dance): Roots of Cajun and Zydeco Music.* Brazos Films: BF-103 DVD. 2003. DVD.

267 *J'ai été au Bal (I Went to the Dance): The Cajun and Zydeco Music of Louisiana.* Arhoolie: CD 331,CD 332. 1928, 1990. 2 CDs.

Zydeco

INDIVIDUAL ARTISTS AND GROUPS

268 Ardoin, Amadé. *I'm Never Comin' Back* (Dennis McGee). Arhoolie Folklyric: CD 7007. 1995. CD.

269 Buckwheat Zydeco. *Buckwheat's Zydeco Party* (Stanley "Buckwheat" Dural). Rounder: 11528. 1987. CD.

270 Chavis, Boozoo. *The Lake Charles Atomic Bomb.* Original Goldband Recordings. Rounder: CD 2097. 1955, 1990. CD.

271 Chenier, Clifton. *Louisiana Blues and Zydeco.* Arhoolie: CD 329. 1964, 1990. CD.

272 Delafose, John. *Joe Pete Got Two Women.* Arhoolie: CD 335. 1980, 1990. CD.

273 Queen Ida. *Queen Ida and the Bon Temps Band on Tour.* GNP Crescendo: GNPD 2147. 1986. CD.

274 Simien, Terrance. *Live Worldwide* (Zydeco Experience). Aim: 5016. 2007. CD.

ANTHOLOGIES

275 *Zydeco: The Early Years, Vol. 1.* Arhoolie: CD 307. 1949, 1989. CD.

276 *Zydeco Champs: Over 60 Minutes of Historic Zydeco.* Arhoolie: CD 328. 1928, 1992. CD.

HAWAIIAN

INDIVIDUAL ARTISTS AND GROUPS

277 Beamer, Keola. *Soliloquy: Ka Leo O Loko.* Dancing Cat: 08022-38012-2. 2002. CD.

278 Gilliom, Amy. *Generation Hawaii.* Hanaiali'I: HANA 8556. 2006. CD.

279 Helm, Raiatea. *Sweet and Lovely.* Raiatea Helm: RHCD 8518. 2004. CD.

280 Hoopii, Sol. *Master of the Hawaiian Guitar, Vol. 1.* Rounder: CD 1024. 1977, 1991. CD.

281 Hui Aloha. *Hui Aloha.* Hawaiian Slack Key Guitar Masters Series. Dancing Cat: 08022 38053-2. 1999. CD.

282 Kalama's Quartet. *Early Hawaiian Classics.* Arhoolie Folklyric: CD 7028. 1927, 1993. CD.

283 Kamakawiwo'ole, Israel
   283.1 *Alone in IZ World.* Bigboy: BBCD 5907. 2001. CD.
   283.2 *Wonderful World.* Mountain Apple: BBCD 5911. 2007. CD.

284 ★Kiona, Kaulaheaonamiku. *Hawaiian Chant, Hula, and Music.* Custom Compact Disc Series. Smithsonian Folkways: FW 8750. 1962, 2000s. CD.

285 Ku, Tony. *Original Hawaiian Steel Guitar.* Custom Compact Disc Series. Smithsonian Folkways: FW 8714. 1979, 2003. CD.

286 Pahinui, Bla. *Windward Heart: Live Solo.* Hawaiian Slack Key Guitar Masters Series. Dancing Cat: 08022 38052-2. 2000. CD.

287 Raiatea. *Hawaiian Blossom.* Raiatea Helm: RHCD 8601. 2007. CD.

288 Reichel, Keali'i
   288.1 *Kamahiwa: Keali'i Reichel, Collection One.* Punahele Productions: PPCD 010. 1999, 2005. CD.
   288.2 *Ke'Alaokamaile.* Punahele Productions: PPCD 009. 2003. CD.

289 Rose Ensemble. *Nā Mele Hawai'i: A Rediscovery of Hawaiian Vocal Music.* Rose Ensemble: Rose 00008. 2007. CD.

290 Shimabukuro, Jake
   290.1 *Dragon.* Hitchhike: HRCD-1104. 2005. CD.
   290.2 *Gently Weeps.* Hitchhike: HRCD-1105. 2006. CD.

291   Taj Mahal and the Hula Blues Band. *Hanapepe Dream.* Tone-Cool; Artemis: 751 173-2. 1999, 2003. CD.

292   Tau Moe Family. *Ho'omana'o i na mele o ka wa u'i (Remembering the Songs of Our Youth).* Rounder: CD 6028. 1988. CD.

293   Wolfgramm, Nani. *The Seductive Sounds of Hawaii: Polynesian Girl* (Islanders). Monitor: MON 71826. 1993. CD.

ANTHOLOGIES

294   *Festival of Japanese Music in Hawaii.* Custom Compact Disc Series. Smithsonian Folkways: F 8885-6. 1962, 2000. 2 CDs. *See also* Middle Eastern and Asian Immigrants, Anthologies.

295   *Hawaii: Music from the Islands of Aloha.* Mountain Apple: MACD 2077. 2001. CD.

296   *Hawaiian Chants, Hula, and Love Dance Songs.* Custom Compact Disc Series. Smithsonian Folkways: FE 4271. 1972, 1999. CD.

297   *Hawaiian Drum Dance Chants: Sounds of Power in Time* (Elizabeth Tater, compiler). Smithsonian Folkways: CD SF 40015. 1923, 1989. CD. *See also* Oceania.

298   *Hawaiian Playground.* Putumayo World Music: PUT-274-2. 2008. CD.

299   *Hawaiian Slack Key Guitar Masters Collection, Vol. 2* (Ray Kane and others). Hawaiian Slack Key Guitar Masters Series. Dancing Cat: 08022-38046-2. 1999. CD.

300   *Hawaiian Steel Guitar Classics.* Arhoolie Folklyric: CD-7027. 1927, 1993. CD.

301   *The History of Slack Key Guitar* (Gabby Pahinui and others). Vintage Hawaiian Treasures, Vol. 7. Hana Ole: HOCD 24000. 1946, 1995. CD.

302   *Legends of Ukulele.* Rhino: R2 75278. 1927, 1998. CD.

303   *Music of the Orient in Hawaii.* Custom Compact Disc Series. Smithsonian Folkways: FW 8745. 1963, 2000s. CD.

304   *Musics of Hawai'i: Anthology of Hawaiian Music, Special Festival Edition* (Clyde Sproat and others). Custom Compact Disc Series. Smithsonian Folkways: SF 40016. 1989, 1999. CD.

305   *Puerto Rican Music in Hawaii* (Ted Solis, compiler; Latin Gentlemen; Latin Five; Bobby Castillo,

cond.). Smithsonian Folkways: CD SF 40014. 1989. CD.

306   *Slack Key Guitar, Vol. 2.* Palm: PRCD 4017. 2003. CD.

307   *Vintage Hawaiian Music: The Great Singers, 1928–1934.* Rounder: CD 1053. 1989. CD. *See also* Oceania.

308   *Vintage Hawaiian Music: Steel Guitar Masters, 1928–1934.* Rounder: CD 1052. 1989. CD.

309   Wolfgramm, Nani. *20 Golden Hits of Hawaii* (Islanders). Music of the World. Monitor: MON 61804. 1900, [1981]. CD.

NATIVE AMERICAN

Contemporary and Intertribal

INDIVIDUAL ARTISTS AND GROUPS

310   Black Eagle
    310.1   *Flying Free.* SOAR Corp.: SOAR 213 CD. 2003. CD.
    310.2   *Voice of the Drum.* SOAR Corp.: SOAR 228. 2006. CD.

311   Black Lodge Singers
    311.1   *Pow-Wow Highway Songs.* SOAR Corp.: SOAR-125-CD. 1991. CD.
    311.2   *Weasel Tail's Dream.* Canyon: CR-6337. 2001. CD.

312   Cody, Robert Tree, and Will Clipman. *Heart of the Wind: Music for Native American Flute and Drums.* Canyon: CR-7072. 2006. CD.

313   Coyote Oldman. *In Medicine River.* Rock Bottom. 2008. CD.

314   Fire Crow, Joseph, Jr. *Cheyenne Nation.* Makoche: MM 154 D. 2000. CD.

315   Gordon, David. *Gratitude: Relaxing Native American Flute Music.* Sequoia Records: X709. 2010. CD.

316   Gu-Achi Fiddlers. *Old Time O'odham Fiddle.* Canyon Records Vintage Collection, Vol. 7. Canyon: CR-8082. 1988, 1997. CD.

317   Littlefeather, Kyle. *The Unconquered Spirit: Chants and Trances of the Native American Indian.* Fuel 2000: 302 061 409 2. 2004. 2 CDs.

318   Miller, Bill. *Spirit Songs: The Best of Bill Miller.* Vanguard: 797292. 2004. CD.

319 Mirabal, Robert
   319.1 *Indians, Indians.* Silver Wave: SD 935. 2003. CD.
   319.2 *Music from a Painted Cave* (Rare Tribal Mob). Silver Wave: SD 927. 2001. CD.
   319.3 *Totemic Flute Chants* (Johnny Whitehorse). Silver Wave: SD 948. 2007. CD.

320 Nakai, R. Carlos
   320.1 *Big Medicine* (R. Carlos Nakai Quartet). Canyon: CR-7024. 1998. CD.
   320.2 *In Beauty, We Return: 20 Years of Native American Flute Music.* Canyon: CR-7064. 2004. CD.

321 Redheart. *Indian Summer.* Natural Visions: NVR 139. 2007. CD.

322 Smith, Alex E., and Cheevers Toppah. *Intonation: Harmonized Songs from the Southern Plains.* Canyon: CR-6395. 2005. CD.

323 Stuart, Marty. *Badlands: Ballads of the Lakota.* Superlatone, Universal South: B 0004960-02. 2005. CD.

324 Trudell, John. *Bone Days.* Astis Productions: DAM 19035. 2001. CD.

325 Walela. *Walela: Live in Concert* (Rita Coolidge, Priscilla Coolidge, and Laura Satterfield). Rich-Heape Films: 652645700137. 2004. CD.

326 Youngblood, Mary. *Feed the Fire.* Silver Wave: SD 939. 2004. CD.

ANTHOLOGIES

327 *Discovering American Indian Music.* Discovering Music Series. AIMS Multimedia: SKU 873257. 2007. DVD. *See also Native American* General Anthologies.

328 *Gathering of Nations Pow Wow, 1999.* SOAR Corp.: SOAR 200 CD. 2000. CD.

329 *Moving within the Circle: Contemporary Native American Music and Dance* (Bryan Burton, compiler). World Music Press: WMP 012 CD. 1994. CD.

330 *Tribal Dreams: Music from Native Americans.* EarthBeat: R2 74269. 2001. CD.

331 *Tribal Waters: Music from Native Americans.* EarthBeat: R2 75540. 1998. CD.

Great Basin, Plateau, California, and Northwest Coast Cultures

INDIVIDUAL ARTISTS AND GROUPS

332 Bear Creek. *XI: Pow-Wow Songs Recorded Live at San Manuel.* Canyon: CR-6474. 2010. CD, DVD.

ANTHOLOGIES

333 *Canada: Inuit Games and Songs.* Smithsonian Folkways: UNES 08032. 1976, 2014. CD.

334 *The Eskimos of Hudson Bay and Alaska* (Laura Boulton, compiler). Smithsonian Folkways Archival. Smithsonian Folkways: FE 4444. 1954, 2006. CD.

335 *Indian Music of the Pacific Northwest Coast* (Ida Halpern, compiler). Ethnic Folkways Library; Custom Compact Disc Series. Smithsonian Folkways: FE 4523. 1967, 2003. 2 CDs.

336 *Kwakiutl: Indian Music of the Pacific Northwest* (Ida Halpern, compiler). Custom Compact Disc Series. Smithsonian Folkways: FE 4122. 1981, 2001. CD.

337 *Music of the Alaskan Kutchin Indians* (Craig Mishler, compiler). Smithsonian Folkways: FE 4070. 1974, 2004. CD.

338 *Songs and Dances of the Flathead Indians* (Alan P. Merriam and Barbara Williams Merriam, compilers). Custom Compact Disc Series. Smithsonian Folkways: FE 4445. 1953, 2001. CD.

339 *Songs of Love, Luck, Animals, and Magic: Music of the Yurok and Tolowa Indians* (Charlotte Heth, compiler). New World: 80297-2. 1977, 1992. CD. Recorded Anthology of American Music.

340 *Utes: Traditional Ute Songs.* Canyon Records Vintage Collection, Vol. 10. Canyon: CR-6113. 1998. CD.

Northeast and Southeast Cultures

INDIVIDUAL ARTISTS AND GROUPS

341 Northern Cree Singers. *Temptations: Cree Round Dance Songs.* Canyon: CR-6443. 2010. CD.

ANTHOLOGIES

342 *Canada: Inuit Games and Songs.* Smithsonian Folkways: UNES 08032. 1976, 2014. CD.

343 *Plains Chippewa/Métis Music from Turtle Mountain* (Nicholas Curchin Vrooman, compiler). Smithsonian Folkways: SF 40411. 1984, 1992. CD.

344 *Seneca Social Dance Music* (Mary Riemer, compiler). Custom Compact Disc Series. Smithsonian Folkways: FE 4072. 1980, 2000. CD.

345 *Songs and Dances of the Eastern Indians from Medicine Springs and Allegany* (Charlotte Heth, compiler). New World: 80337-2. 1985, 1993. CD. Recorded Anthology of American Music.

346 *Songs and Dances of the Great Lakes Indians* (Gertrude Prokosch Kurath, compiler). Custom Compact Disc Series. Smithsonian Folkways: FE 4003. 1956, 2001. CD.

347 *Songs of the Chippewa, Vol. 1: Minnesota Chippewa Game and Social Dances*. Custom Compact Disc Series. Smithsonian Folkways: FE 4392. 1977, 2001. CD.

348 *Songs of the Seminole Indians of Florida* (Frances Densmore, compiler). Custom Compact Disc Series. Smithsonian Folkways: FE 4383. 1972, 2001. CD.

Plains Cultures

INDIVIDUAL ARTISTS AND GROUPS

349 Bear, Keith. *People of the Willows*. Makoche: 333401482. 1999. CD.

350 Black Lodge Singers. *Tribute to the Elders*. Canyon: CR-6318. 1999. CD.

351 Evarts, Mark. *Music of the Pawnee*. Custom Compact Disc Series. Smithsonian Folkways: F-4334. 1936, 1999. CD.

352 Horncloud, William. *Traditional Lakota Songs*. Canyon Records Vintage Collection, Vol. 15. Canyon: CR-6150. 1976, 1998. CD.

353 Kiowa Dance Group Singers. *Kiowa: Traditional Kiowa Songs*. Canyon Records Vintage Collection, Vol. 14. Canyon: CR-6145. 1975, 1998. CD.

354 Nevaquaya, Doc Tate. *Comanche Flute Music*. Collector's Series. Smithsonian Folkways: SFW CD 50403. 1978, 2004. CD.

355 Northern Cree Singers. *Still Rezin'*. Canyon: CR-6358. 2002. CD.

356 Wood, Randy. *Our Love Will Never Die: Round Dance Songs*. Canyon: CR-6388. 2005. CD.

ANTHOLOGIES

357 *An Historical Album of Blackfoot Indian Music* (Bruno Nettl, compiler). Custom Compact Disc Series. Smithsonian Folkways: FE 34001. 1979, 1990s. CD.

358 *Kiowa*. Custom Compact Disc Series. Smithsonian Folkways: FE 4393. 1964, 1999. CD.

359 *Indian Music of the Canadian Plains* (Kenneth Peacock, compiler). Custom Compact Disc Series. Smithsonian Folkways: F-4464. 1995, 2000. CD.

360 *Peyote Ceremonial Songs*. Canyon Records Vintage Collection, Vol. 12. Canyon: CR-6054. 1970s, 1998. CD.

361 *Powwow Songs: Music of the Plains Indians*. New World: 80343-2. 1975, 1986. CD.

362 *Takini: Music and Songs of the Lakota Sioux*. Chant du Monde: CMT 2741000. 1994. CD.

Southwest Cultures

INDIVIDUAL ARTISTS AND GROUPS

363 Cassadore, Patsy and Philip. *Apache: Traditional Apache Songs*. Canyon Records Vintage Collection, Vol. 5. Canyon: CR-6053. 1977, 1998. CD.

364 Cody, Herman and Radmilla. *Seed of Life*. Canyon: CR-6345. 2001. CD.

365 Kinlechene, Kee, and Yatza. *Songs of the Navaho*. JVC World Sounds. JVC: VICG-5334. 1994. CD.

ANTHOLOGIES

366 *Hopi Butterfly* (Ben Setima, compiler). Canyon Records Vintage Collection, Vol. 3. Canyon: CR-6072. 1967, 1998. CD.

367 *Indian Music of the Southwest* (Laura Boulton, compiler). Custom Compact Disc Series. Smithsonian Folkways: FW 8850. 1957, 2001. CD.

368 *Music of New Mexico: Native American Traditions*. Smithsonian Folkways: CD SF 40408. 1990, 1992. CD.

369 *Music of the American Indians of the Southwest* (Willard Rhodes, compiler). Custom Compact Disc Series. Smithsonian Folkways: FE 4420. 1951, 2001. CD.

370 *Music of the Plains Apache*. Custom Compact Disc Series. Smithsonian Folkways: F-4252. 1966, 1983. CD.

371 *Navajo Songs: Recorded by Laura Boulton in 1933 and 1940* (Laura Boulton, compiler). Smithsonian Folkways: SFW 40403. 1992. CD.

372   *Navajo Songs from Canyon de Chelly*. New World: 80406-2. 1975, 1990. CD.

373   *Oku Shareh: Turtle Dance Songs of San Juan Pueblo* (Alfonso Ortiz, notes). New World: 80301-2. 1879, 1993. CD. Recorded Anthology of American Music.

374   *The Pueblo Indians: In Story, Song and Dance.* Custom Compact Disc Series. Smithsonian Folkways: F-7200. 1972, 2001. CD.

375   *Traditional Navajo Songs.* Canyon Records Vintage Collection, Vol. 2. Canyon: CR-6064. 1998. CD.

376   *Yaqui Ritual and Festive Music.* Canyon Records Vintage Collection, Vol. 8. Canyon: CR-6140. 1976, 1998. CD.

NATIVE AMERICAN
GENERAL ANTHOLOGIES

377   *American Indian Dances* (Ronnie Lipner and Stu Lipner, compilers). Custom Compact Disc Series. Smithsonian Folkways: F-6510. 1958. CD. Released between 1983 and 1999.

378   *American Warriors: Songs for Indian Veterans.* Smithsonian Folkways Archival. Smithsonian Folkways: HRT 15014. 1977, 2010. CD.

379   ★*An Anthology of North American Indian and Eskimo Music* (Michael Asch, compiler). Custom Compact Disc Series. Smithsonian Folkways: FE 4541. 1973, 1990s. 2 CDs.

380   *Creation's Journey: Native American Music.* National Museum of the American Indian. Smithsonian Folkways: CD SF 40410. 1992, 1994. CD.

381   *A Cry from the Earth: Music of the North American Indians* (John Bierhorst, editor). Smithsonian Folkways: F-37777. 1894, 1998. CD.

382   *Discovering American Indian Music.* Discovering Music Series. AIMS Multimedia: SKU 873257. 2007. DVD. *See also* Contemporary and Intertribal, Anthologies.

383   *Healing Songs of the American Indians* (Frances Densmore, compiler; Charles Hofmann, editor). Custom Compact Disc Series. Smithsonian Folkways: F-4251. 1965, 2000. CD.

384   *Heartbeat: Voices of First Nations Women.* Smithsonian Folkways: CD SF 40415. 1995. CD.

385   *Heartbeat 2: More Voices of First Nations Women.* Smithsonian Folkways: CD SF 40455. 1991, 1998. CD.

386   *Music of the Native American Indians.* ARC Music: EUCD 1484. 1998. CD.

387   *Music of the Sioux and the Navajo* (Willard Rhodes, compiler). Custom Compact Disc Series. Smithsonian Folkways: F-4401. 1949, 1983. CD.

388   *Native American Meditations.* New World: NWCD 469. 1999. CD.

389   Periwinkle. *The Promised Land: American Indian Songs of Lament and Protest.* Custom Compact Disc Series. Smithsonian Folkways: FHS 37254. 1981, 2000s. CD.

390   *Pow Wow Trail.* Arbor. 2004. 11 DVDs, teacher's helper.

391   *Traditional Voices: Historic Recordings of Traditional Native American Music.* Canyon Records Vintage Collection, Vol. 20. Canyon: CR-7053. 1950s, 1998 CD.

392   *Under the Green Corn Moon: Native American Lullabies.* Silver Wave: SC 916. 1997. CD.

IMMIGRANT DIASPORAS

German and Swiss

INDIVIDUAL ARTISTS AND GROUPS

393   Britton, George. *Pennsylvania Dutch Folk Songs.* Custom Compact Disc Series. Smithsonian Folkways: FA 2215. 1961, 2000s. CD.

ANTHOLOGIES

394   *Ach Ya! Traditional German-American Music from Wisconsin.* Center for the Study of Upper Midwestern Cultures: CSUMC 023--CSUMC 024. 1985, 2005. 2 CDs.

395   *Swissconsin, My Homeland: Swiss Folk Music in Wisconsin.* Center for the Study of Upper Midwestern Cultures: CSUMC 002. 1988, 2004. CD.

Irish

INDIVIDUAL ARTISTS AND GROUPS

396   Carroll, Liz. *Liz Carroll* (Dáithi Sproule). Green Linnet: GLCD 1110. 1988. CD.

397   Dan Sullivan's Shamrock Band. *From Galway to Dublin: Traditional Irish Music* (Frank Quinn, Paddy Killoran, Michael Coleman, Tom Morrison, James Mullen, and others). Rounder: CD 1087. 1993. CD.

398   Green Fields of America. *Live in Concert* (Mike Moloney, Eileen Ivers, Seamus Egan, Jimmy Keane, and others). Green Linnet: GLCD 1096. 1989. CD.

ANTHOLOGIES

399   *Come Dance with Me in Ireland: Classic Irish Dance Music.* Claddagh Records, Atlantic: 83273-2. 1900s, 2000. CD.

400   *Dear Old Erin's Isle: Irish Traditional Music from America.* Nimbus: NI 5350. 1992. CD.

401   *I'm Leaving Tipperary: Classic Irish Traditional Music Recorded in America in the '20s and '30s* (Hugh Gillespie, James Morrison, Michael Hanafin, Tom Ennis, Dan Sullivan, Flanagan Brothers, John McGettigan, and others). GlobeStyle: CDORBD 082. 1994. CD.

402   *Irish Dance Music.* Custom Compact Disc Series. Smithsonian Folkways: FW 8821. 1973, 2000s. CD.

403   *Irish Music from Cleveland, Vol. 1* (Tom Byrne, Tom McCaffrey, and others). Custom Compact Disc Series. Smithsonian Folkways: FS 3517. 1977, 2000s. CD.

404   *Irish Music from Cleveland, Vol. 2: The Community Tradition* (Richard Carlin, Tom Byrne, Tom McCaffrey, and others). Custom Compact Disc Series. Smithsonian Folkways: FS 3521. 1979, 2000s. CD.

405   *Irish Music from Cleveland, Vol. 3: The Continuing Tradition* (Tom Byrne, Tom McCaffrey, and others). Custom Compact Disc Series. Smithsonian Folkways: FS 3523. 1980, 2000s. CD.

406   *Traditional Irish Music in America: Chicago* (Mick Moloney, compiler). Rounder: 82161-6006-2. 1978, 2001. CD.

407   *Traditional Irish Music in America: The East Coast* (Mick Moloney, compiler). Rounder: 82161-6005-2. 1977, 2001. CD.

408   *Wheels of the World: Classics of Irish Traditional Music from the 1920's & 30's, Vol. 1.* Yazoo: 7008. 1997. CD.

Italian

INDIVIDUAL ARTIST

409   Banda Ionica. *Procession Music of Southern Italy / Passion of Mysteries.* Fine Tune, LLC. 2001. CD.

ANTHOLOGIES

410   *Italian Folk Music Collected in New York, New Jersey and Rhode Island, Vol. 2: Calabria Bella, Dove T'hai Lasciate.* Custom Compact Disc Series. Smithsonian Folkways: FES 34042. *1979,* 2000s. CD.

411   *Italian Folk Music in New York and New Jersey, Vol. 1: In Mezz'una Strada Trovai Una Pianta Di Rosa.* Custom Compact Disc Series. Smithsonian Folkways: FES 34041. 1979, 2000s. CD.

412   *Italian Folk Songs Collected in Italian-Speaking Communities in New York City and Chicago.* Custom Compact Disc Series. Smithsonian Folkways: FE 4010. 1965, 2000. CD.

413   *Italian String Virtuosi.* Rounder: CD 1095. 1908, 1995. CD.

Scandinavian, Finnish, and Baltic

INDIVIDUAL ARTISTS AND GROUPS

414   Ameriikan Poijat. *Finnish Brass in America.* Global Village: CD 810. 1994. CD.

415   Berntsons. *One Hundred Years of Norwegian-American Music.* Azalea City Recordings: ACCD-0703. 2007. CD.

416   Goose Island Ramblers. *Midwest Ramblin'.* Center for the Study of Upper Midwestern Cultures: CSUMC 001. 1990, 2004. CD.

417   The Latvian Folk Ensemble of New York
   417.1   *Latvian Folk Songs & Dances, Vol. 1.* Custom Compact Disc Series. Smithsonian Folkways, Monitor: MFS 466. 1960s, 2001. CD.
   417.2   *The Latvian Folk Songs & Dances, Vol. 2.* Custom Compact Disc Series. Smithsonian Folkways, Monitor: MFS 495. 1960s, 2001. CD.

418   Solgård, Karen Torkelson. *Norse Fiddle in Concert.* Karen Solgård: 664241023831. 2007. CD.

ANTHOLOGIES

419   *Finnish Tunes and Songs* (Adolf Stark and Aino Karelia). Custom Compact Disc Series. Smithsonian Folkways: FW 6856. 1957, 2003. CD.

420   *Lithuanian Folk Songs in the United States.* Custom Compact Disc Series. Smithsonian Folkways: F-4009. 1955, 2000. CD.

Slavic and Balkan

INDIVIDUAL ARTISTS AND GROUPS

421 Boston Baroque. *Lost Music of Early America: Music of the Moravians* (Martin Pearlman, cond.). Telarc: CD-80482. 1997, 1998. 2 CDs.

422 Humeniuk, Pawlo. *King of the Ukrainian Fiddlers.* Arhoolie Folklyric: CD 7025. 1925, 1993. CD.

423 Moskowitz, Joseph. *The Art of the Cymbalom: The Music of Joseph Moskowitz.* Rounder: CD 1126. 1916, 1996. CD.

424 The Nama Orchestra. *Best of Nama: Balkan, Klezmer, and American Songs and Dance Music: The Nama Orchestra, 1974–1983.* NAMA. 1974, 1999. 5 CDs.

ANTHOLOGIES

425 *Polish Village Music: Historic Polish American Recordings.* Arhoolie Folklyric: CD-7031. 1927, 1995. CD.

426 *Texas Bohemia: Polkas, Waltzes, Schottisches, 1959–1993.* Trikont: US-0201. 1994. CD.

427 *Texas-Czech Bands, 1929–1959.* Arhoolie Folklyric: CD 7026. 1929, 1993. CD.

Polka

INDIVIDUAL ARTISTS AND GROUPS

428 Brave Combo
  428.1 *Musical Varieties.* Rounder: CD 11546. 1981, 1987. CD.
  428.2 *Polkas for a Gloomy World.* Rounder: CD 9045. 1995. CD.
  428.3 *Polkasonic.* Cleveland International Records: CIR-1023-2. 1999. CD.

429 Floren, Myron. *24 of Polka's Greatest Hits* (orchestra, vocalists). Ross: 6627-2. 1996. CD.

430 Meixner, Al, and Alex Meixner
  430.1 *Digitally Yours, Vol. 1.* Al and Alex Meixner: CD-072. 2007. CD.
  430.2 *Digitally Yours, Vol. 2.* Al and Alex Meixner: CD-073. 2007. CD.
  430.3 *Digitally Yours, Vol. 3.* Al and Alex Meixner: CD-074. 2007. CD.

431 Mrozinski Brothers Aleatoric Ensemble. *The Mrozinski Brothers 2-CD Collector Set.* Push. 2006. 2 CDs.

432 Rotondi
  432.1 *Play On.* ROM: ROM 26001. 1986, 1988. CD.
  432.2 *Polka Changed My Life Today!* (Tony Patellis). Five Star: 1002 CD. 2003. CD.

433 Six Fat Dutchmen
  433.1 *Greatest Hits, Vol. 1.* Polka City: 6656-2. 1998. CD.
  433.2 *Greatest Hits, Vol. 2.* Polka City: 1028-2. 2006. CD.

434 Solek, Walt. *Crown Prince of Polkas* (Walt Solek and his orchestra). Polka Hall of Fame Series. Kielbasa Polka: KCD-7222. 1993. CD.

435 Sturr, Jimmy
  435.1 *Live at Gilley's!* (Jimmy Sturr Orchestra, Johnny Karas). Ranwood Records: RDS-1006. 1992. CD.
  435.2 *Polka Favorites* (Jimmy Sturr Orchestra). Hamilton Records: 3016-2. 1995. CD.

436 Wilfahrt, Whoopee John. *The Whoopee John Story, Vol. 1* (Whoopee John Orchestra). Polka City: 1004-2. 1997. CD.

437 Yankovic, Frankie
  437.1 *48 Polka and Waltz Medleys.* Ross: 6626-2. 1995. CD.
  437.2 *Frankie Yankovic and His Yanks' Greatest Hits.* Sony BMG: 886972438825. 1987, 2008. CD.
  437.3 *70 Years of Hits.* Our Heritage: 200-2. 1985, 2000. CD.

ANTHOLOGIES

438 *Deep Polka: Dance Music from the Midwest.* Smithsonian Folkways: SF 40088. 1983, 1998. CD.

439 *Deeper Polka.* Smithsonian Folkways: SF 40140. 2002. CD.

440 *16 Most Requested Polkas.* Columbia: VRCD 343. 1989. CD.

Middle Eastern and Asian

INDIVIDUAL ARTISTS AND GROUPS

441 Hagopian, Richard, and Buddy Sarkisian
  441.1 *Kef Time: Detroit* (Kef Time Band). Traditional Crossroads: 80702-4315-2. 2002. CD.

441.2   *Kef Time: Exciting Sounds of the Middle East* (Kef Time Band). Traditional Crossroads: CD 4269. 1968, 1994. CD.

ANTHOLOGIES

442   *Armenians on 8th Avenue.* Traditional Crossroads: CD 4279. 1996. CD.

443   *Festival of Japanese Music in Hawaii.* Custom Compact Disc Series. Smithsonian Folkways: F-8885-6. 1962, 2000. 2 CDs. *See also* Hawaii, Anthologies.

444   *Music of Arab Americans: A Retrospective Collection.* Rounder: CD 1122. 1916, 1997. CD.

Traditional and Popular Music of the Americas and the Caribbean

Compiled by JOE C. CLARK, SUZANNE FLANDREAU, ANDREW JUSTICE,
MARK MCKNIGHT, RICHARD MCRAE, and TOM MOORE

Anthologies of music from the Americas and the Caribbean are spread throughout these regional sections and are included in chapter 7. *See also* the African diaspora section, chapter 5, which covers Garifuna, circum-Caribbean, and Latin American titles. Volume 28 of *The JVC Video Anthology of World Music and Dance* series covers the Americas. For more information about the music of these regions, readers should consult the *Garland Handbook of Latin American Music* (Routledge, 2008) and the *Rough Guide* series. For music from North America, see chapter 1.

MEXICO AND THE SOUTHWESTERN UNITED STATES

Compiled by Joe C. Clark

Mexico possesses a rich musical heritage that incorporates elements from other Latin American countries, including Colombia's *cumbia* and Cuba's *danzón*. Important genres of Mexican music include the *son* (many varieties exist), *norteños*, *banda*, *cumbia*, *corridor*, and *canción*, and each genre may have numerous regional variations. The southwestern United States was once part of Mexico, and these roots still influence the region's music. Tex-Mex combines various Mexican styles (primarily *norteños*) with the waltz and polka music of Polish, Czech, and German immigrants in south Texas.

California-based Arhoolie Records, which specializes in vernacular music from the Americas, offers both modern and historic recordings of Tex-Mex music, along with many historical mariachi reissues. The Mexico City based label Corasón provides contemporary traditional music releases from various regions of Mexico. Other labels for Mexican and Tex-Mex music include Smithsonian, Rounder, Fonovisa, and BMG. Titles are fairly easy to obtain in the United States, and online vendors, such as Barnes and Noble and Amazon, offer a good selection. Smithsonian Folkways Records recently made many of their older recordings available on custom CDs and digital downloads and launched a Folkways Latino series that highlights music from Mexico and other Latin American countries.

MEXICO

INDIVIDUAL ARTISTS AND GROUPS

445 Baldovinos, Salvador (cond. and perf.). *Los campesinos de Michoacán.* Arhoolie: CD-9035. 1985, 2003. CD.

446 Banda el Recodo de Don Cruz Lizárraga. *Tengo una ilusion.* Fonovisa Records: FDCD-80742. 1998. 2 CDs.

447 Los Bukis. *Greatest Hits.* Fonovisa Records: 0883504992. 2001. CD.

448 Café Tacuba. *Re.* WEA Latina: 96784-2. 1994. CD.

449 Caifanes. *El nervio del volcán.* RCA: 74321-21411-2. 1994. CD.

450 Los Camperos de Valles. *El ave de mi soñar: Mexican sones huastecos.* Smithsonian Folkways: SFW CD 40512. 2005. CD.

451 Cárdenas, Guty. *Guty Cárdenas, 1928–1932: El ruiseñor Yucateco.* Alma Criolla Records: ACCD 801. 1990. CD.

452 Conjunto Alma de Apatzingan. *Arriba! Tierra caliente.* Music of Mexico, Vol. 2. Arhoolie: CD-426. 1994. CD.

453 Conjunto Alma Jarocha. *Sones jarochos.* Music of Mexico, Vol. 1. Arhoolie: CD-354. 1994. CD.

454 Dinastía Hidalguense. *Sones huastecos.* Corasón: CORA130. 1996. CD.

455 Jiménez, José Alfredo. *Lo mejor de José Alfredo Jiménez.* Antología De La Música Mexicana. RCA: 2254-2-RL. 1987, 1990. 2 CDs.

456 Lara, Agustín. *Serie platino: 20 éxitos.* BMG: 74321459272. 1997. CD.

457 Lopez, Joaquín. *Mexico: Imágenes cotidianas = Contemporary Mexican Folksongs.* Custom Compact Disc Series. Smithsonian Folkways: FH 5448. 1979, 2000. CD.

458 Mariachi Coculense Rodríguez de Cirilo Marmolejo, Mariachi Coculense de Cirilo Marmolejo, and Cuarteto Coculense. *Mariachi coculense de Cirilo Marmolejo.* Mexico's Pioneer Mariachis, Vol. 1. Arhoolie: CD-7011. 1908, 1993. CD.

459 Mariachi Reyes del Aserradero. *Sones de jalisco.* Corasón: COCD 108. 1994. CD.

460 Mariachi Tapatío. *Mariachi Tapatío de José Marmolejo: El auténtico.* Mexico's Pioneer Mariachis, Vol. 2. Arhoolie: CD-7012. 1994. CD.

461 ★Mariachi Vargas. *Mariachi Vargas de Tecalitlán.* Mexico's Pioneer Mariachis, Vol. 3. Arhoolie: CD-7015. 1937, 1992. CD.

462 ★*Mexico* (Eduardo Llerenas, compiler). Rough Guide. World Music Network: RGNET 1098 CD. 2002. CD.

463 ★*Mexico: Fiestas of Chiapas and Oaxaca* (David Lewiston, compiler). Explorer Series. Nonesuch: 79732-2. 1976, 2003. CD.

464 Negra Graciana. *Sones jarochos.* Corasón: COCD 109. 1994. CD.

465 Negrete, Jorge. *Lo mejor de lo mejor.* BMG: 74321-72830. 2000. 2 CDs.

466 Reyes, Lucha. *Serie platino: 20 éxitos.* BMG U.S. Latin: 74321-60512-2. 1998. CD.

467 Reynoso, Juan. *El paganini de la tierra caliente.* Corasón: COCD 105. 1972, 1993. CD.

468 Solis, Javier. *15 autenticos éxitos: 20 años, 1966–1986.* Serie De Coleccion, Vol. 11. Sony: RMK-82811/-2-1053. 1958, 1998. CD.

469 Tigres del Norte
    469.1 *Corridos prohibidos.* Fonovisa Records: 883501072. 2001. CD.
    469.2 *Raíces.* Fonovisa Records: 883534882. 2007. CD.

470 Tres Ases. *40 temas originales.* Mejor de lo Mejor. BMG: 74321-72836-2. 2000. 2 CDs.

471 Trio Los Panchos. *Nuestras mejores 30 canciones.* Sony BMG Europe: 493685. 2004. 2 CDs.

ANTHOLOGIES

472 *Antología del son de México = Anthology of Mexican Sones.* (Baruj Lieberman, Eduardo Llerenas, and Enrique Ramírez de Arellano, compilers). Corasón: COCD 101–COCD 103. 1985. 3 CDs.

473 *Indian Music of Mexico.* Custom Compact Disc Series. Smithsonian Folkways: FE 4413. 1900s, 1952. CD.

474 *Mexican Indian Traditions.* Smithsonian Folkways: UNES 08304. 1992, 2014. CD.

475 *Mexico: The Real Mexico in Music and Song.* Explorer Series. Nonesuch: 79724-2. 1966, 2003. CD.

476 *Pure Purepecha: Pirekuas, the Purepecha Indian Love Songs and Abajeño Dance Music.* Corasón: COCD 119. 1994. CD.

477 ★*Putumayo Presents Mexico.* Putumayo World Music: PUT 187-2. 2001. CD.

VIDEOS

478 *The JVC/Smithsonian Folkways Video Anthology of Music and Dance: The Americas II, Vol. 28: Mexico, Cuba, Bolivia, and Argentina.* JVC, Victor Co. of Japan; dist. by Multicultural Media: VTMV-58. 1998, 2005. DVD.

479 Vichules, Ruth, and the Mariachi Band. *Mariachi.* Sunburst Visual Media. 2004. DVD, VHS.

TEX-MEX AND OTHER HISPANIC AMERICAN MUSIC OF THE SOUTHWESTERN UNITED STATES

INDIVIDUAL ARTISTS AND GROUPS

480 Ayala, Ramón. *Antología de un rey.* Freddie Records: JMCD 1890. 2004. 2 CDs.

481 Fender, Freddy. *Canciones de mi barrio.* Arhoolie: CD-366. 1959, 1993. CD.

482 Jiménez, Flaco
   482.1 *Ay te dejo en San Antonio y mas!* Arhoolie: CD-318. 1979, 1990. CD.
   482.2 *Un mojado sin licencia.* Arhoolie: CD-396. 1977, 1993. CD.

483 Jiménez, Flaco, and Max Baca. *Flaco & Max: Legends & Legacies.* Smithsonian Folkways: SFW 40569. 2014. CD.

484 Jiménez, Santiago, Jr.
   484.1 *El mero, mero de San Antonio.* Arhoolie: CD-317. 1990. CD.
   484.2 *Purely Instrumental.* Arhoolie: CD-466. 1998. CD.
   484.3 *Viva seguin.* Historic Mexican-American Music, Vol. 12. Arhoolie: CD-7023. 1947, 2001. CD.

485 Jordan, Steve
   485.1 *The Many Sounds of Steve Jordan.* Arhoolie: CD-319. 1963, 1990. CD.
   485.2 *The Return of El Parche.* Rounder: CD 6019. 1976, 1988. CD.

486 Longoria, Valerio. *Caballo viejo.* Arhoolie: CD-336. 1990. CD.

487 López, Isidro. *15 Original Hits.* Arhoolie: CD-9042. 2004. CD.

488 Mazz. *30 del recuerdo = Memorable 30.* EMI Televisa Music: H2 0946 3 60468 22. 2006. 2 CDs.

489 Mendoza, Lydia
   489.1 *The Best of Lydia Mendoza: La alondra de le frontera.* Arhoolie: CD-536. 1934, 008. CD.
   489.2 *Mal hombre.* Arhoolie: CD-7002. 1928, 1992. CD.

490 Navaira, Emilio. *De nuevo.* Universal Music Latino: B 0009895-02. 2007. CD.

491 Pérez, Rubén. *Mi unico camino* (Conjunto Bernal). Tejano Roots. Arhoolie: CD-9060. 2007. CD.

492 Pingüinos del Norte and Trio San Antonio. *Conjuntos norteños.* Arhoolie: CD-311. 1989. CD.

493 Ronstadt, Linda
   493.1 *Canciones de mi padre.* Asylum: 60765-2. 1987. CD.
   493.2 *Mas canciones.* Elektra: 61239-2. 1991. CD.

494 Rosa, Tony de la. *Así si baila en Tejas.* Rounder: CD 6046. 1991. CD.

495 Selena. *Greatest Hits.* EMI Latin: H2 7243 5 90397 25. 1989, 2003. CD.

496 Valdéz, Chayito. *20 éxitos.* Sony Discos: 84086. 2000. CD.

497 Villa, Beto. *Beto Villa, Father of Orquesta Tejana, Vol. 1.* Arhoolie: CD-9059. 1948, 2007. CD.

498 Ybarra, Eva. *A mi San Antonio.* Rounder: CD 6056. 1993. CD.

ANTHOLOGIES

499 *Accordion Conjunto Champs of Tejano and Norteño Music.* Arhoolie: CD-342. 2004. CD.

500 ★*Borderlands: From Conjunto to Chicken Scratch.* Smithsonian Folkways: SF CD 40418. 1946, 1993. CD.

501 ★*Conjunto! Texas-Mexican Border Music, Vol. 1.* Rounder: 6023. 1988, 1992. CD.

502 *Conjunto! Texas-Mexican Border Music, Vol. 2.* Rounder: 6024. 1988, 1992. CD.

503 *Conjunto! Texas-Mexican Border Music, Vol. 3.* Rounder: 6030. 1990, 1992. CD.

504 *Conjunto! Texas-Mexican Border Music, Vol. 4.* Rounder: 6034. 1990, 1992. CD.

505 *Corridos and tragedias de la frontera: First Recordings of Historic Mexican-American Ballads, 1928–1937.* Mexican-American Border Music, Vols. 6–7. Arhoolie: CD-7019–CD7020. 1994. 2 CDs.

506 *Dark and Light in Spanish New Mexico.* New World: 80292-2. 1978, 1995. CD.

507 *The Devil's Swing = El columpio del diablo.* Arhoolie: CD-480. 1994, 2000. CD.

508   *15 Early Tejano Classics.* American Masters Series, Vol. 9. Arhoolie: CD-109. 1997. CD.

509   *Heroes and Horses: Corridos from the Arizona-Sonora Borderlands.* Smithsonian Folkways: SFW 40475. 2002. CD

510   *Mexican-American Border Music, Vol. 1: An Introduction, the Pioneer Recording Artists.* Arhoolie: CD-7001. 1928, 1994. CD.

511   *Mexican-American Border Music, Vol. 3: Norteño and Tejano Accordion Pioneers, 1929–1939.* Arhoolie: CD-7016. 1929, 1995. CD.

512   ★*Music of New Mexico: Hispanic Traditions.* Smithsonian Folkways: CD SF 40409. 1973, 1992. CD.

513   *Spanish and Mexican Folk Music of New Mexico.* Custom Compact Disc Series. Smithsonian Folkways: FE 4426. 1959, 2001. CD.

514   *Taquachito Nights: Conjunto Music from South Texas.* Smithsonian Folkways: SFW CD 40477. 1998, 1999. CD.

515   ★*Tejano Roots.* Arhoolie: CD-341. 1991. CD.

516   *Tejano Roots: Orquestas Tejanas.* Arhoolie: CD-368. 1947, 1992. CD.

517   *Tejano Roots: The Women.* Arhoolie: CD-343. 1946, 1991. CD.

VIDEOS

518   *Chulas fronteras.* Roots of Tex-Mex Music. Brazos Films: BF-104. 2003, 1976. DVD.

519   *Tex-Mex: Music of the Texas Mexican Borderlands.* Beats of the Heart. Shanachie: 1206. 1982, 2001. DVD.

CARIBBEAN POPULAR AND TRADITIONAL

Compiled by Richard McRae

This section comprises traditional and popular music from the Caribbean region and from U.S. regions that have significant cultural influences stemming from the Caribbean. The styles and countries covered include salsa, Latin jazz, and related styles (including New York City, Miami, and Pan-Caribbean artists); Cuba, Dominican Republic; Haiti; Jamaica; Puerto Rico; Trinidad and Tobago (steel band, calypso); and other Caribbean islands (including the Bahamas, Barbados, Guadeloupe, Martinique, St. Lucia, and the U.S. Virgin Islands). Just a few of the vibrant styles include French Antillean zouk (a blend of pop, African guitar, and funk), soca, and reggae, which have spawned many fusion styles. Creole, Afro-Brazilian, Afro-Cuban, and other cross-cultural influences abound.

Distributors and sources include Reyes Records (www.reyesrecords.com), Universal Music Group (www .universalmusic.com, Allmusic (www.allmusic.com), and *World Music: The Rough Guide, Vol. 2: Latin and North America, Caribbean, India, Asia, and Pacific,* edited by Simon Broughton and Mark Ellingham (Rough Guides, 2000). Local recordings sources include Parrot Fish Records and Tapes in the Virgin Islands, St. Thomas (tel: 340-776-4514). In Trinidad, see Rhyner's Music Store (www.rhyners.com).

SALSA, LATIN JAZZ, AND RELATED STYLES (INCLUDING NEW YORK CITY, MIAMI, AND PAN-CARIBBEAN ARTISTS)

INDIVIDUAL ARTISTS AND GROUPS

520   Allegre All-Stars. *Te invita.* Fania: 773 130 137-2. 1993, 2006. CD.

521   Anthony, Marc. *Desde un principio.* Sony Discos: TRK-83580. 1999. CD.

522   Armenteros, Alfredo "Chocolate." *Mejor de Chocolate, Vol. 1.* SAR: SCD-1009. 1990. CD.

523   Barretto, Ray
       523.1   *Acid.* Fania: SLP 346. 2006. CD.
       523.2   *Ancestral Spirits* (New World Spirit). Concord Picante: CCD-4549. 1993. CD.
       523.3   *Essential Ray Barretto.* Fania, Emúsica: 773 130 283-2. 2007. 2 CDs.
       523.4   *Rican/Struction.* Fania: JM 552. 1995. CD.

524   Bauzá, Mario
       524.1   *My Time Is Now.* Messidor: CD 15824 2. 1993. CD.
       524.2   *Tanga.* Messidor: CD 15819-2. 1992. CD.

525   Blades, Rubén
       525.1   *Bohemio y poeta.* Fania: 773 130 025-2. 1979, 2006. CD.
       525.2   *Maestra vida.* Fania: 773 130 034-2, 773 130 047-2. 2006. 2 CDs.
       525.3   *Poeta del pueblo.* A Man and His Music. Fania: 773 130 342-2. 2008. 2 CDs.

525.4 *Rubén Blades y Son del Solar . . . Live!* (Son del Solar). Elektra: 60868-2. 1990. CD.

526 Chirino, Willy. *Willy Chirino, 20 originales éxitos.* Sony BMG Music Entertainment (U.S. Latin): SMK 95875 (disc 1), SMK 95919 (disc 2). 2005. 2 CDs.

527 Colón, Willie
   527.1 *Essential Willie Colón.* Fania: 773 130 299-2. 2008. 2 CDs.
   527.2 *Siembra* (Rubén Blades). Fania: 773 130 030-2. 1978, 2006. CD.
   527.3 *Willie* (Hector Lavoe). Fania: SLP 00464. 1974. CD.

528 Cortijo, Rafael. *Cortijo and His Time Machine.* Coco: SNAP 031 CD. 2001. CD.

529 Cruz, Celia
   529.1 *Celia and Johnny* (Tito Puente). Fania: 773-130 004-2. 1974, 2006. CD.
   529.2 *Celia Cruz* [1966–1992]. Rough Guide. World Music Network: RGNET 1150 CD. 2007. CD.
   529.3 *Cuba y Puerto Rico son . . .* (Tito Puente). Fania: 773-130 004-2. 1966, 2006. CD.
   529.4 *Incomparable Celia* (Sonora Matancera). Seeco: STR 90506. 1991. CD.
   529.5 *Latin Music's First Lady: Her Essential Recordings.* Manteca: MANTDBL501. 2006. 2 CDs.
   529.6 *Only They Could Have Made This Album* (Willie Colón). Fania: 773 130 110-2. 1977, 2006. 2 CDs.
   529.7 *Ritmo en el corazón* (Ray Barretto). Fania: 773 130 205-2. 1988, 2007. CD.

530 D'Rivera, Paquito
   530.1 *Habana: Rio conexión.* Pimienta: 245 360 711-2. 2005. CD.
   530.2 *Reunion* (Arturo Sandoval). Pimienta: 245 360 610-2. 2004. CD.

531 ★Familia RMM. *Combinación perfecta.* Sony, RMM: CDT-841126. 1993. CD.

532 Fania All-Stars
   532.1 ★*Best of Fania All-Stars.* Charly: SNAD523CD. 2001. 2 CDs.
   532.2 *Live at the Cheetah, Vols. 1–2.* Fania, Emúscia: 773 130 042-2 (vol. 1), 773 130 111-2 (vol. 2). 2006. 2 CDs.

533 Feliciano, Cheo. *Cheo.* Universal Music Latino: 440066148-2. 2007. 2 CDs.

534 Gonzalez, Jerry. *Rumba para Monk.* Sunnyside: SSC 1036D. 2001. CD.

535 Harlow, Larry. *La herencia.* Fania: 773 130 270-2. 2007. CD. Remastered compilation.

536 Lavoe, Hector. *La voz* (Willie Colón). A Man and His Music. Fania: 773 130 144-2. 2007. 2 CDs.

537 ★Machito. *Ritmo caliente.* Proper: P1289-P1292. 2002. 4 CDs.

538 Marin, Orlando
   538.1 *Orlando Marin's Saxofobia: Two Piano Descarga* (Charlie Palmieri, Louie Ramirez). Mucho Music: MMICD 1024. 1993. CD.
   538.2 *Se te quemó la casa.* Alegre: LPA-8140. 1961, 1999. CD.

539 Miguel, Luis. *Grandes éxitos.* Warner Music Latina: 62753-2. 2005. 2 CDs.

540 Orchestra Rytmo Africa-Cubana. *La charanga 1980.* Orquestra Rytmo Africa-Cubana: 7779VOL1. 1992. CD.

541 Orquesta Batachanga. *Mañana para los niños.* Bembé EarthBeat!: 9 42513-2. 1995. CD.

542 Orquesta Conexión Latina. *Mambo Nights.* Enja: ENJ-9402 2. 2001. CD.

543 Pacheco, Johnny
   543.1 *Johnny Pacheco, el maestro.* A Man and His Music. Fania, Emúsica: 773 130 144-2. 2006. 2 CDs.
   543.2 *Los compadres* (Pete Rodríguez). Fania: 773 130 013-2. 1972, 2006. CD.

544 Palmieri, Charlie. *A Giant Step.* M.I.L. Multimedia: ESP 8523. 1997. CD.

545 Palmieri, Eddie
   545.1 *Mozambique* (Ismael Quintana). Tico: SLP 1126. 1965, 2008. CD.
   545.2 *Palmas.* American Explorer Series. Elektra Nonesuch: 61649-2. 1994. CD.
   545.3 *Sun of Latin Music* (Lalo Rodriquez). Musical Productions: MP-3109 CD. 1974, 1990. CD.
   545.4 *Unfinished Masterpiece* (Lalo Rodriquez). Musical Productions: MP-3120. 1974, 1990. CD.

546 Pozo, Chano. *Legendary Sessions* (Arsenio Rodríguez and Machito). Tumbao Cuban Classics: TCD-017. 1992. CD. Originally recorded [1947–1953] in New York and Havana.

547　Puente, Tito
　　547.1　*Dance Mania.* RCA Latin. BMG: 82876-72001-2. 1958, 2005. CD.
　　547.2　*The Essential Tito Puente* [1949–1962]. Sony BMG Music Entertainment: 82876 69243 2. 2005. 2 CDs.
　　547.3　*50 Years of Swing* [1946–1996]. RMM: RMD3-82050. 1997. 3 CDs.

548　Rodríguez, Arsenio. *Arsenio Rodríguez, el alma de Cuba: Grabaciones completas RCA Victor, 1940–1956.* Tumbao Cuban Classics: TCD 315 (TCD 316–TCD 318). 2007. 6 CDs.

549　Rodriguez, Tito
　　549.1　*La herencia.* Fania: 773 130 293-5. 2007. CD.
　　549.2　*Mambo Madness.* Sonido: TRLP 1004. 1959, 1999. CD.

550　Rosario, Willie. *Willie Rosario.* Oro Salsero. Universal Music Latino: 863 673 130-2. 1994, 2002. 2 CDs.

551　Ruiz, Frankie. *La leyenda.* Universal: 314 547 038-2. 1999. 2 CDs.

552　Ruiz, Hilton. *Manhattan Mambo.* Telarc Jazz: CD-83322. 1992. CD.

553　Ruiz, Rey. *Mis 30 mejores canciones.* Sony Discos: T2K 87697. 2003. 2 CDs.

554　Sanabria, Bobby. *Afro-Cuban Dream: Live and in Clave!!!* Arabesque: AJ0149. 2000. CD.

555　★Sanchez, Poncho. *Ultimate Latin Dance Party.* Concord Picante: CCD2-2153-2. 2002. 2 CDs.

556　Sandoval, Arturo. *Very Best of Arturo Sandoval.* Verve Music Group: B0001700-02. 2004. CD.

557　Santa Rosa, Gilberto. *A dos tiempos de un tiempo.* Sony: DCC-80895 2-46954. 1992. CD.

558　Santamaria, Mongo
　　558.1　*Afro Roots.* Prestige: PCD-24018-2. 1958, 1989. CD.
　　558.2　*Afro-Indio.* Fania: 7731300722. 1975, 2006. CD.
　　558.3　*Greatest Hits.* Columbia Legacy: CK 63920. 2000. CD.
　　558.4　*Our Man in Havana.* Fantasy: FCD-24729-2. 1960, 1993. CD.

559　Tjader, Cal. *Ultimate Cal Tjader.* Ultimate Verve. Verve: 314 559 702-2. 1999. CD.

560　Valdez, Carlos "Patato." *Patato and Totico* (Eugenio "Totico" Arango and others). Verve: V6-5037. 1968, 2004. CD.

ANTHOLOGIES

561　*Boogaloo* (Pete Rodríguez y su Conjunto, Tito Puente y su Orchestra, Charlie Palmieri, Ralph Robles, Lebron Brothers Orchestra, Bobby Valentin, Joe Cuba Sextet, Fania All-Stars, Celia Cruz, Ismael Rivera y sus Cachimbo, Willie Colon, Ray Barretto, Bobby Valentin, and Gilberto Sextet). Rough Guide. World Music Network: RGNET 1097 CD. 2005. CD.

562　★*Caliente (Hot): Puerto Rican and Cuban Musical Expression in New York.* New World: 244. 1992. CD.

563　*Latin Jazz* (Cannonball Adderley Machito, Poncho Sanchez, Tomas Einarsson, Tito Puente, Chico Alvarez, Ray Barretto, Hilton Ruiz, Manny Oquendo and Libre, and Chocolate Armenteros). Putumayo World Music: PUT 265-2. 2007. CD.

564　★*Latin Legends* (Tito Puente, Celia Cruz, Tito Rodriguez, Orquesta Guayacan, Joe Cuba Sextet, Beny More, Machito and His Orchestra, Hector Lavoe, Willie Colón and Ruben Blades, Eddie Palmieri, Perez Prado and his Orchestra, Oscar D'León, Fania All-Stars, Ray Barretto, Desi Arnaz, and Tito Nieves). Medalist: 8053860015-2-4. 2001. 2 CDs.

565　★*Mambo Mania! The Kings and Queens of Mambo* (Celia Cruz con La Sonora Matancera, Perez Prado and His Orchestra, Tito Rodriguez, Mongo Santamaria Orchestra, Hector Rivera, Beny More, Desi Arnaz, Ray Barretto, La India de Oriente, Tito Puente, Machita, Cachao, Cal Tijader, Xavier Cugat, and Septeto Nacional Ignacia Piñeiro). Rhino: R2 71881. 1995. CD.

566　*Oye Listen! Compacto caliente* (Linda Leida y la Bahia con Javier Vasquez, Bobby Rodriguez, Alfredo Valdes, Monguito "El Unico," La Sonora de Baru, Virgilio Marti, Rolando la Serie, Rudy Calzado, Guaracheros de Oriente, and La India de Oriente, and Super All Star). Caiman: CDORB 014. 1987. CD.

567　*Revolucion en la casa: The Essential Latin House Collection.* Music Collection International: NSCD 047. 1999. CD.

568　*Rough Guide to Salsa Dance* (Conjunto Imagen, Grupo Gale, Los Nemus, Fruko y Sus Tesos,

Johnny Polanco y Su Conjunto Amistad, Rigo y Su Orba Maestra, Africando, Bibby Rivas, Los Titanes, Conjunto Colores, Mercadonegro, Charlie D'Cali y Su Salsa, Merengada, Jorge Cordero, Sonora Carruseles and Jimmy Bosch). Rough Guide. World Music Network: RGNET 1156 CD. 2005. CD.

569   *Rough Guide to Salsa Dura NYC* (Eddie Palmieri, Wayne Gorbea, Soneros del Barrio, Jimmy Delgado, Pablo Chino Nuñez, Chico Álvarez, Jimmy Bosch, George Delgado, Don Ramón, Estrellas Cobo, Ricky González, and Joe Quijano and His Conjunto Cachan). Rough Guide. World Music Network: RGNET 1177 CD. 2007. CD.

570   ★*¡Salsa!* (Poncho Sanchez, Chico Álvarez, Eddie Palmieri, Cheo Feliciano, Jose Conde, Ricardo Lemvo, and Juanito). Putumayo World Music: PUT 289-2. 2009. CD.

571   ★*Salsa Explosion! The New York Salsa Revolution, 1968–1985* (Willie Colón, Héctor Lavoe, Mongo Santamaria, Tito Puente, Celia Cruz, Johnny Pacheco, Ralfi Pagan, Eddie Palmieri, Ray Barretto, Louie Ramirez, and Rafael Valenzuela). Fania Essential Recordings Strut: STRUT 068 CD. 2010. CD.

572   *Salsa Fresca: Dance Hits of the '90s* (Hansel " El Gato" Martinez, Pupy Santiago, Frankie Ruiz, Alex Leon, Rey Ruiz, Grupo Niche, Johnny Ray y Salsa con Clase, Pete "El Conde" Rodriquez, Willie Rosario, Luis Enrique, Gilberto Santa Rosa, Eddie Santiago, Giro, and Tommy Olivencia). Rhino: R2 72195. 1996. CD.

573   ★*Salsa: A Musical History*. Fania: 463 950 8007-2. 1964, 2010. 4 CDs.

574   ★*Viva Salsa* (Ray Barretto, Fania All-Stars, Willie Colon, Orchestra Harlow, Tito Puente, Roberto Roena, Eddie Palmieri, Johny Pacheco, Richie Ray, Bobby Valentín, Sonora Ponceña, Pete "Condel" Rodríguez, Adalberto Santiago, Celia Cruz, and Ruben Blades). Charly: CD HOT BOX 1. 1991. 4 CDs.

VIDEOS

575   *Calle 54* (Eliane Elias, Michel Camilo, Chucho Valdés, Cachao, Paquito D'Rivera, Tito Puente, and Jerry Gonzalez). Miramax Home Entertainment: 22597. 2001. DVD.

576   ★*Latin Music USA*. PBS Distribution: LMUS 601. 2009. 2 DVDs.

577   *The Rhythmic Construction of a Salsa Tune* (Pablo Chino Nuñez). Latin Percussion: LPVC201D. 2010. 2 DVDs.

578   ★*Salsa: Latin Music of New York and Puerto Rico* (Celia Cruz, Tito Puente, Reuben Blades, Charlie Palmieri, and Ray Barretto). Beats of the Heart. Shanachie: 1203. 1979, 2000. DVD.

CUBA

INDIVIDUAL ARTISTS AND GROUPS

579   ★Buena Vista Social Club. *Buena Vista Social Club* (Compay Segundo, Eliades Ochoa, Ibrahim Ferrer, Ry Cooder, and Rubén González). World Circuit, Nonesuch: 79478-2. 1997. CD.

580   ★Cachao. *Last Mambo: La leyenda en vivo*. Eventus: 81171201212. 2007, 2011. 2 CDs.

581   Calzado, David, y La Charanga Habanera. *Tremendo Delirio*. Universal Music: LATD-40068. 1997. CD.

582   Conjunto Matamoros. *Bailaré tu son*. Tumbao Cuban Classics: TCD-070. 1995. CD.

583   Conjunto Son 14. *La máquina musical: 20th Anniversary*. Tumi Cuban. Tumi: TUMI 086. 1999. CD.

584   ★Cruz, Celia. *Azúcar!* (Tito Puente, Johnny Pacheco, Justo Betancourt, and Willie Colón). Código Music: 463 950 7012-2. 2010. 2 CDs.

585   Estrellas de Areito. *Estrellas de Areito: Heroes*. World Circuit, Nonesuch: 79551-2. 1998. 2 CDs.

586   Fellove, Francisco. *Cuban Gold, Vols. 1–5*. Qbadisc: QB-9006 (vol. 1), QB-9016 (vol. 2), QB-9024 (vol. 3), QB-9025 (vol. 4), QB-9027 (vol. 5). 1993–1998. 5 CDs.

587   Ferrer, Ibrahim. *Buenos Hermanos* (Celia Cruz). World Circuit, Nonesuch: 79650-2. 2003. CD.

588   González, Rubén. *Introducing—Rubén González*. World Circuit, Nonesuch: 79477-2. 1997. CD.

589   Grupo Irakere
589.1   *Irakere*. Egrem: CD 0145–CD 0155. 1980s, 1995. 11 CDs.
589.2   *Live at Ronnie Scott's*. World Pacific Presents the Music of Cuba. World Pacific: CDP 0777 7 80598. [1996]. CD.

590   Milanés, Pablo. *Cancionero*. World Pacific: CDP 0777 7 80596 2 2. 1993. CD.

591 Moré, Beny. *The Very Best of Beny Moré and His All Star Afro Cuban Big Band, Vols. 1–3* [1955–1958]. Tropical Series. BMG: 74321-26029-2 (vol. 1), 74321-26238-2 (vol. 2), 74321-63752-2 (vol. 3). 1994–1998. 3 CDs.

592 ★Munequitos de Matanzas. *Rumba Caliente 88/77.* Qbadisc: QB 9005. 1992. CD.

593 ★Orquesta Aragón. *The Heart of Havana, Vols. 1 and 2.* Tropical Series. RCA: 3204-2-RL (vol. 1), 3488-2-RL (vol. 2). 1956, 1992. 2 CDs.

594 Orquesta Reve. *La explosion del momento!* Real World; dist. by Caroline Records: Carol 2303-2. 1989. CD.

595 Prado, Pérez
595.1 *Kuba-Mambo.* Tumbao Cuban Classics: TCD-006. 1991. CD.
595.2 *Mondo Mambo! The Best of Pérez Prado and His Orchestra.* Rhino: R2 71889; DRCI-1242. 1995. CD.

596 Puebla, Carlos. *Carlos Puebla y Sus Tradicionales.* Egrem-Artex: CD-013. 1992. CD.

597 Rodriguez, Silvio
597.1 *Cuba Classics 1: Canciones urgentes los grandes éxitos.* Luaka Bop, Warner Bros: 9 26480-2. 1991. CD.
597.2 *Días y flores.* Hannibal: HNCD 1322. 1975, 1988. CD.

598 Segundo, Compay. *Gracias Compay.* Warner Music Latina: 60884-2. 2003. 2 CDs.

599 Sexteto Habanero. *Grabaciones completas, 1925–1931.* Tumbao Cuban Classics: TCD 300. 1998. 4 CDs.

600 Sierra Maestra. *Tíbiri tábara.* World Circuit, Nonesuch: 79497-2. 1997. CD.

601 Sonora Matancera. *Celebrando con la Sonora Matancera: 65 aniversario.* TH-Rodven: TH-2630. 1989. CD.

602 ★Los Van Van. *La colección Cubana.* Music Club: 50082. 1998. CD.

603 Varela, Carlos. *Monedas al Aire.* Qbadisc: QB 9010. 1993. CD.

ANTHOLOGIES

604 *A toda Cuba le gusta* (Ibrahim Ferrer, Pío Leyva, Mañuel "Puntillita" Licea, Raúl Planas, José Antonio "Maceo" Rodríguez, Félix Valoy, Rubén González, and Afro-Cuban All-Stars). Nonesuch: 79476-2. 1997. CD.

605 ★*Afro-Cuba* (Cheikh N'Digël Lô, Ricardo Lemvo and Makina Loca; Africando, Cuarteto Patria and Manu Dibango, Super Cayor de Dakar, Orchestra Baobab, Super Eagles, Septeto Nacional Ignacia Piñeiro, Sierra Maestra, Balla et ses Balladins, E. T. Mensah, Lázaro Ros, Afro-Cuban All Stars, and Patato featuring Samba Mapangala). Rough Guide. World Music Network: RGNET 1070 CD. 2001. CD.

606 ★*Antología de la nueva trova, vols. 1–4.* Coleccion Trovadores. Egrem: CD 0295-CD 0298. 1960s, 1998. 4 CDs.

607 ★*A Carnival of Cuban Music* (Afro Cuba de Matanzas, Carnival Comparsa Group, Los Muñequitos de Matanzas, Isaac Oviedo, Duo del Bodequita del Medio, Bing Crosby with Xavier Cugat, Enrique Jorrin, Los Van Van, Son de la Loma, Don Azpiazu and his Havana Casino Orchestra, Chano Pozo and Dizzy Gillespie's Big Band, Grupo Irakere, Perez Prado, Arsenio Rodríguez, Celia Cruz with Tito Puente and Orchestra, and Ruben Blades). Routes of Rhythm, Vol. 1. Rounder: CD 5049. 1990. CD.

608 ★*Cuba Classics 2: Dancing with the Enemy* (Celeste Mendoza, María Teresa Vera, Orquesta Original de Manzanillo, Orquesta Riverside, Chapottín y sus Estrellas, Los Van Van, Conjunto Rumbavana, Orquesta Reve "Changüí '68," Caridad Hierrezuelo y Conjunto Caney, Los Zafiros, Orquesta Pancho el Bravo, and El Jilguero de Cienfuegos). Luaka Bop, Sire, Warner Bros: 9 26580-2. 1991. CD.

609 ★*Cuba Classics 3: Diablo al infierno!* (Grupo Irakere, Grupo Síntesis, Los Van Van, Pío Leyva, Lázaro Ros with Mezcla, Los Blues, Grupo Vocal Sampling, Dan Den, N.G. La Banda, Pablo Milanés, Carlos Varela, and Zeus). Luaka Bop, Warner Bros: 9 45107-2. 1974, 1992. CD.

610 ★*Cuba I Am Time.* Blue Jackel Entertainment: BJAC 5101-2-BJAC 5014-2. 1997. 4 CDs.

611 ★*Cuban Counterpoint: History of the Son Montuno.* Rounder: CD 1078. 1992. CD.

612 ★*Cuban Dance Party* (Grupo Irakere, Los Van Van, Estrellas Cubanas, Septeto Nacional Ignacia Piñero, Orquesta Orestes Lopez, Isaac Oveido, and Son de la Loma). Routes of Rhythm, Vol. 2. Rounder: CD 5050. 1990. CD.

613 *The Cuban Danzón: Its Ancestors and Descendants*
(La Orquesta Folklórica Cubana, Charanga Típica,
Antonio Arcaño y Sus Maravillas, Orquesta de
Enrique Jorrín, and Orquesta Ritmo Oriental).
Smithsonian Folkways: FE 4066. 1982, 2007. CD.

614 *Cuban son* (Septeto Nacional Ignacia Piñeiro,
Afro-Cuban All Stars, Vieja Trova Santiaguera,
Ñico Saquito, Orquesta Melodías del 40, Beny
Moré, Sierra Maestra, Septeto Santiaguero,
Orquesta Aragón, Los Van Van, Son de la Loma,
Sexteto Habanero, Maria Teresa Vera, Familia
Valera Miranda, Cañambú, Cubanismo!, and Los
Jubilados). Rough Guide. World Music Network:
RGNET 1046 CD. 2000. CD.

615 *Hot Dance Music from Cuba.* Flex Media
Entertainment: KBOX3471. 2006. 3 CDs.

616 *Jesús Alemañy's Cubanismo!* (Jesús Alemañy,
Alfredo Rodriguez, and Tata Güines). Hannibal:
HNCD 1390. 1996. CD.

617 *Mambo* (Snowboy and the Latin Section, Tito
Puente, Mario Bauza, Cal Tjader, Noro Morales,
Bobby Matos and John Santos, Mamborama,
Pérez Prado, Bebo Valdés, Jack Costanzo, Eddie
Palmieri, Xavier Cugat, Machito, Poncho Sanchez,
Manny Oquendo and Libre, Orquesta Tabaco y
Ron, and Fruko y Sus Tesos). Rough Guide. World
Music Network: RGNET 1136 CD. 2004. CD.

618 *A Night in Cuba: The Music of Cuba* (Trio
Matamoros, Perez Prado, El Original Cuarteto
D'Aida, Beny More, Orquesta Aragón, Xiomara
Alfaro, Gloria Estevan, Willie Chirinno and Celia
Cruz, Arturo Sandoval, Cachao, Hansel and Raul
with Rolando Laserie, Paquito D'Rivera, Albita,
Donato Poveda, and Paquito Hechavarria). Sony
BMG Music Entertainment: 8869 735299 2.
2008. CD.

619 *Oriente de Cuba* (Familia Valera Miranda,
Folkloyuma, Estudiantina Invasora, and Trio
Yagua). Nimbus: NI 1746. 1999. 5 CDs.

620 *Putumayo Presents Cuba* (Ibrahim Ferrer, Eliades
Ochoa, Cuarteto Patria, Septeto Nacional Ignacia
Piñeiro, Afro-Cuban Jazz Project, Orquesta
Sublime, Mi Son, Todos Estrellas, Grupo Irakere,
Sierra Maestra, and Guaracheros de Oriente).
Putumayo World Music: PUTU
149-2. 1999. CD.

621 *The Rough Guide to Cuban Street Party* (Pablo
Ellicott Yglesias, Yumurí, Orlando Valle,
Adalberto Alvarez, Teresa Garcia Caturla,

Barbarito Torres, Roberto Torres, La Lupe, Linda
Leida, Chico Álvarez, Edwin Bonilla, Jesús El
Niño Pérez, Roberto Linares Brown, Ernesto
Brooks, and Corey Paul). Rough Guide. World
Music Network: RGNET 1199 CD. 2008. CD.

622 *The Rough Guide to the Music of Cuba.* Special
edition (Estrellas de Arieto, Sierra Maestra, Afro-
Cuban All-Stars, Orlando "Cachaito" Lopez, Afro
Cuban Jazz Project, Los Van Van, Pancho Quinto,
Osdalgia, Azucar Negra, Sama y El Expreso de
Oriente, Elio Revé Jr., Maikel Blanco y su Salsa
Mayor, and Madera Limpia). Rough Guide. World
Music Network: RGNET 1225 CD. 2009. 2 CDs.

623 *Sacred Rhythms of Cuban Santería.* Smithsonian
Folkways: SF 40419. 1995. CD.

VIDEOS

624 Cruz, Celia. *Celia the Queen.* Eventus
Entertainment: 81171201189. 2009. DVD.

625 *Cuba: Island of Music* (Gary Keys, Henry G.
Jarecki, Billy Taylor, Candido, and Chico
O'Farrill). Wienerworld: MVD 5170D. 2000,
2011. DVD.

626 *Roots of Rhythm.* Docudrama: NVG-9476.
2001. DVD.

627 *We Are the Music!* The Cuban Masterworks
Collection. First Run Features: 913188.
2008. DVD.

DOMINICAN REPUBLIC

INDIVIDUAL ARTISTS AND GROUPS

628 Fulanito. *Greatest Hits.* Cutting Records: CD 2059.
2008. CD.

629 Guerra, Juan Luis
    629.1 *Asondeguerra.* Capitol Latin:
        5099924248327. 2010. CD.
    629.2 *Bachata Rosa.* Karen: 10793 0136-2.
        1995. CD.

630 Los Hermanos Rosario. *Los mundialmente famoso
Hermanos Rosario.* EMI Latin: H2 8278 6 50005
2 1. 2003. CD.

631 Pochy. *Pochy y Su Coco Band.* Kubaney: SPKT
296337. 1995. CD.

632 Los Sabrosos de Merengue. *Sabrosos del Merengue,
20 aniversario.* Musical Productions: MP 6418.
2005. CD.

633   Santos, Henry. *Introducing Henry Santos.* Universal Music Latino: 278 655 092-2. 2011. CD.

634   Ulloa, Francisco. *Ultramerengue!* Green Linnet: GLCD 4004. 1992, 1993. CD.

635   Vargas, Wilfrido. *Abusadora* (Sandy Reyes). Karen: K-60. 1981. CD.

636   Ventura, Johnny. *20th Anniversary, 1979–1999.* Sony: TRK-83433. 1999. CD.

637   Viloria, Angel. *Merengues: 21 éxitos originales, Vol. 1.* Ansonia: HGCD 1206. 1989. CD.

ANTHOLOGIES

638   *Aquí está el merengue* (Juan Luis Guerra y Grupo 4:40, Sergio Vargas y Los Hijos del Rey, Hermanos Rosario, Rasputin, Henry Hierro, Rubby Pérez con Wilfrido Vargas, Las Chicas del Can, Carolina, Diómedes y Los Hijos del Rey, Rubby Pérez, Dioni Fernández, Carlos David, Alex Bueno, Charlie Espinal, Tony Medrano, and New York Band). Karen: CDK 112. 1992. CD.

639   *Essential Merengue: Stripping the Parrots* (Rafaelito Arias y su Conjunto, Cuarto Alegres Dominicanos, Cuarteto Hernandez, Sexteto Peravia, and Cachucha y su Conjunto). Corazon; dist. by Rounder: COCD122. 1995. CD.

640   *Merengue Dance* (Jose Peña Suazo, Johnny Ventura, Milly Quezada, Joseíto Mateo, Wilfrido Vargas, Nelson De la Olla, María Díaz, Prodigio, Kinito Mendez, Papi Sanchez, Boy, Krisspy, Chiqui Rodríguez, Charlie Valens, and Carlitos Almonte). Rough Guide. World Music Network: RGNET 1229 CD. 2009. 2 CDs.

641   *Merengue: Dominican Music and Dominican Identity* (Ñico Lora, Orquesta Nilo Menendez, Antonio Morel, Ñiñi Vásquez y sus Rigoleros, Joseíto Mateo, Guandulito y su Conjunto Típico Cibaeño, Angel Viloria, Belkis Concepción, Blas Durán y sus Peluches, El Ciego de Nagua, Juan A. Mercedes Moreno ("Jefe"), E. Pérez, Domingo Azólo, Pascual Salmón Moya, and Gómez Peña). Rounder: CD 1130. 1997. CD.

642   *Revolucion en la casa: The Essential Latin House Collection.* Music Collection International: NSCD 047. 1999. CD.

See Caribbean Popular and Traditional: General Anthologies for additional citations.

VIDEOS

643   *Bachata: Música del pueblo.* Cinema Guild. 2003. DVD.

644   *Duke of Bachata* (Joan Soriano). Horizon Line Documentary. 2009. DVD.

HAITI

INDIVIDUAL ARTISTS AND GROUPS

645   Bissainthe, Toto. *Haïti chanté.* Chant du Monde: LDX 2741014. 1983, 1995. CD.

646   Boukan Ginen. *Jou a rive.* Xenophile: 4024. 1995. CD.

647   Boukman Eksperyans. *Kanaval Rasin—Vodou adjae: A Spiritual and Political Anthology, 1990–2000.* Balenjo Music: 68256004962-2. 2000. CD.

648   Coupé Cloué. *The Best of Coupé Cloué.* BMI, Digital, Geronimo Records: GR0076. 1992. CD.

649   ★Ensemble Nemours Jn. Baptiste. *Musical Tour of Haiti.* Ansonia: HGCD-1280. 1960–1992. CD.

650   Michel, Emeline. *Very Best of Emeline Michel.* Production Cheval de Feu: DDC-460. 1991. CD.

651   Orchestre Septentrional. *Nouvelle vague.* AD Music: AD 081. 2003. CD.

652   Skah Shah. *Skah-Shah #1.* Rotel Records; dist. by Montuno Records: CD 3380. 1992. CD.

653   System Band. *Best of System Band.* Le Son Haïti. Wagram Music: 3040262. 1998. CD.

654   ★Tabou Combo. *Anthology (1979–1986).* Zafem, Mini Records; dist. by Maxison: MRSD1017-MRSD1020. 1992. 4 CDs.

655   Ti-Coca. *Haiti Colibri.* Accords Croisés: AC 127. 2009. CD.

ANTHOLOGIES

656   *Alan Lomax in Haiti.* Alan Lomax Collection. Harte Recordings: HR 103. 1936, 2009. 10 CDs, field notebooks, maps, etc.

657   *Angels in the Mirror: Vodou Music of Haiti.* Musical Expeditions. Ellipsis Arts: CD 4120. 1997. CD.

658   ★*The Beat of Haiti, Vol. 1: 1965–1985* (Les Shleu-Shleu, Tabou Combo, Coupé Cloué, Bossa Combo, GM Connection, Mini All Stars, and Tropicana). Mini: MRSD-1012. 1991. CD.

659 *Caribbean Revels: Haitian Rara and Dominican Gaga.* Smithsonian Folkways: CD SF 40402. 1978, 1991. CD.

660 *Haiti* (Coupé Cloué, Masters of Haiti, Ti Coca and Wanga Negess, Les Fantaisistes de Carrefour, Orchestre Tropicana, Haitiando, Mini All Stars, Ram, Mizik Mizik, Boukman Eksperyans, Nemours Jean-Baptiste, Super Jazz des Jeunes, D. P. Express, Tabou Combo, and Issa El Saieh et Son Orchestre). Rough Guide. World Music Network: RGNET 1067 CD. 2002. CD.

661 *Haiti chéri* (Beethova Obas, Tabou Combo, D. P. Express, Caribbean Sextet, Magnum Band, Boukan Ginen, Le Gypsies, Michel Martelly, Coupé Cloué, Zin, and Emeline Michel). Déclic: 50403-2. 1995. CD.

662 ★*Konbit: Burning Rhythms of Haiti* (Ensemble Nemours Jean-Baptiste, Dadou, Magnum Band, Skah Shah, Sakad Neville Brothers and Les Freres Parents, Manno Charlemagne, Sanba Yo, Tabou Combo, Mini All Stars, and D. P. Express). A&M: CD 5281. 1989. CD.

663 *Rara in Haiti* (Frederick Frednel, Lauture Arnaud, Jozil J. Rebert, Harold Laurenceau, Gerald Michel, Aja Saintil, Jean Claude Annee, Jean Vital, Onil Jean Baptiste, Enide George, and Marie Michel George). Soul Jazz Records: SJR CD230. 2010. CD.

664 *Rhythms of Rapture: Sacred Musics of Haitian Vodou.* Smithsonian Folkways: SF 40464. 1947, 1995. CD.

See Caribbean Popular and Traditional: General Anthologies for additional citations.

VIDEO

665 *Haitian Song.* Documentary Educational Resources. 2005. DVD.

JAMAICA

INDIVIDUAL ARTISTS AND GROUPS

666 Banton, Buju. *Before the Dawn.* Gargamel Music: GGM 0171. 2010. CD.

667 Black Uhuru. *Ultimate Collection.* Universal Music Enterprises: 314 542 348-2. 2000. CD.

668 Brown, Dennis. *Absolutely the Best of Dennis Brown: The King of Lover's Rock.* Burning Bush Records: 302 061 119 2. 1970s, 2001. CD.

669 Burning Spear. *The Burning Spear Experience.* Burning Music Production: BM332. 2007. 2 CDs.

670 Cliff, Jimmy. *Jimmy Cliff.* 20th Century Masters. Universal Music: B0001964-02. 2004. CD.

671 Count Ossie. *Tales of Mozambique* (Mystic Revelation of Rastafari). Dynamic Sounds: DYCD 3358. 199? CD.

672 Culture. *Two Sevens Clash.* Shanachie: 45065. 2007. CD.

673 Dekker, Desmond. *Rockin' Steady: The Best of Desmond Dekker.* Rhino: R2 70271. 1992. CD.

674 Griffiths, Marcia. *Put a Little Love in Your Heart: The Best of Marcia Griffiths, 1969 to 1974.* Classic Reggae Recordings. Trojan: 6076802412. 2001. CD.

675 Heptones. *Peace and Harmony.* Trojan: 06076-80487-2. 2004. 2 CDs.

676 Higgs, Joe. *Blackman Know Yourself* (Wailers). Shanachie: SH 43077. 1990. CD.

677 Jolly Boys. *Pop'n' Mento.* Rykodisc: RCD 10185. 1989. CD.

678 Marley, Bob, and the Wailers
    678.1 *Catch a Fire.* Tuff Gong. 1973, 2015. CD.
    678.2 *Exodus.* Island Records. 1977, 2015. CD.
    678.3 *Legend.* Island Records. 1984, 2015. CD.
    678.4 ★*Songs of Freedom.* Tuff Gong: CD1 314-512 281-2–CD4 314-512 284-2. 1999. 4 CDs.

679 Mighty Diamonds. *Best of the Mighty Diamonds.* Times Square: TSQ-CD 9044. 2005. 2 CDs.

680 Pablo, Augustus. *The Mystic World of Augustus Pablo: The Rockers Story* [1971–1990]. Shanachie: 45068. 2008. 4 CDs, DVD.

681 Paul, Frankie. *Frankie Paul.* Ras Portraits. RAS: RAS 3316. 1987, 1997. CD.

682 Perry, Lee "Scratch." *An Introduction to Lee Perry.* Varese Sarabande: 3020615812. 2006. CD.

683 Skatalites. *Foundation Ska.* Heartbeat: CD HB 185/186. 1964, 1997. 2 CDs.

684 Third World. *Reggae Ambassadors.* Mercury, Chronicles: 314518295-2. 1993. 2 CDs.

685 Tosh, Peter. *The Best of 1978–1987.* EMI: 72435-82795-2-8. 2003. CD.

686 Wailer, Bunny. *Retrospective.* Shanachie: 45021. 1995. CD.

See Caribbean Popular and Traditional: General Anthologies for additional citations.

ANTHOLOGIES

687 *Conscious Ragga, Vol. 1* (Luciano and Louie Culture, Captain Barkey, Bunny Rugs, Beenie Man, Frankie Paul, Simpleton, Cocoa Tea, Garnett Silk, Bounty Killer, Anthony Malvo, Mykal Rose, Red Rose, and Luciano). Greensleeves: GRELCD220. 1995. CD.

688 *Drums of Defiance: Maroon Music from the Earliest Free Black Communities of Jamaica.* Smithsonian Folkways: CD SF 40412. 1977, 1992. CD. *See also* Afro-Caribbean.

689 ★*First Family of Reggae* (Joe Higgs, Lucky Dube, Bunny Wailer, Rita Marley, Judy Mowatt, Yellow-man, Alpha Blondy, Mutabaruka, Augustus Pablo, Dennis Brown, Linton Kwesi Johnson, Culture, Eek-a-Mouse, Gregory Isaacs, and Ras Mitchell). Shanachie: SH 9100. 1991. CD.

690 *The Harder They Come* (Jimmy Cliff, Scotty, The Melodians, The Maytals, The Slickers, Desmond Dekker, The Uniques, The Ethiopians, Dave and Ansel Collins, and Eric Donaldson). Hip-O, Island: 440 069 495-2. 2003. 2 CDs.

691 ★*Jamaica* (Laurel Aitken, Basil Gabbidon, Maytals, Baba Brooks, Ken Boothe and Stranger Cole, Phyllis Dillon, Lord Creator, Roland Alphonso, John Holt, Impact All Stars featuring Tommy McCook, I-Roy, Cornel Campbell, Dennis Brown, Big Youth, Lopez Walker, Triston Palma, Junior Reid, Home T., Cocoa Tea and Shabba Ranks, Yami Bolo, and Luciano). Rough Guide. World Music Network: RGNET 1056 CD. 2001. CD.

692 *Reggae Dance Party* (Natural Beauty, Barrington Levy, Michigan and Smiley, Don Carlos, Wayne Smith, Black Uhuru, Paul Blake and Bloodfire Posse, Sugar Minott, Horace Andy, J. C. Lodge, and Gregory Isaacs). RAS: RAS CD 3018. 1987. CD.

693 *Reggae Ska and Rastafari.* Dejavu: 5X002. 2006. 5 CDs.

694 *Rock Steady* (Hopeton Lewis, Alston Ellis and the Flames with Tommy McCook and the Supersonics Band, Justin Hinds and the Dominoes, Prince Buster, Honey Boy Martin, Techniques, Jamaicans, Ken Boothe with Lyn Taitt and the Jets, Delroy Wilson, Keith and Tex, Melodians with the Gaytones, Paragons, Uniques with Bunny Lee All-Stars, Gaylettes, Bob Andy, Melodians, and Hugh Roy). Roots of Reggae, Vol. 2. Rhino: R2 72439. 1996. CD.

695 *Rough Guide to Reggae* (Flames, Don Drummond and the Skatalites, Paragons, Melodians, Augustus Pablo, King Tubby and Soul Syndicate, Yabby You and the Prophets, Burning Spear, Congos, Aswad, Gregory Isaacs, General Echo, Triston Palmer, Smiley Culture, Janet-Lee Davis and Peter Hunnigale, Barrington Levy and Bounty Killer, Buju Banton, and Lucky Dube). Rough Guide. World Music Network: RGNET 1016 CD. 1997. CD.

696 *Ska* (Laurel Aitken, Derrick Morgan, Bunny and Skitter, Prince Buster, Stranger Cole, Stranger and Patsy, Higgs and Wilson, Eric "Monty" Morris with Byron Lee and the Dragonaires, The Blues Busters, Ska Kings, Alcapone, Carlos Malcolm and His Afro-Jamaican Rhythm, Justin Hinds and the Dominoes). Roots of Reggae, Vol.1. Rhino: R2 72438. 1996. CD.

697 *Ska Bonanza: The Studio One Ska Years.* Heartbeat: CD HB 86, CD HB 87. 1991. 2 CDs.

698 ★*This Is Reggae Music.* Trojan, Sanctuary: 06076-80470-2. 2004. 4 CDs.

699 ★*Tougher Than Tough: The Story of Jamaican Music.* Mango: 518 399-2. 1993. 4 CDs.

VIDEOS

700 *Deep Roots Music.* Screen Edge; dist. by MVD Visual: EDGE49D–EDGE51D. 2006–2007. 3 DVDs.

701 *History of Reggae, Vol.1* (Ken Booth, Junior Murvin, Johnny Clarke, Errol Dunkly, Eddie Fitzroy, Leroy Brown, Sugar Minott, Leroy Sibbles, Little John, Tarrus Riley, Leroy Brown, Frankie Paul, and Max Romeo). MVD: LY55526. 2011. DVD.

702 *Rocksteady: The Roots of Reggae.* Lightyear Entertainment: LIT-DV-56418. 2010. DVD.

PUERTO RICO

INDIVIDUAL ARTISTS AND GROUPS

703 Batacumbele. *Con un poco de songo.* Disco Hit: DHTLP-008-CD. 1989. CD.

704 Ecos de Borinquen. *El alma de Puerto Rico = The Soul of Puerto Rico: Jíbaro Tradition.* Smithsonian Folkways: SFW 40570. 2016. CD.

705 ★Gran Combo de Puerto Rico. *30 aniversario: Bailando con el mundo.* Combo Records: RSCD 2091. 1992. 2 CDs.

706 Grupo Afro Boricua. *Bombazo.* Blue Jackel Entertainment: BJAC 5027-2. 1998. CD.

707 Manuelle, Victor. *Historia de un sonero.* Norte: 8869 730684 2. 1993, 2008. CD.

708 Padilla, Pablo. *Vuelva en alas del placer = Return on Wings of Pleasure.* Rounder: CD 5003. 1975, 1997. CD.

709 Paracumbe. *Tambó.* Ashé: ASHE CD 2005. 1997. CD.

710 Plena Libre. *Juntos y revueltos.* RykoLatino: RLCD 1005. 1999. CD.

711 ★Los Pleneros de 21 and Conjunto Melodia. *Puerto Rico, Puerto Rico, mi tierra natal.* Shanachie: SH 65001. 1990. CD.

712 Sonora Ponceña. *Sonora Ponceña: 30th Anniversary, Golden Age.* Inca: JMIS 1092. 2005. CD.

ANTHOLOGIES

713 ★*The Music of Puerto Rico, 1929–1947* (Trio Armonico, Trio Boricua, Los Borinquenos, Canario y Su Grupo, Los Jardineros, Sexteto Flores, Sexteto Okeh, Cuarteto Marcano, Sexteto Pellin, Conjunto La Plata, Los Reyes de la Plena, Cuarteto Mayari, Pedro Marcano y Su Grupo, Los Jibaros, and Conjunto Tipico Ladi). Harlequin: HQ CD 22. 1992. CD.

714 *Puerto Rican Plenas.* Disco Hit: DHCD-1026. 1992. CD.

715 *Putumayo Presents Puerto Rico* (Eddie Palmieri, Andrés Jiménez, Jimmy Bosch, Ramito, Modesto Cepeda, Edwin Colón Zayas, Pepe Castillo, Julius Meléndez, and Ismael Miranda). Putumayo World Music: RSCD2091. 2000. CD.

VIDEOS

716 Gran Combo de Puerto Rico. *Salsa: Un homenaje a el gran combo.* Popular. 2010. DVD.

717 *Plena Is Work, Plena Is Song.* Cinema Guild. 2002. DVD.

TRINIDAD AND TOBAGO

INDIVIDUAL ARTISTS AND GROUPS

718 ★Arrow. *Classics.* Arrow Music: 042 CD. 1990. CD.

719 Burning Flames. *Dig.* Mango: 162539914-2. 1991. CD.

720 Calliste, Leroy (Black Stalin). *Roots, Rock, Soca.* Rounder: CD 5038. 1991. CD.

721 Calypso Rose. *Soca Diva.* Ice: 931202. 1993. CD.

722 ★Mighty Sparrow. *Mighty Sparrow, Vols. 1–4.* Ice: 921002 (v.1–3), 941702 (v.4). 1992–1994. 4 CDs.

723 Our Boys Steel Orchestra. *Pan Progress.* Mango: 162 539 916-2. 1991. CD.

724 Rootsman. *The Best of Rootsman and Bally.* J. W. Productions: JWCD 1005. 1992. CD.

725 Rudder, David. *Gilded Collection, Vols. 1–3.* Lypsoland: CRO 019 (v.1), CR 024 (v.2), CRO 34 CD (v.3). 1993–1998. 3 CDs.

726 ★Shadow. *The Best of Shadow.* Straker's Records: GS2389CD. 1995. CD.

ANTHOLOGIES

727 *Calypso Breakaway* (Keskidee Trio, King Radio, Felix and his Krazy Kats, The Growler, The Lion, Lord Executor, Al Philip's Iere Syncopators, Tiger, Lord Beginner, Atilla the Hun, Lord Invader, Lionel Belasco, Wilmoth Houdini, The Caresser, and Codallo's Top Hatters). Rounder: CD 1054. 1990. CD.

728 *Carnival Jump-Up: Steelbands of Trinidad and Tobago* (Solo Harmonites, Silver Stars, Phase II Pan Groove, Carib Tokyo, Amoco Renegades, and Neal and Massy Trinidad All Stars). Caribbean Carnival Series. Delos; dist. by A&M Records: DE-4014. 1989. CD.

729 *Chutney Gold* (Sally Edwards, JMC Triveni, Chris Garcia, Kanchan, Parvatie Seeram, Pundar Popo, Anand Yankaran, Ramrajie Prabhoo, Salima, and Nisha). J.M.C.: JMC 1145. 2001. CD.

730 ★*Rough Guide to Calypso and Soca* (Lord Pretender, Chris "Tambu" Herbert, Mighty Sparrow, David Rudder, Brother Resistance, Hunter and Laventille Rhythm Section, Ajala, Singing Sandra, Shadow, Kitchener, Square One, Andre Tanker, 3 Canal, and Sharlene Boodram). Rough Guide. World Music Network: RGNET 1040 CD. 1999. CD.

731 *Rough Guide to Calypso Gold* (Sir Lancelot, King Radio, Lord Pretender, Calypso Rose, Caresser, The Mighty Bomber, Lion, Relator, Lord Kitchener, Duke of Iron, Tiger, Kiskedee Trio, Atilla, Sam Manning, Belasco's Orchestra, Wilmoth Houdini, and Monrose's String Orchestra). Rough Guide. World Music Network: RGNET 1213 CD. 2008. CD.

732 ★*Soca Music from Trinidad* (Johnny King, Shadow, Bally, All Rounder, Singing Francine, and Chalkdust). Rounder: CD5041. 1990. CD.

733 *Trinidad & Tobago: Trinidad: Music from the North Indian Tradition.* Smithsonian Folkways: UNES 08278. 1999, 2014. CD.

734 *The Ultimate Soca Gold Collection.* VP Music: VP1940. 2011. 3 CDs.

735 ★*Wind Your Waist: The Ultimate Soca Dance Party* (Arrow, Shadow, Burning Flames, Drupatee, Spice, Tambu, Organizer, and Kitchener). Shanachie: 64034. 1991. CD.

VIDEO

736 *Calypso Music History: One Hand Don't Clap* (Lord Kitchener and Calypso Rose). EforFilms: 2869017. 1991, 2004. DVD.

OTHER CARIBBEAN ISLANDS (INCLUDING THE BAHAMAS, BARBADOS, GUADELOUPE, MARTINIQUE, ST. LUCIA, AND THE U.S. VIRGIN ISLANDS)

INDIVIDUAL ARTISTS AND GROUPS

737 Coppet, Hurard. *Best of Hurard Coppet, Léona Gabriel, Saint-Hilaire* (Archange Saint-Hilaire, Léona Gabriel, and Orchestre Printemps Jazz de Saint-Hilaire). Sully Cally, Collection Patrimoine: HUSC93. 1962, 1993. CD.

738 Gazoline. *Zouk Obsession.* Shanachie: SH 64021. 1990. CD.

739 Kassav'. *Double Best of Kassav'.* New Deal: 184692MU790. 1994. 2 CDs.

740 Malavoi. *Légende.* Déclic: 302389. 1994. 2 CDs.

741 Mona, Eugène. *Eugène Mona, Vols. 1 and 2.* Collection Prestige de la Musique Caribeenne. Hibiscus: 191213-2 (v.1), 191212-2 (v.2). 1990, 1995. 2 CDs.

742 Vikings Guadeloupe. *Vikings Guadeloupe 1974–1978.* Collection Prestige de la Musique Caribeenne. Hibiscus: 88054-2. 1974, 1990s. CD.

ANTHOLOGIES

743 *Junkanoo Band: Key West.* Smithsonian Folkways: FW 04492. 1964, 2004. CD.

744 *Tumbélé! Biguine, Afro and Latin Sounds from the French Caribbean, 1963–1974* (Loups Noirs D'Haïti, Robert Mavounzy Quartet, Orchestre Jeunesse de Paul-Emile Haliar, Orchestre Combo Zombi, Kings, West Indian Combo, Leopards, Ensemble la Perfecta, Ry-Co Jazz, Aiglons de Basses Terre, Gentlemens Ensemble Abricot, and Guitar Boys). Soundway: SNDWCD017. 2009. CD.

745 *West Indies: An Island Carnival.* Explorer Series. Elektra Nonesuch: 9 72091-2. 1991. CD.

746 *Zouk Attack* (Rosier and Gazoline, Patrick Parole, Love Stars; Ramon Pyrmée, Typical, Tanya St. Val, Luc Leandry, Tatiana and Zouti, Jules-Henri Malacquis, and Frédéric Caracas). Rounder: CD 5037. 1992. CD.

VIDEO

747 *Caribbean Eye 3: La Musique Antillaise.* Banyan Archives. 1999. DVD.

CARIBBEAN POPULAR AND TRADITIONAL GENERAL ANTHOLOGIES

748 *Beginner's Guide to Caribbean.* Nascente: NSBO X080. 2011. 3 CDs.

749 ★*Caribbean Beat.* Intuition Records: INT 3112 2, INT 3197 2. 1992–1997. 6 CDs.

750 *Caribbean Folk Music, Vol. 1.* Ethnic Folkways Library. Smithsonian Folkways: FE 4533. 1960, 2007. CD.

751 ★*Caribbean Party* (Tabou Combo, Krosfyah Bago, Coalishun, Bunny Wailer, Eric Virgal, Patsy Geremy and Souskay, Ralph Thamar, and Arrow). Putumayo World Music: PUTU 132-2. 1997. CD.

752 *Mento Merengue Méringue.* Original Music: OMCD 028. 1995. CD.

VIDEOS

753 *Caribbean Eye 9: Caribbean Carnivals*. Banyan Archives. 1999. DVD.

754 ★*The JVC/Smithsonian Folkways Video Anthology of Music and Dance of the Americas, Vol. 4: The Caribbean*. JVC, Victor Co. of Japan; dist. by Multicultural Media: VTMV-228. 1995, 2005. DVD.

AFRO-CARIBBEAN TRADITIONAL

Compiled by Suzanne Flandreau

The Caribbean area is musically rich and diverse: the colonial history of the region has provided for the unique intersection of European, Native, and African musics. This list of recordings is intended to provide specific examples for the study of a vast array of interconnected music while also highlighting important local genres. The traditional music of the Caribbean is important for what it says about the creolization process on a local scale. Its importance grows because many local styles have become international popular music genres whose roots need to be understood. At the same time, the Caribbean is a laboratory for the study of musical retentions, especially in the various African-derived religious practices.

There are three types of recordings on this list. Most are commercial issues of field recordings by scholars and ethnographers: Harold Courlander, John Storm Roberts, Kenneth Bilby, and, above all, Alan Lomax, whose trip to the region in 1962 resulted in a rich archive of recordings, many of which have been issued by Rounder Records in its *Caribbean Voyage* series. Other ethnographic labels—Nonesuch Explorer, and especially Smithsonian Folkways—are also represented. Also included are collections of reissues of early commercial recordings. These are important because they present the earliest recordings of traditional genres (calypso, merengue) that have evolved into popular styles. Finally, there are a few studio recordings by groups or performers who keep important traditions alive. Such recordings are often local productions that go out-of-print very quickly and must be acquired from specialist vendors, but they testify both to the continuing importance of local recordings and to the vitality of local traditions.

Smithsonian Folkways, which has issued field recordings from the Caribbean since the 1950s, keeps its catalog in print through its custom compact disc series and also through MP3 downloads available commercially.

Many Folkways recordings are listed because of their documentary importance, but it is important to note that though the original liner notes may be provided with the custom CDs, no effort has been made to update them. Therefore, the original dates, as well as dates for custom reissues, have been provided here. Related citations for popular music may be found in the "International Anthologies" and "Caribbean Popular" music sections.

BAHAMAS

INDIVIDUAL ARTISTS AND GROUPS

755 Saunders, Nat, and Thomas Cartwright. *The Bahamas: Islands of Song*. Smithsonian Folkways: 40405. 1995, 1997. CD.

756 Spence, Joseph. *Music of the Bahamas: The Complete Folkways Recordings, 1958* (Samuel Barclay Charters, compiler). Smithsonian Folkways: CD SF 40066. 1959, 1992. CD.

ANTHOLOGIES

757 *Bahamas 1935: Chanteys and Anthems from Andros and Cat Island* (Alan Lomax, and Mary Elizabeth Barnicle, compilers). Alan Lomax Collection; Deep River of Song. Rounder: 11661-1822-2. 1935, 1999. CD.

758 *Bahamas 1935, Vol. 2: Ring Games and Round Dances* (Alan Lomax and Mary Elizabeth Barnicle, compilers). Alan Lomax Collection; Deep River of Song. Rounder: 11661-1832-2. 1935, 2002. CD.

759 *Music of the Bahamas, Vol. 2: Anthems, Work Songs and Ballads* (Samuel Barclay Charters, compiler). Custom Compact Disc Series. Smithsonian Folkways: F-3845. 1958, 2001. CD.

760 *Music of the Bahamas, Vol. 3: Instrumental Music from the Bahamas Islands* (Samuel Barclay Charters, compiler). Custom Compact Disc Series. Smithsonian Folkways: F 3846. 1959, 2001. CD.

761 *The Real Bahamas, Vol. 1. The Bahamas: The Real Bahamas in Music and Song* (Peter K. Siegel and Jody Stecher, compilers). Explorer Series; Latin America/Caribbean. Nonesuch: 79725-2. 1966, 2003. CD.

762 *The Real Bahamas, Vol. 2* (Peter K. Siegel and Jody Stecher, compilers). Explorer Series. Nonesuch: 79733-2. 1978, 2003. CD.

763 *Religious Songs and Drums in the Bahamas* (Marshall Winslow Stearns, compiler). Custom

Compact Disc Series. Smithsonian Folkways: F-4440. 1953, 2001. CD.

CARRIACOU ISLAND (GRENADA)

ANTHOLOGIES

764   *The Big Drum and Other Ritual and Social Music of Carriacou* [1971–1972] (Donald R. Hill, compiler). Custom Compact Disc Series. Smithsonian Folkways: FE 34002. 2003. CD.

765   *Carriacou Calaloo* [1962] (Alan Lomax, compiler). Alan Lomax Collection; Caribbean Voyage. Rounder: 11661-1722-2. 1962, 1999. CD.

766   *Saraca: Funerary Music of Carriacou* [1962] (Alan Lomax, compiler). Alan Lomax Collection; Caribbean Voyage. Rounder: 11661-1726-2. 1962, 2000. CD.

767   *Tombstone Feast: Funerary Music* [1962] (Alan Lomax, compiler). Alan Lomax Collection; Caribbean Voyage. Rounder: 11661-1727-2. 1962, 2001. CD.

CAYMAN ISLANDS

ANTHOLOGIES

768   *Traditional Music of the Cayman Islands* (Radley Gourzong and the Happy Boys and "Aunt" Julia Hydes). Cayman National Cultural Foundation: MUC4714-MUC4715. 2010. 2 CDs.

769   *Under the Coconut Tree: Music from Grand Cayman and Tortola* [1982] (John Storm Roberts, compiler). Original Music: OMCD 025. 1985. CD.

See Afro-Caribbean General Anthologies for additional citations.

CUBA

ANTHOLOGIES

770   ★*Afro-Cuba: A Musical Anthology*. Rounder: CD 1088. 1994. CD. *See also* Carribbean Popular and Traditional.

771   Conga de los Hoyos de Santiago de Cuba. *Carnival Music of Eastern Cuba: Afro-Cuban Music from the Roots*. World Audio Foundation; Soul Jazz Records: WAF CD1. 2009. CD. Recorded 2005.

772   *Cuban Danzon: Before There Was Jazz*. Arhoolie: CD 7032. 1999. CD.

773   *Havana and Matanzas, Cuba, ca. 1957: Bata, Bembe, and Palo Songs* (Lydia Cabrera and Josefina Tarafa, compilers). Smithsonian Folkways: SFW CD 40434. 1957, 2003. CD.

774   *Havana, Cuba, ca. 1957: Rhythms and Songs for the Orishas* (Lydia Cabrera and Josefina Tarafa, compilers). Smithsonian Folkways: SFW CD 40489. 1957, 2001. CD.

775   *Matanzas, Cuba, ca. 1957: Afro-Cuban Sacred Music from the Countryside* (Lydia Cabrera and Josefina Tarafa, compilers). Smithsonian Folkways: SFW CD 40490. 1957, 2001. CD.

776   ★*Sacred Rhythms of Cuban Santeria = Ritmos sagrados de la santeria Cubana* (Olavo Alen, ed.). Smithsonian Folkways: SF 40419. 1983, 1995. CD.

777   *Sextetos Cuabanos: Sones, vol. 2*. Arhoolie Folklyric: CD-7006. 1926, 1995. CD.

DOMINICA

ANTHOLOGY

778   *Dominica: Creole Crossroads* [1962] (Alan Lomax, compiler). Alan Lomax Collection; Caribbean Voyage. Rounder: 11661-1724-2. 1962, 1999. CD.

DOMINICAN REPUBLIC

ANTHOLOGIES

779   *Afro-Dominican Music from San Cristobal, Dominican Republic* (Morton Marks, compiler). Custom Compact Disc Series. Smithsonian Folkways: FE 4285. 1981, 2002. CD.

780   *Merengue: Dominican Music and Dominican Identity* (Paul Austerlitz, prod.). Rounder: CD 1130. 1928, 1997. CD.

781   *Music from the Dominican Republic, Vol. 1: The Island of Quisqueya* (Verna Gillis, compiler). Custom Compact Disc Series. Smithsonian Folkways: FE 4281. 1976, 2001. CD.

782   *Music from the Dominican Republic, Vol. 2: The Island of Española* (Verna Gillis, compiler). Custom Compact Disc Series. Smithsonian Folkways: FE 4282. 1976, 2001. CD.

783   *Music from the Dominican Republic, Vol. 3: Cradle of the New World* (Verna Gillis, compiler). Custom

Compact Disc Series. Smithsonian Folkways: FE 4283. 1976, 2001. CD.

784   *Music from the Dominican Republic, Vol. 4: Songs from the North* (Verna Gillis, compiler). Custom Compact Disc Series. Smithsonian Folkways: FE 4284. 1978, 2001. CD.

VIDEO

785   *The Culture of Palo: Palo Music and Oral Traditions from the Dominican Republic* (Giovanni Savino, prod.). Magnetic Art Productions; Earthcds Partners: DVD NTSC 525. 2005. DVD.

See Afro-Caribbean: Haiti and General Anthologies for additional citations.

GRENADA
ANTHOLOGY

786   *Grenada: Creole and Yoruba Voices* [1962] (Alan Lomax, compiler). Alan Lomax Collection; Caribbean Voyage. Rounder: 11661-1728-2. 1962, 2001. CD.

See Afro-Caribbean: Carriacou Island (Grenada) for additional citations.

GUADELOUPE
ANTHOLOGY

787   *Guadeloupe: Le Gwoka: Soiree Lewoz a Jabrun.* Ocora Radio France: c-560030. 1992. CD.

See Afro-Caribbean: Trinidad and Tobago and General Anthologies for additional citations.

HAITI
ANTHOLOGIES

788   *Caribbean Revels: Haitian Rara and Dominican Gaga* [1976–1978] (Verna Gillis, compiler). Smithsonian Folkways: CD SF 40402. 1978, 1992. CD.

789   ★*The Haiti Recordings* [1936] (Alan Lomax, Elizabeth Lyttleton, and Gage Averill, compilers). Alan Lomax Collection. Harte Recordings: HR 103. 2009. 10 CDs, 2 books, map.

790   *Rhythms of Rapture: Sacred Musics of Haitian Vodou (Elizabeth McAlister, compiler)*. Smithsonian Folkways: SF 40464. 1947, 1995. CD.

See Afro-Caribbean General Anthologies for additional citations.

JAMAICA
ANTHOLOGIES

791   *Bongo, Backra, and Coolie: Jamaican Roots, Vol. 1* (Kenneth M. Bilby, compiler). Custom Compact Disc Series. Smithsonian Folkways: FE 4231. 1975. CD.

792   *Bongo, Backra, and Coolie: Jamaican Roots, Vol. 2* (Kenneth M. Bilby, compiler). Custom Compact Disc Series. Smithsonian Folkways: FE 4232. 1975, 2000. CD.

793   *Churchical Chants of the Nyabingi* [1982]. Heartbeat: CD HB 20. 1997. CD.

794   ★*Drums of Defiance: Maroon Music from the Earliest Free Black Communities of Jamaica* (Kenneth M. Bilby, compiler). Smithsonian Folkways: CD SF 40412. 1977, 1992. CD. *See also* Caribbean Popular and Traditional.

795   *Jamaican Cult Music* (George Eaton Simpson, ed.). Custom Compact Disc Series. Smithsonian Folkways: FW 4461. 1954, 2000. CD.

796   *John Crow Say . . . : Jamaican Music of Faith, Work, and Play* (John Storm Roberts, compiler). Custom Compact Disc Series. Smithsonian Folkways: FE 4228. 1981, 2003. CD.

See Afro-Caribbean General Anthologies for additional citations.

MARTINIQUE
ANTHOLOGIES

797   *Au Bal Antillais: Franco-Creole Biguines from Martinique* [1929–1951]. Arhoolie Folklyric: CD-7013. 1929, 1992. CD.

798   *Les maitres du Bele de Sainte-Marie: Tambours de Martinique.* Buda: 860146. 2006. CD.

799   *Martinique: Cane Fields and City Streets* [1962] (Alan Lomax, compiler). Alan Lomax Collection; Caribbean Voyage. Rounder: 11661-1730-2. 1962, 1999. CD.

See Afro-Caribbean General Anthologies for additional citations.

PUERTO RICO
INDIVIDUAL ARTISTS AND GROUPS

800   Hermanos Ayala. *Bomba de Loiza.* Blue Jackel Entertainment: 54527-2. 2001, 2002. CD.

801 Padilla, Pedro. *Vuelva en alas del placer = Return on Wings of Pleasure.* Rounder: CD 5003. 1997. CD.

802 Zayas, Edwin Colon, and Taller Campesino. *Bien jibaro!* Rounder: CD 5056. 1994. CD.

ANTHOLOGIES

803 *Lamento Borincano: Puerto Rican Lament* [1916–1936]. Arhoolie: 7037-7038. 1916, 2001. 2 CDs.

804 *Songs and Dances of Puerto Rico* (William S. Marlens, compiler). Custom Compact Disc Series. Smithsonian Folkways: F-8802. 1956, 2000s. CD.

VIDEO

805 ★*Plena Is Work, Plena Is Song* (Susan Zeig, prod. and dir.). Cinema Guild. 2002. DVD. *See also* Caribbean Popular and Traditional.

SAINT-BARTHÉLEMY

See Afro-Carribean General Anthologies.

SAINT KITTS AND NEVIS

ANTHOLOGY

806 *Nevis and St. Kitts: Tea Meetings, Christmas Sports, and the Moonlight Night* [1962] (Alan Lomax, compiler). Alan Lomax Collection; Caribbean Voyage. Rounder: 82161-1731-2. 1962, 2002. CD.

SAINT LUCIA

ANTHOLOGY

807 ★*Musical Traditions of St. Lucia, West Indies: Dances and Songs from a Caribbean Island* [1975–1987] (Jocelyne Guilbault, Embert Charles, and Manfred Kremser, compilers). Smithsonian Folkways: CD SF 40416. 1975, 1993. CD.

TRINIDAD AND TOBAGO

INDIVIDUAL ARTISTS AND GROUPS

808 Lara Brothers. *Sweet Parang: Lara Brothers Live at the Normandie Hotel.* Sanch: CD 9505. 1988, 1995. CD.

ANTHOLOGIES

809 *Bamboo Tamboo, Bongo and the Belair.* Custom Compact Disc Series. Smithsonian Folkways, Cook Laboratories: C 5017. 1956, 2000s. CD.

810 ★*Calypso Awakening: The Emory Cook Collection, 1956–1962* (Emory Cook, compiler). Smithsonian Folkways: SFW CD 40453. 1956, 2000. CD.

811 *Cult Music of Trinidad* (George Eaton Simpson, ed.). Custom Compact Disc Series. Smithsonian Folkways: FE 4478. 1961, 2003. CD.

812 *East Indian Music in the West Indies* [1962] (Alan Lomax, compiler). Alan Lomax Collection; Caribbean Voyage. Rounder: 11661-1723-2. 1962, 1999. CD.

813 ★*Peter Was a Fisherman: The 1939 Trinidad Field Recordings of Melville and Frances Herskovits.* Rounder: CD 1114. 1939, 1998. CD.

814 *Rastlin Jacob: The Music of the Spiritual Baptists of Trinidad and Tobago* [1939] (Melville Herskovits and Frances Herscovits, compilers). Rounder: 82161-1115-2. 1939, 2003. CD.

815 *Trinidad Carnival Roots* [1962] (Alan Lomax, compiler). Alan Lomax Collection; Caribbean Voyage. Rounder: 11661-1725-2. 1962, 2000. CD.

VIRGIN ISLANDS

INDIVIDUAL ARTISTS AND GROUPS

816 Blinky. *Crucian Scratch Band Music* (Blinky and the Roadmasters). Rounder: CD 5047. 1990. CD.

817 Brewster, James. *We Don Skylark* [2004] (Jamesie and the All Stars). Rounder: 11661-6114-2. 2008. CD.

818 Stanley and the Ten Sleepless Knights.
  818.1 *Pumpin'.* Ten Sleepless Knights: TSK-003-2. 1994. CD.
  818.2 *Quelbe! Music of the U.S. Virgin Islands.* Smithsonian Folkways: SFW 40568. 2016. CD.

ANTHOLOGIES

819 ★*Zoop Zoop Zoop: Traditional Music and Folklore of St. Croix, St. Thomas, and St. John* [1957–1985] (Mary Jane Soule, compiler). New World: 80427-2. 1957, 1993. CD.

VIDEO

820   Leland, Andrea E (prod. and dir.), and James
       Brewster (perf.). *Jamesie King of Scratch* (James
       Brewster; Jamesie and the All Stars). Nine
       Morning Productions. 2006. DVD.

AFRO-CARIBBEAN
GENERAL ANTHOLOGIES

821   ★*Brown Girl in the Ring* [1962] (Alan Lomax,
       compiler). Alan Lomax Collection; Caribbean
       Voyage. Rounder: CD 1716. 1961, 1997. CD.

822   *Caribbean Sampler* [1962] (Alan Lomax,
       compiler). Alan Lomax Collection; Caribbean
       Voyage. Rounder: 1166-1172-12. 1999. CD.

823   *The French Antilles: We Will Play Love Tonight*
       [1962] (Alan Lomax, compiler). Alan Lomax
       Collection; Caribbean Voyage. Rounder Select:
       82161-1733-2. 1962, 2004. CD.

824   ★*Island Songs and Dances* (John Storm Roberts,
       compiler). Explorer Series. Nonesuch: 79731-2.
       1972, 2003. CD.

825   *Mento Merengue Meringue: Country Dance Music
       from Jamaica, Grand Cayman, Haiti, and the
       Dominican Republic.* Original Music: OMCD 028.
       1971, 1995. CD.

826   *West Indies: An Island Carnival* (Krister Malm,
       compiler). Explorer Series. Nonesuch: 79734-2.
       1977, 2003. CD.

CENTRAL
AND SOUTH AMERICA

*Compiled by Andrew Justice,
Mark McKnight, and Tom Moore*

The vast territory of Central and South America includes
a broad array of varying climates and terrains—from
dense, steamy jungles to rugged Andean highlands
stretching over five thousand miles, to fertile prairies and
pampas, to the forbidding yet fascinating sub-Antarctic
regions of Patagonia and Tierra del Fuego at the tip of
the continent—the very "end of the world." While the
Spanish-speaking countries of Central and South America may share a common language and background, their
geographic diversity is matched by equally distinctive
musical styles and genres. These distinctions derive,

to a large extent, from the various political, historical,
geographic, cultural, and socioeconomic conditions that
helped shape each country, as well as the intersection
of Native, African, and European influences (much like
that of the Caribbean). These intersections may be seen,
for example, in such recordings as those of the Garifuna ("black Carib") people from Belize and Honduras,
the Maya-Quiche of Guatemala, the tango tradition of
Argentina, or Andean *huayño* music. It should also be
recognized that within each of these various styles lies
a wide range of historical and stylistic diversity, in the
way the tango, for example, moved from the slums of
Buenos Aires to the capitals of Europe in the early twentieth century or the manner in which the *huayño* tradition evolved from its Peruvian pre-Colombian roots
as it spread to parts of Bolivia, Argentina, Ecuador,
and Chile. In addition to traditional regional and ethnic genres, included are recordings that represent more
current popular styles, including calypso, salsa, tango,
cumbia, vallenato, and so on. Guyana is represented in
the sub-Saharan Africa chapter (African diaspora list),
as well as other Central and South American music.

Many of the titles in these lists represent commercial issues of field recordings by such major labels
as Smithsonian Folkways, Nonesuch, and Arhoolie, as
well as some specialty labels such as Discos Fuentes
from Colombia, Sony Discos, and Warner Music Chile.
Note that recordings issued as part of the Smithsonian
Folkways recording project are issued on demand as
custom CDs, custom cassettes, or digital downloads,
available from the website www.folkways.si.edu.

Brazil is the largest country in Latin America, and
one of the largest in the world—the fifth most populous,
after China, India, the United States, and Indonesia,
and the fifth largest in terms of land area. Nevertheless,
Brazil and its culture remain relatively invisible in the
United States, where the cultural space for Latin America
tends to be occupied by Spanish-speaking immigrants
from Mexico and Central America.

Brazil has many things in common with the United
States—size, its origins as a European colony, centuries
with a slave-based economy, transition from agriculture
to industry in the twentieth century, the major presence
of immigration, and the force of the African diaspora in
shaping its culture. One major difference is that, while
the United States boasts the ideology of the melting pot,
it nevertheless (arguably) keeps its cultural and ethnic
strains largely separate. In Brazil, cultures integrate,
with an ideology of anthropophagy, which is reflected
in the musical life of the region.

Brazil boasts a large variety of musics, some of
which are considered regional, such as *sertanejo* (a kind

of Brazilian "country" music), and others that have been adopted as expressions of national culture, such as *choro* and *samba*. The latter must have been present in the two major metropolitan centers, Rio de Janeiro and São Paulo. Choro began as a performance tradition for the salon dances of the middle and upper classes (waltzes, polkas, schottisches, mazurkas) in the later nineteenth century, with music arranged for an ensemble of flute, cavaquinho, and percussion. It has continued to develop its own tradition of virtuoso instrumental performance. Samba, a genre of vocal music and dance, had its roots in the music brought from Bahia to Rio in the first two decades of the twentieth century and quickly became so popular that it was impossible to say whether it belonged to the Afro-descended working classes or to the city of Rio as a whole, becoming a national expression of Brazilianity with the sambas of Ary Barroso. Other important popular genres include the nationally-popular music known as *forró*, with its roots in the northeast of the country, and local folk genres, such as *frevo* and *maracatu*, present primarily in the Northeast.

It may be easier to acquire materials directly from major bookstores and record stores in Rio de Janeiro. One to consider is Livraria da Travessa (www.travessa.com.br), a large general-interest bookstore that also carries CDs and DVDs.

Tom Moore contributed the Brazil portion of this list. The Central and South American section was prepared with the help of students Katie Buehner, Leah Cole, Anna Perkins Griner, and James Wintle.

CENTRAL AMERICA

Belize

INDIVIDUAL ARTIST

827 Palacio, Andy. *Wátina* (Garifuna Collective). Stonetree: CMB-CD-3. 2007. CD.

ANTHOLOGIES

828 *Cult Cargo: Belize City Boil Up.* Numero Group: N 006. 1970s, 2005. CD.

829 *Dabuyabarugu: Inside the Temple: Sacred Music of the Garifuna of Belize* (Carol Lynn Jenkins and Travis Jenkins, compilers). Custom Compact Disc Series. Smithsonian Folkways: FW 04032. 1982. CD.

830 ★*Garifuna Music: Field Recordings from Belize.* ARC Music: EUCD 1913. 2002, 2005. CD. *See also* Sub-Saharan Africa, Diaspora.

831 *Shine Eye Gal: Brukdon Belizian Calypso.* Corasón: COCD 118. 1978, 1994. CD.

832 *Traditional Music of the Garifuna (Black Carib) of Belize* (Carol Lynn Jenkins and Travis Jenkins, compilers). Custom Compact Disc Series. Smithsonian Folkways: FW 04031. 1982, 2001. CD.

833 *Umalali: The Garifuna Women's Project.* Cumbancha: CMB-CD-6. 2002, 2008. CD.

Costa Rica

INDIVIDUAL ARTISTS AND GROUPS

834 Compañía Folklórico Matambú. *Music of Costa Rica.* ARC Music: EUCD 1940. 2005. CD.

835 Gavitt, Walter Ferguson (composer and perf.). *Mr. Gavitt: Calypso of Costa Rica.* Custom Compact Disc Series. Smithsonian Folkways: FW 31309. 1982, 2001. CD.

ANTHOLOGY

836 *Ambiances du Costa-Rica: Bosques Tropicales de Costa Rica = Costa-Rica Soundscapes.* Frémeaux et Associés: FA 617. 1992, 2011. CD.

El Salvador

INDIVIDUAL ARTISTS AND GROUPS

837 ★Banda Tepeuani. *El Salvador libre.* Custom Compact Disc Series. Smithsonian Folkways: MON 00823. 1984, 2004. CD.

838 Cutumay Camones. *Por eso luchamos: Songs of the Salvadoran Struggle.* Smithsonian Folkways: PAR 01050. 1985, 2006. CD.

839 ★Hermanos Lovo. *¡Soy salvadoreño! Chanchona Music from Eastern El Salvador.* Smithsonian Folkways: SFW CD 40535. 2011. CD.

840 Yolocamba I-Ta. *Cara o cruz.* Flying Fish: FF 70503. 1988. CD.

ANTHOLOGY

841 *The Pipil Indians of El Salvador* (David Blair Stiffler, compiler). Custom Compact Disc Series. Smithsonian Folkways: FW 04244. 1983, 2000. CD.

Guatemala

INDIVIDUAL ARTISTS AND GROUPS

842 Arjona, Ricardo. *Independiente*. Mexico Metamorfosis Enterprises: 529011. 2011. CD.

843 Grupo Ibimeni. *Garifuna: Traditional Music from Guatemala*. Sub Rosa: SR273. 2008. CD.

844 Peña, Carlos. *Con una canción*. Adrenaline Music: 21748. 2008. CD.

ANTHOLOGIES

845 *Forêts Mayas (Mayan Forests): Soundscapes from Guatemala*. Frémeaux et Associés: FA 612. 1995, 2006. CD.

846 *Guatemala: Marimba*. Instruments of the World. Voyager: CRG 140189. 2007. CD.

847 *Marimba Music of Guatemala*. Smithsonian Folkways: SFW CD 40542. 2007. CD.

848 ★*Music of Guatemala, Vol. 1*. Asch Mankind Series; Custom Compact Disc Series. Smithsonian Folkways: FW 04212. 1964, 1999. CD.

849 ★*Music of Guatemala, Vol. 2*. Custom Compact Disc Series. Smithsonian Folkways: FW 04213. 1964, 1999. CD.

850 *Music of the Maya-Quiche of Guatemala: The rabinal achi and baile de la canastas* (Henrietta Yurchenco, compiler). Custom Compact Disc Series. Smithsonian Folkways: FW 04226. 1978, 2000. CD.

Honduras

INDIVIDUAL ARTIST

851 Aurelio. *Laru Beya*. Sub Pop: NXA 002. 2011. CD.

ANTHOLOGIES

852 *The Black Caribs of Honduras* (Doris Stone, ed.). Custom Compact Disc Series. Smithsonian Folkways: FE 4435. 1953, 2000. CD.

853 *Paranda*. Stonetree: STR CD-018. 2000. CD.

854 ★*Songs and Dances of Honduras*. Custom Compact Disc Series. Smithsonian Folkways: FW 06834. 1955, 1999. CD.

Nicaragua

INDIVIDUAL ARTISTS AND GROUPS

855 Enrique, Luis. *Ciclos*. Top Stop Music: TOPS8910. 2009. CD, DVD.

856 ★Godoy, Mejía, and Luis Enrique. *Un son para mi pueblo: Songs from the New Nicaragua* (Mantocal). Custom Compact Disc Series. Smithsonian Folkways: PAR01048. 1983, 1999. CD.

ANTHOLOGIES

857 *Antología musical Nicaragüense*. Discos Fenix: FE CD-2010. 1990s. CD.

858 *Caribbean Rhythms*. Custom Compact Disc Series. Smithsonian Folkways: FW 08811. 1957, 1999. CD.

859 *Music of the Miskito Indians of Honduras and Nicaragua* (David Blair Stiffler, compiler). Custom Compact Disc Series. Smithsonian Folkways: FW 04237. 1981, 2001. CD.

860 *Nicaragua Presente! Music from Nicaragua Libre*. Rounder: CD 11564. 1989. CD.

Panama

INDIVIDUAL ARTISTS AND GROUPS

861 Flex
    861.1 *La Evolución Romantic Style*. EMI Televisa Music: 50999 2 67917 2 2. 2009. CD.
    861.2 *Romantic Style: Desde la esencia, Parte 3*. Capitol Latin: 5099962868723. 2010. CD.

862 El General. *Grandes éxitos*. BMG U.S. Latin: 74321-54364-2. 1998. CD.

ANTHOLOGIES

863 Los De Azuero. *Traditional Music from Panama*. Nimbus: NI 5579. 1997, 1999. CD.

864 *Music of the Indians of Panama* (David Blair Stiffler, compiler). Custom Compact Disc Series. Smithsonian Folkways: FW 04326. 1983, 2001. CD.

865 *Panama! Latin, Calypso, and Funk on the Isthmus, 1965–1975*. Soundway: SNDWCD 007. 1965, 2006. CD.

866 *Panama! 2: Latin Sounds, Cumbia Tropical, and Calypso Funk on the Isthmus, 1967–1977.* Soundway: SNDWCD013. 2009. CD.

867 *Panama! 3: Calypso Panameño, Guajira Jazz, and Cumbia Tipica on the Isthmus, 1960–1975.* Soundway: SNDWCD018. 2009. CD.

**CENTRAL AMERICA
GENERAL ANTHOLOGY**

868 *Umalali: The Garifuna Women's Project* (Ivan Duran, compiler). Cumbancha: CMB-CD-6. 2008. CD.

SOUTH AMERICA

Andes Region

INDIVIDUAL ARTISTS AND GROUPS

869 ★Alpamayo. *Flutes and Panpipes from the Andes.* ARC Music: ARC-CD-2179. 2008. CD.

870 Torres, Osvaldo (dir.). *Les Flûtes du Soleil* (Sayri Tupac). Air Mail Music. Sunset-France: SA 141181. 2008. CD.

Argentina

INDIVIDUAL ARTISTS AND GROUPS

871 Bajofondo. *Mar dulce.* Surco Records: B0011443-02. 2008. CD.

872 ★Castro, Segundo, and Una Ramos. *Folk Dances and Dance Songs of Argentina* (Segundo Castro and His Trovadores de Angaco). Custom Compact Disc Series. Smithsonian Folkways: FW 08841. 1958, 2004. CD.

873 Cerati, Gustavo. *Fuerza natural.* Sony Music Latin: 8869 756779 2. 2009. CD.

874 Chalchaleros. *En Europa.* DBN: CDE 51254. 1992. CD. Vol. 2 available as MP3 only.

875 Chancha Via Circuito. *Río arriba.* Ultra Pop: 86. 2010. CD.

876 De Caro, Julio. *Instrumental Tangos of the Golden Age* (Francisco Canaro, Anibal Triolo, Roberto Firpo, Carlos di Sarli, and others). Harlequin: HQ CD 45. 1994. CD.

877 Deluigi, Silvana. *Yo!* American Clave: amcl 1025. 2000, 2004. CD.

878 Los Fabulosos Cadillacs. *La luz del ritmo.* Nacional Records: 718122028399. 2009. CD.

879 Gardel, Carlos
   879.1 *Carlos Gardel, Le createur du tango Argentin.* Forlane: UCD 19032. 1991. CD.
   879.2 *Celebridades.* EMI Televisa Music: H2 50999 5 15297 27. 2008. CD.

880 ★Los Hermanos Abalos. *Traditional Dances of Argentina, Vol. 2.* Custom Compact Disc Series. Smithsonian Folkways: FW 08842. 1958, 1999. CD.

881 ★Lara, Roberto. *Argentina: The Guitar of the Pampas.* Lyrichord Presents Outstanding Music from around the World. Lyrichord: LYRCH 7253. 1998. CD.

882 Montenegro, Soema. *Passionaria.* Western Vinyl: WEST084. 2011. CD.

883 Paz, Suni. *Bandera mía: Songs of Argentina* (Rafael Manríquez, Ramiro Fauve, Ulises Pineda, Alejandro Scarpino, and Julio Montero). Smithsonian Folkways: SFW 40532. 2006. CD.

884 Piazzolla, Astor
   884.1 ★*La historia del tango, Vol. 1.* Polydor: 314 511 638-2. 1978, 1994. CD.
   884.2 *Tango: Zero Hour* (New Tango Quintet). Nonesuch: 79469-2. 1986, 1998. CD.

885 Sosa, Mercedes
   885.1 ★*Cantora 1* (Joan Manuel Serrat, Luis Alberto Spinetta, Jorge Drexler, Caetano Veloso, and Shakira). Sony BMG Entertainment Cono Sur: 88697 56785 2. 2009. CD.
   885.2 *Cantora 2* (Gustavo Cerati, Charly García, Gabriel Fernández Capello, and Fito Páez). Sony BMG Entertainment Cono Sur: 88697 53364 2. 2009. CD.
   885.3 *Deja la vida volar: En gira.* Sony Music Latin: 8869 780278 2. 2011. CD.
   885.4 *Gracias a la vida.* Philips: 832 314-2. 1987. CD.

886 Spasiuk, Chango. *Pynandí: Los descalzos.* World Village: WV 468083. 2009. CD.

887 Yupanqui, Atahualpa. *Mis 30 mejores canciones.* Microfon: 2-493688. 2000. 2 CDs.

ANTHOLOGIES

888 *Bailemos tango!* Rhino: R2 79840. 1930, 2000. CD.

889 *Buenos Aires by Night: 20 Historic Tangos by Argentina Musical Legends.* EMI: 0777 7 89180 2 8. 1993. CD.

890 *A Night in Argentina.* Sony BMG Latin: 8869 735347 2. 2008. CD.

891 *A Passion for Tango: Authentic Tangos from Argentina* (Sexteto Mayor Orchestra, Daniel Bouchet, Alberto del Solar, and Yeni Patino). Angel: CDC 7 54857 2 1. 1993, 1994. CD.

892 *The Piazzolla Project* (Jacques Ammon and Artemis Quartet; Astor Piazzolla, composer). Virgin: 5099926729206. 2009. CD.

893 *Tango Argentino: Original Cast Recording.* Atlantic: 81636-2. 1986. CD.

894 *The Tango Project.* Nonesuch: 79030-2. 1982. CD.

VIDEOS

895 ★Piazzolla, Astor. *Astor Piazzolla in Portrait.* Opus Arte: OA 0905 D. 2005. DVD.

896 *Tango Our Dance = Tango baile nuestro* (Gabriel Perosino, Marcelo Camarino, Juan Carlos Lenardi, Pablo Mari, and Daniel Binelli). Facets Video: DV 88579. 1988, 2006. DVD.

Bolivia

INDIVIDUAL ARTISTS AND GROUPS

897 Grupo Aymara. *Aliriña.* Flying Fish: FF 70535. 1991. CD.

898 Pujak Wayra. *Music from Bolivia.* Lyrichord: LYRCH 7361. 1980s. CD.

899 Rumillajta. *Urupampa: Andean Music from Bolivia.* Rumillajta Records: RUMI 911CD. 1991. CD.

900 Los Rupay. *Folklore de Bolivia* (Lucho Cavour). ARC Music: EUCD 2246. 2009. CD.

901 ★Ukamau. *Traditional Music from Bolivia.* ARC Music: EUCD 2138. 2008. CD.

ANTHOLOGIES

902 *Bolivia: Charangos and Guitarillas from Norte Potosí.* AIMP, 41. VDE: VDE CD-871. 1991, 1995. CD.

903 *Bolivia y su folklore.* Horizons, Vol. 21. ANS Records: ANS 13027-2. 1998. CD.

904 ★*Instruments and Music of Indians of Bolivia.* Custom Compact Disc Series. Smithsonian Folkways: FW 04012. 1962, 2000s. CD.

905 ★*Songs and Dances of Bolivia.* Custom Compact Disc Series. Smithsonian Folkways: FW 06871. 1959, 1999. CD.

Brazil

INDIVIDUAL ARTISTS AND GROUPS

906 Barroso, Ary
   906.1 *Ary Barroso.* Harlequin: HQ CD 151. 2000. CD.
   906.2 *Ary Barroso: Songbook.* Lumiar Editora. 1994. Score, 2 vols.
   906.3 *O mais Brasileiro dos Brasileiros.* Revivendo: CD-040. [1990–1994]. CD.

907 Buarque, Chico
   907.1 *As cidades.* BMG Brasil: 7432163233-2. [1990–2003]. CD.
   907.2 *Carioca.* Biscoito Fino: BF-646. 2006. CD.
   907.3 *Chico Buarque: Songbook.* Lumiar Editora. 1999. Score, 4 vols.
   907.4 *Paratodos.* BMG Ariola Discos: V120.046. 1993. CD.
   907.5 *Vida.* Philips: 518 218-2. 1980, 1993. CD.

908 Callado, Joaquim. *Leonardo Miranda toca Joaquim Callado* (Leonardo Miranda). Acari Records: AR 2. 2000. CD.

909 Cartola
   909.1 *Ney Matogrosso interpreta Cartola* (Ney Matogrosso). Universal Music: 4400380772. 2002, 2003. CD. *See also* Videos.
   909.2 *O melhor de Cartola.* Irmãos Vitale: 261 A. 1998. Score.
   909.3 *O sol nascerá.* Revivendo: RVCD-131. 1929, 1998. CD.
   909.4 *Raízes do samba.* EMI Brazil: 522168 2. 2000. CD.

910 Costa, Gal
   910.1 *Água viva.* Série Colecionador. Philips: 510 004-2. 1978. CD.
   910.2 *Aquarela do Brasil.* Philips: 836 017-2. 1988. CD.
   910.3 *Domingo.* Verve: 838 555-2. 1967, 1990. CD.

911 Djavan
   911.1 *Djavan.* Lumiar Editora. 1997. Score, 2 vols.
   911.2 *Novena.* Sony: CDZ 81572. 1995. CD.
   911.3 *Voz e violão.* Gala: 4162-2. 1996. CD.

912 Gil, Gilberto
  912.1 *The Eternal God of Change.* WEA International: WH 56620. 1989. CD.
  912.2 *Gil Luminoso.* DRG Brazil: 31618. 1999, 2006. CD.
  912.3 *Music from the Film* Me, You, Them. Atlantic: 83430-2. 2000. CD.
  912.4 *Quanta.* Mesa: 92778-2. 1997. CD.
  912.5 *Songbook.* Lumiar Editora. 1992. Score, 2 vols.

913 Gilberto, João
  913.1 *João Gilberto.* PolyGram: 837 589-2. 1988. CD.
  913.2 *João Gilberto.* PolyGram/Verve: 848 507-2. 1991. CD.
  913.3 *João Gilberto in Tokyo.* Verve: B 0002545-02. 2004. CD.
  913.4 *João voz e violão.* Verve: 314 546 713 2. 2000. CD.
  913.5 *The Legendary João Gilberto.* World Pacific: CDP 7 93891 2. [1990]. CD.

914 Gonzaga, Chiquinha.
  914.1 *O melhor de Chiquinha Gonzaga: Pecas.* Irmãos Vitale: 265A. 1998. Score.
  914.2 *Olivia Hime canta Chiquinha Gonzaga: Serenata de uma mulher.* Biscoito Fino: BF-522. 1998, 2002. CD.

915 Gonzaga, Luís
  915.1 *50 años de Chão.* RCA Victor: 7432129416-2. 1988. 3 CDs.
  915.2 *O melhor de Luiz Gonzaga.* Irmãos Vitale: 287-A. 2000. Score.

916 Jackson, do Pandeiro. *50 años de carreira.* EMI Brazil: 145550. 2 CDs.

917 Jacob do Bandolim
  917.1 *Mandolin Master of Brazil, Vol. 1* (Jacob Pick Bittencourt). Acoustic Disc: ACD-3. 1991. CD.
  917.2 *Mandolin Master of Brazil, Vol. 2* (Jacob Pick Bittencourt). Acoustic Disc: ACD-13. 1994. CD.

918 Jobim, Antonio Carlos
  918.1 *Cancioneiro Jobim: Obras completas, arranjos para piano = Complete Works, Piano Arrangements.* Jobim Music. 2001, 2007. Score, 5 vols.
  918.2 *Elis and Tom* (Elis Regina). Verve: 824 418-2. 1974, 1989. CD.

919 Lenine
  919.1 *Na pressão.* BMG Brasil: 74321-71076-2. 1999. CD.
  919.2 *O dia em que faremos contato.* BMG Brasil: 7432150211-2. 2000. CD.

920 Mestre Ambrósio. *Mestre Ambrósio.* Mestre Ambrósio Produções e Edições: 10101. 1995. CD.

921 Miranda, Carmen
  921.1 *The Brazilian Recordings.* Harlequin: HQ CD 33. 1993. CD.
  921.2 *Carmen Miranda.* Revivendo: CD-003. [1990–1994]. CD.

922 Moraes, Vinícius de
  922.1 *Cancioneiro Vinícius de Moraes.* Jobim Music, Instituto Antonio Carlos Jobim. 2007. Score, 2 vols.
  922.2 *Cancioneiro Vinícius de Moraes: Orfeu.* Jobim Music. 2003. Score.
  922.3 *Maria Bethânia Sings the Vinícius de Moraes Songbook.* DRG Brazil: 31616. 2006. CD.
  922.4 *Vinícius de Moraes.* Lumiar Editora. 1993. Score, 3 vols.

923 Nazareth, Ernesto
  923.1 *Brazilian Tangos and Dances.* Alfred Masterwork Edition. Alfred Pub.: 16775. 1997. Score.
  923.2 *O melhor de Ernesto Nazareth.* Irmãos Vitale: 245 A. 1997. Score.

924 Nóbrega, Antonio
  924.1 *Madeira que qupim não rói.* Brincante Produções Artisticas: BR 0002. 1997. CD.
  924.2 *Nove de frevereiro.* Brincante Produções Artisticas: BR 0007-2. 2004. CD.

925 Pixinguinha
  925.1 *No tempo dos Oito Batutas.* Revivendo: RVCD-064. [1995–1997]. CD.
  925.2 *O melhor de Pixinguinha.* Irmãos Vitale: 242-A. 1997. Score.

926 Regina, Elis
  926.1 *Elis.* Philips: 510 007-2. 1974. CD.
  926.2 *Elis.* Philips: 836 009-2. 1988. CD.
  926.3 *O melhor de Elis Regina.* Irmãos Vitale: 8484782. 1991. CD.
  926.4 *O melhor de Elis Regina.* Irmãos Vitale Score.
  926.5 *Saudades do Brasil.* WEA: M250678-2. 2001. 2 CDs.
  926.6 *Transversal do tempo.* Philips: 838 285-2. 1989. CD.

927 Rosa, Noel
  927.1 *A dama do encantado: Tributo a Aracy de Almeida* (Olivia Byington). WEA: 398420455-2. 1997. CD.

927.2 *Coisas Nossas*. Revivendo: CD-106. 1997. CD.

927.3 *Noel Rosa* (Mário Reis and Aracy de Almeida). Revivendo: CD-027. [1990–1994]. CD.

927.4 *Noel Rosa: Songbook*. Lumiar Editora. 1991. Score, 3 vols.

928   Veloso, Caetano

928.1 *Caetano Veloso: Songbook*. Lumiar Editora. 1994. Score, 2 vols.

928.2 *Cinema Transcendental*. Verve: 314 512 023-2. 1979, 1989. CD.

928.3 *Cores Nomes*. Polygram do Brasil: 838 464-2. 1982. CD.

928.4 *Livro*. Nonesuch: 79557-2. 1997. CD.

928.5 *Tropicália 2*. Nonesuch: 79339-2. 1993, 1994. CD.

ANTHOLOGIES

929   *Bossa Nova*. Songbook. Lumiar Editora. 1990. Score, 5 vols.

930   *Cadernos de choro*. Cadernos De Choro, Vols. 1 and 2. Acari Records. 2001. Score, 2 vols.

931   *Memórias musicais*. Biscoito Fino: BF 601-1–BF 601-15. 2002. 15 CDs.

932   *The Music of Capoeira: Mestre Acordeon*. Smithsonian Folkways: FE 4332. 1985, 2007. CD.

933   *O melhor do choro Brasileiro*. Irmãos Vitale. 1997. Score, 3 vols.

934   *Princípios de choro*. Acari Records, Biscoito Fino: BF 600-1--BF 600-15. 2001. 15 CDs.

935   *Princípios do choro*. Cadernos De Choro. EdUERJ. 2003–. Score, 5 vols.

936   *The Rough Guide to Samba*. Rough Guide. World Music Network: RGNET 1289 CD. 2013. 2 CDs. Special edition.

VIDEOS

937   Bethânia, Maria. *Maricotinha ao vivo*. Sarapui Produções Artisticas: DVD 701. 2003. DVD.

938   Cartola. *Ney Matogrosso interpreta Cartola ao vivo*. Universal Music: 44003806894. 2002. DVD.

939   Djavan

939.1 *Djavan ao vivo*. Sony Music Entertainment, Epic: 132.059/9-495871. 2000. DVD.

939.2 *Milagreiro*. Sony Music Entertainment, Epic: 132188/9-201909. 2002. DVD.

940   Gonzaga, Luís. *Danado de bom*. BMG Brasil. 2003. DVD.

941   Nóbrega, Antonio. *Lunário perpétuo*. Brincante Produções Artisticas: BR 0006-5. 2003. DVD.

Chile

INDIVIDUAL ARTISTS AND GROUPS

942   Advis, Luis. *Chile: The Siege of Santa Maria de Iquique: A People's Cantata of the Chilean Nitrate Miners* (Hector Duvachel Quilapayún). Custom Compact Disc Series. Smithsonian Folkways: PAR01019. 1974, 2001. CD.

943   Alarcón, Rolando. *Traditional Chilean Songs*. Custom Compact Disc Series. Smithsonian Folkways: FW 08748. 1999. CD.

944   ★Conjunto Folclórico "Danzamérica" de Chile. *Beautiful Songs of Chile*. ARC Music: EUCD 2313. 2010. CD.

945   ★Díaz, Martina and María. *Songs of Chile*. Custom Compact Disc Series. Smithsonian Folkways: FW 08817. 1957, 2000. CD.

946   Hernández, Myriam. *Seduccion*. Universal Music Latino: B0015484-02. 2011. CD.

947   Inti-Illimani. *Antologia I: 1973–1978*. Warner Music Chile: 857382820-2. 2000. CD.

948   Jara, Victor

948.1 *Antología musical*. Warner Music Chile: 8573 89067-2. 1960, 2001. 2 CDs.

948.2 *El canto libre de Victor Jara*. Música de esta América. Casa de las Américas: CMA 003. 2009. CD.

949   Kudai. *Nadha*. EMI Televisa Music: 50999 2 27509 21. 2008. CD.

950   Manns, Patricio, and Daniel Viglietti, Ángel Parra, Karaxu, and José Durán (composers). *Chile: Songs for the Resistance*. Custom Compact Disc Series. Smithsonian Folkways: P-1030. 1975, 2001. CD.

951   Manríquez, Rafael. *Que viva el canto! Songs of Chile*. Smithsonian Folkways: SFW 40549. 2008. CD.

952   Quilapayún. *Latitudes*. Alerce: CDA-0149. 1992. CD.

953   Trujillo, Chico. *Chico de oro*. Barbès Records: BR0026. 2010. CD.

954   Yáñez, Gonzalo. *Gonzalo Yáñez*. Nacional Records: NCL 20016. 2008. CD.

ANTHOLOGY

955 ★*The Amerindian Music of Chile.* Custom Compact Disc Series. Smithsonian Folkways: FW 04054. [1975, 2007]. CD.

VIDEOS

956 Inti-Illimani. *Lugares comunes.* Warner Music Chile: 5046-68201-2. 2002, 2003. DVD.

957 Quilapayún. *Quilapayún: El reencuetro.* Warner Music: 9782564619010. 2003. DVD.

Colombia

INDIVIDUAL ARTISTS AND GROUPS

958 Alarcón, Niyireth. *Musica Colombiana andina.* ARC Music: EUCD 2198. 2009. CD.

959 Arroyo, Joe
    959.1 *Grandes éxitos = Greatest Hits* (La Verdad). Discos Fuentes; Miami Records: 11004. 1999. CD.
    959.2 *Live! (2004).* Miami Records: 696211125528. 2006. CD.

960 Aterciopelados. *Rio.* Nacional Records: NCL 20014. 2008. CD.

961 Bomba Estéreo. *Blow Up.* Nacional Records: 718122028092. 2009. CD.

962 Cabrera, Jorge. *Grandes éxitos con Banda y Norteño.* Fonavisa: 0883 51631 2. 2005. CD.

963 Celedón, Jorge. *De lo nuevo . . . Lo mejor* (Jimmy Zambrano). Norte: 8869 730245 2. 2008. CD.

964 Los Corraleros de Majagual. *De vallenato a cumbia.* Miami Records: 696211120325. 2006. CD.

965 Cuesta, Ivan. *A ti, Colombia.* Arhoolie: CD-388. 1992, 1993. CD.

966 Díaz, Diomedes. *30 grandes éxitos en concierto.* Sony: TR2K-82821/2-485660. 1998. 2 CDs.

967 Gaiteros de San Jacinto. *Un fuego de Sangre Pura.* Smithsonian Folkways: SFW 40531. 2003, 2006. CD.

968 ★Grupo Cimarrón. *¡Cimarrón! Joropo Music from the Plains of Colombia.* Smithsonian Folkways: SFW CD 40557. 2011. CD.

969 Grupo Niche. *10 de colección.* Norte: 8869 727739 2. 2008. CD.

970 Guayacán Orquesta. *Xtremo.* Sony BMG: 8287 678264 2. 2005. CD.

971 Juanes. *La vida . . . Es un ratico.* Universal Music Latino: B0012316-02. 2008. CD.

972 Lu, Fanny. *Felicidad y perpetua.* Universal Music Latino: B0016308-02. 2011. CD.

973 Manjarrés, Peter. *Tu número uno* (Sergio Luis Rodríguez). Tropisounds: 84265602362. 2011. CD.

974 Meliyara, La India. *La sonora Meliyara.* Women of the World. Riverboat: TUGCD 1005. 1992. CD.

975 Meza, Lisandro. *Made in Colombia.* Sony Discos: JNK 97631. 2002. CD.

976 Peregoyo y su Combo Vacaná. *El rey del currulao.* Otraband: OTB 05. 2004. CD.

977 Paíto. *The Rough Guide to Colombian Street Party* (Joe Arroyo and David Dely). Rough Guide. World Music Network: RGNET 1217 CD. 2008. CD.

978 Sexteto Tabalá. *Colombia, the Kings of the Son Palenquero.* Musique du Monde. Buda: 1979312. 1999, 2001. CD.

979 Sonora Dinamita
    979.1 *Super éxitos! Vol.1.* Disco Fuentes: 11002. 1999. CD.
    979.2 *30 pegaditas de oro, vol. 1.* Disco Fuentes: 11021. 2001. CD.

980 Torres, Roberto. *Lo mejor de Roberto Torres.* SAR: SCD-1057. 1994. CD.

981 Vives, Carlos
    981.1 *Canta los clásicos del vallenato.* Universal Music Latino: 440 014 870-2. 1994. CD.
    981.2 *10 de colección.* Norte: 8869 731793 2. 2008. CD. Remastered.

ANTHOLOGIES

982 *¡Ayombe! The Heart of Colombia's Música Vallenata.* Smithsonian Folkways: SFW CD 40546. 2008. CD.

983 *Cartagena! Curro Fuentes and the Big Band Cumbia and Descarga Sound of Colombia, 1962–1972.* Soundway: SNDWCD026. 2010. CD.

984 *Colombia! The Golden Age of Discos Fuentes, the Powerhouse of Colombian Music, 1960–1976.* Soundway: SNDWCD 008. 1960, 2007. CD.

985 ★*Music of Colombia.* Custom Compact Disc Series. Smithsonian Folkways: FW 6804. 1954. CD.

986 *A Night in Colombia*. Sony BMG Music Entertainment: 8869 735291 2. 2008. CD.

987 *The Original Sound of Cumbia: The History of Colombian Cumbia and Porro*. Soundway: SNDWCD032. 2011. 2 CDs.

988 *Pacífico Colombiano: Music Adventures in Afro-Colombia*. Otrabanda: OTB09. 2008. CD.

989 *Palenque Palenque: Champeta Criolla and Afro Roots in Colombia, 1975–1991*. Soundway: SNDWCD022. 2010. CD.

990 *Sacred and Profane Music of the Ika*. Custom Compact Disc Series. Smithsonian Folkways: FW 04055. 1976, 2000. CD.

VIDEOS

991 Arroyo, Joe. *Joe Arroyo: La historia, Vol. 1*. Sony Discos: SVD-D89368. 2003. DVD.

992 Celedón, Jorge. *Grandes éxitos* (Jimmy Zambrano). Sony US Latin: 886972976693. 2009. DVD.

Ecuador

INDIVIDUAL ARTISTS AND GROUPS

993 Benítez-Valencia Trio. *Ecuador* (Gonzalo Benítez and Luis Alberto Valencia). Smithsonian Folkways: COOK01120. 1958, 2006. CD.

994 Ecuador Manta
  994.1 *Caminando en la imaginación*. Condor: 618604400326. 1998. CD.
  994.2 *Sounds of the Andes*. 707541000697. 2008. CD.

995 Hatun Kotama. *¡Asi Kotama! The Flutes of Otavalo, Ecuador*. Smithsonian Folkways: SFW CD 40564. 2013. CD.

996 Karu Ñan. *Chimbaloma*. Tumi: TUMI CD027. 1993. CD.

997 Jatari. *Ecuador: The Cry of Freedom! = El grito de libertad!* Custom Compact Disc Series. Smithsonian Folkways: PAR01034. 1976, 2001. CD.

998 Villarroel, Ligia. *Equateur: Musique des Andes*. Air Mail Music. Sunset-France: SA 141214. 2011. CD.

ANTHOLOGIES

999 *Lowland Tribes of Ecuador*. Custom Compact Disc Series. Smithsonian Folkways: FW 04375. 1986, 2001. CD.

1000 *Music of the Jívaro of Ecuador*. Ethnic Folkways Library. Smithsonian Folkways: FW 04386. 1973, 2001. CD.

Ecuador and Bolivia

INDIVIDUAL ARTISTS AND GROUPS

1001 Mañachi, Ñanda, Savia Andina, and Sukay. *Cultural Legacy: Traditional Music from Ecuador and Bolivia*. Condor: 618604900259. 2006. 2 CDs.

Ecuador, Colombia, and Brazil

ANTHOLOGY

1002 ★*South America: Black Music in Praise of Oxalá and Other Gods* (David Lewiston, compiler). Explorer Series. Nonesuch: 79729-2. 1970, 2003. CD.

Ecuador and Peru

INDIVIDUAL ARTIST

1003 Alpamayo. *Music from Peru and Ecuador*. ARC Music: EUCD 1184. 1991. CD.

French Guiana

ANTHOLOGY

1004 ★*Music from Aluku: Maroon Sounds of Struggle, Solace, and Survival* (Kenneth M. Bilby, compiler). Smithsonian Folkways: SFW CD 50412. 2010. CD.

Paraguay

INDIVIDUAL ARTISTS AND GROUPS

1005 Basaldúa, Papi, and Grupo Cantares. *Tiempo de amar*. Alula: ALU-5003. 2005. CD.

1006 Los Chiriguanos. *Paraguay: Guaraní Songs and Dances*. Explorer Series. Nonesuch: 79727-2. 1968, 2003. CD.

1007 Elenco Ko'eti. *Paraguay: Traditional Songs and Dances*. ARC Music: EUCD 2323. 2011. CD.

1008 Gill, Eralio. *The Art of the Paraguayan Harp*. Oliver Sudden Productions: K10-12CD. 1998. CD.

1009 Rojas, Marcelo. *Maiteí América: Harps of Paraguay* (Martín Portillo, Kike Pedersen,

Miguel Ángel Valdéz, and Nicolás Caballero). Smithsonian Folkways: SFW CD 40548. 2009. CD.

Peru

INDIVIDUAL ARTISTS AND GROUPS

1010 Allyu Sulca. *Music of the Incas: Andean Harp and Violin Music from Ayacucho, Peru.* Lyrichord: LYRCD 7348. 1970–[1979]. CD.

1011 Ayllón, Eva. *Kimba fá.* Four Quarters Entertainment: FQT-CD-1815. 2009. CD.

1012 Baca, Susana. *Afrodiaspora* (Calle 13 and Quetzal). Luaka Bop: 6 80899 0077-2-6. 2011. CD.

1013 Chocolate and Peru Jazz. *Chocolate: Peru's Master Percussionist.* Lyrichord: LYRCD 7417. 1990. CD.

1014 Grupo Belen de Tarma. *Chicha.* Tumi: TUMI CD045. 1994. CD.

1015 Juaneco y Su Combo. *Masters of Chicha 1.* Barbès Records: BR0020. 2008. CD.

1016 Manzanita. *The Roots of Chicha: Psychedelic Cumbias from Peru 2.* Barbès Records: BR0028. 2010. CD.

1017 Montes, Eduardo. *Montes y Manrique, 1911– 2011: Cien años de música Peruana* (César Augusto Manrique). Colección Travaux de l'Institut Français d'Études Andines. Instituto de Etnomusicologia, Pontificia Universidad Católica del Perú. 2010. 2 CDs.

1018 Novalima. *Karimba.* ESL Music: ESL 190. 2012. CD.

1019 Peña. *Peña.* Secret Stash: SSR CD-274. 2010. CD, DVD.

1020 Perú Negro. *Jolgorio.* Times Square: TSQD 9035. 2004. CD.

ANTHOLOGIES

1021 ★*The Ayacucho Region* (Raúl R. Romero, compiler). Traditional Music of Peru, 6. Smithsonian Folkways: SFW 40449. 2001. CD.

1022 ★*Celebrating Divinity in the High Andes* (Raúl R. Romero, compiler). Traditional Music of Peru, 5. Smithsonian Folkways: SFW 40448. 1999. CD.

1023 *Corazón: Songs and Music Recorded in Peru by Rosalind Solomon* [1985] (Pablo Maldonado and Delinas Salas). Folkways: FW 34035. 1985, 2001. CD.

1024 *Cumbia Beat, Vol. 1: Tropical Sounds from Peru, 1966–1976.* Vampi Soul: CD 116. 2010. 2 CDs.

1025 *Huaynos and Huaylas: The Real Music of Peru.* Worldwide Tourguide and Globe Trails: CDORBD 064. 1991. CD.

1026 *Huayno Music of Peru, the Discos Smith Recordings, Vol. II.* Arhoolie: CD 338. 1957, 1991. CD.

1027 ★*Huayno Music of Peru, Vol. 1, 1949–1989.* Arhoolie: CD 320. 1949, 1989. CD.

1028 ★*The Lima Highlands* (Raúl R. Romero, compiler). Traditional Music of Peru, 7. Smithsonian Folkways: SFW 40450. 2001. CD.

1029 *Mountain Music of Peru, Vol. 1.* Smithsonian Folkways: CD SF 40020. 1991. CD.

1030 ★*Mountain Music of Peru, Vol. 2.* Smithsonian Folkways: CD SF 40406. 1964, 1994. CD.

1031 *Music of Peru.* Ethnic Folkways Library. Smithsonian Folkways: FW 04415. 1950, 2007. CD.

1032 *Peru and Bolivia: The Sounds of Evolving Traditions: Central Andean Music and Festivals.* Music of the Earth. Multicultural Media: MCM 3009. 1992, 1997. CD.

1033 *Peru: Andean Music of Life, Work and Celebration.* Smithsonian Folkways: UNES 08307. 2015. CD.

1034 *Peru Fiestas: Music of the High Andes* (David Lewiston, compiler). Explorer Series. Nonesuch: 79730-2. 1972, 2003. CD.

1035 *Peru—Kingdom of the Sun: The Inca Heritage* (David Lewiston, compiler). Explorer Series. Nonesuch: 79728-2. 1969, 2003. CD.

1036 *Peru: Music from the Land of Macchu Picchu.* Lyrichord: LYRCD 7294. 1980s. CD.

1037 *Peru: Music of the Awajun and Wampis Amazonia, Cenepa Valley.* Archives Internationales de Musique Populaire, 92. VDE Gallo: VDE CD-1279. 2009. CD.

1038 *Piñata Party Presents Music of Peru.* Custom Compact Disc Series. Smithsonian Folkways: FW 08749. 1962, 2000. CD.

1039 ★*Piura* (Raúl R. Romero, compiler). Traditional Music of Peru, 8. Smithsonian Folkways: SFW 40451. 2002. CD.

1040 ★*Traditional Music of Peru.* Ethnic Folkways Library. Smithsonian Folkways: FW 04456. 1958, 2001. CD.

1041 ★*Traditional Music of Peru, Vol. 1: Festivals of Cusco.* Smithsonian Folkways: SFW 040466. 1992, 1995. CD.

1042 ★*Traditional Music of Peru, Vol. 2: The Mantaro Valley* (Raúl R. Romero, compiler). Smithsonian Folkways: SFW 40467. 1985, 1995. CD. Previously released in Peru by the Pontificia Universidad Católica del Perú in 1985.

1043 ★*Traditional Music of Peru, Vol. 3: Cajamarca and the Colca Valley* [1980s] (Raúl R. Romero, compiler). Smithsonian Folkways: SF 40468. 1997. CD.

1044 ★*Traditional Music of Peru, Vol. 4: Lambayeque* [1990–1991] (Raúl R. Romero, compiler). Smithsonian Folkways: SFW 40469. 1996. CD.

Suriname

INDIVIDUAL ARTISTS AND GROUPS

1045 ★*The Creole Music of Surinam.* Custom Compact Disc Series. Smithsonian Folkways: FW 04233. 1978, 1999. CD.

1046 *Music from Saramaka: A Dynamic Afro-American Tradition.* Custom Compact Disc Series. Smithsonian Folkways: FW 04225. 1977, 2002. CD.

Uruguay

INDIVIDUAL ARTISTS AND GROUPS

1047 Cuareim 1080. *Uruguay: Tambores del candombe, Vol. 2.* Musique du Monde. Buda: 3017816. 2009. CD.

1048 Drexler, Jorge. *Cara B.* Warner Music Latina: 493436. 2008. CD.

1049 Gauchos de Roldán. *Button Accordion and Bandoneón Music From Northern Uruguay.* Smithsonian Folkways: SFW 40561. 2012. CD.

1050 ★Marino Rivero, René. *Bandoneon Pure: Dances of Uruguay.* The World's Musical Traditions, 5. Smithsonian Folkways: CD SF 40431. 1991, 1993. CD.

1051 No Te Va Gustar. *Por lo menos hoy.* Nacional Records: 753182545417. 2010. CD.

1052 Raimondo Vayo. *Tango Universal.* Pantaleón: PAN-1012. 2010. CD.

ANTHOLOGY

1053 *Uruguay: Tambores del candombe.* Buda: 92745-2. 1999. CD.

Venezuela

INDIVIDUAL ARTISTS AND GROUPS

1054 Los Amigos Invisibles. *Commercial.* Nacional Records: 718122031092. 2009. CD.

1055 Barradas, Huáscar. *Folk Music from Venezuela* (Maracaibo). ARC Music: EUCD 1565. 1999. CD.

1056 Chino & Nacho. *Supremo.* Machete Music: B0016190-02. 2011. CD.

1057 Díaz, Simón. *Mis canciones (My Songs).* World Village: 468042. 2005. CD.

1058 D'León, Oscar
    1058.1 ★*Tranquilamente: Tranquilo.* Sony International: 31367. 2008. CD.
    1058.2 *Fuzionanado.* Norte: 03762 96867 2. 2006. CD.

1059 Granados, Marco. *Music of Venezuela* (Jorge Clem, Roberto Koch, Manuel Rangel, and Leonardo Granados). Soundbrush: SR1014. 2008. CD.

1060 Los Melodicos. *Nenes con las nenas.* MSI Music Corp.: 825083163127. 2004. CD.

1061 Ochoa, Rafael, and Rafael Aponte. *Arpa: Venezuela.* Air Mail Music. Sunset-France: SA 141120. 1991, 2005. CD.

1062 Orquesta de la Luz. *La historia de la luz.* RMM: CDZ-81132. 1993. CD.

1063 Vita, Franco de. *Primera fila.* Sony Music Latin: 8869 778112 2. 2011. CD.

ANTHOLOGIES

1064 ★*Dances of Venezuela.* Custom Compact Disc Series. Smithsonian Folkways: FW 08844. 1958, 1999. CD.

1065 *Music of the Venezuelan Yekuana Indians.* Custom Compact Disc Series. Smithsonian Folkways: FW 04104. 1975, 2000s. CD.

1066 *Venezuela: Afro-Venezuelan Music, Vols. 1 and 2.* Smithsonian Folkways: UNES 08318. 2014. 2 CDs.

1067 ★*¡Y que viva Venezuela! Maestros del joropo oriental*. Smithsonian Folkways: SFW CD 40551. 2009. CD.

SOUTH AMERICA
GENERAL ANTHOLOGIES

1068 Ambar Music Group. *El diablo suelto* (Moscow Chamber Orchestra). Delos: DE 4031. 2010. CD.

1069 *Music of the Andes*. Hemisphere: 7243 8 28190 2 8. 1994. CD.

1070 Mendoza, Jorge Aníbal. *Bachata and Cachata* (Pablo Cárcamo). ARC Music: EUCD 2164. 2008. CD

1071 ★*Los Parajos Perdidos: The South American Project* (L'Arpeggiata; Christina Pluhar, dir.). Virgin: 5099907095023. 2012. CD.

VIDEO

1072 ★*The JVC/Smithsonian Folkways Video Anthology of Music and Dance of the Americas*. JVC, Victor Co. of Japan; dist. by Multicultural Media: JVCAIIVOL01-06. 1995, 2005. 6 DVDs.

3

Classical, Traditional, and Popular Music of Asia and Oceania

Compiled by **MI-HYE CHYUN, JOE C. CLARK, ALEC McLANE, KEVIN C. MILLER, JEFF SCHWARTZ,** *and* **LIZA VICK**

Asia and Oceania enjoy rich and widely varying musical traditions. East Asian styles stem from traditional (folk), dramatic and religious forms, and classical and popular genres both homegrown and Western-influenced. Disparities in size reflect the availability of commercial recordings overseas. The organization of heading reflects the categories mentioned above, which are, as in other areas, imperfect. Japan, Korea, China, Taiwan, and Indonesia are subdivided along these lines for ease of use. South Asia is arranged like so: Northern (Hindustani) and Southern (Carnatic) India, Bollywood film music, with surrounding areas (Himalayas, Pakistan, Sri Lanka, Bangladesh, Bhutan, Nepal, and Tibet). Like Africa, the Asian diaspora is widespread and you will find anthologies listed both here and in chapter 7, International Anthologies.

NORTH AND EAST ASIA

CHINA AND TAIWAN

Compiled by Alec McLane

Although it could certainly be said that China, with one-fifth of the world's population and covering a region stretching from Central Asia to islands in the Pacific, is characterized by great diversity, an even more striking characteristic is the relative homogeneity of culture spread over such a huge area and population. This phenomenon owes itself to the influence of a Han ethnic majority in all but two provinces and a sense of national identity that is perhaps the oldest in the world. The great majority of available recordings of Chinese traditional music feature very rich instrumental and operatic traditions that are spread all over the country, but each province possesses its own unique brand. The instrumental traditions include several classical instruments with repertoires extending back to the third century CE and much earlier—*dizi, pipa, qin, and zheng,* for instance—and some, like the *erhu* now very popular in the

West, have arrived in the "classical" tradition relatively recently. Most provinces have their own characteristic genres of opera, but the best known are the ancient *Kunqu*, from Jiangsu Province, and the more recent *Jingju*, or Peking Opera, from the capital city.

Despite the Han dominance, the government recognizes some fifty-five different ethnic minority groups. Chinese musicology has generally celebrated the existence of these groups, with abundant collecting and attempts at preservation. There are excellent recordings of minority music from Guizhou and Yunnan Provinces, as well as from the Uighur minority in Xinjiang Province. In Taiwan, there has been similar attention paid to aboriginal groups, as well as a large Hakka-speaking population that emigrated from Fujian Province on the mainland. In the twentieth century, through contacts with the West, many unique styles of popular music have arisen, first in Hong Kong with its film industry–inspired "Cantopop" and most recently in a thriving underground rock-music scene in Beijing. European classical music has also been a shaping force in twentieth-century Chinese music, with many internationally known Chinese composers producing works with a mix of Western and Chinese instruments and styles.

Although many of the recordings on this list are not easy to find through conventional channels, several vendors on the Internet carry the labels that have produced major collections of Chinese music: JVC, King Records, Lyrichord, Hugo, and so on. Two of these are Farside Music (www.farsidemusic.com) and Multicultural Media's World Music Store (www.worldmusicstore.com). Popular music from China and Taiwan is even more difficult to find, but YesAsia.com (www.yesasia.com) and Malmusic.com (www.malmusic.com) carry most of the performers on the current scene.

CHINA

General Anthologies

1073 *Chinese Music of the Han and the Uighurs.* World Music Library. Seven Seas: KICC 5141. 1985, 1988. CD.

1074 *Music of the Dynasties of China.* Inside Sound Classics: ISC-2895 CD. 1995. CD.

1075 ★*The Silk Road: A Musical Caravan.* Smithsonian Folkways: FW CD 40438. 1980, 2002. 2 CDs.

See also Central Asia (China).

VIDEOS

1076 *The JVC Video Anthology of World Music and Dance: East Asia, Vols. 3–5.* JVC, Victor Co. of Japan; dist. by Multicultural Media: VTMV-33–VTMV-35, JVCVOL 03–JVCVOL05. 1988, 2005. 3 DVDs.

1077 *Mosuo Song Journey* (Diedie Weng, dir. and prod.). Diedie Weng. 2007. DVD.

Traditional and Folk

INDIVIDUAL ARTISTS AND GROUPS

1078 ★Abing. *Min jian yin yue jia Hua Yanjun (Abing) ji nian zhuan ji, 1893–1950 = Commemoration of the Renowned Folk Musician Hua Yan-Jun; Ah Bing.* ROI Productions: RC-961002-2C. 1996. 2 CDs.

1079 Ancient Music Band of Nanjian. *Unnan dokei ongaku = Dongjing Music in Yunnan, China.* World Music Library, 89–90. King: KICW 85179. 1995, 2008. 2 CDs.

1080 Ensemble du Conservatoire Supérieur de Xian (Changan). *Chine: musique ancienne de Chang'an.* Inédit. Maison des Cultures du Monde: W 260036. 1991. CD. Available for download only.

1081 Fei, Jianrong, and Qundi An. *Music of the Ruan Xien, Zhuong Ruan and Da Ruan.* JVC World Sounds. JVC: VICG-5463-2. 1998. CD.

1082 Guo Brothers and Shung Tian. *Yuan* Realworld: 91345-2. 1990. CD.

1083 Guo, Jingqiang, and the Chinese Music Ensemble of New York. *Beloved Chinese Songs.* Chesky: WO 121. 1995. CD.

1084 He, Baoquan, and Sun Wenjian. *Guzheng: The Art of Sun Wenjian and He Baoquan.* World Music Library. King: KICC 5233. 2008. CD.

1085 He, Shufeng. *Chinese Pipa.* World Music Library, 43. Seven Seas: KICC 5143. 2008. CD.

1086 Hu, Zhihou. *Music of the Guanzi.* JVC World Sounds. JVC: VICG-5260. 1993. CD.

1087 Jiang, Xiaoqing. *China World Sounds: Music of the Guzheng.* JVC World Sounds. JVC: VICG-5464-2. 1998. CD.

1088 Jing Ying Soloists
  1088.1 *Evening Song: Traditional Chinese Instrumental Music.* Saydisc: CD-SDL 368. 1987. CD.

1088.2 *Like Waves against the Sand* (Leung-tak Tong, cond.). Saydisc: CD-SDL 325. 1986. CD.

1089 Li, Zhengui, Xin Tian, Jianhui Wang, Yue Sun, and Shuo Li. *Thundering Dragon: Percussion Music from China.* Welt Musik. Haus der Kulturen der Welt: SM 1519-2. 1994. CD.

1090 ★Liang, Tsai-Ping. *The Chinese Cheng: Ancient and Modern.* Lyrichord Presents Outstanding Music from around the World. Lyrichord Discs: LYRCD 7302. 1998. CD. Available for download only.

1091 Liang, Tsai-Ping, et al. *China's Instrumental Heritage.* Lyrichord Presents Outstanding Music from around the World. Lyrichord: LYRCD 792. [1986–1993]. CD.

1092 Liu, Hongjun. *Pipes of the Minority Peoples.* JVC World Sounds. JVC: VICG-5017. 1990. CD.

1093 ★Liu, Mingyüan. *China World Sounds: Music of the Erhu and the Bowed Stringed Instruments.* JVC World Sounds. JVC: VICG-5461-2. 1998. CD.

1094 Liu, Tianhua, composer. *Liu Tianhua er hu qu shi shou: Erhu Pieces of Liu Tian-Hua by George Gao (Shaoqing Gao).* ROI: RA-001010C. 2000. CD.

1095 Lui, Pui-Yuen. *Floating Petals—Wild Geese—The Moon on High: Music of the Chinese Pipa.* Explorer Series. Elektra; Nonesuch: 72085. 1980. CD.

1096 Mamat, Ayshamgul, Abdurashid Nâdirev, and Abdulaziz Hashimov. *Asie Centrale: musique des ouïgours: traditions d'ili et de kachgar.* Maison des Cultures du Monde: W 260113. 2003. CD.

1097 Min, Huifen, and Xiaofen Min. *Ni Shang Qu: The Gossamer Song.* First Impression Music: FIM SACD M 032. 2004. CD.

1098 Ming de chuang yi ji tuan. *Ren yu zi ran de he sheng = People and Nature in Harmony.* Guizhou wen hua yin xiang chu ban she: 9787885825164. 2008. CD, DVD.

1099 Society of Jiangnan Sizhu of Shanghai. *Chinese Chamber Music of Jiangnan Sizhu.* World Music Library, 136. King: KICW 85115-6. 2008. 2 CDs.

1100 Song, Fei. *Song Fei er hu yan zou zhuan ji.* Ming jia zou ming qu xi lie. Gong an bu hua sheng yin xiang chu ban she: 140016. 2003. CD, VCD.

1101 Sou, Si-tai. *Chine: "Le pêcheur et le bûcheron": Le qin, cithara des lettrés = China: "The Fisherman and the Woodcutter": The Qin, Zither of the Literati.*

Archives Internationales de Musique Populaire, 82. VDE-Gallo: VDE CD-1214. 2006. CD.

1102 Uyghur Musicians of Xinjiang. *Music from the Oasis Towns of Central Asia.* GlobeStyle Recordings: CDORBD 098. 2000. CD.

1103 Wu, Man, Tien-Juo Wang, Yi Yang, and Qi-Chao Liu. *Pipa: Chinese Traditional and Contemporary Music.* Nimbus Records: NI 5368. 2000. 2 CDs.

1104 Wu, Wenguang. *Music of the Qin.* JVC World Sounds. JVC: VICG-5213. 1992. CD.

1105 Xinjiang Mukam Art Ensemble. *Music of the Uighur/Mukam and Folk Songs.* World Music Library. Seven Seas: KICW 85081-3. 2008. 3 CDs.

1106 Yuan, Lily. *The Ancient Art Music of China.* Lyrichord Discs: LYRCD 7409. 1990. CD.

1107 Zhang, Qiang. *Music of the Piba.* JVC World Sounds. JVC: VICG-60380. 2000. CD.

1108 Zhu, Changyao. *Erhu: The Art of Zhu Changyao.* World Music Library. Seven Seas: KICC 5231. 2008. CD.

ANTHOLOGIES

1109 *Chinese Folk Songs.* Collection of Chinese Music. CRC Jianian: RCD-02. 2008. 4 CDs.

1110 *Chinese Instrumental Performance Series.* Collection of Chinese Music. CRC Jianian: CCD-2533. 2008. 4 CDs.

1111 *Chinese Instrumental Tone Picture Series.* Collection of Chinese Music. CRC Jianian: CCD-2529. 2008. 4 CDs.

1112 *Guizhou miao zu yin yue: Ren yu zi ran de he sheng = Miao Music: Miao Folk Music: People and Nature in Harmony.* Ming de chuang yi chu ban she: 9789889767570. 2000. CD.

1113 ★*The Hugo Masters: An Anthology of Chinese Classical Music.* Celestial Harmonies: 13042-2. 1992. 4 CDs.

1114 *The Music of Ethnic Groups in Yunnan.* World Music Library. King: KICW 85119-21. 2008. 3 CDs.

1115 *Music of the Silk Road in China.* World Music Library. King: KICW 85033-5. 2008. 3 CDs. *See also* Central Asia (China).

1116 *Sizhu: Silk Bamboo: Chamber Music of South China.* Anthology of Music in China, 3. Pan: PAN 2030 CD. 1994. CD. Available for download only.

1117 *Tibetan Music.* Collection of Chinese Music. CRC Jianian: RCD-98. 2008. 4 CDs.

1118 *Turkestan chinois: le muqam des Dolan = Chinese Turkestan: The Melody Type of the Dolan.* Inédit. Maison des Cultures du Monde: W 260126. 2006. CD.

Theatrical, Religious

INDIVIDUAL ARTISTS AND GROUPS

1119 Chi, Yang, and Li Ping. *Opéra de Pékin: La Forêt en Feu; La Princess Cent-Fleurs = Peking Opera: The Forest on Fire; The Princess Hundred Flowers* (Members of the Peking Opera, Dalian Troupe). Musique du Monde. Buda: 92618-2. 1995. CD. Available for download only.

1120 Rnam-rgyal Grwa-tshan (Monks of Namgyal Monastery). *Buddhist Liturgy of Tibet: The Monks of Namgyal Monastery.* World Music Library, 37. Seven Seas: KICC-5137. 2008. 2 CDs.

1121 Suzhou Kunju Theatre. *Kunqu Opera of China.* King: KICW 85117. 2008. CD.

1122 Tang, Xianzu, composer. *Le Pavillon aux Pivoines: opéra classique Chinois Kunqu* (Wen-yi Hua, Huilan Gao, and Troupe Lan Ding). Inédit. Maison des Cultures du Monde: W 260060. 1995. 2 CDs.

1123 Tianjin Buddhist Music Ensemble. *Buddhist Music of Tianjin.* Nimbus Records: NI 5416. 1994. CD.

1124 Traditional Ensemble of the Beijing National Music Academy. *Buddhist Music of the Ming Dynasty: Zhihuasi Temple, Beijing.* JVC World Sounds. JVC: VICG-5259. 1993. CD.

1125 Wang, Fenxun (adapt.). *Opéra du Sichuan: la légende de serpent blanc* (Chengdu shi Chuan ju yuan [Chengdu Sichuan opera company]). Musique du Monde. Buda: 92555-2. [1992–1994]. 2 CDs.

ANTHOLOGIES

1126 ★*An Introduction to Chinese Opera, Vols. 1, 2, and 4.* Chinese Opera Series. Marco Polo: 8.223930, 8.223931, 8.223933. 1994. 3 CDs (vol. 3 never released).

1127 *Peking Opera.* CRC Jianian: CCD-2537. 2010. 4 CDs.

1128 *Rain Dropping on the Banana Tree.* Rounder: CD 1125. 1996. CD.

1129 ★*Voice of the Dragon: A Journey through Musical China.* Stemra: 92804. 2005. 2 CDs.

VIDEOS

1130 *Peking Opera.* Quintessential Chinese Culture. HUWA Publishing House: 978159882005844455. 2003. DVD.

1131 *What Is the Chinese Opera?* Insight Media: DAH 3688. 2004. DVD.

Popular and Western-Influenced

INDIVIDUAL ARTISTS AND GROUPS

1132 Chan, Wing-wah, Dun Tan, An-Lun Huang, Jordan Cho-tung Tang, Xiao-Gang Ye, and Xiaosong Qu. *First Contemporary Chinese Composers Festival 1986* (Various soloists, Hong Kong Philharmonic Orchestra; Kenneth Schermerhorn, cond.). Chinese Contemporary Series. Marco Polo: 8.223915. 1995. CD.

1133 Cheung, Leslie. *Leslie Cheung Forever.* Rock Records: RD1811. 2007. CD.

1134 Cui, Jian. *Best of Cui Jian, 1986–1996.* EMI: 94636729220. 2006. CD.

1135 Huaxia Chinese Chamber Ensemble. *Huaxia: Contemporary Music for Traditional Chinese Instruments.* Delos: DE 3299. 2004. CD.

1136 Mei, Yanfang (Anita Mui). *Faithfully.* East Asia Music. 2008. 3 CDs, DVD.

1137 Tang chao yue dui. *Meng Hui Tang Chao = A Dream of Returning to the Tang Dynasty.* Zhong guo yin le jia yin xiang chu ban she. 2008. CD, DVD.

1138 Yin, Chengzhong, and Lina Yu. *Butterfly Lovers: Violin Concerto; The Yellow River: Piano Concerto.* Marco Polo: 8.008. 2000s. CD.

1139 Zhou, Long, composer. *Tales from the Cave.* Music from China. Delos: DE 3335. 2004. CD.

ANTHOLOGY

1140 *Music from the People's Republic of China: Sung and Played on Traditional Instruments* (Guy Carawan and Candie Carawan, compilers). Rounder: CD 4008. 1990. CD.

CENTRAL ASIA

ANTHOLOGY

1141 *Ethnic Minority Music of Northwest Xinjiang, China.* Sublime Frequencies: SF057. 2009. CD.

TAIWAN

Traditional and Folk

ANTHOLOGIES

1142 *Music of Taiwan Aborigines = Sekai no minzoku ongaku.* Seven Seas: GXC-5002. 2008. CD.

1143 *Taiwan: musique des Hakka: chants montagnards et musique instrumentale bayin = Taiwan: Music of the Hakka: Mountain Songs and Bayin Instrumental Music.* Maison des Cultures du Monde: W 260127. 2006. CD.

Popular and Western-Influenced

INDIVIDUAL ARTISTS AND GROUPS

1144 Deng, Lijun. *Chuan qi de dan sheng.* Universal. 2008. 3 CDs.

1145 Zhang, Huimei. *Mei li zui jing xuan = A-mei best, 1996–2002.* Forward music: 02-20245-1. 2002. 2 CDs.

1146 Zhou, Jielun. *Initial: Jay Chou Greatest Hits.* Sony: SICP 88. 2008. CD.

JAPAN

Compiled by Joe C. Clark

Japan offers a rich and varied musical culture. Music of Japan's Muromachi period (fourteenth through sixteenth centuries) includes *gagaku*, which means "elegant music." It is most commonly associated with ancient court music and is sometimes used in Buddhist temples and Shinto shrines. Other musical forms from this period include *shōmyō* (Buddhist chant) and *nō* theater art, which combine music, dance, and drama.

Traditional musical theater genres from the premodern period (1573–1867) include *kabuki* and the melodramatic puppet theater *bunraku*. The premodern period also witnessed the development of chamber music on instruments, such as the *shakuhachi* (bamboo flute), the *koto* (long zither), and the *shamisen* (three-stringed plucked lute).

During the modern era, which began in 1868 with the Meiji Reformation, influences from around the world began to find their way into the music of Japan. Japanese musicians also contributed to rock, jazz, pop, world, and Western orchestra music.

The availability of Japanese music in the United States is somewhat problematic, as many classic titles are currently out of print. CDs and DVDs, including imports, are available through normal channels, including the online vendors CD Universe (www.cduniverse.com) and Amazon (www.amazon.com). Prices for imports can be exorbitant. Record labels featuring traditional music of Japan include Camerata, Celestial, Denon, Fontec, King Records, Lyrichord, Nonesuch, and Ocora. Contemporary CDs are primarily on Japanese labels, but some artists record with U.S. or U.K. labels and are much easier to obtain. Smithsonian Folkways recently made many of their older recordings of Japanese music available as custom CDs and digital downloads.

Traditional and Folk

INDIVIDUAL ARTISTS AND GROUPS

1147 Ensemble Kineya. *Nagauta.* Japon. Ocora: C 560144. 1997, 2000. CD.

1148 ★Ensemble Nipponia. *Kabuki and Other Traditional Music.* Explorer Series. Nonesuch: 266108-2. 1978, 2007. CD.

1149 Hirayasu, Takashi, and Bob Brozman. *Jin Jin: Firefly.* World Music Network, Riverboat Records: TUGCD 1012. 1999. CD.

1150 Iwamoto, Yoshikazu. *Japon: l'esprit du vent = Japan: The Spirit of Wind.* Musique du Monde. Buda: 92640-2. 1995. CD.

1151 Izutsuya, Koishimaru. *Japan: Koishimaru Izutsuya: Master of the Kawachi Ondo Epics.* Smithsonian Folkways: UNES 08319. 2015. CD.

1152 Kikusui, Kofu, Noriko Noda, and Yayoi Nishimura. *Japanese Koto Consort: Koto, Shamisen, Shakuhachi and Voice.* Lyrichord: 7205. 1993. CD.

1153 Kodo
    1153.1 ★*Best of Kodo.* Tristar Music: WK 57776. 1988, 1993. CD.
    1153.2 *Tataku: Best of Kodo II, 1994–1999.* Sony: WK 1391. 1994, 2000. CD.

1154 ★Kyoto Imperial Court Music Orchestra. *Gagaku: The Imperial Court Music of Japan.* Lyrichord: 7126. 1980, 1989. CD.

1155 Kyoto Nogakukai. *Japanese Noh Music.* Lyrichord: 7137. 1980–[1989]. CD.

1156 Miyata, Kohachiro. *Japan: Shakuhachi, the Japanese Flute.* Explorer Series. Elektra Nonesuch: 9 72076-2. 1977, 1991. CD.

1157 Nihon Daiko. *The Japanese Drums.* ARC: EUCD 1483. 1998. CD.

1158 ★Nihon Ongaku Shudan. *Japan: Traditional Vocal and Instrumental Music: Shakuhachi, Biwa, Koto, Shamisen.* Explorer Series. Elektra Nonesuch: 72072-2. 1976, 1980s. CD.

1159 Reigakusha. *Gagaku Suites.* Celestial Harmonies: 13223-2. 2002. CD.

1160 Saeki, Satomi, and Alcvin Ramos. *Japanese Traditional Koto and Shakuhachi Music.* Oliver Sudden Productions: K10-22 CD. 2006. CD.

1161 Sakamoto, Tsuyoshi, Kazuko Tsukushi, and Mitsuhashi Koto (Koto ensemble of the Ikuta-ryu). *Japanese Koto Orchestra.* Lyrichord: 7167. 1989, 1993. CD.

1162 Tokyo Gakuso. *Gagaku and Beyond.* Celestial Harmonies: 13179-2. 2000. CD.

1163 Yamada, Isshi, and Fuzan Sato. *Koto, Music of the One-String Ichigenkin.* Custom Compact Disc Series. Smithsonian Folkways: FW 8746. 1967, 2003. CD.

1164 Yamaguchi, Goro. *Japan Shakuhachi Music: A Bell Ringing in the Empty Sky.* Explorer Series. Nonesuch Records: 130364-2. 1969, 2007. CD.

1165 Yamato Ensemble
 1165.1 *The Art of Japanese Bamboo Flute and Koto: A Selection of Japanese Chamber Music.* ARC: EUCD 1248. 1993–1995. CD.
 1165.2 *The Art of the Japanese Koto, Shakuhachi and Shamisen: A Selection of Old and New Japanese Chamber Music.* ARC: EUCD 1364. 1996. CD.

1166 Yasuda, Shinpu. *Music of the Shakuhachi.* Smithsonian Folkways: FE 4218. 1975, 1999. CD.

1167 Yoshimura, Nanae, and Kifu Mitsuhashi. *The Art of the Koto, Vol. 3: Works for Nijugen.* Celestial Harmonies: 13188-2. 2003. CD.

1168 Yuize, Shin'ichi. *The Japanese Koto.* Custom Compact Disc Series. Smithsonian Folkways: C-1132. 1955, 2000. CD.

1169 Zumi-Kai Original Instrumental Group. *Koto Music of Japan.* Delta Laserlight: 12 184. 1993. CD.

ANTHOLOGIES

1170 *Buddhist Drums, Bells, and Chants.* Lyrichord: 7200. 1993, 2005. CD.

1171 *Folk Music of Japan* (Edward Norbeck, compiler). Custom Compact Disc Series. Smithsonian Folkways: FE 4429. 1952, 2003. CD.

1172 *Folk Music of the Amami Islands.* Custom Compact Disc Series. Smithsonian Folkways: F-4448. 2000. CD.

1173 *Japan: Gagaku, Court Music.* Cultural Traditions. Voyager: CRG 140206. 2007. CD.

1174 *Japan Musical Traditions.* Voyager. Columbia River Entertainment: CRG 140196. 2007. CD.

1175 *Japanese Buddhist Ritual.* Custom Compact Disc Series. Smithsonian Folkways: FE 4449. 1954, 2003. CD.

1176 *Japanese Masterpieces for the Shakuhachi.* Lyrichord: 7176. 1980–[1989]. CD.

1177 *Lullaby for the Moon: Japanese Music for Koto and Shakuhachi.* Hemisphere: 7243 8 59271 2 6. 1997. CD.

1178 ★*Noh and Kyogen Plays* (Zeami, perf.; Jacob Feuerring, compiler). Custom Compact Disc Series. Smithsonian Folkways: AH 9572. 1969, 2002. 2 CDs.

1179 *The Rough Guide to the Music of Japan.* Rough Guide. World Music Network: RGNET 1211 CD. 2008. CD.

1180 *Sakura: A Musical Celebration of the Cherry Blossoms.* Smithsonian Folkways: SFW CD 40509. 1900s, 2003. CD.

1181 *The Soul of the Koto* (Katsumasa Takasago, compiler). Lyrichord Presents Outstanding Music from around the World. Lyrichord: 7218. 1994, 2006. CD.

1182 *Traditional Folk Dances of Japan* (Mary L. Evans, compiler). Smithsonian Folkways: F-4356. 1990s. CD.

1183 *Traditional Folk Songs of Japan* (Ryutaro Hattori, compiler). Custom Compact Disc Series. Smithsonian Folkways: F-4534. 1961, 2000s. 2 CDs.

1184 *The Way of Eiheiji: Zen Buddhist Ceremony.* Smithsonian Folkways Recordings. Smithsonian Folkways: F-8980. 1987. 2 CDs.

VIDEOS

1185 Kuribayashi, Hideaki. *Aoku (Deep Blue): Hideaki Kuribayashi, Koto Player and Composer.* Sound of Japan. Films for the Humanities and Sciences: FFH 30228. 2003. DVD.

1186 Sawai, Kazue, and Tadao Sawai. *Art of Kazue Sawai.* Sound of Japan. Films for the Humanities and Sciences: FFH 30229. 2003. DVD.

Popular

INDIVIDUAL ARTISTS AND GROUPS

1187 Boredoms. *Pop Tatari.* Reprise: 9 45416-2. 1992. CD.

1188 Cornelius. *Point.* Matador: OLE 332-2. 2002. CD.

1189 Itsuki, Hiroshi. *Itsuki Hiroshi 2003 zenkyokushu: bokyo no uta.* Five's Entertainment: FKCX-5008. 2003. CD.

1190 Jero. *Umiyuki.* Bikuta: VICL-36394. 2008. CD.

1191 Kaji, Meiko. *Zenkyokusyu.* Teichiku: TECE-30463. 2004. CD.

1192 Kina, Shokichi, and Champloose. *The Music Power from Okinawa.* Shinko Music: CDORBD 072. 1977, 1991. CD.

1193 Matsutoya, Yumi. *Yuming's Neue Musik.* Toshiba-EMI Limited. 1998. 2 CDs.

1194 Melt-Banana. *Cell-Scape.* A-Zap Records: AZCD-0005. 2003. CD.

1195 Miyako, Harumi. *Fusetsu meotobana: Miyako Harumi meikyokusen.* Columbia: COCP-34309. 2007. CD.

1196 Miyazawa, Kazufumi. *Deeper Than Oceans.* Stern's Music: STCD 4002. 2003. CD.

1197 Nenes. *Akemodoro unai.* Ace Records: CDORDB 096. 1997, 1998. CD.

1198 Orquesta de la Luz. *Lo Esencial.* Norte: 886971162721. 2007. CD. Japanese salsa tracks.

1199 Parsha Club. *Okinawa Paradise Radio.* Toshiba EMI: TOCT-10930. 1997, 2003. CD.

1200 Pizzicato Five. *The Sound of Music.* Matador: OLE 166-2 92622-2. 1995. CD.

1201 Puffy. *Nice.* Bar/None Records: BRN-CD-142. 2003. CD.

1202 Shonen Knife. *Let's Knife.* Virgin: 86638 2. 1992. CD.

1203 Yoshida, Kyodai. *Best of Yoshida Brothers.* Domo Records: 73081-2. 2008. CD.

ANTHOLOGIES

1204 *Japan: The Greatest Songs Ever.* The Greatest Songs Ever Collection; Music from EMI. EMI America Records: 09463 92531 28. 2007. CD.

1205 *The Rough Guide to the Music of Japan.* Rough Guide. World Music Network: RGNET 1211 CD. 2008. CD.

VIDEO

1206 *Sukiyaki and Chips: The Japanese Sounds of Music.* Beats of the Heart. Shanachie Home Video: 1213. 1984, 2003. DVD.

Contemporary Art Music

INDIVIDUAL ARTISTS AND GROUPS

1207 Regan, Marty. *Forest Whispers—: Selected Works for Japanese Instruments, Vol. 1.* Navona Records: N5831. 2010. CD.

1208 Takemitsu, Toru, composer. *In an Autumn Garden* (Katsuya Yokoyama and Kinshi Tsuruta). Echo 20/21. Deutsche Grammophon: 471 590-2. 1974, 2002. CD.

1209 Tokyo-to Kokyo Gakudan. *Japanese Orchestral Favourites.* Naxos: 8.555071. 2000, 2002. CD

1210 ★Toyama, Michiko, composer. *Waka and Other Compositions: Contemporary Music of Japan.* Custom Compact Disc Series. Smithsonian Folkways: F-8881. 1960, 2000. CD.

KOREA

Compiled by Mi-Hye Chyun

The selections in this discography of Korean music are divided into three categories. The first, traditional music, includes court music (*Chongmyo cheryeak* = the Royal Ancestral Shrine music), aristocratic genres (*Kagok, Kasa, Sijo, Yŏngsanhoesang*), folk music (*Minyo, Pansori, Samulnori Sanjo*), religious music (Buddhist chant, Rituals music), and theatrical music (*Pongsan* mask dance music). The second, popular music from the 1920s to the present, includes recordings by performers such as Yi Mi-ja, Cho Yong-pil, Sŏ T'ae-ji wa Aidŭl, and Girls' Generation. The third, Western-style contemporary art music, includes An Ik-t'ae, Yun Isang, and Chin Unsuk. With the exception of the works music by a few Korean composers who are active abroad, compositions by contemporary composers are underrepresented here due to the lack of commercially available recordings.

Some recordings in this discography are available through online stores such as Amazon (www.amazon.com) and YesAsia (www.yesasia.com). There do not appear to be English-speaking vendors of Korean music in the United States (online or otherwise) who deal exclusively with recordings of indigenous Korean music. Seoul Selection (www.seoulselection.com), a source of print and audiovisual materials, provides service in English at its website. Questions about acquiring Korean traditional recordings may also be directed to Mr. Chang Kwan Jung's Korean Traditional Music CD World at www.gugakcd.kr or email ckjungck@hanafos.com. In some cases, out-of-print items are available through these sources.

Traditional and Folk

INDIVIDUAL ARTISTS AND GROUPS

1211 Cho, Kong-nye, and Ki-ran Kim. *Corée: chants rituels de l'Île de Chindo = Korea: Ritual Songs from the Island of Chindo.* Archives Internationales de Musique Populaire, 28. VDE-Gallo: CD-756. 1990, 1993. CD.

1212 Chŏn, T'ae-yong. *A Selection of Kyŏnggi Sori Performed by the Late Chŏn T'ae-Yong.* Top: TOPCD-031. 2000. CD.

1213 Chŏng, Tae-sŏk. *Dalmuri: Chŏng Tae-Sŏk kŏmun'go tokchukokchip.* Seoul Records: SRCD-1607. 2005. CD.

1214 Hwang, Pyŏng-gi. *Pyŏng-Gi Hwang: kayagŭm chakp'umjip = Byungki Hwang: Kayagŭm Masterpieces.* C&L Music: CNLR 0103-2–CNLR 0106-2. 1985, 2001. CD.

1215 ★Jae-Hwa, Lee. *Corée: l'art du sanjo de geomungo = Korea: The Art of the Geomungo Sanjo.* Inédit. Maison des Cultures du Monde: W 260146. 2013. CD.

1216 JongNongAkHoe. *Yŏngsanhoesang.* Synnara Music: NSSRCD-009. 2001. 4 CDs.

1217 Kang, Ŭn-il. *Mirae ŭl kiŏk = Remembering the Future.* Seoul Records: SRCD-1636. [2007]. CD.

1218 Kang, Kwŏn-Sun. *Kang Kwon Soon, Female Gagok: Sounds of Heaven.* C&L Music: CNLR 0423/4-2. 2004. 2 CDs.

1219 Kim, Chŏng-ja. *Korean Zither Solo for Classical Songs by Kim Chong-Ja : Echoes to Heaven.* C&L Music: CNLR-0729/32-2. 2007. 4 CDs.

1220 Kim, Chŏng-nim. *Kim Chŏng-nim haegŭm tokchugokchip 6: Sŏ Yong-Sŏk Nyu.* Sinnara: DDSA-130C. 2011. CD.

1221 Kim, Ho-sŏng. *Ancient Poems, Walk on the Clouds: Kim Ho-seong's Sijo Collection.* Gugak FM Broadcasting System: Korean Music Series toward New Millennium, Vol. 23. Seoul Records: SRCD 1631. 2006. 2 CDs.

1222 Kim, Hye-ran. *The Seoul Gut and Its Orchestra Performance with Kim Hye-Ran.* Top: TOPCD-083. 2004. CD.

1223 Kim, Ki-su. *A Collection of Kim Ki-Su's Music.* YBM: SRCD-1555. [2004]. CD.

1224 Kim, Kyŏng-bae. *12 Kasa.* Sinnara: NSC-235/7. 2011. 3 CDs.

1225 Kim, Myŏng-sin. *Kim Myŏng-sin kat sŭmul e sumŏbŏrin sanjo: Unknown Performance of Two Gayageum Sanjo Presented by the Age of 21, Kim Myeong-Shin.* Top: TOPCD-048. 2002. CD.

1226 Kim, So-hŭi
    1226.1 *P'ansori: Korea's Epic Vocal Art and Instrumental Music.* Explorer Series. Elektra Nonesuch: 72049-2. 1988. CD.
    1226.2 *Simch'ŏngga.* Seoul Media: SRCD-1299–SRCD-1302. 1995. 4 CDs.

1227 Kim, Tŏk-su. *On the Road: The 50th Anniversary of Kim Duk Soo's Debut.* Synnara Music: NSC 175. 2007. CD.

1228 Kim, Yŏng-im. *Arirang.* Sinnara: NSC-122. 2005. CD.

1229 Kim, Yŏng-jae. *Kim Yŏng-jae kugak insaeng 50-chunyŏn kinyŏm ŭmban: chiptaesŏng ŭm.* Sinnara: NSC-240. 2011. CD.

1230 Kim, Yŏng-dong. *The Buddhist Meditation Music of Korea.* Seoul Records: SRCD-3013. [1988]. CD.

1231 Kungnip Kugagwŏn. *Chŏngak.* Yejŭn Media: SKCD-K-0004. [198-]. 2 CDs.

1232 Pak, Pong-sul. *Park Bong-sul's Pansori: Chunhyangga.* Top: TOPCD-096. 1971, 2005. 4 CDs.

1233 ★Pak, Pyŏng-ch'ŏn. *Ssitgim-gut (Kukak hanmadang)*. Top: TOPCD-115. 2002. CD.

1234 Pyŏn, Kye-wŏn. *Pyŏn Kye-wŏn Kugak ch'angjakkokchip III*. Loen: L-100004296. 2011. CD.

1235 Sŏ, Yŏng-ho. *Sŏ Yŏng-ho a-jaeng sanjo*. Aktang Iban: ADSACD-281. 2010. CD.

1236 Sookmyung Gayageum Orchestra. *For You: Sookmung Gayageum Orchestra's Best Collection 2006*. Sookmyung Gayageum Orchestra, Vol. 6. Seoul Records: SRCD-1624. 2006. CD.

1237 Yi, Chi-yŏng. *8 Scenes: Contemporary Music for Gayageum*. C&L Music: CNLR 0407-2. 1994, 2004. CD.

1238 Yi, Saeng-gang. *Commemorative Record of the 60th Anniversary of Great Musician Lee Saeng Kang's Musical Life*. Synnara Music: SBC-003. 2005. 2 CDs.

1239 Yi, Ŭn-gwan. *Hoesimgok*. Jigu: KCDS-0448. 1995. CD.

1240 Yun, Chin-ch'ŏl. *Chŏkpyŏkka*. Open Music: LMCD-0007. 2011. 3 CDs.

1241 Yun, Sŏn-suk. *Two Cycles of the Geomungo Sanjos*. Top: TOPCD-121. 2007, 2008. CD.

ANTHOLOGIES

1242 *Chakko myŏngin yŏnjujip = Folk Songs Played by Masters*. YBM: SRCD-1518. 2003. CD.

1243 *Chŏngga Akhoe p'ungnyu III (Kagok)*. Aktang Iban: ADSACD-610. 2011. CD.

1244 *Corée: Jongmyo jeryeak, musique rituelle pour les ancêtres royaux = Korea: Ritual Music for the Royal Ancestors*. Ocora Records: C 560242. 2011. CD.

1245 *Dansim: Danga of Yu Mi-li; Park Ae-ri; Jang Moon-hee; Kim Ji-sook*. Seoul Records: SRCD-1641. 2007. CD.

1246 *Kŏmungo, kayagŭm pyŏng-ch'ang*. YBM: SRCD-1539. 2004. CD.

1247 ★*Korean Traditional Music in the John Levy Collection*. Han'guk ŭmak sŏnjip; che 33 chip. Just Music: JMICD-1001/10. 2010. 10 CDs.

1248 *Minyo: le chant profond de la Coree = The Deep Song of Korea*. Musique du Monde. Buda: 3017407. 2007. CD.

1249 *Simun: danga of Jeon In-sam, Jeong Hoe-seok, Wang Ki-seok*. Kugak Pangsong: SDT-0002. 2007. CD.

1250 *21c Korean Music Project*. Universal Music: DU-8574. 2010. CD.

VIDEOS

1251 *Samul-nori*. Jigu: JMDVD-001. 2004. DVD.

1252 ★*Sanjo Collection*. Our Cultural Heritage Traditional Folk Music Series, Vol. 2. Jigu: JMDVD-002. 2004. DVD.

Popular

INDIVIDUAL ARTISTS AND GROUPS

1253 BoA. *Girls on Top*. SM Entertainment: SMCD-110. 2005. CD.

1254 Chang, Sa-ik. *Saram i kŭriwŏsŏ: Jang Sa-ik, Vol. 5*. Seoul Records: SRCD-1632. 2006. CD.

1255 ★Cho, Yong-p'il. *Cho Yong Pil Best 1st*. Jigu: JMCD-0022. 2005. 2 CDs.

1256 Chŏng, T'ae-ch'un and Pak Ŭn-ok. *Chŏng T'ae-ch'un and Pak Ŭn-ok: Koldŭn*. Jigu: JCDS-0030. 2005. 2 CDs.

1257 Girls' Generation. *The Boys*. S. M. Entertainment: B0016474-02. 2012. CD.

1258 H.O.T. *H.O.T. 3*. Sinnara: KSC-8060 PA. 1990s. CD.

1259 Kim, Kŏn-mo. *Kim, Kŏn-mo, 20th Anniversary: 13th Chasŏjŏn*. KMP Holdings: MLK0078. 2011. 3 CDs.

1260 Kim, Min-gi. *Past Life of Kim Min-gi*. Seoul Records: SRCD-3774. 2004. 6 CDs.

1261 Kim, P'aet'i. *Patti Kim: Super Star Hit Song Collection*. Kŏsŏng: DMKD-0185-0187. [1990]. 3 CDs.

1262 Na, Hun-a. *Na Hun-a Goldŭn*. Jigu: JMCD-44. 2005. 2 CDs.

1263 Pi. *Back to the Basic*. CJ E&M: CMCC 9501. 2010. CD.

1264 Sanullim. *Sanullim tasi tŭtki*. Doremi Midiŏ: DRMCD-2067. 2005. 3 CDs.

1265 Sin, Chung-hyŏn. *Shin Jung Hyun and Yup Juns Instrumental Best*. Jigu: JSCDS-0453. 1994. CD.

1266 ★Sŏ T'e-ji wa Aidŭl. *Seotaiji and Boys*. Pando Ŭmban: BDCD-023. 1994. CD.

1267   Song, Ch'ang-sik. *Sesibong ch'in'gudŭl.* Goldmind: DK-0650. 2011. 3 CDs.

1268   Tongbang Sin'gi. *Rising Sun.* SM Entertainment: SMCD 114. 2005. CD.

1269   ★Yi, Mi-ja. *Yi Mi-ja Original Best.* Jigu: JG5-1-4. 2002. 4 CDs.

ANTHOLOGIES

1270   *Pikt'ŏ yusŏnggi wŏnban sirijŭ kayo 2: 30-yŏndae sin minyo.* Seoul Media: SRCD-1232. 2003. 2 CDs.

1271   ★*Yusŏnggiro dŭtdŏn kayosa (1925–1945).* Sinnara: SYNCD-015. 1992. CD.

1272   *Yusŏnggiro dŭtdŏn kayosa (Haebang-1960).* Sinnara: NSSRCD-012. 2000. 12 CDs.

Contemporary Art Music

INDIVIDUAL ARTISTS AND GROUPS

1273   An, Ik-t'ae. *Symphonic Fantasy Korea* (Los Angeles Philharmonic Orchestra). Ene Media: SCO-079ETACD. CD.

1274   Jo, Sumi. *Cho Su-Mi: Kŭnyŏŭi Ch'ŏtpŏntchae Sunsu Han'guk Kagokjip.* Ene Media: ENEC 023. 2002. CD.

1275   Kim, Hyelim. *Nim: Hyelim Kim: Taegum Collection.* Universal Music: DU 42057. 2013. CD.

1276   Min, Klara. *Pa-Mun (Ripples on Water): Korean Piano Music.* Naxos: 8.572406. 2011. CD.

1277   Paek, Byŏng-dong. *Byung-dong Paik and Hwaum Chamber.* Sony: SB70218C. 2007. CD.

1278   Yi, Yŏng-jo. *Korean Piano Music* (My Kim). Asv: CDDCA 1088. 2000. CD.

1279   ★Yun, Isang. *Chamber Symphony I* (Korean Chamber Ensemble). 21st Century Classics. Naxos: 8.557938. 2005, 2006. CD.

ANTHOLOGY

1280   ★*Han'guk kagok besŭt'ŭ.* Naturally Music. 2011. 2 CDs.

VIDEO

1281   Chin, Unsuk, composer. *Alice in Wonderland.* Euro Arts: 2072418. 2008. DVD.

SOUTH ASIA

HIMALAYAS

Compiled by Jeff Schwartz

The overtone singing of Buddhist monks dominates the catalog of Himalayan music available in the West. The recordings of the Tibetan Gyoto Monks produced by Grateful Dead drummer Mickey Hart capture this sound in extraordinary fidelity and are an excellent first purchase, but there is considerable diversity between Tibet, Nepal, and Bhutan, as well as among the monasteries in each nation, requiring a fuller collection. There are many meditation/relaxation CDs on the market blending monk recordings with electronics, guitars, bamboo flutes, wind chimes, and so on, which may not serve the purposes of library collections and are not listed. They are abundant in new age bookstores for those desiring to collect them. Selected hybrids of Tibetan music and Western pop with Tibetan artists as leaders or equal partners are listed: Yungchen Lhamo and Choying Drolma, for example.

Recordings of other musical forms are scarcer. Several collections of the music of the Gaines, a Nepalese Hindu caste of itinerant bards, are available, but the folk music of ethnic groups including the Newar, Sherpa, Tamang, and Tharu is represented mainly on survey anthologies. Also scarce, but worth pursuing, are recordings of the Nepalese wedding music *panchai baja*, played by an ensemble of oboes, large metal horns, and percussion, and Tibetan opera, which presents Buddhist narratives accompanied by percussion.

Bhutan

INDIVIDUAL ARTIST

1282   Drukpa, Jigme. *Endless Songs from Bhutan.* Grappa Musikforlag: HCD 7143. 1998. CD.

ANTHOLOGIES

1283   *Music from the Mountains of Bhutan.* Smithsonian Folkways: SFW 50405. 2014, 2015. CD.

1284   *Music of Bhutan.* Custom Compact Disc Series. Smithsonian Folkways: FW 04030. 1978, 2001. CD.

1285   *Tibetan Buddhist Rites from the Monasteries of Bhutan*
1285.1   *Vol. 1: Rituals of the Drupka Order from Thimpu and Punakha.* Lyrichord: LYRCD-7255. 1971, 1990s. CD.

1285.2 *Vol. 2: Sacred Dances and Rituals of the Nyingmapa and Drupka Orders.* Lyrichord: LYRCD-7256. 1971, 1990s. CD.

1285.3 *Vol. 3: Temple Rituals and Public Ceremonies.* Lyrichord: LYRCD-7257. 1971, 1990s. CD.

1285.4 *Vol. 4: Tibetan and Bhutanese Instrumental and Folk Music.* Lyrichord: LYRCD-7258. 1971, 1990s. CD.

Nepal

INDIVIDUAL ARTISTS AND GROUPS

1286 Gaïnés de Hyangja. *Chants et danses du Népal = Songs and Dances of Nepal.* Musique du Monde. Buda: 82493-2. 1990s. CD.

1287 Sonam, Kirkiyap, and Dawa. *Music of a Sherpa Village.* Custom Compact Disc Series. Smithsonian Folkways: FW 04320. [1972]. CD.

ANTHOLOGIES

1288 *Folk Songs of Nepal.* Lyrichord: LYRCD-7330. 1970s, 2004. CD.

1289 ★*Folksongs and Sacred Music from Nepal.* Arc Music: EUCD 1517. 1973, 1999. CD.

1290 *The Gaines of Nepal.* Custom Compact Disc Series. Smithsonian Folkways: FW 04078. 1982, 2001. CD.

1291 *Harmika Yab-yum: Folksongs from Nepal.* Sublime Frequencies: SF 017. 2004. CD.

1292 *Songs and Dances of Nepal.* Custom Compact Disc Series. Smithsonian Folkways: FW 04101. 1964, 1999. CD.

VIDEOS

1293 *Adaptable Kingdom: Music and Dance in Nepal* (Deben Bhattacharya, dir.). Unwritten Music of the Orient. Lyrichord: LYRDV-1005. 1972, 2003. DVD.

1294 *Village and Town Music of India and Nepal* (Roderic C. Knight, prod.). Lyrichord: LYRDV-2003. 1982, 2007. DVD, data CD.

Tibet

INDIVIDUAL ARTISTS AND GROUPS

1295 Buddhist Monks of Sherab Ling Monastery. *Sacred Tibetan Chant.* Naxos World: 76044-2. 2003. CD.

1296 Drolma, Choying, and Steve Tibbetts. *Selwa.* Six Degrees Travel Series. Six Degrees: 65703611042. 2004. CD.

1297 Gyoto Monks
1297.1 *Freedom Chants from the Roof of the World.* Rykodisc: RCD 20113. 1988, 1989. CD.
1297.2 ★*Tibetan Tantric Choir.* Windham Hill: WD-2001. 1987. CD.

1298 Gyuto Tantric Choir. *Tibetan Chants for World Peace.* White Swan: 717147008621. 2008. CD.

1299 Lhamo, Yungchen
1299.1 *Ama.* Real World: RLW33300. 2006. CD.
1299.2 *Coming Home.* Real World: 7243 8 45785 27. 1998. CD.
1299.3 *Tibet Tibet.* Real World: 2363-2. 1996. CD.

1300 Monks of Khampagar Monastery. *Tibetan Buddhism: The Ritual Orchestra and Chants.* Explorer Series. Nonesuch: 72071. 1976, 1995. CD.

1301 Nangi Gompa Monastery, Chorus of Nuns. *Les nonnes du Tibet = Tibetan Nuns.* Air Mail Music. Sunset-France: SA 141149. 2007. CD.

1302 Sangeet, Gaines Gandhara, and Ga-Kyi. *Music from the Roof of the World: Tibet, Nepal* (Nyingmapa Monks). Playasound: PLS 360711. 2007. 3 CDs.

1303 Sherap Dorjee. *Tibet: Chansons des six hautes vallées = Songs from the Six High Valleys* (Shang Shung Da Yang). Musique du Monde. Buda: 3016784. 2003. CD.

1304 Techung. *Songs from Tibet* (Tashi Dhondup). Arc Music: EUCD 2014. 2006. CD.

ANTHOLOGIES

1305 *Anthology of World Music: The Music of Tibetan Buddhism.* Anthology of World Music. Rounder: CD 5129/30/31. 1999. 3 CDs.

1306 *Celestial Female: Parts from Tibetan Opera.* Anthology of Music in China. Pan Records: Pan 2046CD. 1996. CD.

1307 ★*Rough Guide to the Music of the Himalayas.* Rough Guide. World Music Network: RGNET 1105 CD. 2002. CD.

1308 *Songs and Music of Tibet.* Custom Compact Disc Series. Smithsonian Folkways: FW 04486. [1962–1999]. CD.

1309 *Tibetan Ritual Music* [1961]. Lyrichord: LYRCD-7181. [1980–1989]. CD.

VIDEO

1310 *Echoes from Tibet.* Films of Deben Bhattacharya. Lyrichord: LYRDV-1008. 1992, 2004. DVD.

PAKISTAN

Compiled by Jeff Schwartz

Western perception of the music of Pakistan is dominated by Nusrat Fateh Ali Khan and *qawwali*, a Sufi musical style, which uses virtuoso ornamentation and metaphors of romantic love to describe the worshipper's relationship to God. There are dozens of Khan recordings in print, including collaborations with rock stars Peter Gabriel and Eddie Vedder as well as with numerous dance, ambient, and new age electronic musicians, some of these latter assembled without Khan's active participation or permission. All but the most comprehensive collections should be satisfied with Khan's recordings for Western labels, particularly Gabriel's Real World, which offers excellent sound and packaging in contrast to many of the Khan discs on the market.

Beyond Nusrat Fateh Ali Khan, the group Rizwan-Muazzam Qawwali is his designated heir, but many collections of *qawwali* and other Sufi musical styles are available. Other communities are less well represented on recordings in print, but the Folkways and Rough Guide compilations provide well-documented and easily available samplings.

INDIVIDUAL ARTISTS AND GROUPS

1311 Ali, Mehr. *Qawwali: Expression de l'essentiel désir = Qawwali: The Essence of Desire.* Musique du Monde. Buda: 92611-2. 1995. CD.

1312 Aziz, Razia. *Songs of Love and Devotion from Pakistan: Between Heaven and Earth.* ARC Music: EUCD 2127. 2007, 2008. CD.

1313 Baluchi Ensemble of Karachi. *Love Songs and Trance Hymns.* Shanachie: 66016. 1996, 1999. CD.

1314 Bhatti, Asif. *Traditional Music from Pakistan.* ARC Music: EUCD 2033. 2006. CD.

1315 Jogi, Iqbal. *The Passion of Pakistan.* Tradition: TCD 1045. 1950s, 1997. CD.

1316 Khan, Mohammad Sharif. *The Music of Pakistan.* Anthology of World Music. Rounder: ROUN 5147. 2003. CD.

1317 Khan, Nusrat Fateh Ali
  1317.1 *Body and Soul.* Real World: 7243 8 10996 2 9. 2001. CD.
  1317.2 *Devotional and Love Songs.* Real World: CAROL 2300-2. 1992. CD.
  1317.3 *Dust to Gold.* Real World: 72438-49178-2-1. 1997, 2000. CD.
  1317.4 *Rapture.* Nascente: NSCD 013. 1997. CD.
  1317.5 *Rough Guide to Nusrat Fateh Ali Khan: Sufi Sounds from the Qawwali King.* World Music Network: RGNET 1078 CD. 2002. CD.
  1317.6 *Shahbaaz.* Real World: CAROL 2315-2. 1991. CD.
  1317.7 ★*Shahen-Shah.* Real World: CAROL 2302-2. 1988, 1989. CD.
  1317.8 *The Ultimate Nusrat Fateh Ali Khan: The Early Years, Rare Recordings*
    1317.8.1 *Vol. 1: 1978–1982.* Narada: 72435-63962-2-7. 2005. 2 CDs.
    1317.8.2 *Vol. 2: 1983–1984.* Narada: 72435-63965-2-4. **2005–?** 2 CDs.

1318 Khan, Shafqat Ali. *Sufi Songs from India and Pakistan.* ARC Music: EUCD 2293. 2010. CD.

1319 Khan, Ustad Bary Fateh Ali. *The Music of Islam, Vol. 13: Music of Pakistan, Lahore, Pakistan.* Celestial Harmonies: 13153-2. 1998. CD.

1320 Parvin, Abida. *The Meeting: Mystic Poets from the Hind and the Sind.* World Village: 479 010. 2002. CD.

1321 Rizwan-Muazzam Qawwali. *Day of Colours.* Real World: 72435 71170 2 3. 2004. CD.

1322 Sabri Brothers. *Ya Habib.* Real World: 91346-2. 1990. CD.

1323 Sindhi Music Ensemble. *Sufi Music from Sindh* [1992]. Weltmusik. Wergo: SM 15152. 1994, 1995. CD.

ANTHOLOGIES

1324 *Bards from the Makrân.* Musique du Monde. Buda: 92633-2. 1995. CD.

1325 *Flight of the Soul: Qawwali from Pakistan.* Weltmusik. Wergo: SM 15342. 1997, 2001. CD.

1326 ★*Folk Music of Pakistan.* Custom Compact Disc Series. Smithsonian Folkways: FW 04425. 1951, 1999. CD.

1327 *Land of the Sufis: Soul Music from the Indus Valley.* Shanachie: SH 66017. 1999. CD.

1328 *Liturgies musicales du Pakistan-Panjab = Musical Liturgies of Pakistan-Panjab.* Musique du Monde. Buda: 92681-2. [1992–1998]. CD.

1329 *Pakistani Soul Music.* Weltmusik. Wergo: SM 15292. 1996, 1997. CD.

1330 ★*Rough Guide to the Music of Pakistan.* Rough Guide. World Music Network: RGNET 1116 CD. 2003. CD.

1331 *Troubadours of Allah: Sufi Music from the Indus Valley.* Weltmusik. Wergo: SM 16172. 1996, 1999. 2 CDs.

NORTH INDIA (HINDUSTANI)

Compiled by Jeff Schwartz

Hindustani classical music features extended virtuoso improvisation based on a system of scalar/melodic and rhythmic patterns (*ragas* and *talas*). Performances are conventionally described by the *raga* and *tala* used. The classical music of north India is abundantly represented on CD. During its initial vogue in the West during the 1960s, Ravi Shankar, Ali Akbar Khan, and other artists recorded for commercial labels such as Prestige, Columbia, and World Pacific. Many of these albums have been reissued, and there are numerous north Indian titles available from Folkways and other ethnomusicological labels, as well as several specialist labels, including AMMP, Moment, Raga, Water Lily Acoustics, and Nimbus. Some older archival recordings have challenging audio quality, but many of the specialist labels are run by devoted audiophiles and feature superb sound.

Because this music is based on prolonged improvisations with slowly paced development, it is not well represented by compilations. Basic collection building should begin with some of the Ravi Shankar and Ali Akbar Khan titles, then sample vocalists and other instruments: *bansuri, shenai, sarangi, surbahar, santur, vina, dilruba,* and slide guitar, as well as other players of the sitar and sarod. There are notable differences of technique and interpretation between the major schools on each instrument. It is desirable both to represent a variety of ragas in a collection to show the breadth of the musical system and to include multiple performances of the same raga to show the range of possible interpretations. Percussion will be prominent in the accompaniment on most Hindustani classical recordings, and there are also very interesting recordings led by drummers.

Regional folk music is documented on several Folkways and Lyrichord discs, while Sublime Frequencies' Radio India collage captures a chaotic mass media soundscape in great contrast to the focused intensity of classical music.

INDIVIDUAL ARTISTS AND GROUPS

1332 Banerjee, Nikhil
  1332.1 *The Hundred-Minute Raga* (Swapan Chadhuri). Raga: RAGA-207 A. 1991. 2 CDs.
  1332.2 *Live-to-Air Broadcast, KPFA: 1967* (Mahapurush Misra). Raga: RAGA-201. 1967, 1988. CD.

1333 Bhawalkar, Uday. *Uday Bhawalkar: raga shri, raga malkauns* (Manik Munde). Hindustani Classical Vocal. Nimbus: NI 5489. 1994, 1997. CD.

1334 Brhaspati, Sulocana, Shruti Katkar, and Girija Devi. *Hindustani Classical Vocal.* Nimbus: NI 1740. 1992, 2000. 3 CDs.

1335 Chaurasia, Hariprasad
  1335.1 *Four Dhuns* (Shiv Shankar Ray). Indian Classical Masters. Nimbus: NI 5527. 1996, 1997. CD.
  1335.2 *Rag ahir bhairav = Marriage Song* (Sabir Khan and others). Indian Classical Masters. Nimbus: NI 5111. 1987, 1988. CD.

1336 Dagar, Sayeeduddin. *India: The Art of Dagarvani Dhrupad.* Musique du Monde. Buda: 1984912. 2000. CD.

1337 Dagar, Zia Mohiuddin. *Raga yaman, raga shuddha todi.* Nimbus: NI 7047/8. 1990. 2 CDs.

1338 Doedhar, B. R. *Dr. B. R. Deodhar Presents the Ragas of India.* Custom Compact Disc Series. Smithsonian Folkways: F-8368. 1962, 2000. CD.

1339 Ghosh, Shankar. *Tabla: Shankar Ghosh: Nasruk Tal, Tintal.* India Archive: IAM CD 1054. 2002. CD.

1340 Hussain, Zakir. *Selects.* Moment: MR 1021. 2002, 1994. CD.

1341 Jairazbhoy, Nazir Ali. *Theory of Classical Hindusthani Instrumental Music.* Smithsonian Folkways: FI 8366. 1955, 2000. CD.

1342 Jasraj, Pandit. *Hussaini kanra, bhajan* (Swapan Chadhuri). Moment: MR 1009. 1993, 1992. CD.

1343 Khan, Ali Akbar
    1343.1 *Then and Now* (Chatur Lal and Zakir Hussain). AMMP: CD 9507. 1955, 1995. 2 CDs.
    1343.2 ★*Three Ragas* (Mahapurush Misra). Signature Series, Vol. 1. AMMP: CD 9001. 1990. CD.
    1343.3 *Ustad Ali Akbar Khan Plays Alap: A Sarod Solo.* AMMP: CD 9303. 1992, 1993. 2 CDs.

1344 Khan, Ali Akbar, and L. Subramaniam. *Duet* (Zakir Hussain and Ramnad V. Raghavan). Ravi Shankar Music Circle: RSMC-D-103. 1993. CD.

1345 Khan, Amjad Ali. *Homage to Mother Theresa* (Zakir Hussain). Moment: MR 1019. 1999. CD.

1346 Khan, Asad Ali. *Raga jaijaivanti* (Mohan Shyam Sharma). Indian Classical Masters. Nimbus: NI 5601. 1999. CD.

1347 Khan, Bade Ghulam Ali. *Regal Resonance.* Dunya: fy 8080. 2004. CD.

1348 Khan, Ghulam Mustafa. *Ghulam Mustafa Khan: raga bilaskhani todi, raga puriya, raga pilu.* Hindustani Classical Vocal. Nimbus: NI 5409. 1992, 1994. CD.

1349 Khan, Keramatullah. *42 Lessons for Tabla.* Custom Compact Disc Series. Smithsonian Folkways: FM 8369. 1973, 2000s. CD.

1350 Khan, Nishat. *Rag bhimpalasi, rag tilak kamod* (Imrat Khan, Shafaatullah Khan, and Irshad Khan). Indian Classical Masters. Nimbus: NI 5233. 1989, 1990. CD.

1351 Khan, Sabri. *Master of the Indian Sarangi* (Sarvar Sabri). ARC Music: EUCD 2192. 2000. CD.

1352 Khan, Shujaat. *Raga bairagi, bhairavi* (Samir Chatterjee). India Archive: IAM CD 1085. 2007. CD.

1353 Khan, Sultan
    1353.1 *Bhupali* (Zakir Hussain). Moment: MR 1006. 1991. CD.
    1353.2 *Sarangi: The Music of India* (Shri Rij Ram). The World. Rykodisc: RCD 10104. 1974, 1988. CD.

1354 Khan, Vilyat. *Captivating Melodies of Sitar* (Zakir Hussain). Oriental: CD-120. [1900–1990]. CD.

1355 Mallik, Bidur, and Sons. *The Fast Side of Dhrupad.* Welt Musik. Wergo: SM 1517-2. 1994. CD.

1356 Misra, Gopal Shankar. *Out of Stillness* (Ramkumar Mishra and Padmaja Misra). Real World: 7243 8 49707 27. 2000. CD.

1357 Narayan, Aruna. *Sarangi: raga bairagi bhairav, raga shuddh sarang, raga madhuvanti* (Sanjay Jhalla and others). Nimbus: NI 5447. 1993, 1995. CD.

1358 Narayan, Brij. *Raga lalit, raga bairagi bhairav* (Zakir Hussain and various artists). Indian Classical Masters. Nimbus: NI 5263. 1990. CD.

1359 ★Narayan, Ram. *Rag bhupal tori, rag patdip* (Suresh Talwalkar and various artists). Indian Classical Masters. Nimbus: NI 5119. 1987, 1988. CD.

1360 Nath, Pran
    1360.1 *Midnight: Raga Malkauns* (Terry Riley and others). Just Dreams: JD 003. 2002. 2 CDs.
    1360.2 *The Raga Cycle, Palace Theatre, Paris 1972: Ragas Shudh Sarang and Kut Todi* (Terry Riley and others). Sri Moonshine: 003. 2006. CD.

1361 Rakha, Alla, and Zakir Hussain. *Tabla Duet in Tintal* (Ramesh Misra). Moment: MR 1001. 1991. CD.

1362 Sabri, Sarvar. *Master Drummer of India* (Vishwa Prakash). ARC Music: EUCD 1719. 2002. CD.

1363 Sachdev, G. S.
    1363.1 *Bansuri: The Bamboo Flute of India* (Gay Kagy and Elb Souders). Lyrichord: LYRCD 7405. 1980. CD.
    1363.2 ★*Flights of Improvisation* (Zakir Hussain). Lyrichord: LYRCD 7416. 1980s. CD.

1364 Senior Dagar Brothers
    1364.1 *Bihag kamboji Malkosh, Calcutta 1955.* Raga: RAGA-221. 2000. 2 CDs.
    1364.2 ★*Rag Todi in Concert, Calcutta 1957.* Raga: RAGA-220. 1999. CD.

1365 Shankar, Ravi
    1365.1 ★*A Morning Raga / An Evening Raga* (Alla Rakha and Kamala Chakvravarty). The Ravi Shankar Collection. Angel: 7243 5 67437 2 4. 1968, 2001. CD.
    1365.2 *The Sounds of India* (Chatur Lal and Nodu C Mullick). Columbia: CK 9296. 1968, 1989. CD.
    1365.3 *Three Ragas* (Chatur Lal and Pradjot Sen). Angel: 7243 5 67310 2 8. 2000. CD.

1366 Shankar, Ravi, and Ali Akbar Khan. *Ragas* (Kanai Dutta and others). Fantasy: FCD-24714-2. 1973, 1990. CD.

ANTHOLOGIES

1367 *Cachemire: Le sūfyāna kalām de Srinager = Kashmir: Sūfyāna Kalām from Srinagar.* Archives Internationales de Musique Populaire, 106. VDE-Gallo: VDE CD-1410. 2013. CD.

1368 *Folk Music of Kashmir.* Custom Compact Disc Series. Smithsonian Folkways: FE 4350. 1963, 2000. CD.

1369 *India: Traveling Artists of the Desert, the Musical Culture of Rajasthan.* Music of the Earth. Lyrichord: MCM-3002. 1993, 1997. CD.

1370 *Indian Folk Music from Uttar Pradesh.* Lyrichord: LYRCD 7452. 2006. CD.

1371 *North India: Vocal Music: Dhrupad & Kyhal = Inde du nord: Musique vocale: Dhrupad et khyal.* Smithsonian Folkways: UNES 08076. 2014. CD.

1372 ★*The Raga Guide: A Survey of 74 Hindustani Ragas* (Hariprasad Chaurasia); Joep Bor, et al., eds. Nimbus: NI 5536/9. 1991, 1999. 4 CDs.

1373 *Tribal Music of India: The Muria and Maria Gonds of Madhya Pradesh.* Smithsonian Folkways: FE 4028. 1983, 1999. CD.

1374 *Vintage Music from India: Early 20th Century Classical and Light Classical Music.* Rounder: CD 1083. 1906, 1993. CD. *See also* India (South, Carnatic).

1375 *Voices for Humans, Ancestors and Gods: A Musical Journey through India's Interior (East and North-East).* Topic Records: TSCD933. 2006. CD.

VIDEOS

1376 *Khan, Ali Akbar. Summer Solstice: Five Classical Ragas* (Swapan Chadhuri). AMMP: DVD 88-1. 2003. DVD.

1377 *Raga* (Halim Jaffer Khan and Deben Bhattacharya, prod.). Music and Society Series. Lyrichord: LYRCD-1006. 1969, 2004. DVD.

1378 Shankar, Ravi. *Concert for World Peace* (Partho Sarthy and Zakir Hussain). A&E Home Video: AAAE 101330. 2007. DVD.

1379 Shankar, Ravi. *In Portrait* (Anoushka Shankar, Bikram Ghosh, and Tanmoy Bose). BBC: OA 0864 D. 2001, 2002. 2 DVDs.

SOUTH INDIA (CARNATIC), BANGLADESH, AND SRI LANKA

Compiled by Alec McLane

Southern India includes the states of Tamil Nadu, Kerala, Karnataka, and Andhra Pradesh. Although the Carnatic region comprises a much smaller area—limited to Tamil Nadu and adjacent portions of Karnataka and Andhra Pradesh—the presence of Carnatic music extends throughout the southern region as a "classical" tradition, distinguished from the Hindustani classical music of northern India. The two traditions share the general concepts of *raga* and *tala,* along with the principle of composed and improvisatory sections of musical pieces, but there are many differences in the forms that these take in the music of each region. Carnatic music has a much stronger emphasis on singing, and there are several instruments unique to the tradition: the *vina* and the *mrdangam* (a two-headed drum), for example, are used in place of the north Indian sitar and *tabla,* respectively; also, the European violin appears both as a solo instrument and as accompaniment to singing.

In addition to Carnatic music, there are widespread folk traditions from the various states, as well as a Chennai-based Tamil film industry that rivals Bollywood in output and has produced a great abundance of composers and performers of film songs.

Indian, specifically Tamil, culture has also spread to Sri Lanka, resulting in a similar pop music industry growing up around film music, but there are more distinctive Sri Lankan musical traditions represented here: dance and song styles influenced by Portuguese colonialism and dating from the fifteenth century, as well as the strong influence of Buddhism, dating from the second century and now claiming 70 percent of the population as adherents.

The country of Bangladesh, separated from India in 1947 as the eastern part of Pakistan and then achieving unique independence in 1971, is part of a larger cultural area that includes the Indian state of West Bengal. Among the distinctive musical traditions in this region are the solo singing styles of the *Bauls,* a group of religious minstrels, and the composed songs of Rabindranath Tagore.

Although many of the recordings represented here are difficult to find through normal channels such as Amazon, there are many independent distributors of south Asian music that carry recordings often indicated as out-of-print or unavailable elsewhere. Some recommended vendors for Indian music are Charsur Digital Workstation (www.charsur.com) and Shrimati's (www.shrimatis.com). Many Sri Lankan CDs can be found at Kapruka (www.lanka.info/shops/musicStore/sinhala SongSelec tionMain.jsp).

Carnatic

INDIVIDUAL ARTISTS AND GROUPS

1380 ★Babu, Chitti. *Vina of Southern India.* World Roots Music Library, 61. King: KICW 85086-87. 1994. 2 CDs.

1381 Balachander, S. *Veena Virtuoso.* World Music Library, 19. King: KICC 5119. 1982. CD.

1382 Balakrishna, and Anand Mohan. *Ragas: Songs of India.* Custom Compact Disc Series. Smithsonian Folkways: F-3530. 1957, 2000. CD.

1383 Balamurali Krishna, M. *Raga Sudha Rasa, Vols. 1 and 2.* Sangeetha: KDV 049, KDV 055. 1995, 1996. 2 CDs.

1384 Chinna Moulana, Sheik, T. V. Venkatesan, and P. Raman. *Shaik Chinna Moula Live in Concert 1973.* Paddhatti, the Tradition of Burnished Gold. Charsur Digital Work Station: CDW 136 D. 2005, 1973. 3 CDs.

1385 Civan, Papanacam, composer. *Papanasam Sivan Songs* (Maharajapuram Santhanam and Vellore Ramabadran). Vani: V-063. 2000. CD.

1386 Dīkṣita, Muttusvāmi, composer
  1386.1 ★*An Audio Documentation of the Compositions of Shri Muttusvami Dikshitar from the Sangita Sampradaya Pradarshini, Audio Book One* (T. M. Krishna, R. S. Jayalakshmi, R. K. Shriramkumar, and K. Arun. Prakash; Subbarāmadīkṣitula, compiler). Jnanarnava Trust. 2006. CD.
  1386.2 ★*An Audio Documentation of the Compositions of Shri Muttusvami Dikshitar from the Sangita Sampradaya Pradarshini, Audio Book Two and Three* (T. M. Krishna, R. S. Jayalakshmi, R. K. Shriramkumar, and K. Arun. Prakash; Subbarāmadīkṣitula, compiler). Jnanarnava Trust. 2006. 2 CDs.

1387 Doresvami Ayyangar, Vi., and Vellore Ramabadran. *V. Doreswamy Iyengar [Veena].* Maestro's Choice, Ser. 1. Living Media India. 1991. CD.

1388 Gopalnath, Kadiri. *Gem Tones: Saxophone Supreme, South Indian Style.* GlobeStyle: CDORBD 097. 2000. CD.

1389 Hyderabad Brothers. *Annapoorne.* Asia One Stop: KDV-016. 1994. CD.

1390 Jayaraman, Lalgudi G., and Lalgudi Krishnan. *Singing violins, South Indian Classical Music.* Felmay: fy 8094. 2005.CD.

1391 Kanyakumari, A. *O'rajeevaksha.* Koel: KDI 047. 1995. CD.

1392 Kassebaum, Gayathri Rajapur, Dorothy Moskowitz, and Harihar Rao. *Ragas: Classical Music of South India.* Custom Compact Disc Series. Smithsonian Folkways: FW 8854. 1967, 2000s. CD.

1393 Krishnan, Ramnad. *Ramnad Krishnan, Vidwan: Music of South India: Songs of the Carnatic Tradition.* Explorer Series. Nonesuch: HB-72023. 1988. CD.

1394 Nathamuni Brothers. *Madras 1974.* Fire Museum: 643157390169. 2007. CD.

1395 Rajagopalan, Ranganayaki. *South India: Ranganayaki Rajagopalan: Continuity in the Karaikudi Vina Style.* Smithsonian Folkways: UNES 08311. 2014. CD.

1396 Ramani, N., A. Kanyakumari, Dandamoodi Ramamohana Rao, and E. M. Subramaniam. *Master of the Flute.* Music of South India. Sangeetha: KDI 032. 1994. CD.

1397 Ravikiran, N., Mysore Nagarajan, V. Nagarajan, and Vizianagaram Satishkumar. *Latangi: ragam tanam pallavi: a pallavi in 8 kalai.* Charsur Digital Work Station: CDW 020. 2000. CD.

1398 Shankar, Lakshminarayana, T. H. Vinayakram, and Zakir Hussain. *Eternal Light.* Moment: MRCD 1020. 2000. CD.

1399 Sikkil Sisters. *Flute.* Magnasound: D 5 C 15003. 1994. CD.

1400 Srinivas, U., and Sikkil Bhaskaran. *Mandolin Ecstasy.* Classical Music of India. Ancient & Modern Sound: CD-111. 1986. CD.

1401 ★Subramaniam, L. *Three Ragas for Solo Violin.* Indian Classical Masters. Nimbus: NI 5323. 1991. CD.

1402 Subramaniam, L., and V. Kamalakar Rao. *Le violon de l'Inde du Sud: Karnatic Violin.* Inde Du Sud. Ocora Radio France: C 582029. 2001. CD.

1403 ★Subulakshmi, M. S. *M. S. Subbulakshmi: Live at Carnegie Hall.* Dancing Dolphin: 147808. 2006. 2 CDs.

1404 Viswanathan, T., and Trichy S. Sankaran. *Tribute.* Performing and Media Arts: PMA 1048. 2000. CD.

ANTHOLOGIES

1405 *Inde, le chant du Mohini Attam: Danse classique du Kerala = India, Singing the Mohini Attam: Classical Dance of Kerala.* Inédit. Maison des Cultures du Monde: W 260145. 2012. CD.

1406 *Swara Bushani.* Ancient and Modern Sound. Oriental: CD166–CD 167. 1992. 2 CDs.

1407 *Vintage Music from India: Early Twentieth-Century Classical anad Light-Classical Music.* Rounder: CD 1083. 1993. CD.

VIDEOS

1408 Krishna, T. M., T. K. V. Ramanujacharyalu, and Vellore Ramabadran. *December Season 2004: T. M. Krishna Live in Concert.* Kutcheri. Charsur Digital Work Station: CDW 109 DVD. 2005. DVD.

1409 Krishnan, T.N. *At Home with Master Musicians of Madras, Vol. 1* (Viji Krishnan, Palghat T.S. Mani Iyer). Aspara Media for Intercultural Education: 45849983. 2000. VHS.

1410 *South Indian Classical Music House Concert* (M.D. Ramanathan, T.N. Krishnan, and Umayalpuram Sivaraman). Aspara Media for Intercultural Education: 32721465. 1994. VHS.

Folk and Film (Tamil)

INDIVIDUAL ARTISTS AND GROUPS

1411 Ilaiyaraja, composer. *Legends.* Saregama: CDF 158530. 2003. 5 CDs.

1412 Balasubramaniam, S. P. *Legends, Vol. 4.* Saregama: CDF 158541. 2009. CD.

1413 Balasubramanyam, S. P., Malgudi Subha, and Mano. *Folk Songs of Andhra Pradesh.* Music Today: CDF-02024 CD. 2002. CD.

1414 Karnataka College of Percussion, K. Raghavendra, R. A. Ramamani, and T. A. S. Mani. *River Yamuna.* Music of the World: MOW 145. 1997. CD.

1415 Mazalu, Karadi, Makbul Jagi, and Yellappa Jogi. *Inde: rythmes et chants du Nord-Karnataka = India: Rhythms and Songs from North Karnataka.* Musique du Monde. Buda: 1978542. 2001. CD.

1416 Peruvanam Kultan Marar and Party. *Drummers from Heaven: Panchari Melam, the Ritual Percussion Ensemble of Kerala.* Pan: 2074. 1999. CD.

1417 Rahman, A. R., and Sivamani. *Live in Dubai.* Sony: 497666 2. 2000. CD.

ANTHOLOGIES

1418 ⋆*Ho tuki rav yofi! shire nashim yehudiyot mikeralah = Oh, Lovely Parrot! Jewish Women's Songs from Kerala.* Antologyah Shel Masorot Musikah Be-Yisrael, 18. Jewish Music Research Centre, Hebrew University of Jerusalem: AMTI 0403. 2004. CD.

1419 *Inde: percussions rituelles du Kerala, Vol. 1: kshetram vadyam = India: Ritual Percussion of Kerala, Vol. 1: kshetram vadyam.* Archives Internationales de Musique Populaire, 54. VDE: VDE CD-971. 1998, 1995. CD.

1420 *Inde: percussions rituelles du Kerala, Vol. 2: tayambak = India: Ritual Percussion of Kerala, Vol. 2: Tayambak.* Archives Internationales de Musique Populaire, 60. VDE-Gallo: VDE CD-972. 1998. CD.

VIDEOS

1421 Ilaiyaraja, composer. *Thalapathi* (Prajinikanth, Mamooty, Arvind Swamy, Shobana, and Sivakumar). Pyramid International: PYDVD 1011. 2002. DVD.

1422 Mahadevan, K. V., composer. *Sankarabharanam* (J. V. Somayajulu, Manju Bhargavi, Allu Ramalingaiah, and Tulasi Ram). EVP International: 56210456. 2001. DVD.

1423 Rahman, A. R., composer.
1423.1 *Alaipayuthey* (Madhavan, Shalini, Aravinda Samy, Kushboo, and Jeyasutha). Ayngaran International: AYNDVD 010. 2001. DVD.
1423.2 *Indian* (Kamalhasan, Manisha Koirala, Sukanya, and Goundamani and Senthil). Ayngaran International. 2001. DVD.
1423.3 *Kandukondain Kandukondain: I Have Found It* (Mammootty, Ajith, Tabu, Aishwarya Rai, Abbas Manivannan, Srividya Raghuvaran, and Nizhalgal Ravil Shamili). Kino on Video: K 395. 2005. DVD.

Bangladesh

INDIVIDUAL ARTISTS AND GROUPS

1424　Bauls of Bengal and Purna Chandra Das, et al. *Bauls of Bengal.* Empire Musicwerks: 545 450 762-2. 2005. CD.

1425　Chakravarty, Ajoy. *Soulful Tagore.* Music Today: 829410764476. 2007. CD.

1426　Dey, Anjana. *Anjana Dey Presents More Songs from Tagore, Vol. 2.* Creek Recording. 2008. CD.

ANTHOLOGIES

1427　*Bauls of Bengal.* ARC Music: EUCD 1923. 2005. CD.

1428　★*Echoes from Bangladesh.* Deben Bhattacharya Collection. Frémeaux & Associés: FA 161. 2003. 2 CDs.

Sri Lanka

INDIVIDUAL ARTISTS AND GROUPS

1429　Amaradeva. *Amara Gi Sara.* Singlanka Ltd.: SLCD 002094. 1995. CD.

1430　Edirisimha, Sunil. *Best of Sunil Edirisinghe.* Singlanka: SLCD 200030. [2000–2003]. CD.

ANTHOLOGIES

1431　*Best Sixteen Calypso Hits of Sri Lanka.* Torana Music Box: SPSK 1026. 1990–2000. CD.

1432　★*Maitres de Sri Lanka = Masters of Sri Lanka.* Frémeaux: FA 5168. 2007. CD.

1433　*Sevali pirita saha atavisi pirita.* Torana Music Box: SPSK 1107. 2002. CD.

ANDAMAN ISLANDS

ANTHOLOGY

1434　*The Moken: Sea Gypsies of the Andaman Sea.* Topic World Series. Topic: TSCD 919. 2001. CD.

BOLLYWOOD AND BHANGRA

Compiled by Jeff Schwartz

Since the 1930s, musicals have been a major part of the Indian film industry. Known as "Bollywood," a combination of Hollywood and Bombay, a phenomenal number of these long, extravagant movies are made each year, featuring huge production numbers openly lip-synched by the actors to recordings made by studio vocalists known as playback singers, who have become stars in their own right. Unlike the traditional Broadway musical, the numbers in a Bollywood film often do not directly support or advance the plot, functioning more as pure spectacle. Thus most collections can cover this area with CD anthologies. There are general surveys as well as discs devoted to the major playback singers (Asha Bhosle, Lata Mangeshkar, and Mohammed Rafi), composers (R. D. Burman and A. R. Rahman), and various periods and styles. The extremely quirky collections on Sublime Frequencies and Normal Records document Bollywood's assimilation of steel guitar and 1970s funk. Collection development guidance for films can be found in the recent spate of publications from U.S. academic presses, including *Global Bollywood: Travels of Hindi Song and Dance,* edited by Sangita Gopal and Sujata Moorti (University of Minnesota Press, 2008), *Global Bollywood,* edited by Anandam P. Kavoori and Aswin Punathambekar (New York University Press, 2008), *Cinema India: The Visual Culture of Hindi Film,* by Rachel Dwyer, (Rutgers University Press, 2002), and *Encyclopedia of Indian Cinema,* new rev. ed., edited by Ashish Rajadhyaksha and Paul Willemen (Routledge, 1999).

Originally a Punjabi festival music, bhangra has become the label for a hybrid dance club music of the international Indian community, particularly in the United Kingdom. Incorporating techno, hip-hop, and reggae beats, it is as difficult to collect as any other club music, driven by rapidly changing trends and dependent on DJs to bring the records alive through creative mixing. Anthologies can periodically provide a snapshot of the genre; the Rough Guide series is readily available.

INDIVIDUAL ARTISTS AND GROUPS

1435　Bhosle, Asha
　1435.1　*The Rough Guide to Bollywood Legends: Asha Bhosle.* Rough Guide. World Music Network: RGNET 1131 CD. 2003. CD.
　1435.2　*The Very Best of Asha Bhosle: The Queen of Bollywood.* Nascente: NSCDB 001. 2004. 2 CDs.

1436　Burman, R. D. *A Bollywood Legend: The Best of the EMI Years.* Times Square: TSQ-CD-9064. 1957, 2007. 2 CDs.

1437　Mangeshkar, Lata. *The Rough Guide to Bollywood Legends: Lata Mangeshkar.* Rough Guide. World Music Network: RGNET 1132 CD. 2004. CD.

1438　Rafi, Mohammed. *The Rough Guide to Bollywood Legends: Mohd. Rafi.* Rough Guide. World Music Network: RGNET 1133 CD. 2004. CD.

1439   Rahman, A. R. *Introducing A. R. Rahman: Original Soundtracks from the Musical Genius of Indian Cinema.* Times Square: TSQ-CD-9053. 1992, 2006. 2 CDs.

ANTHOLOGIES

1440   *Beginner's Guide to Bhangra.* Nascente: NSBOX 038. 2008. 3 CDs.

1441   ★*Beginner's Guide to Bollywood, Vols. 1 and 2.* Nascente: NSBOX 003, NSBOX 024. 2003, 2006. 6 CDs.

1442   *The Best of Bollywood.* Hip-O: B 0000359-02. 2003. CD.

1443   *Bhangra: Original Punjabi Pop.* ARC Music: EUCD 1765. 2003. CD.

1444   *Bhangra: The Sound of Bollywood.* ARC Music: EUCD 1862. 2004. CD.

1445   *Bollywood: An Anthology of Songs from Popular Indian Cinema.* Silva Screen: SILCD 1204. 1949, 2005. 2 CDs.

1446   *Bollywood Dance: Bhangra.* ARC Music: EUCD 1989. 2006. CD.

1447   *The Bombay Connection*
1447.1   *Vol. 1: Funk from Bollywood Action Thrillers, 1977–1984.* Normal: BC 001. 2007. CD.
1447.2   *Vol. 2: Bombshell Baby of Bombay: Bouncin' Nightclub Grooves.* Normal: BC 002. 2007. CD.

1448   *Golden Voices from the Silver Screen, Vols. 1–3.* Worldwide Tourguide. Globestyle: CDORBD 054, CDORBD 056, CDORBD 059. 1949, 1951, 1955; 1990. 3 CDs.

1449   *I Love Bollywood.* Manteca: MANTCD 029. 1958, 2001. CD.

1450   *Kings and Queens of Bollywood.* Nascente: NSCD 090. 2001. CD.

1451   ★*The Rough Guide to Bhangra.* Rough Guide. World Music Network: RGNET 1054 CD. 2000. CD.

1452   *The Rough Guide to Bhangra Dance.* Rough Guide. World Music Network: RGNET 1154 CD. 2006. CD.

1453   *The Rough Guide to Bollywood.* Rough Guide. World Music Network: RGNET 1074 CD. 2002. CD.

1454   *The Rough Guide to Bollywood Gold.* Rough Guide. World Music Network: RGNET 1182 CD. 2007. CD.

SOUTHEAST ASIA

Compiled by Liza Vick, Alec McLane

Southeast Asia consists of many distinct cultures, including mainland, lowland and upland, island, and hundreds of minority ethnic and language groups. Cultures and influences include Malay-Indonesian, Malayo-Polynesian, aboriginal peoples, Muslims, and immigrant groups such as Arabs, Chinese, Eurasians, Europeans, and Indians, and many more, all of which influence musical characteristics and make Southeast Asia challenging to generalize about (*Garland Encyclopedia of World Music*, Vol. 4 (Garland, 1998), 594).

Traditional forms range from folk to court music, from Cambodian classical dance and *pinpeat* (court music) to Thai pop and country to Laotian *mor lam* (sung) to Vietnamese opera and puppetry, the imperial music of Hué, and the vibrant Vietnamese pop scene. As in other Asian countries, these strands (in particular, court music and various pop strains) are culturally important. Moving across the ocean, figures like the Vietnamese performer Nhu Quynh and the Cambodian-influenced group Dengue Fever of Los Angles represent both transplanted artists and pop fusion.

Labels such as Sublime Frequencies, Auvidis, Ocora, King, Seven Seas, and Celestial Harmonies carry recordings, as do the mainstream CD vendors, such as Amazon. Many of the Malaysian recordings listed have gone out-of-print. Some may be available in Malaysia, but this listing represents artists and genres to watch.

Indonesia is the fourth most populous country in the world, comprising over seventeen thousand islands on which live approximately three hundred ethnic groups, each with an indigenous language. Yet Indonesia manages to remain a nation by virtue of an adopted national language, *Bahasa Indonesia.* Of the slightly more than two hundred million people in Indonesia, more than half live on the island of Java, so it is not surprising that most recordings of Indonesian music tend toward both *Javanese* traditions (mostly from central Java) and *Sundanese* traditions (from west Java). Much more surprising is that the tiny island of Bali, making up barely 1.5 percent of the country's population, accounts for nearly as many recordings. This is probably because of its huge reputation for Western tourists as an island paradise and also some unique musical and religious traditions of its own. Bali has an overwhelming Hindu majority, while the rest of the nation is largely Muslim.

This list of recordings is dominated by several large series that have gone to great lengths to document much of the traditional music of Indonesia. Because the recordings are so unique, each title from these series is given separately; it is not necessary to acquire the entire series unless collecting comprehensively. The largest of these is from Smithsonian Folkways, a twenty-disc set titled *Music of Indonesia* that covers nearly every island in the archipelago and includes music that has rarely appeared elsewhere on disc. Other smaller series include those from Celestial Harmonies and King Records. While the Smithsonian Folkways series covers primarily folk traditions and avoids the better-known classical traditions featuring bronze *gamelan* orchestras from Java and Bali, a series on the Italian label Felmay concentrates exclusively on central Javanese *gamelan* music, which has become perhaps the most studied Indonesian music in the West. *Gamelan* orchestras often accompany dance dramas or puppet theater, generally known as *wayang*, and so several examples of these on CD and DVD are included.

Historically, Indonesia has been far from an insular country, and many of its older musical traditions and modern popular music show influences from other cultures. India has provided not only the dominant religion in Bali but also the primary narrative themes for the *wayang* and dance dramas (found in both Java and Bali) by means of its two epics, the *Mahabharata* and *Ramayana*. Additionally, a modern popular music genre, *dangdut*, is influenced by Indian popular music. Another older genre of popular music, *keroncong*, was influenced by Portuguese colonists. The huge and thriving local Indonesian music industry has been issued on cassettes for many years, and these are not easy to acquire. Traditional music recordings from European labels are available from Farside Music (www.farsidemusic.com) and Multicultural Media's World Music Store (www.worldmusicstore.com), while many locally produced recordings of popular music can be found at The Indonesian Music Shop (http://indonesianmusic.com).

Read more about southeast Asian music in the *Garland Handbook of Southeast Asian Music* (Routledge, 2008). Alec McLane contributed the Indonesia portion of this list.

CAMBODIA

INDIVIDUAL ARTISTS AND GROUPS

1455 Chorus and Orchestra of the Royal Ballet (Cambodia). *Les musiques du Ramayana, Vol. 2: Cambodge.* Ocora Radio France: C 560015. 1964, 1990. CD.

1456 Chum, Ngek. *Homrong: Classical Music from Cambodia* (Joanna Pecore, prod.). Celestial Harmonies: 13237-2. 2004. CD.

1457 Dengue Fever. *Dengue Fever Presents Electric Cambodia: 14 Rare Gems from Cambodia's Past.* Minky Records: MKY1. 1960s, 2009. CD.

1458 Musicians of the National Dance Company of Cambodia. *Musicians of the National Dance Company of Cambodia: Homrong.* Real World: 2-91734. 1990, 1991. CD.

1459 Sam-ang Sam Ensemble
    1459.1 *Echoes from the Palace.* Music of the World: CDT-140. 1996. CD.
    1459.2 *Mohori: Khmer Music from Cambodia.* Latitudes: LAT 50609. 1997. CD.
    1459.3 *Silent Temples, Songful Hearts: Traditional Music of Cambodia* (Sam-ang Sam and Patricia Shehan Campbell, compilers). World Music Press: WMP 008 CD. 1991. CD, book.

ANTHOLOGIES

1460 *Cambodge: Musique classique, théâters d'ombres, chants de mariage.* Inédit. Maison des Cultures du Monde: W 260002. 1991, 1995. CD.

1461 *Cambodia Rock Spectacular! Groove Club, Vol. 2.* Traffic Entertainment Group. 2011. CD.

1462 ★*Cambodia Traditional Music: Instrumental and Vocal Pieces, Vols. 1 and 2* (Chinary Ung, compiler). Custom Compact Disc Series. Smithsonian Folkways: FE 4081, FE 4082. 1978, 1979, 2004. 2 CDs.

1463 *Cambodian Cassette Archives: Khmer Folk and Pop Music, Vol. 1.* Sublime Frequencies: SF 011. 1960, 2004. CD.

1464 *Cambodia Rock Spectacular! Groove Club, Vol. 2.* Traffic Entertainment Group. 2011. CD.

1465 *Cambodian Rocks, Vol. 1.* Khmer Rocks. 2005. CD.

1466 *Ethnic Minority Music of Northeast Cambodia* (Laurent Jeanneau, compiler). Sublime Frequencies: SF 027. 2005. CD.

1467 *The Music of Cambodia*
    1467.1 *Vol. 1: 9 Gong Gamelan* (David Parsons and Kay Parsons, prods.). Celestial Harmonies: 13074-2. 1993. CD.

1467.2 *Vol. 2: Royal Court Music* (David Parsons, prod.) Celestial Harmonies: 13075-2. 1993. CD.

1467.3 *Vol. 3: Solo Instrumental Music* (David Parsons and Kay Parsons, prods.). Celestial Harmonies: 13076-2. 1994. CD.

EAST TIMOR

ANTHOLOGIES

1468 *Liberdade: Viva East Timor.* Mushroom Records: MUSH 332632. 1999. CD.

1469 *Ne'e hau nia moris: Songs from the Lautem District, Timor-Leste.* Plan. 2008. CD.

LAOS

INDIVIDUAL ARTISTS AND GROUPS

1470 Keaopidom, Wannaa, and Khamsaen Wongsimuang. *Mohlam of Siiphandon.* Seven Seas; World Music Library. King: KICC 5225. 1996, 1997. CD.

1471 Molam Lao. *Music from Southern Laos.* Nimbus: NI 5401. 1993, 1994. CD.

1472 Mua, Boua Xou. *The Music of the Hmong People of Laos.* Arhoolie: CD 446. 1995. CD.

1473 Phimvilayphong, Nouthong. *Visions of the Orient: Music from Laos.* Secret World Series. Amiata: ARNR 0195. 1981, 1995. CD.

1474 Xyooj, Maiv Lug. *Yuav tsawg tus niam thiaj txaus koj siab.* Vang International Travel: SKU 16758. 2009. CD. Available at Hmong Bookstore: www.hmongabc.com.

1475 Yaj, Maiv Tooj Yi. *Kev ntshaw ntawm txijnkawm.* MTYY-V11-2008. 2009. CD. Available at Hmong Bookstore: www.hmongabc.com.

1476 Yaj, Suab Nag. *Noog toj siab.* Hmoob 2000 Xyoo Production: SKU 16767. 2009. CD. Available at Hmong Bookstore: www.hmongabc.com.

ANTHOLOGIES

1477 *Anthology of World Music: The Music of Laos.* Rounder: CD 5119. 1999. CD.

1478 *Bamboo on the Mountains: Kmhmu Highlanders from Southeast Asia and the U.S.* (Frank Proschan, compiler). Smithsonian Folkways: SFW 40456. 1999, 1982. CD.

1479 *Ethnic Minority Music of Southern Laos* (Laurent Jeanneau, compiler). Sublime Frequencies: SF 036. 2007. CD.

1480 *Laos: Lam saravane: Musique pour Le Khène* (Soubane Vongath, Singphet Souryavongxay, Nouthong Phimvilayphong, and Khamsy Knounsavath; Jacques Brunet and Pierre Toureille, compilers). Ocora: C 559 058. 1989. CD.

1481 *Laos: Molams et Mokhènes: Chant et orgue à bouche = Laos: Molams and Mokhenes: Singing and Mouth Organ.* Inédit. Maison des Cultures du Monde: W 260137. 2009. CD.

1482 *Laos: Musique de l'ancienne cour de Luang Prabang = Laos: Music of the Ancient Royal Court of Luang Prabang* (Tiao Phun Muang). Archives Internationales de Musique Populaire, 81. VDE-Gallo: VDE CD-1213. 2007, 2008. CD.

1483 *Musiques du Laos.* Inédit. Maison des Cultures du Monde: W 206118. 2004. CD.

MALAYSIA

INDIVIDUAL ARTISTS AND GROUPS

1484 Liang, Jingru. *Bai quan nu wang zhi qing ge wu shuang.* Xiang xin yin yue: BD 0022. 2009. CD.

1485 Madun, Roslan. *Lagu rakyat.* Anggun Performing Arts: APA 05-002. 2005. CD.

1486 Majid, Sheila. *Lengenda.* EMI: CD-FH 30055. 1990. CD.

1487 Ramlee, P.
1487.1 ★*Lagu dan filem.* Siri murah hati. EMI: 7243 834142 22. 1995, 2002. CD.
1487.2 ★*Terunggul.* EMI. 2008. 4 CDs.

ANTHOLOGIES

1488 ★*Dream Songs and Healing Sounds in the Rainforests of Malaysia* (Marina Roseman, compiler). Smithsonian Folkways: SF 40417. 1981, 1995. CD.

1489 ★*Murut Music of North Borneo* (Ivan Polunin, compiler). Smithsonian Folkways: F-4459. 1961, 2000. CD.

1490 *The Rough Guide to the Music of Malaysia.* Rough Guide. World Music Network: RGNET 1176 CD. 2006. CD.

1491 *Sawaku: Music of Sarawak.* Pan: PAN 2067 CD. 1997, 1998. CD.

1492 *Silat Rancak: muzik tradisional Kelantan.* Sincere Musical Trading. 2009. CD.

1493 ★*Temiar Dream Songs from Malaya.* Custom Compact Disc Series. Smithsonian Folkways: FE 4460. 1955, 2000. CD.

MYANMAR

INDIVIDUAL ARTISTS AND GROUPS

1494 Aung Win. *Burma: musique traditionnelles = Burma: Traditional Music.* Air Mail Music. Providence Music; Production Sunset-France: SA 141156. 2007, 2008. CD.

1495 Kyaw Kyaw Naing
   1495.1 *Bang on a Can Meets Kyaw Kyaw Naing* (Bang on a Can All-Stars). Cantaloupe Music: CA 21023. 2002, 2004. CD.
   1495.2 *The Magic Drum Circle of Burma.* Shanachie: 66005. 1996, 1998. CD.

1496 Moe Moe Yee. *Harpe Birmane: Myanmar Music.* PlayaSound: PS 65135. 1994. CD.

1497 Shwe, Khing Zin, and Shwe Shwe Khaing. *Voice over the Bridge.* White Swan: ES 0031. 2010. CD.

ANTHOLOGIES

1498 *Birmanie: Musique d'art* (Pierre Toureille, compiler). Ocora: C 559019. 1975, 1989. 2 CDs.

1499 *Burmanie: musique du théâtre classique = Burma: Classical Theatre Music* (Ward Keeler and Philip Yampolsky, compilers). Archives Internationales de Musique Populaire, 96–97. VDE-Gallo: VDE CD-1317; VDE CD-1318. 2005, 2010. 2 CDs.

1500 ★*Burmese Folk and Traditional Music.* Custom Compact Disc Series; Ethnic Folkways Library. Smithsonian Folkways: FE 4436. 1953, 2003. CD.

1501 *Guitars of the Golden Triangle: Folk and Pop Music of Myanmar (Burma), Vol. 2.* Sublime Frequencies: SF 024. 1970, 2005. CD.

1502 *Music of Myanmar.* World Music Library. Seven Seas King: KICC 5132. 1988. CD.

1503 *Music of Myanmar: Buddhist Chant in the Pali Tradition.* Celestial Harmonies: 14219-2. 2008. 2 CDs

1504 *Princess Nicotine: Folk and Pop Music of Myanmar (Burma), Vol. 1.* Sublime Frequencies: SF 006. 1994, 2004. CD.

1505 *White Elephants and Golden Ducks: Enchanting Musical Treasures from Burma.* Shanachie: 64087. 1996, 1997. CD.

PHILIPPINES

INDIVIDUAL ARTISTS AND GROUPS

1506 Aguilar, Freddie. *Greatest Hits.* Legends Series. Ivory: IRC-K-7119. 2001. CD.

1507 APO Hiking Society. *The Best of Apo Hiking Society.* WEA: CDP-94,601. 1991. CD.

1508 Bayanihan Philippine Dance Company. *Monitor Presents the Bayanihan Philippine Dance Company.* Monitor: MCD 71322. 1991. CD.

1509 Clamor, Charmaine. *My Harana: A Filipino Serenade.* FreeHam Records: FH 0806. 2008. CD.

1510 Fiesta Filipina Dance Troupe. *Traditional Music from the Philippines.* ARC Music: EUCD 1491. 1998, 1999. CD.

1511 Nono, Grace. *'Isang Buhay = One Life.* BMG: 2002-359139. 1997. CD. Available from Tao: www.gracenono.com/toomusic/orderinfo.html.

1512 Silos, Juan. *Philippine Folk Dances, Vol. 10* (Rondalla). Villar Records International: MCD-5122. 2009. CD.

1513 World Kulintang Institute Ensemble. *Kulintang: Ancient Gong/Drum Music from the Southern Philippines.* World Kulintang: wkcd 72551. 1991, 1994. CD.

ANTHOLOGIES

1514 *The Best of Pinoy Folk Rock: Ugat.* Vicor Music: VMC-CDS-08-016. 2008. CD.

1515 ★*Hanuno'o Music from the Philippines* (Harold C. Conklin, compiler). Custom Compact Disc Series; Ethnic Folkways Library. Smithsonian Folkways: FE 4466. 1955, 2003. CD.

1516 *Himig Handog Sa Bayaning Pilipino.* Star Recording: 11-20156-2. 2000. CD.

1517 *Music of the Magindanao in the Philippines* (José Montserrat Maceda, compiler). Custom Compact Disc Series. Smithsonian Folkways: F-4536. 1961, 2001. 2 CDs.

1518 *Pagbabalik: Pinoy Folk Rock.* Vicor Music:
VCD-SA-014. 2005. CD.

1519 ★*Utom, Summoning the Spirit* (Manolete Mora,
compiler). Smithsonian Folkways Archival.
Smithsonian Folkways: HRT 15017. 1997,
2010. CD.

SINGAPORE

ANTHOLOGY

1520 *Singapore a-Go-Go.* Sublime Frequencies: SF051.
1963, 2009. CD. Available from Juno Records:
www.juno.co.uk/products.

THAILAND

INDIVIDUAL ARTISTS AND GROUPS

1521 ★Chumbhot, Princess. *Drums of Thailand.* Custom
Compact Disc Series; Ethnic Folkways Library.
Smithsonian Folkways: FE 4215. 1974,
2003. CD.

1522 Damnoen, Chawiwan, and Thongkham Thaikla.
Mo Lam Singing of Northeast Thailand. King: KICC
5123. 1991. CD.

1523 Ensemble Si Nuan Thung Pong. *Chang Saw:
Village Music of Northern Thailand.* Ethnic Series.
Pan: PAN 2075 CD. 1998, 1999. CD.

1524 Fong Naam
    1524.1 *Ancient Contemporary Music from
    Thailand.* Celestial Harmonies: 14098-2.
    1995. 2 CDs.
    1524.2 *Siamese Classical Music, Vol. 5: The
    Mahori Orchestra.* World Classics. Marco
    Polo: 8.223493. 1992, 1994. CD.
    1524.3 *Thai Classical Music.* World Classics.
    Marco Polo: 8.223197. 1991. 4 CDs.

1525 Guitar, Johnny. *Shadow Music of Thailand*
[1960]. Sublime Frequencies: SF042. 1960s,
2009. CD.

1526 Isan Slété. *The Flower of Isan.* GlobeStyle:
CDORBD 051. 1989. CD.

1527 Kruang Sai Thai. *Thailande: Phuket.* Air Mail
Music. Productions Sunset-France: SA 141085.
2003. CD.

1528 Prasit Thawon Ensemble. *Thai Classical Music.*
Nimbus: NI 5412. 1993, 1994. CD.

1529 Thanakoset, Benjarong, and Chaloem
Muangphresi. *Ayutaya tsuiso: Tai kokyoku ongaku
no kyosho = Virtuosi of Thai Classical Music.*
World Music Library, 58. Seven Seas: KICC 5158.
1992. CD.

ANTHOLOGIES

1530 *Classical Music of Thailand.* World Music Library.
King: KICC 5125. 1991. CD.

1531 *Instrumental Music of Northeast Thailand.* World
Music Library. King: KICC 5124. 1991. CD.

1532 *Lanna Thai: Instrumental Music of North-West
Thailand.* Ethnic Series. Pan: PAN 2045 CD.
1997. CD.

1533 ★*Music of Thailand* (Howard K. Kaufman,
compiler). Smithsonian Folkways: 4463. 1960,
1999. CD.

1534 *The Musical Heritage of Northeast Thailand*
    1534.1 *Vol. 1: Forgotten Lam Genres* [1973–
    1974] (Terry Miller and Charoenchai
    Chonphairot, compilers). EarthCDs: TH-
    NE1. 2008. CD.
    1534.2 *Vol. 2: Puppet Theater in Isan* [1973–
    1974] (Terry Miller and Charoenchai
    Chonphairot, compilers). EarthCDs: TH-
    NE2. 2008. CD.
    1534.3 *Vol. 3: Ritual Voices: Spirit-Curing
    Ceremonies, Rocket Festival, and Buddhist
    Chant* [1973–1974] (Terry Miller and
    Charoenchai Chonphairot, compilers).
    EarthCDs: TH-NE3. 2008. CD.

1535 *Radio Thailand: Transmissions from the Tropical
Kingdom.* Sublime Frequencies: SF 028. 1989,
2006. 2 CDs.

1536 ★*Royal Court Music of Thailand.* (Witthayalai
Nattasin and various artists). Smithsonian
Folkways: SF 40413. 1994. CD.

1537 *Siamese Soul: Thai Pop Spectacular, Vol. 2:
1960s–1980s.* Sublime Frequencies: SF050.
2009. CD.

1538 *The Sound of Siam: Leftfield Luk Thung, Jazz
and Molam in Thailand, 1964–1975.* Soundway:
SNDWCD 027. 1964, 2010. CD.

1539 *Thai Pop Spectacular, 1960s–1980s.* Sublime
Frequencies: SF 032. 1960s, 2007. CD.

1540 *Thailand.* Rough Guide. World Music Network:
RGNET 1095 CD. 2003. CD.

1541 *Thailand: The Music of Chieng Mai.* Smithsonian Folkways: UNES 08007. 1988, 2014. CD.

VIDEOS

1542 *Isan: Folk and Pop Music from Northeast Thailand.* Sublime Frequencies: SF 015. 2004. DVD.

1543 Sumbatcharon, Surachai. *Two Faces of Thailand: A Musical Portrait* (Jeremy Marre, dir. and prod.). Beats of the Heart. Shanachie: 1214. 1983, 2003. DVD.

VIETNAM

INDIVIDUAL ARTISTS AND GROUPS

1544 Duy, Phạm. *Phạm Duy: Ngày tr'o' ve, Vol. 1.* Phu'o'ng Nam Phim. 2005. CD. Western-influenced pop.

1545 Khac Chi Ensemble. *Moonlight in Vietnam.* Rounder: HSR 0005. 1997. CD.

1546 Nguyên, Vinh Bao, and Van Khê Trân. *Vietnam: Tradition of the South = Tradition du sud.* Unesco Collection; Anthology of Traditional Musics. Auvidis: D 8049. 1993. CD.

1547 Perfume River Traditional Ensemble. *Vietnam: Music from the Lost Kingdom, Huế.* Lyrichord Presents Outstanding Music from around the World. Lyrichord: LYRCD 7440. 1998. CD.

1548 Quy Bon Family. *Vietnamese Folk Theatre: Hát chèo.* King: KICC 5122. 1991. CD.

1549 Thanh, Huong. *Musique du Théâtre Cai Luong = Cai Luong Theatre Music.* Collection Ocora Radio France. Ocora Radio France: C 560222. 2008. CD.

1550 Thanh, Huong, and Nguyên Lê. *Fragile Beauty.* ACT Music: 9451-2. 2007. CD.

1551 Trân, Van Khê, and Thi Thuy Ngoc Trân. *Vietnam: Poésies et chants.* Ocora Radio France: C 560054. 1994. CD.

ANTHOLOGIES

1552 *Anăk Č' ư' Čhiăng: The Original People of Vietnam's Central Highlands.* Montagnard Culture Group. 2006. CD.

1553 *Ethnic Minority Music of North Vietnam* (Laurent Jeanneau, compiler). Sublime Frequencies: SF 037. 2007. CD.

1554 ★*Folk Songs of Vietnam* (Phạm Duy and Stephen Addiss, compilers). Custom Compact Disc Series. Smithsonian Folkways: FTS 31303. 1968, 1999. CD.

1555 *Gongs du Vietnam = Vietnamese Gongs* (Patrick Kersalé, compiler). Air Mail Music. Sunset-France: SA 141178. 2002, 2009. CD.

1556 *Hò! Roady Music from Vietnam 2000, Vol. 1.* Trikont: US-0249. 1998. CD.

1557 *Instrumental Music of Vietnam.* World Music Library, 60. King: KICC 5160. 1991, 1992. CD.

1558 ★*Music from North and South Vietnam: Sung Poetry of the North; Theater Music of the South* (Stephen Addiss, compiler). Custom Compact Disc Series. Smithsonian Folkways: FE 4219. 1971, 2000. CD.

1559 *Music from Vietnam: Minorities from the Central Highland and Coast, 5.* World Caprice. Caprice: CAP 21674. 2003. CD.

1560 *The Music of Vietnam* (Van Khê Trân, compiler) Anthology of World Music. Rounder: CD 5140/41. 1999. 2 CDs.

1561 *The Music of Vietnam.* Celestial Harmonies: 13082-2. 1994–1995. 3 CDs.

1562 *The Rough Guide to the Music of Vietnam.* Rough Guide. World Music Network: RGNET 1183 CD. 2007. CD.

1563 *Stilling Time: Ngu' ò'i Ngòi Ru Thò'i Gian: Traditional Musics of Vietnam* (Philip Blackburn, compiler). Innova: 112. 1994. CD.

1564 *String Instruments of Vietnam.* World Music Library, 21. King: KICC 5121. 1991. CD.

1565 *Vietnam: Ca tru and quan ho (Traditional Music = Musique Traditionnelle)* (Van Khê Trân, compiler). Musiques and Musiciens du Monde. Auvidis Unesco: D 8035. 1978, 1991. CD.

1566 *Vietnam: Musique des Montagnards = Vietnam: Music of the Montagnards* (Hugo Zemp, compiler). Collection C.N.R.S., Musée de l'Homme. Chant du Monde: CNR 2741085. 1963, 1997. 2 CDs.

1567 *Viêt-Nam: musiques et chants des minorités du nord = Northern Vietnam: Music and Songs of the Minorities* (Patrick Kersalé, compiler). Musique du Monde. Buda: 92669-2. 1997. CD.

1568 *Vietnam: musiques vocales des plaines du nord = Vocal Music from the Northern Plains: Ca trú,*

Hát chèo, Quan ho (Yves Defrance, compiler). Archives Internationales de Musique Populaire. VDE-Gallo: VDE CD-1207. 2006. CD.

1569 *Viet Nam: Traditions of the South (Trần Văn Khê, compiler).* Smithsonian Folkways: UNES 08070. 1984, 2015. CD.

SOUTHEAST ASIA
GENERAL ANTHOLOGY

1570 ★*The JVC Video Anthology of World Music and Dance: Southeast Asia, Vols. 6–8.* JVC, Victor Co. of Japan; dist. by Multicultural Media. 1990, 2005. 30 DVDs, 9 booklets.

INDONESIA

Traditional and Folk

GROUP

1571 ★Temu, Gandrung, and Basuki. *Songs before Dawn: Gandrung Banyuwangi* [1990] (Philip Yampolsky, compiler). Music of Indonesia, 1. Smithsonian Folkways: CD SF 40055. 1991. CD.

ANTHOLOGIES

1572 *Batak of North Sumatra.* New Albion: NA 046 CD. 1992. CD.

1573 *Gongs and Vocal Music from Sumatra* (Philip Yampolsky, compiler). Music of Indonesia, 12. Smithsonian Folkways: SF CD 40428. 1996. CD.

1574 *Indonesian Guitars* (Philip Yampolsky, compiler). Music of Indonesia, 20. Smithsonian Folkways: SF CD 40447. 1999. CD.

1575 *Indonésie: Chants de Biboki (Timor occidental) = Indonesia: Songs of Biboki (Western Timor).* Archives Internationales de Musique Populaire, 102. VDE-Gallo: VDE CD-1351. 2011. CD.

1576 *Indonésie: Chants des îles de Flores et Solor = Indonesia: Songs from the Islands of Flores and Solor.* Archives Internationales de Musique Populaire, 95. VDE-Gallo: VDE CD-1304. 2010. CD.

1577 *Kalimantan: Dayak Ritual and Festival Music* (Philip Yampolsky, compiler). Music of Indonesia, 17. Smithsonian Folkways: SF CD 40444. 1998. CD.

1578 *Kalimantan Strings* (Philip Yampolsky, compiler). Music of Indonesia, 13. Smithsonian Folkways: SF CD 40429. 1997. CD.

1579 *Lombok, Kalimantan, Banyumas: Little-Known Forms of Gamelan and Wayang* (Philip Yampolsky, compiler). Music of Indonesia, 14. Smithsonian Folkways: SF CD 40441. 1997. CD.

1580 *Melayu Music of Sumatra and the Riau Islands* (Philip Yampolsky, compiler). Music of Indonesia, 11. Smithsonian Folkways: SF CD 40427. 1996. CD.

1581 ★*Music for the Gods.* Endangered Music Project. Rykodisc: RCD 10315. 1994. CD.

1582 *Music from the Forests of Riau and Mentawai* (Philip Yampolsky, compiler). Music of Indonesia, 7. Smithsonian Folkways: SF CD 40423. 1995. CD.

1583 *Music from the Outskirts of Jakarta: Gambang Kromong* (Philip Yampolsky, compiler). Music of Indonesia, 3. Smithsonian Folkways: CD SF 40057. 1991. CD.

1584 *Music from the Southeast: Sumbawa, Sumba, Timor* (Philip Yampolsky, compiler). Music of Indonesia, 16. Smithsonian Folkways: SF CD 40443. 1998. CD.

1585 *Music of Biak, Irian Jaya* (Philip Yampolsky, compiler). Music of Indonesia, 10. Smithsonian Folkways: SF 40426. 1996. CD.

1586 *Music of Indonesia: Flores* [1994–1996] (Margaret Kartomi, compiler). Celestial Harmonies: 13175-2. 1999. CD.

1587 *Music of Indonesia: Maluku and North Maluku.* Celestial Harmonies: 14232-2. 2003. 2 CDs.

1588 *Music of Maluku: Halmahera, Buru, Kei* (Philip Yampolsky, compiler). Music of Indonesia, 19. Smithsonian Folkways: SF CD 40446. 1999. CD.

1589 *Music of Nias and North Sumatra: Hoho, Gendang Karo, Gondang Toba* (Philip Yampolsky, compiler). Music of Indonesia, 4. Smithsonian Folkways: CD SF 40420. 1992. CD.

1590 *Music of Timor* [1990] (Margaret Kartomi, compiler). Celestial Harmonies: 13182-2. 2000. CD.

1591 *Night Music of West Sumatra: Saluang, Rabab Pariaman, Dendang Pauah* (Philip Yampolsky, compiler). Music of Indonesia, 6. Smithsonian Folkways: CD SF 40422. 1994. CD.

1592 *Songs from the Uma: Music From Siberut Island (Mentawai Archipelago), Indonesia.* Ethnic Series. Pan Records: PAN 2111/12. 2009. 2 CDs.

1593 *South Sulawesi Strings* (Philip Yampolsky, compiler). Music of Indonesia, 15. Smithsonian Folkways: SF CD 40442. 1997. CD.

1594 *Sulawesi: Festivals, Funeral and Work* (Philip Yampolsky, compiler). Music of Indonesia, 18. Smithsonian Folkways: SF CD 40445. 1999. CD.

1595 *Vocal and Instrumental Music from East and Central Flores* (Philip Yampolsky, compiler). Music of Indonesia, 8. Smithsonian Folkways: SF CD 40424. 1995. CD.

1596 *Vocal Music from Central and West Flores* (Philip Yampolsky, compiler). Music of Indonesia, 9. Smithsonian Folkways: SF CD 40425. 1995. CD.

Gamelan Music
Java

INDIVIDUAL ARTISTS AND GROUPS

1597 Danuredjo VII, Prince of Yogyakarta. *Java: Langen mandra wanara: opéra.* Ocora: C 559014/15. 1975, 1987. 2 CDs.

1598 ★Malati, Linkung Seni, and Ida Widawati. *Classical Music from West Java: Tembang Sunda.* Celestial Harmonies: 13134-2. 1996. CD.

1599 ★Mardawa, Kawedanan Hageng Punakawan Kridha. *Yogyakarta, Gamelan of the Kraton.* Celestial Harmonies: 13161-2. 1997. CD.

1600 Pawiyatan Kraton Surakarta (G. R. A. Koes Murtiyah, leader). *Central Java: Court Music of Kraton Surakarta (Solo).* World Music Library, 51. King: KICW 85016-8. 1992, [2008]. 3 CDs.

1601 Sarasehan Karawitan Surakarta, Saptono, and Tukinem. *Chamber Music of Central Java.* World Music Library, 52. King: KICW 85161-3. 1992, 1995, [2008]. 3 CDs.

1602 Wasitodiningrat, K. R. T. *The Music of K. R. T. Wasitodiningrat* (Gamelan Sekar Tunjung). CMP: CS 3007. 1992. CD.

ANTHOLOGIES

1603 *Betawi and Sundanese Music of the North Coast of Java: Topeng Betawi, Tanjidor, Ajeng* (Philip Yampolsky, compiler). Music of Indonesia, 5. Smithsonian Folkways: CD SF 40421. 1994. CD.

1604 *Gamelan of Central Java*
  1604.1 *Vol. 1: Classical Gendings* (Nyi Cendaniraras and faculty members of the Music Conservatory [Sekolah Tinggi Seni Indonesia] Surakarta). Felmay: FY 8041. 2001. CD.
  1604.2 *Vol. 2: Ceremonial Music* (Musicians of the Kraton Surakarta and Istana Mangkunagaran). Felmay: FY 8042. 2002. CD.
  1604.3 *Vol. 3: Modes and Timbres* (Joko Purwanto and musicians of Sekolah Tinggi Seni Indonesia Surakarta). Felmay: FY 8073. 2004. CD.
  1604.4 *Vol. 4: Spiritual Music* (Joko Purwanto and musicians of Sekolah Tinggi Seni Indonesia Surakarta). Felmay: FY 8074. 2004. CD.
  1604.5 *Vol. 5: Gaya Yogyakarta* (Musicians and gamelan of RRI [Radio Republik Indonesia] Yogyakarta). Felmay: FY 8075. 2005. CD.
  1604.6 *Vol. 6: Kraton Surakarta* (Nyi Cendaniraras, Joko Purwanto, and faculty members of the Music Conservatory [Sekolah Tinggi Seni Indonesia] Surakarta). Felmay: FY 8103. 2006. CD.
  1604.7 *Vol. 7: Edge of Tradition* (Nyi Cendaniraras, Nyi Suparsih, Joko Purwanto, and faculty members of the Music Conservatory [Sekolah Tinggi Seni Indonesia] Surakarta). Felmay: FY 8104. 2006. CD.
  1604.8 *Vol. 8: Court Music Treasures* (Nyi Cendaniraras, Joko Purwanto, and faculty members of the Music Conservatory [Sekolah Tinggi Seni Indonesia] Surakarta). Felmay: FY 8119. 2007. CD.
  1604.9 *Vol. 9: Songs of Wisdom and Love* (Joko Purwanto and musicians of Sekolah Tinggi Seni Indonesia Surakarta). Felmay: FY 8120. 2007. CD.

1605 *Gamelan of Cirebon.* World Music Library, 30. King: KICW 85100. 1988, [2008]. CD.

1606 *Gamelan of Java*
  1606.1 *I: Kraton Kasunanan.* Lyrichord: LYRCD 7456. 2009. CD.
  1606.2 ★*II: Contemporary Composers* (Aloysius Suwardi, Darno Kartawi, Joko Purwanto, Prasadiyanto, Sri Harta, Supardi, Agus

Prasetyo, Bagong Pujiono, Heni Savitri Nurwanto, Rudy Triatmoko, and Sigit Prasetyo Sriyati). Lyrichord: LYRCD 7457. 2009. CD.

1606.3   *III: Yogyakarta* (K. R. T. Wasitodipuro, Gamelan Kyai Sekar Tunjung, Ensemble "Karawitan Raras Raos Irama"; Mas Riyo Muryowinoto, dir.). Lyrichord: LYRCD 7458. 2009. CD.

1606.4   *IV: Puspa Warna* (Gamelan Kyai Gedhong Gedhe). Lyrichord: LYRCD 7460. 2002, 2010. CD.

1606.5   *V: Cirebon Tradition in America* (Gamelan Sinar Surya, Deni Hermawan; Richard North, dir.). Lyrichord: LYRCD 7461. 2010. CD.

1607   *Indonésie, Java Centre: Gamelan de solo: Le jeu des sentiments = Indonesia, Central Java: Solenese Gamelan: A Garland of Moods.* Inédit. Maison des Cultures du Monde: W 260125. 2006. 4 CDs.

1608   ★*Javanese Court Gamelan.* Explorer Series. Elektra Nonesuch: 9 72044-2. 1991. CD.

1609   *Java—Sunda, musiques savantes: l'art du gamelan degung, vol. II (Java).* Ocora: C 560097. 1996. CD.

1610   *Sundanese Classical Music: Tembang and Degung.* World Music Library, 31. King: KICW 85101-2. 1986, [2008]. 2 CDs.

VIDEO

1611   *Traditional Dance from Central Java: Pamungkas, Gambyong Pangkur* (Ngaliman S., Sri Endah Wahyuningsih; Blacius Subono and Supardi, dirs.). Resonance Media: RM 206. 1997, 2007. DVD.

Bali

INDIVIDUAL ARTISTS AND GROUPS

1612   Alit, Dewa Ketut, Wayan Jebeg, Gede Manik, and Pan Wandres. *Cudamani: The Seven-Tone Gamelan Orchestra from the Village of Pengosekan, Bali.* Vital: VR 440. 2002. CD.

1613   Gong gedé of the Temples of Batur and Tampaksiring. *Bali: musique pour le gong gedé.* Ocora: C 559002. 1987. CD.

1614   Gamelan Semar Pegulingan Gunung Jati. *Gamelan Semar Pegulingan of Gunung Jati.* World Music Library, 80. King: KICW 85108-9. 1990, [2008]. 2 CDs.

1615   I Nyoman Sumandhi and Banjar Tunjuk Klod "Kusma Sari"

1615.1   *Gong leko: tunjuk-tabanan tabuh-tabuh leko.* Nippon Acoustic: NARD 5012. 1997, 2008. CD.

1615.2   *Gong leko: tunjuk-tabanan tari leko.* Nippon Acoustic: NARD 5013. 1997, 2008. CD.

1616   Gamelan Semar Pegulingan Saih Pitu. *The Heavenly Orchestra of Bali.* CMP: CD 3008. 1991. CD.

1617   Sekehe Legong Bidadari Indra Parwati. *Music of Bali: Gamelan Semar Pegulingan from the Village of Ketewel.* Lyrichord: LYRCD 7408. 1989. CD.

1618   Seka Gambuh Pura Desa Adat Batuan. *Music of the Gambuh Theater.* Vital: VR 501. 1999. CD.

ANTHOLOGIES

1619   ★*Bali 1928, Vols. 1–5 (1. Gamelan Gong Kebyar; 2. Tembang Kuna: Songs From an Earlier Time; 3. Lotring and the Sources of Gamelan Tradition; 4. Music for Temple Festivals and Death Rituals; 5. Vocal Music in Dance Dramas).* World Arbiter: 2011, 2014–2017. 5 CDs.

1620   *Bali: Gamelan and Kecak.* Explorer Series, Indonesia. Nonesuch: 79814-2. 2003. CD.

1621   *From Kuno to Kebyar: Balinese Gamelan Angklung.* Smithsonian Folkways: SFW 50411. 2011. CD.

1622   *Les grands gong kebyar des années soixante* [1969, 1970, 1971]. Bali. Ocora: C 560057/58. 1994. 2 CDs. Recorded by Jacques Brunet.

1623   ★*Music from the Morning of the World: The Balinese Gamelan and Ketjak: The Ramayana Monkey Chant.* Explorer Series. Elektra Nonesuch: 9 79196-2. 1988. CD.

1624   *The Music of Bali.* Celestial Harmonies: 13136-2—13138-2. 1997. 3 CDs.

VIDEOS

1625   *The JVC Video Anthology of World Music and Dance*

1625.1   *IV Southeast Asia, Vol. 9.* JVC, Victor Co. of Japan; dist. by Multicultural Media: VTMV-39, JVCVOL09. 1988, 2005. DVD.

1625.2   *V Southeast Asia, Vol. 10.* JVC, Victor Co. of Japan; dist. by Multicultural Media: VTMV-40, JVCVOL10. 1988, 2005. DVD.

Classical, Theatrical, and Religious

INDIVIDUAL ARTISTS AND GROUPS

1626 *Kecak: A Balinese Music Drama* (Kecak Ganda Sari, perf.; I Gusti Putu Putra, dir.). Bridge: BCD 9019. 1990. CD.

1627 Sekehe Gender Bharata Muni and Sading. *Gender Wayang Pemarwan: Music for the Balinese Shadow Play "The Mahabharata."* CMP: CD 3014. 1989. CD.

1628 ★Sunarya, Asep Sunandar. *Indonesia: Wayang Golek: The Sound and Celebration of Sundanese Puppet Theater*. Music of the Earth. Multicultural Media: MCM3019/24. 2001. 6 CDs.

ANTHOLOGIES

1629 *The Music of Islam, Vol. 15*. Celestial Harmonies: 14155-2. 1998. 2 CDs.

1630 *Music of Islamic Festival, Solo*. King: KICW 85164. 1992, 2008. CD.

1631 *Wayang Kulit of Java, "Banjaranjali" Story*. King: KICW 85054-6. 1992, [2008]. 3 CDs.

1632 *Wayang Kulit Sukawati "Tasik Kencana."* King: KICW 85059-60. 1990, [2008]. 2 CDs.

VIDEOS

1633 *Island of Temples*. Asian Notebook; Films of Deben Bhattacharya; Music and Society Series. Lyrichord: LYRDV-1004. 1973, 2003. DVD.

1634 *The Prosperity of Wibisana*
    1634.1 ★*A Performance of Javanese Wayang Kulit* (Widiyanto S. Putro; A. L. Suwardi, dir.). Resonance Media: RM 205. 1997, 2007. DVD.
    1634.2 ★*A Study Guide and Analysis of Javanese Wayang Kulit*. (Widiyanto S. Putro; A. L. Suwardi, dir.). Resonance Media: RM 204. 1997, 2007. DVD.

1635 *Wayang Kulit: The Shadow Puppet Theatre of Java* (Dalang Omartopo and Gamelan Kyai Kumbal). American Gamelan Institute. 1995. VHS.

Popular and Western-Influenced

INDIVIDUAL ARTISTS AND GROUPS

1636 Dody Satya, Ekagustdiman, Nano S., Afryanto Suhendi, and Harry Roesli. *New Music of Indonesia, Vol. 1: Asmat Dream*. Lyrichord: LYRCD 7415. 1993. CD.

1637 Gumbira, Gugum, composer. *Indonesia: West Java: Sundanese Popular Music* (Idjah Hadidjah and Suwanda). Explorer Series, Indonesia. Nonesuch: 79815-2. 1987, 2003. CD.

1638 Kurnia, Detty. *Dari Sunda*. Women of the World. Riverboat: TUGCD1011. 1995. CD.

1639 Nano S. *Music of Sunda, Nano S.* World Music Library. King: KICW 85103. 1996, [2008]. CD.

1640 Sadra, I Wayan. *New Music of Indonesia, Vol. 3: Karya*. Lyrichord: LYRCD 7421. 1990. CD.

1641 Sadra, I Wayan, Blacius Subono, Otok Bima Sidarta, and Pande Made Sukerta. *New Music of Indonesia, Vol. 2: Mana 689*. Lyrichord: LYRCD 7420. 1993. CD.

1642 Sukaesih, Elvy. *The Dangdut Queen*. Rice: RAS-104. 2005. CD.

ANTHOLOGY

1643 ★*Indonesian Popular Music: Kroncong, Dangdut, and Langgam Jawa* (Philip Yampolsky, compiler). Music of Indonesia, 2. Smithsonian Folkways: CD SF 40056. 1991. CD.

ASIA
GENERAL ANTHOLOGIES

1644 *Asia*. Buda: 860194. 2010. CD.

1645 *Asian Beat Box: Bhangra, Bollywood, India, Asian Underground*. Rough Guide. World Music Network: WMN 339005. 2003. 4 CDs.

1646 *Asian Underground*. Rough Guide. World Music Network: RGNET 1096 CD. 2003. CD.

1647 *Music of Central Asia: Popular Classics from Bukhara and Beyond, Vol. 7: In the Shrine of the Heart*. Smithsonian Folkways: SFW CD 40526. 2010. CD, DVD.

1648 *The Rough Guide to the Music of India*. Rough Guide. World Music Network: RGNET 1091 CD. 2002. CD.

1649 *The Rough Guide to the Music of India and Pakistan*. Rough Guide. World Music Network: RGNET 1008 CD. 1996. CD.

1650 *La route de la soie (Silk Road)*. Air Mail Music. Sunset-France: SA 141189. 2009. CD.

OCEANIA

Compiled by Kevin C. Miller

The recording of Oceanic music began in 1893, soon after the invention of the wax cylinder. Today a wealth of diverse recordings exists in the archives of universities, museums, and Pacific-based radio stations, only a small portion of which is available for commercial purchase. It follows that the primary challenge to building a basic library of Oceanic music is acquiring an audiovisual collection diverse enough to represent the region's great variety of ethnic groups. According to convention, the recordings suggested herein are divided into the geographical/cultural areas of Melanesia, Micronesia, and Polynesia, with a separate category for Australia. Melanesia (Greek for "black islands") includes New Guinea and the island region to its southeast; Micronesia ("small islands") encompasses the scattering of islands to the north of Melanesia, mostly north of the equator; and Polynesia ("many islands") includes numerous island groups within a large triangle formed by New Zealand, Hawaii, and Easter Island. As colonial constructs, these divisions often fail to contain the cultural migrations that lace Oceania together as a "sea of islands." Fiji, for example, is a transitional island group—phenotypically Melanesian, but culturally Polynesian—and there are numerous Polynesian outliers within the "borders" of Melanesian states, including Bellona in the Solomon Islands and West Futuna in Vanuatu.

The recordings listed reflect these musical journeys, encompassing a wide range of genres and styles and including music to accompany dance, traditional chants, polyphonic church music, and neotraditional popular music. Several instruments stand out among these recordings, including the didjeridu of Aboriginal Australia, the slack-key guitar of Hawaii, and the widespread string bands of guitars and ukuleles, yet the most pervasive and stylistically diverse Pacific instrument remains the human voice.

These recordings also reveal an apparent disparity: nearly half of the list is dedicated to recordings of Polynesian music, whereas other regions—particularly Micronesia—are represented by only a handful of citations. In part, this reflects the respective population sizes of these regions, but more to the point, commercially-available recordings from Micronesia and parts of Melanesia are simply harder to come by. Local cassette and CD industries often lack international distribution and libraries have become dependent on collections of Oceanic field recordings and popular music released by labels in the United States, the United Kingdom, the Netherlands, France, Japan, and Australia. These sources include the Australian Institute of Aboriginal and Torres Strait Islander Studies (www .aiatsis.gov.au), ARC Music (www.arcmusic.co.uk), Pan Records (www.arhoolie.com/imports/pan-records), and Smithsonian Folkways Recordings (www.folkwayssi .edu). Several historic Oceanic recordings on Folkways Records are now available through Smithsonian Folkways Recordings as custom CDs with professional packaging and downloadable liner notes. Furthermore, many of the smaller island cultures are represented on anthologies of Oceanic music, many of which are included in the list. The one hundred CDs and DVDs that compose this list include a range of traditional, folk, religious, and popular music from all regions of Oceania. Librarians are encouraged to consult the discography maintained by the Society for Ethnomusicology (www.ethnomusicology .org/?0G_CurrentDisco).

AUSTRALIA

New South Wales

INDIVIDUAL ARTISTS

1651 Carmody, Kev. *Pillars of Society*. Larrikin: CDLRF 237. 1990. CD.

1652 Young, Dougie. *The Songs of Dougie Young*. Australian Institute of Aboriginal and Torres Strait Islander Studies, the National Library of Australia: AIAS 19 CD. 1994. CD.

Northern Territory

INDIVIDUAL ARTISTS AND GROUPS

1653 Blekbala Mujik. *Blekbala Mujik*. CAAMA: 244 CD. 1993. CD.

1654 Maralung, Alan. *Bunggridj-Bunggridj: Wangga Songs* (Peter Manaberu). World's Musical Traditions, 4. Smithsonian Folkways: SWF 40430. 1988, 1993. CD.

1655 Yothu Yindi. *Tribal Voice*. Mushroom: 61288-2. 1992. CD.

ANTHOLOGIES

1656 *Songs from the Northern Territory* (Alice M. Moyle, compiler). Australian Institute of Aboriginal and Torres Strait Islander Studies: AIAS 1–5. 1964, [1995]. 5 CDs.

1657 *Tribal Music of Australia* (A. P. Elkin, compiler). Custom Compact Disc Series. Smithsonian Folkways: F-4439. 1953, 2000s. CD.

VIDEOS

1658 *Groote Eylandt Music and Dance* (Alice M. Moyle, compiler). Australian Institute of Aboriginal and Torres Strait Islander Studies. 1969, 2000s. DVD.

1659 *A Walbiri Fire Ceremony, Ngatjakula Yuendumu, Central Australia, August, 1967* (Nicolas Peterson, compiler). Australian Institute of Aboriginal and Torres Strait Islander Studies. 1977, 2000s. DVD.

Queensland

ANTHOLOGY

1660 *The Bora of the Pascoe River, Cape York Peninsula, Northeast Australia* (Wolfgang Laade, compiler). Custom Compact Disc Series. Smithsonian Folkways: F-4211. 1975, 2000s. CD.

VIDEO

1661 *Lurugu*. Australian Institute of Aboriginal and Torres Strait Islander Studies. 1973, 2000s. DVD.

Torres Strait

INDIVIDUAL ARTIST

1662 Anu, Christine. *Stylin' Up*. Mushroom: MUSH32059.2. 1995. CD.

ANTHOLOGY

1663 *Modern Music of the Torres Strait* (Jeremy Beckett, compiler). Australian Institute of Aboriginal and Torres Strait Islander Studies: AIAS-15. 1981, 2000s. CD.

Western Australia

ANTHOLOGY

1664 *Songs from the Kimberleys* (Alice M. Moyle, compiler). Australian Institute of Aboriginal and Torres Strait Islander Studies: AIAS 13 CD. 1968, 1996. CD.

Australia

GROUP

1665 Not Drowning, Waving. *Tabaran* (George Telek). WEA: 903172999-2. 1990, 2005. CD.

MELANESIA

Fiji

INDIVIDUAL ARTISTS AND GROUPS

1666 Black Rose. *Voices of Nature*. Mangrove: MGVCD 1220. 2000. CD.

1667 Nawaka Entertainment Group and Rewases Entertainment Group. *Bula Fiji Bula: Music of the Fiji Islands*. ARC Music: EUCD 1651. 2001. CD.

1668 Vuatalevu, Saimone. *My Originals*. Mangrove: MGV CD 1330. 2001. CD.

ANTHOLOGIES

1669 *Fiji: Songs of Love and Homeland: String Band Music*. Smithsonian Folkways: UNES 08316. 2014. CD.

1670 *Tautoga: And Other Songs and Dances of Rotuma* (Ad Linkels and Lucia Linkels, compilers). Anthology of Pacific Music, 12. Pan: PAN 2097 CD. 1996, 1998. CD.

1671 *Viti Levu: The Multi-Cultural Heart of Fiji* (Ad Linkels and Lucia Linkels, compilers). Anthology of Pacific Music, 14. Pan: PAN 2096 CD. 1986, 2000. CD.

Indonesia

ANTHOLOGY

1672 *Music of Biak, Irian Jaya* (Philip Yampolsky, compiler). Music of Indonesia, 10. Smithsonian Folkways: SFW 40426. 1993, 1996. CD.

New Caledonia

ANTHOLOGIES

1673 *La Compil Choc*. Mangrove: MGV CD 1240. 2000. CD.

1674 *New Caledonia: Kanak Dance and Music* (Raymond Ammann, compiler). Archives Internationales de Musique Populaire, 48. VDE-Gallo; AIMP: VDE CD-923. 1993, 1997. CD.

Papua New Guinea

INDIVIDUAL ARTIST

1675 Telek, George. *Telek*. Origin: OR 30. 1994. CD.

ANTHOLOGIES

1676 *Bosavi: Rainforest Music from Papua New Guinea* (Steven Feld, compiler). Smithsonian Folkways: SFW 40487. 1976, 2001. 3 CDs.

1677 *Dema: Music of the Marind Anim: The Verschueren Collection 1962.* Anthology of Music from West Papua, 2. Pan Records: 4018. 2008. CD.

1678 *Healing, Feasting and Magical Ritual: Songs and Dances from Papua New Guinea* (John Thornley, compiler). Topic World Series. Topic: TSCD 918. 1987, 2001. CD.

1679 *The Living, Dead and Dying: Music of the New Guinea Wape* (William E. Mitchell, compiler). Custom Compact Disc Series. Smithsonian Folkways: F-4269. 1978, 2000s. CD.

1680 *Muo Remé: Dance of the Cassowary: The Anceaux Collection.* Anthology of Music from West Papua, 1. Pan Records: 4013. 2002. CD.

1681 *Music from South New Guinea* (Wolfgang Laade, compiler). Custom Compact Disc Series. Smithsonian Folkways: F-4216. 1971, 2000s. CD.

1682 *Sacred Flute Music from New Guinea, Vol. 1: Madang* (Ragnar Johnson and Jessica Mayer, compilers). Rounder: CD 5154. 1976, 1999. CD.

1683 ★*Voices of the Rainforest* (Steven Feld, compiler). Rykodisc: RCD 10173. 1991. CD.

VIDEO

1684 *Kawelka: Ongka's Big Moka.* Disappearing World. Shanachie Entertainment Corp.: 925. 1974, 2003. DVD.

Solomon Islands

GROUPS

1685 Choir of All Saints, Honiara and Melanesian Brotherhood, Tabalia. *Chants from the Thin Red Line: Melanesian Choirs: The Blessed Islands.* RCA Victor: 09026-63470-2. 1999. CD.

1686 Narasirato Pan Pipers. *Solomon Islands: Cry of the Ancestors.* Phantom Sound & Vision. 2008. CD.

ANTHOLOGIES

1687 *Polynesian Dances of Bellona (Mungiki) Solomon Islands* (Jane Mink Rossen and Hugo Zemp, compilers). Custom Compact Disc Series. Smithsonian Folkways: FE 4274. 1978, 2000s. CD.

1688 *Polynesian Songs and Games from Bellona (Mungiki), Solomon Islands* (Jane Mink Rossen, compiler). Custom Compact Disc Series. Smithsonian Folkways: FE 4273. 1976, 2000s. CD.

1689 *Solomon Islands: Fataleka and Baegu Music from Malaita = Iles Salomon: musique fataleka et baegu de Malaita* (Hugo Zemp, compiler). Musiques & Musiciens du Monde. Auvidis: D 8027. 1969, 1990. CD.

1690 *Solomon Islands: The Sounds of Bamboo: Instrumental Music of the 'Are'are People of Malaita.* Music of the Earth. Multicultural Media: MCM 3007. 1988, 1997. CD.

Vanuatu

INDIVIDUAL ARTIST

1691 Quai, Vanessa. *Best of Vanessa Quai.* Mangrove: MGV CD 1820. 2004. CD.

ANTHOLOGIES

1692 *Musiques du Vanuatu: Fêtes et mystères = Music of Vanuatu: Celebrations and Mysteries.* Inédit. Maison des Cultures du Monde: W 260147. 2013. CD.

1693 *Vanuatu: The Music Tradition of West Futuna.* Unesco Collection. Auvidis: D 8274. 1998. CD.

1694 *Vanuatu: New Hebrides (Nouvelles-Hebrides): Singsing-Danis Kastom (Musiques Coutumieres; Custom Music)* (Peter Crowe, compiler). Archives Internationales de Musique Populaire, 34. VDE-Gallo; AIMP: VDE CD-796. 1972, 1994. CD.

MELANESIA
GENERAL ANTHOLOGY

1695 ★*Spirit of Melanesia* (David Fanshawe, compiler). Saydisc: CD-SDL 418. 1978, 1998. CD.

MICRONESIA
Kiribati

ANTHOLOGY

1696 *Rabi: The New Home of the Exiled Banabans from Ocean Island* (Ad Linkels and Lucia Linkels, compilers). Anthology of Pacific Music, 15. Pan: PAN 2095. 2000. CD.

Micronesia (Federated States)

INDIVIDUAL ARTIST

1697 Benian, Dano. *Pohnpei Time*. Unisound Recordings: UNI-9201 C. 2000–[2008]. CD.

MICRONESIA GENERAL ANTHOLOGIES

1698 ★*Spirit of Micronesia* (David Fanshawe, compiler). Saydisc: CD-SDL 414. 1995. CD.

1699 *Music of Micronesia: Guam, Northern Marianas, F.S.M., Marshal Islands* (Hikaru Koide, compiler). JVC World Sounds Special. Victor Entertainment: JVC: VICG-5277. 1993. CD.

POLYNESIA

Austral Islands (French Polynesia)

INDIVIDUAL ARTISTS AND GROUPS

1700 Tahitian Choir. *The Tahitian Choir: Rapa Iti*. Triloka: 7192-2. 1992. CD.

1701 Tubuai Choir. *Tubuai Choir: From the Polynesian Odyssey*. Shanachie: 64049. 1993. CD.

Cook Islands

ANTHOLOGIES

1702 *Imene Tapu: And Other Choral Music of the Cook Islands* (Ad Linkels and Lucia Linkels, compilers). Anthology of Pacific Music, 13. Pan: PAN 7099 CD. 1992, 1999. CD.

1703 *Te Kuki 'Airani: The Cook Islands Songs, Rhythms and Dances* (Ad Linkels and Lucia Linkels, compilers). Anthology of Pacific Music, 10. Pan: PAN 2099 CD. 1992, 1998. CD.

Easter Island

GROUP

1704 Hotu Family. *Chants de l'Île de Paques (Songs from Easter Island)*. Musique du Monde. Buda: 92553-2. 1993. CD.

ANTHOLOGY

1705 *Te pito o te henua: End of the World: Easter Island Songs and Dances*. Ethnic Series. Pan: PAN 2077 CD. 1996. CD.

Hawaii

INDIVIDUAL ARTISTS AND GROUPS

1706 Kamakawiwo'ole, Israel. *Facing Future*. Mountain Apple: BBCD-5901. 1993. CD.

1707 Kanaka'ole, Aunty Edith. *Hi'Ipoi I Ka 'Ain Aloha: Cherish the Beloved Land (Na 'Oiwi)*. Legendary Classic Series. Hula: CDHS-568. 1979, 2003. CD.

1708 Kane, Ray. *Punahele*. Hawaiian Slack Key Guitar Masters Series. Dancing Cat: 08022 380001-2. 1994. CD.

ANTHOLOGIES

1709 ★*The Descendants (Original Motion Picture Soundtrack)*. Sony Classical: 98456. 2011. CD.

1710 *Hana Hou—Do It Again: Hawaiian Hula Chants and Songs*. Anthology of Pacific Music, 3. Pan: PAN 2033 CD. 1993. CD.

1711 *Hawaiian Slack Key Guitar Masters: Instrumental Collection*. Hawaiian Slack Key Guitar Masters Series. Dancing Cat: 08022 38032-2. 1995. CD.

1712 *Vintage Hawaiian Music: Steel Guitar Masters, 1928–1934*. Rounder: CD 1052. 1989. CD.

1713 *Vintage Hawaiian Music: The Great Singers, 1928–1934*. Rounder: CD 1053. 1989. CD.

1714 *Hawaiian Drum Dance Chants: Sounds of Power in Time* (Elizabeth Tater, compiler). Smithsonian Folkways: SF 40015. 1923, 1989. CD.

VIDEOS

1715 *Hawaiian Rainbow*. Fox Lorber Associates: WHE 73032. 1987, 1999. DVD.

1716 *Holo Mai Pele* (Halau o Kekuhi; Catherine Tatge, dir.). Great Performances, Dance in America. Pacific Islanders in Communications and International Cultural Programming. 2001, 2004. DVD.

New Zealand

INDIVIDUAL ARTISTS AND GROUPS

1717 Oceania. *Oceania*. Point Music: 536 775-2. 1999. CD.

1718 Te Runga Rawa. *New Zealand: Maori Songs = Nouvelle-Zelande: chants Maoris*. Air Mail Music. Sunset-France: SA 141139. 2000, 2007. CD.

1719 Te Vaka. *Ki Mua*. Spirit of Play. 1999. CD.

ANTHOLOGIES

1720   ★*Maori Songs of New Zealand.* Custom Compact Disc Series. Smithsonian Folkways: F-4433. 1952, 2000s. CD.

1721   *Once Were Warriors: Soundtrack Album.* Tangata: TANG 514. 1994. CD.

1722   *Songs of New Zealand.* World of Music. Wizard Entertainment: 500142. 1996. CD.

VIDEO

1723   *Maori Culture, Traditions, and History.* Dove Video Productions. 2003. DVD.

Samoa

ANTHOLOGIES

1724   *Fa'a-Samoa, the Samoa Way: Between Conch Shell and Disco.* Anthology of Pacific Music, 6. Pan: PAN 2066. 1982, 1995. CD.

1725   *Samoan Songs: A Historical Collection* (Richard M. Moyle, compiler). Music of Oceania. Musicaphon: M 52705. 1999. CD.

Tahiti

ANTHOLOGIES

1726   *Drums of Bora Bora and Songs of Tahiti.* GNP, Crescendo: GNPD 2214. 1950s, 1993. CD.

1727   *Polynesia: From Bora Bora to Tahiti.* Edition Pierre Verger. Playasound: PS 66527. 2006. CD.

1728   *Tahiti, Belle Epoque: All Time Tahitian Favorites* (Eddie Lund, compiler). Manuiti: S 65807. 1991. CD.

1729   *Tahiti: The Gauguin Years: Songs and Dances* (Francis Mazière, compiler). Explorer Series. Nonesuch: 79715-2. 1968, 2003. CD.

Tonga

ANTHOLOGIES

1730   *Afo 'O e 'Ofa, Strings of Love: Tongan Stringband Music.* Anthology of Pacific Music, 9. Pan: PAN 2088 CD. 1997. CD.

1731   *Chants from the Kingdom of Tonga* (David Fanshawe, compiler). ARC Music: EUCD 2159. 2008. CD.

1732   *Faikava: The Tongan Kava Circle.* Anthology of Pacific Music, 2. Pan: PAN 2022 CD. 1993. CD.

1733   *Ko e Temipale Tapu: The Holy Temple: Church Music of Tonga.* Choral Series. Pan: PAN 7007 CD. 1996. CD.

1734   *Tonga: Sounds of Change* (Ad Linkels and Lucia Linkels, compilers). Anthology of Pacific Music, 1. Pan: PAN 2098 CD. 1986, 1998. CD.

Tuvalu

ANTHOLOGY

1735   *Tuvalu: A Polynesian Atoll Society* (Ad Linkels and Lucia Linkels, compilers). Anthology of Pacific Music, 5. Pan: PAN 2055 CD. 1990, 1994. CD.

POLYNESIA
GENERAL ANTHOLOGIES

1736   *Hula, Haka, Hoko! Polynesian Dances* (Ad Linkels and Lucia Linkels, compilers.). Pan: PAN 162 CD. 1997. CD.

1737   *Music of Marginal Polynesia: Fiji, Wallis and Futuna, Tuvalu.* JVC World Sounds Special. JVC: VICG-5276. 1977, 1994. CD.

1738   ★*Pacific Chants: Polynesian Himene [and] the "Singing Reef"* (David Fanshawe, compiler). ARC Music: EUCD 1743. 2002. CD.

1739   *Percussions Polynesiennes.* South Pacific Drums. Playasound: PS 65066. 1990. CD.

1740   *Polynesia* (Ad Linkels and Lucia Linkels, compilers). Pan Glossary, 5. Pan: PAN 1205. 2003. CD.

1741   ★*Spirit of Polynesia* (David Fanshawe, compiler). Saydisc: CD-SDL 403. 1994. CD.

1742   *Australian Folksongs and Ballads* (John Greenway, performer and compiler). Custom Compact Disc Series. Smithsonian Folkways: F-8718. 1959, 2000s. CD.

1743   *Fiafia: Dances from the South Pacific for Children and Adults.* Pan: PAN 150 CD. 1979, 1994. CD.

1744   ★*Island Music* (David Fanshawe, compiler). Explorer Series. Nonesuch: 79723-2. 1981, 2003. CD.

1745   *Music of the South Pacific* (David Fanshawe, compiler). ARC Music: EUCD 1709. 2002. CD.

1746   *Musical Mariner: Pacific Journey* (Steven Isserlis and David Fanshawe, compiler). Mercury: 426 185-2. 1989. CD.

1747 *Reggae Ina Pacific.* Mangrove: MGV CD 880. 1998. CD.

1748 ★*The Rough Guide to Australian Aboriginal Music* (Bruce Elder, compiler). Rough Guide. World Music Network: RGNET 1207 CD. 1999, 2008. CD.

1749 *Songs of Aboriginal Australia and Torres Strait* (Alice M. Moyle, compiler). Custom Compact Disc Series. Smithsonian Folkways: FE 4102. 1994, 2000s. CD.

1750 ★*South Pacific Islands.* Putumayo World Music: PUT 231-2. 2004. CD.

VIDEOS

1751 *Dances of Life.* Pacific Islanders in Communications and International Cultural Programming (Catherine Tatge, dir.). 2005. DVD.

1752 *Musical Mariner: Pacific Journey* (David Fanshawe, compiler). Lucky Country Productions: DVD 02. 1987. 2 DVDs.

1753 *Pacific Video Hits, Vols. 1 and 2.* Mangrove Hits Collection. Mangrove: MGV DVD 001, MGVDVD 004. 2003, 2006. 4 DVDs.

4

Classical, Traditional, and Popular Music of Egypt and North Africa, the Middle East, and Central Asia

Compiled by AARON BITTEL, ROBIN P. HARRIS, ALAN KARASS, CRAIG MACRAE, MAUREEN RUSSELL, *and* JEFF SCHWARTZ

Anthologies are included in this chapter within regional areas and also in chapter 7, "International Anthologies" (including, in particular, devotional and diaspora anthologies). Transnational groups are an important consideration (Jewish, Islamic, and Kurdish music also exists in Eastern Europe and elsewhere around the globe). A few useful older resources include *Archives de la musique Arabe* (Ocora, 1908–20), *Music in the World of Islam* (Topic, 1960–75), and *Le Saint Coran, vols. 1–6* (Artistes Arabes Associés, 1993). As in other chapters, the geographical breakdowns here are for organizational purposes only and should not be construed as musical divisions.

EGYPT AND NORTH AFRICA

Compiled by Alan Karass

Middle Eastern music typically manifests improvisation on elaborate melodic and rhythmic modes, a preference for the voice and sung poetry, and lengthy performances that bring together successions of musical genres, both vocal and instrumental. The music of North Africa and Egypt reflects the rich cultural heritage of the region, colonial influences, and musical traditions of the Arabic world. Important genres of the region include raï (Algeria), chaabi (Morocco and Algeria), Gnawa and Berber music (Morocco), sha'abi (Egypt), and Nubian music (Egypt). Forms of classical, popular, and folk music appear throughout the area. Some sound recordings are available through library approval plans and Amazon, as well as from vendors specializing in North African and Middle Eastern music, such as Maqam (www

.maqam.com). Publishers who carry high-quality traditional music publications are the Institut du Monde Arabe (France); Le Chant du Monde (France); Buda Musique (France); and Maison des Culturesdu Monde (France). Titles that are difficult to obtain are omitted in many cases.

EGYPT

INDIVIDUAL ARTISTS AND GROUPS

1754   Asmahan. *Asmahan. Legends of the 20th Century.* EMI Music Arabia: 94631093128. 1940, 2000. CD.

1755   Asmahan and Farid el Atrache. *Asmahan and Farid.* Baidaphon: BGCD 602. 1990. CD.

1756   Atlas, Natacha
    1756.1   *Ayeshenti.* Mantra Records: MNTCD 1024. 2003. CD.
    1756.2   *Gedida.* Mantra Records: MNTCD 1014. 1998. CD.
    1756.3   *Halim.* Koch: CD 7981. [1997–1998]. CD.
    1756.4   *Something Dangerous.* Mantra Records: MNTCD 1035. 2001. CD.

1757   Atrache, Farid el
    1757.1   *Farid el Atrache—25 ans déjà.* EMI Music Arabia: 07243 526416 2 8. 2000. CD.
    1757.2   ★*Legend: The Best of Farid el Atrache.* MSI Music: 94639385027. 2007. CD.

1758   Diab, Amr
    1758.1   *Bi-adiki Ta'ala.* Rotana: ROT1796. 2011. CD

1758.2 *Tamally Maak*. EMI Music Arabia: 07243 528264 2 1. 2000. CD

1758.3 *Very Best of Amr Diab*. MSI Music: 724353511128. 2001. CD.

1759 Din, Hamza el-
   1759.1 *Eclipse*. Rykodisc: RCD 10103. 1978, 1988. CD.
   1759.2 *Escalay (Waterwheel): Oud Music from Nubia*. Explorer Series. Nonesuch. 1998. CD.
   1759.3 ★*Wish*. Sounds True: STA M 110 D. 1999. CD.

1760 Ensemble al-Tanbûrah. *Simsimiyya of Port Said*. Institut du Monde Arabe: 321026. 1996, 1999. CD.

1761 Fadl, Mahmud Ahmad. *Drummers of the Nile in Town: Cairosonic*. Piranha: CD-PIR 1791. 2000, 2003. CD.

1762 George Sawaya Trio. *Arabic Songs of Lebanon and Egypt*. Custom Compact Disc Series. Smithsonian Folkways: FW 6925. 1956, 2001. CD.

1763 Hafez, Abdel Halim
   1763.1 ★*Abdel Halim Hafez: 20th Anniversary Edition*. EMI Music Arabia: 0946 310642-2 7. 1961, 1997. 2 CDs.
   1763.2 *Kariat al Fengan*. EMI: CD 310502-2. 1996. CD.

1764 Hakim
   1764.1 *Lela*. EMI: 186 830 000 2. 2004. CD.
   1764.2 *Talakik*. Mondo Melodia: 186 850 053 2. 2002. CD.
   1764.3 *Yaho*. Mondo Melodia: 186 850 017 2. 2000. CD.

1765 Kuban, Ali Hassan
   1765.1 *From Nubia to Cairo*. Piranha: EFA 01874-2. 2000. CD.
   1765.2 *Real Nubian*. Piranha: CD-PIR 1575. 2001. CD.
   1765.3 *Walk Like a Nubian*. Piranha: PIR 43-2. 1994. CD.

1766 Kulthum, Umm
   1766.1 *Atlal*. EMI Music Arabia: 724352642625. 1988, 2000. CD.
   1766.2 *Awwalah fī al-Gharām*. Sono Cairo: Sono 150-E. 1999. CD.
   1766.3 *Classics*. EMI Music Arabia: 72432981427. 2000. CD.
   1766.4 *Enta Omri*. Sayyidat al-ghina al-'Arabi Umm Kulthum = The Diva of Arab

Music Oum Kolthoum. Ṣawt al-Qāhirah: 94 SDCD 01 B 60. 1999. CD.
   1766.5 ★*Ruba'iyat al-Khayyam*. Sayyidat al-ghina al-'Arabi Umm Kulthum = The Diva of Arab Music Oum Kolthoum. Ṣawt al-Qāhirah: 94 SDCD 01 B 51. 1990. CD.

1767 ★La Châdhiliyya. *Sufi Chants from Cairo, Egypt* (Mohammed El Helbawy, cond.) Institut du Monde Arabe: 321023. 1999. CD.

1768 Mounir, Mohamed. *Earth—Peace*. Mondo Melodia: 186 850 067 2. 2002. CD.

1769 Murad, Layla. *Ajmal Ughniyāt Laylá Murād = The Best of Leila Mourad*. Cairophon: CXG CD 615. 1990. CD.

1770 Musiciens du Nil. *Charcoal Gypsies*. Real World: CAROL 2366-2. 1996. CD.

1771 Redouane, Aïcha. *Songs of the Arab Renaissance in the Middle East, 19th and 20th Centuries* (al-Adwâr Ensemble). Institut du Monde Arabe: IMACD 17. 1995. CD. *See also* Middle East, Levant.

1772 Ruby
   1772.1 *Eb'a Abelni*. EMI: 7243 874293 2 1. 2004. CD.
   1772.2 *Msheet Wara Ehsasy*. EMI: 0946 379666 2 4. 2007. CD.

1773 Said, Mokhtar al-.
   1773.1 *Amar 14: Jalilah's Raks Sharki 2*. Piranha: 452. 1994. CD.
   1773.2 ★*Raks Sharki: Classic Egyptian Dance Music*. Piranha: PIR 41-2. 1994. CD.

1774 Salamat. *Mambo al Soudani*. Piranha: 71875018812. 1994. CD.

1775 Sayyid Darwish. *Immortel Sheikh Sayed Darwiche*. Baidaphon: BGCD 618. 1996. CD.

1776 ★Soumbati, Riad el-. *Roubaiyat el Khayam*. EMI: 724352994526. 1975, 2000. CD.

1777 Tawfic, Ehab. *Habib el Alb*. EMI Music Arabia: 07243 531759 2 4. 2001. CD.

1778 Wahab, Mohammed Abdel.
   1778.1 *Cleopatra*. Arabian Masters. EMI Music Arabia: 7243 8471382 9.03098. 1999. CD.
   1778.2 ★*Treasures*. EMI: 31076 12. 1998. CD.

ANTHOLOGIES

1779 *'Abd al-Hayy Hilmi, 1857-1912: An Anthology.* Foundation for Arab Music Archiving and Research: P1131188. 1903, 2013. 4 CDs.

1780 ★*Arabian Masters: The Greatest Classics of Arab Music.* Virgin: LC 0542. 1999, 2002. 2 CDs.

1781 *Coptic Music.* Custom Compact Disc Series. Smithsonian Folkways: FR 8960. 1960, 2003. CD.

1782 ★*Egypt: Cairo to Nubia, the Source of Arabic Music.* Rough Guide. World Music Network: RGNET 1114 CD. 2003. CD.

1783 *Music of Upper Egypt: Played on the Rababa, Mizar, Arghul, and Darabuka.* Custom Compact Disc Series. Smithsonian Folkways: FW 8512. 1979, 2001. CD.

1784 *Rabab: Egyptian Singing and Epic Songs.* Custom Compact Disc Series. Smithsonian Folkways: FW 8452. 1982, 2003. CD.

VIDEO

1785 ★*Umm Kulthum: A Voice Like Egypt.* Arab Film Distribution: AFD1188D. 1996, 2006. DVD.

NORTH AFRICA

Algeria

INDIVIDUAL ARTISTS AND GROUPS

1786 Abdelli (Abderrahmane Abdelli)
1786.1 *Among Brothers.* Real World: 7243 5 81313 2 1. 1998, 2003. CD.
1786.2 *New Moon.* Real World: 2353-2. 1995. CD.

1787 Akli D. *Ma Yela.* Because Music: 3113722. 2006. CD.

1788 Amrouche, Taos. *Chants de Taos Amrouche: Chants Berbères de Kabylie.* L'empreinte digitale. 2002. 5 CDs.

1789 Faudel
1789.1 *Autre soleil.* Universal. 2004. CD.
1789.2 *Baïda.* Mondo Melodia: 186 850 045 2. 1997, 1999. CD.
1789.3 *Samra.* Mondo Melodia: 186 850. 2001. CD.

1790 Fella
1790.1 *La Ma Raayto.* Rotana: CD ROT 1341. 2007. CD.

1790.2 *Sahrat Tarab.* Phantasm Imports. 2009. CD.

1791 Hasni, Cheb. *Lover's Rai.* Rounder: Rounder CD 5078. 1997. CD.

1792 Idir
1792.1 *Chasseurs de lumières.* Blue Silver: 095 2. 1993. CD.
1792.2 *Identités.* Saint Georges: SAN 4952852. 1999. CD.

1793 Khaled
1793.1 *Kenza.* Ark21: 186 850 012 2. 1999. CD.
1793.2 *Khaled.* Cohiba: 162 221 101-2. 1992. CD.
1793.3 *Sahra.* Island Records: 314-537 510-2. 1996. CD.

1794 l'Oranaise, Reinette. *Mémoires.* Blue Silver: 50345-2 BS 332. 1994. CD.

1795 Lounes, Matoub. *Lettreouverte aux . . .* Blue Silver: 846327-2. 1998. CD.

1796 Mami, Cheb
1796.1 *Dellali.* Mondo Melodia, Ark 21: 186 850 025 2. 2001. CD.
1796.2 *Layalli.* EMI: EMI 787422. 2006. CD.
1796.3 *Let Me Rai.* H. R. Music: CDL 57142. 1990. CD.
1796.4 *Meli Meli.* Ark21: 1868500072. 1999. CD.

1797 Massi, Souad
1797.1 *Deb = Heartbroken.* Wrasse Records: 96. 2003. CD.
1797.2 *Mesk Elil = Honeysuckle.* Wrasse Records: WRASS 170. 2005. CD.

1798 Menguellet, Ait. *Chants and poesie de Kabylie: 12 titres originaux.* Blue Silver: 313-2. 1994. CD.

1799 Mêzell, Iness. *Wedfel.* Silex: Y225077. 1999. CD.

1800 Remitti, Cheikha
1800.1 *Étoile du raï.* Culture Press: CP 5020. 2000. CD.
1800.2 *Trab Music.* Culture Press: CP 5014. 1999, 2000. CD.

1801 Seba. *Ewa!* Tinder: 860952. 2000. CD.

1802 Taha, Rachid
1802.1 *Diwân.* Island Records: 314-539 953-2. 1998. CD.
1802.2 *Live.* Ark21: 186 850 052 2. 2001. CD.
1802.3 *Made in Medina.* Barclay: 186 850 019 2. 2001. CD.

1803 Takfarinas. *Yal.* Tinder: 42859582. 2000. CD.

1804 Warda
    1804.1 *Fi Youm Wi Leil.* Super D, Phantom Sound: 94631055324. 2008. CD.
    1804.2 *Warda.* Hemisphere: 7243 8 55649 2 5. 1997. CD.

ANTHOLOGIES

1805 *Algerian Berber Music.* Custom Compact Disc Series. Smithsonian Folkways: FE 4341. 1966, 2003. CD.

1806 *Kabylie Au Coeur.* Virgin. 2001. CD.

1807 ★*1, 2, 3 soleils.* Mondo Melodia, Ark 21: 186 850 046 2. 1998, 1999. CD.

1808 ★*Rough Guide to Rai.* Rough Guide. World Music Network: RGNET 1100 CD. 2002. CD.

1809 *Tresors de la musiquealgerienne = Treasures of Algerian Music.* Institut du Monde Arabe: 321.054.055. 2003. CD.

VIDEO

1810 *1, 2, 3 soleils: Khaled, Taha, Faudel en Concert.* Barclay: 060 869 9. 1998. DVD.

Libya

INDIVIDUAL ARTISTS

1811 Aatar, Ayman el-. *Bahibak.* EMI. 2005. CD.

1812 Fewet, Touareg de. *Touareg de Fewet: Lybie, Musiques du Sahara.* Musique du Monde. Buda: 1978312. 2001. CD.

1813 Jilani, Cheb. *Jilani.* EMI. 2004. CD.

1814 Shari, Hamid el-
    1814.1 *Ainy.* Virgin. 1997. CD.
    1814.2 *Ghazaly.* EMI: 724352528325. 2000. CD.

Morocco

INDIVIDUAL ARTISTS AND GROUPS

1815 Aatabou, Najat. *Voice of the Atlas.* GlobeStyle: CDORBD 069. 1994. CD.

1816 Aisha Kandisha's Jarring Effects
    1816.1 *El Buya.* Barraka el Farnatshi: Barbarity 002-CD. 1991. CD.
    1816.2 *Koyo Habib.* Barraka el Farnatshi. 2000. CD.

1817 Aïssawa of Meknès and Tayfa of Cheikh Sidi Mohamed. *Confrérie des Aïssawa = The Aïssawa Confraternity.* Ocora: C 560140. 1998, 2001. CD.

1818 Alaoui, Amina. *Alcantara.* Auvidis: B 6872. 1998. CD.

1819 Compagnies Musicales du Tafilalet. *L'appel des oasis = The Call of the Oases.* Institut du Monde Arabe: 321.061. 2002, 2004. CD.

1820 El Lebrijano (Juan Fernández Peña) and Orquesta Arábigo Andaluza. *Casablanca.* Capitol: 7243 4 93342 2 9. 1998. CD.

1821 Erraji, Hassan, and Arabesque. *Nikriz.* Riverboat: TUGCD 001. 1989. CD.

1822 Had Saïd Berrada Group of Fez. *Rituel de transe des Aïssawa de Fès.* Institut du Monde Arabe: 50312-2. 1994, 1995. CD.

1823 Hakmoun, Hassan. *Gift of the Gnawa.* Flying Fish: FF 70571. 1991. CD.

1824 Hasna. *Hasna.* EMI Music Arabia: 07243 592003 2 3. 2003. CD.

1825 Hassan, Chalf
    1825.1 *Artam el-Arab.* Koch: 743037210522. 2007. CD.
    1825.2 *Rhythms of Morocco.* ARC Music: EUCD 1906. 2005. CD.

1826 Houssaine Kili. *Mountain to Mohamed.* Tropical Music: 68.818. 2001. CD.

1827 Jilala de Fès. *Confrérie des Jilala = Jilala Confraternity.* Ocora: C 560131. 1998, 2000. CD.

1828 Kersit, Cherifa. *Berber Blues.* Long Distance: 3063582. 2000. CD.

1829 Lebrijano, Juan Pena, and Orquesta Andalusi de Tanger. *Encuentros.* Ariola Eurodisc: CDORB 024. 1985. CD.

1830 Maghribi, Hassan Al. *Daftar al Oshaaq.* Africana. 2006. CD.

1831 Nass el Ghiwan
    1831.1 *Best of Nass el Ghiwan.* Super D, Phantom Sound: 0946 389523 2 9. 2008. CD.
    1831.2 *Chants Gnawa du Maroc.* Buda/Ades: 82468-2. 1989. CD.

1832 Nass Marrakech. *Bouderbala.* World Village: 498001. 2001. CD.

1833 Orchestre Moulay Ahmed Loukili de Rabat. *Nawbat al-Ushshāq: Nûbâ al-Ushshâq.* Inédit.

Maison des Cultures du Monde: W 260014. 1989, 1990. 6 CDs.

1834 Rmiki, Ihsan. *Al-Samâa: Audition spirituelle extatique.* Institut du Monde Arabe: HM 321.075. 2004. CD.

1835 Saad, Hoda. *Tayr al-Hob.* Rotana. 2011. CD.

1836 Said, Samira
 1836.1 *Ayaam Hayati.* EMI Arabia: 509923631823. 2008. CD.
 1836.2 *Youm Wara Youm.* Mondo Melodia, Ark 21: 186 850 066 2. 2002. CD.

1837 Salah, Cheik. *Maroc: Musique Arabo-Andalouse.* Buda: 82509-2. 1999. CD.

1838 Sawt el Atlas. *Donia.* Tinder: 861002. 2001. CD.

1839 Soultan, Ahmed. *Code.* CDBY. 2009. CD.

1840 Toulali, Houcine. *Malhûn de Meknès = The Malhûn of Meknès.* Institut du Monde Arabe: 321005. 1994, 1999. CD.

ANTHOLOGIES

1841 *Ballads, Wedding Songs, and Piyyutim of the Sephardic Jews of Tetuan and Tangier, Morocco.* Custom Compact Disc Series. Smithsonian Folkways: F-4208. 1983, 2000. CD.

1842 *Chants du Moyen-Atlas, Maroc = Songs from the Middle Atlas, Morocco.* Institut du Monde Arabe: 321048. 2002. CD.

1843 *Gnawa Music of Marrakesh: Night Spirit Masters.* Axiom: 314-510 147-2. 1990. CD.

1844 *Maroc: Anthologie d'al-Melhun.* Maison des Cultures du Monde: W 260016. 1990. 3 CDs.

1845 *Morocco: Crossroads of Time.* Ellipsis Arts: 1559612894. 1959, 1995. CD.

1846 ★*Music of Islam and Sufism in Morocco.* Rounder: CD 5145. 1970s, 1999. CD.

1847 *Music of Morocco.* Ethnic Folkways Library. Smithsonian Folkways: FE 4339. 1966, 2001. CD.

1848 ★*Rough Guide to the Music of Morocco: Desert Sounds from Casablanca to Marrakech.* Rough Guide. World Music Network: RGNET 1128 CD. 2004. CD.

1849 *Sacred Music of the Moroccan Jews.* Rounder: 82161-5087-2. 1959, 2000. 2 CDs.

1850 ★*World of Gnawa.* Rounder: 82161-5080-2. 2001, 1990. 2 CDs.

VIDEO

1851 Belkani, Brahim el-, and Sirbiri Samake. *Wijdan: Mystery of Gnawa Trance Music.* Possible Pictures. 2008. DVD.

Tunisia

INDIVIDUAL ARTISTS AND GROUPS

1852 Annabi, Amina
 1852.1 *Amina Annabi.* Mercury: 5380842. 1999. CD.
 1852.2 *Nomad: Best of Amina.* Mondo Melodia: 186 850 027 2. 2001. CD.
 1852.3 *Yalil.* Mango: 539 892-2. 1989. CD.

1853 Benali, Ghalia, and Timnaa. *Wild Harissa.* Network: 38817. 2001. CD.

1854 Bouchnak, Lotfi. *Live in Berlin.* Wergo: SM 1532 2. 1998, 2002. CD.

1855 Brahem, Anouar
 1855.1 *Barzakh.* ECM: ECM 1432. 1991. CD.
 1855.2 *Pas du chat noir.* ECM: ECM 1792. 2001, 2002. CD.

1856 Brahem, Anouar, and the Anouar Brahem Trio. *Astrakan Café.* ECM: ECM 1718. 2000. CD.

1857 Chekili, Fawzi. *Bedouine.* Blue Jasmin: OTPDA 395. 1997, 1998. CD.

1858 Fakhet, Amina. *Sultan Hubbak.* EMI Music Arabia: 07243 528352 2 5. 2000. CD.

1859 Hadia
 1859.1 *Hadia* CD.
 1859.2 *Hadia 2007.* MSI Music: 5099950183722. 2007. CD.

1860 Latifa. *Maaloumet Akida.* Universal: 325913017677. 2007. CD.

1861 Lotfi Jormana Group. *Music of Islam, Vol. 8: Folkloric Music of Tunisia.* Naxos Music Library: 13148-2. 2004. CD.

1862 M'barek, Sonia. *Tunisia: Takht.* World Network: 32.375. 1998, 1999. CD.

1863 Rebai, Saber al-
 1863.1 *Ajmal Nissa el Dounya.* Rotana: CD FUN 135. 2006. CD.
 1863.2 *Ghorbah.* Rotana: 6281130204009. 2006. CD.

1863.3 *Khalas Tarak.* EMI Arabia: 724353701406. 2001. CD.

1864 Youseef, Dhafer

1864.1 *Digital Prophecy.* Enja Records: JENJ 3307-2. 2003. CD

1864.2 ★*Divine Shadows.* Jazzland: 6024987772249. 2006. CD

1864.3 *Electric Sufi.* Enja Records: ENJ-9412 2. 2001. CD

1865 Zekra

1865.1 *Wa Tabka Zekra.* EMI Music Arabia: 07243 860529 2 6. 2005. CD.

1865.2 *Wesh Maseeri.* EMI Arabia: 594080. 2003. CD.

1865.3 *Youm Liek.* Super D, Phantom Sound. 2008. CD.

ANTHOLOGIES

1866 ★*Hadhra.* Universal: 468 366-2. 2000. 2 CDs.

1867 *Malouf Tunisien (Inédit).* Maison des Cultures du Monde: W 260053. 1993. CD.

1868 ★*Stambeli: L'héritage des Noirs de Tunisie = Stambeli: The Legacy of the Black Tunisians.* Par les chemins productions: PLC101. 2008, 2010. CD.

1869 *Tunis chante et danse.* Editions du Layeur. 2000. CD.

1870 *Tunisia*

1870.1 ★*Vol. 1: The Classical Arab-Andalusian Music of Tunis.* Smithsonian Folkways: F-8861. 1960, 1999. CD.

1870.2 ★*Vol. 2: Religious Songs and Cantillations: Tunisia.* Custom Compact Disc Series. Smithsonian Folkways: F-8862. 1999. CD.

1870.3 ★*Vol. 3: Folk Music.* Smithsonian Folkways: FW-8863. 1962, 1990s. CD.

**NORTH AFRICA
GENERAL ANTHOLOGIES**

1871 Abdu-el-Hanid and His Orchestra. *Arabian Delight: Music from Egypt, Libya, Algeria and Morocco.* Custom Compact Disc Series. Smithsonian Folkways: MFS 434. 1965, 2001. CD.

1872 ★*Cairo to Casablanca: An Arabian Musical Odyssey.* Putumayo World Music: PUTU 143-2. 1998. CD.

1873 *North African Essentials.* Universal: 602498186114. 2004. CD.

1874 ★*Putumayo Presents Arabic Groove.* Putumayo World Music: PUT 189-2. 2001. CD.

1875 ★*Putumayo Presents North African Groove.* Putumayo World Music: PUT 237-2. 1996, 2005. CD.

1876 ★*Rough Guide to the Music of North Africa.* Rough Guide. World Music Network: RGNET 1011 CD. 1997. CD.

1877 *Secret Museum of Mankind: Ethnic Music Classics, 1925–1948: Music of North Africa.* Yazoo: 7011. 1997. CD.

MIDDLE EAST: ARABIAN PENINSULA, PERSIAN GULF, LEVANT

Compiled by Jeff Schwartz

The Middle East is a rich musical and cultural area, but there are significant obstacles to collecting. First, national, regional, and international politics are frequently unstable; second, there is a strong argument within Islam that musical entertainment is unclean, sinful, and to be avoided; and third, based on unsystematic observation, local music consumption appears to be moving directly from cassettes to MP3 (as downloads or as home-burned CD-Rs), skipping the retail CD format, which is the focus of this volume.

Nevertheless, a representative collection can be assembled. Ethnomusicological labels including Folkways and Lyrichord have covered the region, with French labels such as Musique du Monde and Institut du Monde Arabe offering particularly good documentation of the music of former French colonies, Syria and Lebanon. Also, there are distinguished expatriate performers throughout the West producing excellent recordings. Although there are regional and national variations, one can generalize a continuum of music based on songs using the systems of *maqam* (scales) and *iqaat* (rhythm), ranging from unaccompanied *oud* improvisation to songs accompanied by small groupings of *oud, qanun, ney,* violin, and percussion to larger ensembles incorporating Western orchestral and popular instruments to state-of-the-art electronic dance-pop productions. Divisions among folk, classical, and popular are more interesting as an object of study than for collection development, but libraries should collect across the range of styles.

The back catalogs of many major artists—for example, the great Lebanese diva Fairuz (for whom several alternative spellings are in use)—have not been served well by CD reissues. Packaging and distribution are problematic, and informed selection is difficult. Compilations are a safe option and may remain the best choice for many libraries until a digital alternative develops. A similar situation exists for many current popular titles. The Saudi star Mohammad Abdo has no discs readily available through the U.S. retail market. However, EMI Arabia, which dominates the Arabic pop market, produces a widely distributed and highly recommended compilation series, *Now That's What I Call Arabia!*, which offers a regular snapshot of the hit parade. The spinoffs *Now That's What I Call Love Arabia!* and *Now That's What I Call Dance Arabia!* may also be of interest.

Many items are available from library-oriented distributors such as Baker & Taylor, directly from the labels, or via Amazon, but Maqam (www.maqam.com) is the largest online vendor of Middle Eastern music and is recommended for serious collecting.

Compiler names are not listed in this discography but readers may consult the *Garland Encyclopedia of World Music, Vol. 6* to see further listings and scholars who do field work in the Middle East. Although all the Gulf listings can be considered Arabian Peninsula geographically, the citations labeled as such comprise a more cohesive musical grouping than the Gulf entries as a whole (which diverge, especially in Oman and Yemen). Three major Arabian Peninsula artists—Mohamed Ibn Faris, Dahi Ibn Walid, and Mohamed Zuwayid—are not listed individually due to lack of available recordings. The anthology *La musique de Bahreïn* (Les Artistes Arabes Associés, 1994) represents all three.

ARABIAN PENINSULA

Saudi Arabia

ANTHOLOGY

1878 *Music from South Arabia.* Custom Compact Disc Series. Smithsonian Folkways: FE 4421. 1950, 2000s. CD.

PERSIAN GULF

Bahrain

GROUP

1879 Ensemble Muhammad bin Fâris. *The Sawt in Bahrain.* Bahrain. Institut du Monde Arabe: 321.04. 2001, 2004. CD.

Kuwait

GROUP

1880 Ensemble al-Umayri. *The Sawt in Kuwait.* Institut du Monde Arabe: 321.041. 2001, 2004. CD.

Oman

ANTHOLOGY

1881 *Oman: Traditional Arts of the Sultanate of Oman.* Unesco Collection. Auvidis: D 8211. 1993. CD.

Qatar

GROUP

1882 Lelo, Mohammed Saleh Abd al-Saheb, and Haitham Hasan. *The Music of Islam, Vol. 4: Music of the Arabian Peninsula, Doha, Qatar.* Celestial Harmonies: 13143-2. 1997. CD.

United Arab Emirates

ANTHOLOGY

1883 *Music from the Arabian Gulf.* Jutland Archaeological Society Publications, 42. ARC Music: EUCD-2023. 2002. CD.

Yemen

INDIVIDUAL ARTISTS AND GROUPS

1884 ʿAjami, Hasan al-, and Muhammad al-Khamisi. *The Singing of Sanaa.* Yemen. Ocora: C 560173. 2002, 2003. CD.

1885 Association des Chantres Yéménites. *Sacred Songs from Sanaa.* Yemen. Institut du Monde Arabe: 321035. 1998, 2001. CD.

1886 Harithi, Mohammad al-. *The Hour of Solomon.* Yemen. Institut du Monde Arabe: 321032. 1997, 2001. CD.

1887 Junayd, Hamud. *Traditional Yemeni Songs.* Nimbus: NI 5481. 1995. CD.

1888 Kawkabani Brothers. *Music from Yemen Arabia: Sanaani, Laheji, Adeni.* Rounder: CD 5156. 1973. CD.

1889 Naji, Muhammad Murshid, and Mohammed Khalil Khalil. *The Aden Song.* Yemen. Institut du Monde Arabe: 321047. 2002. CD.

ANTHOLOGIES

1890 *Music from Yemen Arabia: Samar.* Rounder: CD 5157. [1975, 1999]. CD.

1891 *The Music of Islam, Vol. 11: The Music of Yemen, Sanaʾa, Yemen.* Celestial Harmonies: 13151-2. 1998. CD.

1892 ★*Yemen: Music from the Heart of Arabia.* Musique du Monde. Buda: 1978302. 1999. CD.

1893 *Yemen: Music of the High Plateaux.* PlayaSound: PS 65179. 1996. CD.

1894 *Yemen: Traditional Music.* Air Mail Music; Sunset-France: SA 141113. 1996, 2005. CD.

Yemen, Israel

INIVIDUAL ARTIST

1895 Haza, Ofra.
   1895.1 *Shaday.* Sire: 9 25816-2. 1988. CD.
   1895.2 *Yemenite Songs.* GlobeStyle: CDORBM 006. 1985, 1987. CD.

LEVANT

Iraq

INDIVIDUAL ARTISTS AND GROUPS

1896 Aiedy, Fawzy al-
   1896.1 *Le Paris Bagdad.* Buda: 92725-2. 1998. CD.
   1896.2 *Oud Aljazira.* Musique du Monde. Buda: 92750-2. 1999. CD.

1897 Alhaj, Rahim. *When the Soul Is Settled: Music of Iraq* (Souhail Kaspar). Smithsonian Folkways: SFW CD 40533. 2005, 2006. CD.

1898 Bashir, Munir. *The Art of the ʿŪd.* Iraq. Ocora: C 583068. 1971, 2001. CD.

1899 ★Bashir, Munir, and the Iraqi Traditional Music Group. *Munir Bashir and the Iraqi Traditional Music Group.* Chant du Monde: 274 1321. 1982, 2005. CD.

1900 Bashir, Omar. *Taqâsîm: Luth arabe = Arab Lute.* Inédit. Maison des Cultures du Monde: W 260144. 2012. CD.

1901 Farida. *Mawal and Maqamat Iraqi.* New Samarkand Records: SAM CD 9004. 1997, 2000. CD.

1902 Kuwaity, Daoud al-, and Saleh. *Masters of Iraqi Music.* ARC Music: EUCD 2154. 2008. CD.

1903 Madfi, Ilham al-
   1903.1 *Baghdad.* EMI Arabia: 07243 590740 2 3. 2003. CD.
   1903.2 *The Voice of Iraq* (Ilham al-Madfai). EMI Arabia: 7243 560344 2 6. 1900s, 2005. CD.

1904 Mukhtar, Ahmed. *The Road to Baghdad: New Maqams from Iraq.* ARC Music: EUCD 1937. 2005. CD.

1905 Mukhtar, Ahmed, and Sattar al-Saadi. *Rhythms of Baghdad.* ARC Music: EUCD 1781. 2002. CD.

1906 Saher, Kazim al-. *Habibati Wal Matar.* EMI Arabia: 0946 310945 2 1. 1999. CD.

1907 Shamma, Naseer. *The Baghdad Lute.* Institut du Monde Arabe: 321009. 1999. CD.

ANTHOLOGIES

1908 ★*Choubi Choubi! Folk and Pop Sounds from Iraq.* Sublime Frequencies: CD SF 025. 1970s, 2005. CD.

1909 *Give Me Love: Songs of the Brokenhearted, Baghdad, 1925–1929.* Honest Jon's Records: HJRCD35. 2008. CD.

1910 *Shbahoth: Iraqi-Jewish Song from the 1920s.* Honest Jon's Records: REN 0126. 2003. CD.

Israel

See Iran, Israel, Turkey.

Jordan

ANTHOLOGY

1911 ★*Bedouins of the Middle East.* ARC Music: EUCD 1910. 1955, 2005. CD.

Lebanon

INDIVIDUAL ARTISTS AND GROUPS

1912 Bulos, Afif Alvarez
   1912.1 *Afif Bulos Sings Songs of Lebanon, Syria and Jordan.* Custom Compact Disc Series. Smithsonian Folkways: FW 8816. 1961, 1990s. CD.
   1912.2 *Classic Arabic Music: A Recital of Muwashahat* (Afif Bulos and His Ensemble). Custom Compact Disc Series. Smithsonian Folkways: F-8818. 1976, 2000s. CD. Egypt.

1913   Fayruz

    1913.1   *B'hebbak Ya Loubnan*. Voix de l'Orient series. Hollywood Music Center: HMC 96752. 1976, 1988. CD.

    1913.2   *The Lady and the Legend*. Manteca: MANTCD053. 1900s, 2005. CD.

    1913.3   ★*Legend: The Best of Fairuz*. EMI Arabia: 0946 347311 2 6. [2006]. CD.

    1913.4   *The Legendary Fairuz*. Hemisphere: 7243 8 23572 2 3. 1997. CD.

    1913.5   ★*The Life Story of Fairouz*. EMI Arabia. 2007. DVD.

1914   Hajj, Andre. *Instrumental Music from Lebanon: Amaken*. ARC Music: EUCD 2219. 2009. CD.

1915   Hanna, Tony. *Tony Hanna in the Country: Bid'dayaa*. Hollywood Music Center: HMC 10388. 1982. CD.

1916   Khalifah, Marsil. *Promises of the Storm*. Smithsonian Folkways: P-1047. 1983. CD.

1917   Racy, Ali Jihad

    1917.1   ★*Mystical Legacies*. Lyrichord: LYRCD 7437. 1993, 1999. CD.

    1917.2   *Taqasim: The Art of Improvisation in Arabic Music* (Simon Shaheen). Lyrichord: LYRCD 7374. [1980, 1989]. CD.

1918   Rouhana, Charbel. *The Art of the Middle Eastern Oud: New Perspectives on Traditional Maqams*. ARC Music: EUCD 1863. 2004. CD.

1919   Roumi, Majida el-. *E'tazalt el Gharam*. EMI Arabia: 0946 359327 2 0. 2006. CD.

1920   Sawaya Quartet and Chorus. *Love Songs of Lebanon*. Custom Compact Disc Series. Smithsonian Folkways: FW 8815. 1957, 2001. CD.

1921   Warda. *Nagham el Hawa*. EMI Arabia: 7243 8 471322 5. 1999. 2 CDs. Egypt.

ANTHOLOGIES

1922   *Anthology of World Music: Lebanon*. Rounder: 82161-5148-2. 1972, 2003. CD.

1923   *Arabic and Druse Music*. Ethnic Folkways Library. Smithsonian Folkways: FE 4480. 1957, 2001. CD.

1924   *Laments of Lebanon*. Custom Compact Disc Series. Smithsonian Folkways: FE 4046. 1985, 2000s. CD.

1925   ★*Melodies and Rhythms of Arabic Music*. Custom Compact Disc Series. Smithsonian Folkways: FW 8451. 1981, 2000s. CD.

1926   *Music of Lebanon*. Hollywood Music Center: HMC 1362. 2007. CD.

Palestine

INDIVIDUAL ARTISTS AND GROUPS

1927   Adwan, Moneim. *Once upon a Time in Palestine* (Reem Kaleani). Accords Croisés: AC 111. 2005. CD.

1928   Funoun, el-. *Zaghareed: Music from the Palestinian Holy Land* (Trio Joubran). Sounds True: STA M109D. 1999. CD.

1929   Kaleani, Reem. *Sprinting Gazelle: Palestinian Songs from the Motherland and the Diaspora* (el-Funoun). Fuse: CFCD048. 2005. CD.

1930   Shaheen, Simon

    1930.1   *Blue Flame* (Qantara). Ark21: 186 850 022 2. 2001. CD.

    1930.2   ★*Turath: The Masterworks of the Middle East*. Times Square: TSQD 9025. 1992, 2001. CD.

1931   Trio Joubran. *Majaz* (Simon Shaheen). Sheer Sound: 878068000627. 2008. CD.

ANTHOLOGY

1932   *Radio Palestine: Sounds of the Eastern Mediterranean*. Sublime Frequencies: SF-008. 1985, 2004. CD.

Syria

INDIVIDUAL ARTISTS AND GROUPS

1933   Ammouri, Amer. *Oud Mosaics*. Hollywood Music Center: HMC 1367. 2007. CD.

1934   Dayikh, Adib al-. *Courtly Love* (al-Kindi Ensemble). Syria. Institut du Monde Arabe: 321013. 2002, 1995. CD.

1935   ★Fakhri, Sabah. *Master of Andalusian Folklore*. Hollywood Music Center: HMC 1351. 2006. CD.

1936   Jamil, Shadi

    1936.1   *Al Andelib*. Hollywood Music Center: HMC 10682CD.

    1936.2   *Ensa Gharamak*. Hollywood Music Center: HMC 11072CD.

1936.3 *Qudud Halabiyya.* Hollywood Music Center: HMC 13162. 2004. CD.

1937 Joubi, Jalal. *The Music of Syria.* Hollywood Music Center: HMC 1361. 2006. CD.

1938 Jundi, Zein al-. *Traditional Songs of Syria.* ARC Music: EUCD 1898. 2004. CD.

1939 al-Kindi Ensemble
   1939.1 *The Aleppian Music Room.* Chant du Monde: CML 5741108. 1998. 2 CDs.
   1939.2 *Aleppian Sufi Trance.* Chant du Monde: 574 1251.52. 2002, 2003. 2 CDs.
   1939.3 *The Crusades Seen through the Eyes of the Orient.* Chant du Monde: 5741118.19. 2001. 2 CDs.
   1939.4 ★*The Whirling Dervishes of Damascus.* Chant du Monde: CMT 574 1123.24. 1999. 2 CDs.

1940 Kheyri, Mouhammad. *Maa Tarab Assil Estez.* Hollywood Music Center: HMC 10132CD.

1941 Moudallal, Sabri. *Wasla d'Alep: Chants traditionnels de Syrie* (Sabri Moudallal et son Ensemble). Inédit. Maison des Cultures du Monde: W 260007. 1988. CD.

1942 Souleyman, Oman. *Highway to Hassake: Folk and Pop Sounds of Syria.* Sublime Frequencies: CD SF 031. 1996, 2006. CD.

ANTHOLOGIES

1943 *I Remember Syria.* Sublime Frequencies: SF-009. 1998, 2004. 2 CDs.

1944 *Maqams of Syria.* ARC Music: EUCD-1765. 2002. CD.

Turkey

See Iran, Israel, Turkey.

Armenia, Georgia

See chapter 6, Traditional & Popular Music of Europe: Eastern Europe.

MIDDLE EAST (ARABIAN PENINSULA, PERSIAN GULF, AND LEVANT) GENERAL ANTHOLOGIES

1945 Achkar, Elie. *Qanun Songs.* Musique du Monde. Buda: 92558-2. 1991. CD.

1946 Din, Adel Shams el-. *Forty Rhythms from the Middle East.* Musique du Monde. Buda: 1986092. 2002. CD.

1947 *A Musical Anthology of the Arabian Peninsula*
   1947.1 *Vol. 1: Sung Poetry of the Bedouins.* VDE-Gallo: VDE CD-780. 1994. CD.

   1947.2 *Vol. 2: Music of the Pearl Divers.* VDE-Gallo: VDE CD-781. 1994. CD.
   1947.3 *Vol. 3: Sawt, Music from the City.* VDE-Gallo: VDE CD-782. 1930, 1994. CD.
   1947.4 *Vol. 4: Women's Songs.* VDE-Gallo: VDE CD-783. 1994. CD.

1948 Yammine, Habib. *Pléiades: Thurayya: Rythmes Arabes du Levant.* Chant du Monde: 2741550. 2008. CD.

IRAN, ISRAEL, TURKEY

Compiled by Aaron Bittel and Maureen Russell

At first glance, it seems easy to characterize Iran, Israel, and Turkey as cultural—religious, linguistic, and musical—monoliths. As in other regions of the world, the lived reality of music making, both past and present, is multifaceted and fluid across the Middle East. Labels such as World Music Network (producers of the Rough Guide recording series), Smithsonian Folkways, and Traditional Crossroads represent much of the dominant and minority traditional music of the region in their catalogs, and their relatively inexpensive releases should be readily available to libraries.

The music of Israel presents particular selection challenges for the nonspecialist. Some may find it easy to conflate the music of the modern nation with those of the various Jewish diasporic communities (represented in chapter 7, "International Anthologies"). Although these areas share much in common, the past sixty years have witnessed the birth and maturing of distinctly Israeli traditional and popular music. As with Eastern Europe, recordings of Israeli music became widely available in the West with the folk song and dance boom of the 1960s and again with the "world music" trend of the 1990s.

Classical genres are represented in samplings on these lists, in particular Persian *Dastgah,* and a few Turkish/Ottoman recordings (those available in the United States on labels such as Smithsonian, Rounder, and World Music Network). Readers may find more information in *Garland Encyclopedia of World Music, vol. 6,* and other such sources.

IRAN

INDIVIDUAL ARTISTS AND GROUPS

1949 Ensemble Delgosha. *Musique de l'époque Qajare.* Inédit. Maison des Cultures du Monde: W 260149. 2014. CD.

1950 Ensemble Shanbehzadeh and Matthieu Donarier Trio. *Zâr: Jazz and Music from South Iran.* Buda: 2763499. 2011. CD, DVD.

1951 Khaladj, Madjid. *Iran, l'art du Tombak.* Musique du Monde. Buda: 92594-2. 1993, 1994. CD.

1952 Khezri, Hamid. *Iran: Le Dotar du Khorassan = The Dotar of Khorassan.* Archives Internationales de Musique Populaire, 76. VDE-Gallo: VDE CD-1170. 2000, 2005. CD.

1953 Musavi, Mohammad. *Iran: Le ney de Mohammad Musavi = Iran: The Ney of Mohammad Musavi.* Musique du Monde. Buda: 92645-2. 1996. CD.

1954 Parissa. *Gol-e Behesht* (Dastan Ensemble). Network: 29.204. 2005. 2 CDs.

1955 Sadeghi, Manoochehr. *Vision: Improvisation in Dastgah-e Mahur and Chahargah.* Nakisa. 2002. CD.

ANTHOLOGIES

1956 ★*Anthology of Persian Music, 1930–1990.* Mage: CD 22-1. 1991. CD.

1957 ★*Classical Music of Iran: Dastgah Systems.* Smithsonian Folkways: SFW40039. 1991. CD.

1958 *Folk Songs and Dances of Iran.* Custom Compact Disc Series. Smithsonian Folkways: FW08856. 1960, 2003. CD.

1959 *Iran: Bardes du Khorassan: Chants et Luth Dotar.* Ocora: C 560136. 1998. CD.

1960 ★*Iran: Les maitres de la musique traditionnelle.* Ocora: C560024, C560025, C560026. 1991. 3 CDs.

1961 *Iran: Musique Persane.* Ocora: C559008. 1987. CD.

1962 *Kurdish Folk Music from Western Iran.* Smithsonian Folkways Archival. Smithsonian Folkways: FW04103. 1966, 2007. CD.

1963 *Kurdish Folk Songs and Dances.* Custom Compact Disc Series. Smithsonian Folkways: FW04469. 1955, 2000. CD.

1964 *Persian Electronic Music Yesterday and Today: 1966–2006* (Alireza Mashayekhi and Ata Ebtekar, compilers). Sub Rosa: SR277. 2007. CD.

1965 ★*Rough Guide to the Music of Iran.* Rough Guide. World Music Network: RGNET 1165 CD. 2005. CD.

1966 *Silk Road: A Musical Caravan.* Smithsonian Folkways: SFW 40438. 2002. 2 CDs.

VIDEOS

1967 ★*Googoosh: Iran's Daughter.* Atash: 720229911283. 2000. DVD.

1968 ★*The JVC Video Anthology of World Music and Dance, Vol. 16: Middle East and Africa: Turkey/Iran/Iraq/Lebanon/Qatar.* JVC, Victor Co. of Japan; dist. by Multicultural Media: VTMV-46. 1988, 2005. DVD.

ISRAEL

INDIVIDUAL ARTISTS AND GROUPS

1969 Feenjon Group and el Avram Group. *Israeli Popular Hits.* Monitor: MON 71828. 1995. CD.

1970 Gill, Geula. *Holiday Songs of Israel.* Custom Compact Disc Series. Smithsonian Folkways: FW 07738. 1958. CD.

1971 Hillel and Aviva. *Mountain So Fair: Folk Songs of Israel.* Custom Compact Disc Series. Smithsonian Folkways: FW 31305. 1968, 2003. CD.

1972 Raveh, Hillel. *Hillel Raveh Sings Songs of the Israel Defense Army.* Custom Compact Disc Series. Smithsonian Folkways: FW 03051. 1959, 2000s. CD.

1973 Shir. *Israeli Songs.* ARC Music: EUCD 1840. 2003. CD.

1974 Sivann, Sylvie. *Israel: Musiques plurielles = Traditional Jewish Music.* Air Mail Music. Sunset-France: SA 141161. 2008. CD.

ANTHOLOGIES

1975 *Authentic Israeli Folk Songs and Dances.* Legacy International: CD 324. 1988. CD.

1976 *Authentic Israeli-Oriental Folk Songs Featuring Yemenite and Druz Influences.* Hataklit Company: CD 9425. 2006. CD.

1977 ★*Collection of Abraham Zvi Idelsohn (1911–1913).* Tondokumente aus dem Phonogrammarchiv der

Österreichische Akademie Der Wissenschaften; Gesamtausgabe der Historischen Bestände 1899–1950, Ser. 9. Verlag der Osterreichischen Akademie der Wissenschaften: OEAW PHA CD 23. 2005. 3 CDs.

1978 ★*Gadalnu Yaḥad: Osef Ha-Yovel Shel Yiśrael: Ha-Musiḳah = Israel's 240 Greatest Songs in Celebration of Its 50th Anniversary.* Hed Arzi: ACUM 15950. 1998. 11 CDs.

1979 ★*Hazanout.* Inédit. Maison des Cultures du Monde: W 260005. 1989. CD.

1980 *Israeli Vocal and Instrumental Music.* Custom Compact Disc Series. Smithsonian Folkways: FW 37466. 1985, 2000s. CD.

1981 *Music of Israel: Chassidic, Yiddish, Folk.* ARC Music: EUCD 1991. 2006. CD.

1982 *Oytsres = Treasures: Klezmer Music, 1908–1996.* Jewish Music Series. Wergo: SM 1621-2. 1999. CD.

1983 *Putumayo Presents a Jewish Odyssey.* Putumayo World Music: PUT 182-2. 2000. CD.

1984 *Putumayo Presents Israel.* Putumayo World Music: PUT 268-2. 2007. CD.

1985 ★*Rough Guide to the Music of Israel.* Rough Guide. World Music Network: RGNET 1168 CD. 2006. CD.

VIDEOS

1986 *Israel in Songs: 43 Most Popular Israeli Sing-Along Songs.* Hataklit Company: 7051. 2005. DVD.

1987 Malovany, Joseph. *Jewish Music in Jerusalem: A Cantorial Concert with Joseph Malovany.* Jewish Liturgical Treasures. Israel Music. 2005. DVD.

1988 *Night on the Sea of Galilee: Israeli Folk Dance Festival.* Israel Music: IM DVD 3001. 2004. DVD.

TURKEY

INDIVIDUAL ARTISTS AND GROUPS

1989 Beken, Munir Nurettin. *Art of the Turkish Ud.* Rounder: CD 1135. 1997. CD.

1990 Çiçek, Ali Ekber. *Turkish Sufi Music: Folk Lute of Anatolia.* Lyrichord: LYRCD 7392. 2007. CD.

1991 Kartal, Goksel, and Seydo Salifoski. *Art of Taksim.* Traditional Crossroads: CD 4267. 1994. CD.

1992 Longa ve Sirtolar. *Turkish Dances: Longa Ve Sirtolar.* Monitor: MON 71739. 1995. CD.

1993 Necdet Yasar Ensemble. *Music of Turkey.* Music of the World: CDT-128. 1992. CD.

1994 Radio Ankara Ensemble. *Songs and Dances of Turkey.* Monitor: MON 71403. 1996. CD.

1995 Yurdatapan, Sanar. *Songs of Freedom from Turkey: Behind Prison Bars* (Melike Demirag). Smithsonian Folkways: FW 37705. 1982. CD.

ANTHOLOGIES

1996 *Folk and Traditional Music of Turkey.* Custom Compact Disc Series. Smithsonian Folkways: FW 04404. 1953, 2000. CD.

1997 *Great Voices of Constantinople, 1927–1933.* Rounder: CD 1113. 1997. CD.

1998 *Haydar Haydar.* Rounder: 82161-1140-2. 2002–2003. CD.

1999 ★*The Rough Guide to the Music of Turkey.* Rough Guide. World Music Network: RGNET 1057 CD. 2003. CD.

2000 ★*Rough Guide to Turkish Café.* Rough Guide. World Music Network: RGNET 1215. 2008. CD.

2001 *Song Creators in Eastern Turkey.* Traditional Music of the World, 6. Smithsonian Folkways: SFW 40432. 1990, 1993. CD.

2002 *Songs and Dances of Turkey.* Custom Compact Disc Series. Smithsonian Folkways: FW 08801. 1955, 2000s. CD.

2003 *Sufi Music from Turkey.* ARC Music: EUCD 1741. 2002. CD.

2004 *Turkish Groove.* Putumayo World Music: PUT 248-2. 1999, 2006. CD.

2005 *Turquie: la cérémonie des derviches de Konya = Turkey: The Ceremony of the Konya Dervishes.* Archives Internationales de Musique Populaire, 98. VDE Gallo: VDE CD-1324. 2009, 2011. CD.

2006 ★*Women of Istanbul.* Traditional Crossroads: CD 4280. 1998. CD.

VIDEOS

2007 *Crossing the Bridge: The Sound of Istanbul.* Strand Releasing: 2607-2. 2005, 2006. DVD.

2008 ★*The JVC Video Anthology of World Music and Dance, Vol. 16: Middle East and Africa: Turkey/*

Iran/Iraq/Lebanon/Qatar. JVC, Victor Co. of Japan; dist. by Multicultural Media: VTMV-46. 1988, 2005. DVD.

CENTRAL ASIA

Compiled by Craig Macrae and Robin P. Harris

Central Eurasia is one of the great crossroads of humanity. In deep prehistory, the genetic ancestors of most Europeans, Native Americans, and many Asians settled in the river valleys of Transoxiana (present-day Uzbekistan, Tajikistan, and southern Kazakhstan) before moving on to populate much of the planet. The present cultural map has emerged from many centuries of symbiotic interaction between the Persian-speaking agriculturalists of Transoxiana and the Turkic-speaking pastoral nomads of the great Eurasian steppe. In this hub of history's greatest trade and invasion routes, one can find traces of ancient Persian, Hellenistic, Indo-Buddhist, and Chinese civilizations across the region. The dominant influences on today's music, however, can be found in the oral traditions of Turkic nomads, in the cosmopolitan art music of the medieval dynasties who for centuries ruled much of the Muslim world from Transoxiana, and in Western music with a distinctly Soviet Russian inflection.

Globalization has come slowly to this musically rich region. Transmission of local recordings to Western audiences has largely been in the hands of two groups. Most of the available recordings have been made by scholars interested in documenting artifacts of oral tradition. This has resulted in a significant body of high-quality performances released with informative supporting material. The focus of such recordings is on classical art music or rural folk genres. These productions are periodically out-of-print and are worth chasing on the secondary market. In counterpoint to this scholarly activity, a growing number of commercial producers are recording contemporary artists, mostly from Uzbekistan, and tailoring their output for the world beat market. Although the performers are often major stars in their homeland, most of these releases are produced and tuned to Western ears. Librarians should consider these factors and their clientele when making purchasing decisions.

Although the traditional genres and highly westernized pop music remain important for central Asian audiences, these represent two ends of a stylistic spectrum comprising an abundance of fusions between traditional and Western music. Collectively these styles might be called "urban folk music" or "neotraditional."

They might include Azeri or Turkmen dance melodies adapted to accordion and violin during the early twentieth century under the Soviets; simplified Uzbek-Tajik maqam melodies with contemporary social commentary in the lyrics, accompanied by a mix of traditional and contemporary electronic instruments; or even Kazak narrative poetry arranged for rock band. These musicians are heavily influenced by the music of their counterparts in Turkey, Iran, and the Arab world. Most of this music, which is the soundtrack to daily life in contemporary central Asia, reaches its audience at wedding parties and through cassettes sold on the street. Very little is readily available overseas but the Rough Guide series begins to address this deficiency. These recordings are responsibly documented and of general appeal. Also, for a library interested in developing a representative collection, examples of contemporary styles can be found in the more eclectic of the academic anthologies recommended above. Musical boundaries are imprecise. Citations are included from Siberia (Tuva), which overlaps with east and north Asia. A valuable site for finding more recordings from Central Asia is CDRoots (www.cdroots.com/cgi/searchcds.cgi?s=centasia).

For Jewish music, see chapter 7, "International Anthologies." Russian (Siberian, Sakha, Tuvan) citations compiled by Robin P. Harris; all other Central Asia citations by Craig Macrae.

AFGHANISTAN

INDIVIDUAL ARTISTS AND GROUPS

2009 Herawi, Aziz. *Cry of the Mountains: Aziz Herawi, Master of Afghan Lutes* (Izmarai Arifi). Traditional Music of Afghanistan. 7/8 Music: 100211. 2002. CD.

2010 Herawi, Aziz, and Ghulam Abbas Khan. *Master of Afghani Lutes.* World Music in California. Arhoolie: CD 387. 1992. CD.

2011 Herawi, Aziz, Siar Ahmad Hazeq, and Omar Herawi. *Memories of Herat: Instrumental Music of Afghanistan* (Veronica Doubleday and John Baily). New American Series. Latitudes: LT 50602. 1990, 1996. CD.

2012 Madadi, 'Abd al-Vahhab, Veronica Doubleday, and John Baily. *Sweet Nomad Girl.* Metier World: MW 360 01. 2005. CD.

2013 Sakhi, Homayun, and Toryalai Hashimi. *Homayun Sakhi: The Art of the Afghan Rubâb.* Music of Central Asia, Vol. 3. Smithsonian Folkways: CD SF 40522. 2005. CD, DVD.

ANTHOLOGIES

2014   *Afghanistan: Le Rubâb de Hérat = The Rubâb of Herat* (Mohammad Rahim Khushnawaz and Mohammad Naim Khushnawaz; John Baily, compiler). Archives Internationales de Musique Populaire, 25. VDE-Gallo: CD-699. 1993, 2002. CD.

2015   *Afghanistan on Marco Polo's Road: The Musicians of Kunduz and Faizabad* (Tomoaki Fujii and Akihiro Takahashi, compilers). Music of the Earth. Multicultural Media: MCM 3003. 1992, 1997. CD.

2016   *Afghanistan: Traditional Musicians.* World Network, 28. World Network: 56.986. 1994. CD.

2017   ★*Afghanistan Untouched* (Mark Slobin, compiler). Traditional Crossroads: CD 4319. 1968, 2003. 2 CDs.

2018   ★*The Music of Afghanistan* (Alain Daniélou, compiler). Anthology of World Music. Rounder Select: 82161 5121 2. 2003. CD.

VIDEO

2019   Video. *A Kabul Music Diary* (John Baily, prod.). dist. by Royal Anthropological Institute. 2003. DVD.

ARMENIA

See chapter 6, Eastern Europe.

AZERBAIJAN

INDIVIDUAL ARTISTS AND GROUPS

2020   Aliev, Aydin. *Azerbaïdjan: Le garmon de Aydin Aliev = Azerbaïdjan: The Garmon of Aydin Aliev.* Musique du Monde. Buda: 92701-2. 1997. CD.

2021   Karim, Agha, and Malik Mansurov. *Azerbaïdjan, chants du Grand Caucase = Azerbaijan, Songs of the Greater Caucasus.* Musique du Monde. Buda: 1983152. 2001. CD.

2022   Mansurov, Elshan, and Kamran Karimov. *Azerbaijan, Le Kamantcha d'Elshan Mansurov (pièce tradionnelle).* Archives Internationales de Musique Populaire, 83. VDE-Gallo: VDE CD-1240. 1997, 2008. CD.

2023   Mansurov, Malik. *Azerbaïdjan: Le tar de Malik Mansurov = Azerbaïdjan: The Tar of Malik Mansurov.* Musique du Monde. Buda: 926962. 1997. CD.

2024   Qasimov, Alim, and Fargana Qasimova. *Alim and Fargana Qasimov: Spiritual Music of Azerbaijan.* Music of Central Asia, Vol. 6. Smithsonian Folkways: SFW CD 40525. 2007. CD, DVD.

2025   Qasimov, Alim, Malik Mansurov, and Elshan Mansurov

    2025.1   ★*Azerbaïdjan l'art du Mugham.* Ocora: C 560112. 1997. CD.

    2025.2   *Azerbaijan.* Ocora: C 560013. 1993. CD.

ANTHOLOGIES

2026   *Azerbaidjan: Musiques et chants Âschiq = Music and Songs of the Âshiq* (Ashiq Hasan, Emrân Heydari, Alim Qasimov and Ensemble; Jean During, compiler). Archives Internationales de Musique Populaire, 19. VDE-Gallo: CD-613. 1990. CD.

2027   ★*Kür: Instrumental and Vocal Music from Azerbaijan* (Djavanshir Guliev, cond.). Welt Musik. Wergo: 281518-2. 1995. CD.

2028   *The Music of Azerbaijan.* Anthology of World Music. Rounder Select: 82161-5142-2. 2003. CD.

GEORGIA

See chapter 6, Eastern Europe.

KAZAKHSTAN

INDIVIDUAL ARTISTS AND GROUPS

2029   Kulysheva, Kapash, Kairat Baibosynov, and Smagul Unbetbaev. *Music of Kazakhstan I.* World Music Library, 66. Seven Seas: KICC 5166. 1994. CD.

2030   Umbetbaev, Smagul, and Saian Aqmolda. *Kazakhstan: Le Kobyz: L'ancienne viole des chamanes.* Inédit. Maison des Cultures du Monde: W 260115. 2004. CD.

ANTHOLOGIES

2031   *Dombra du Kazakhstan = Dombra from Kazakhstan* (Kui Shertpe of Karatu). Musique du Monde. Buda: 3017266. 2005. CD.

2032   *Dombra Music of Kazakhstan* (Aitzhan Toktaganov, Kapash Kulysheva, Kairat

Baibosynov, and Smagul Unbetbaev). World
Music Library. King: KICC 5199, [KICW 1047].
1999. CD.

2033 *Kazakhstan: Musique d'Almati = Music from
Almati.* Archives Internationales de Musique
Populaire, 46. VDE-Gallo: AIMP CD-910.
1996. CD.

2034 *Songs from the Steppes: Kazakh Music Today*
(Michael Church, compiler). Topic World Series.
Topic: TSCD 929. 2005. CD.

KYRGYZSTAN

GROUP

2035 Kambarkan Folk Ensemble. *The Music of
Kyrgyzstan.* ARC Music: EUCD 1689. 2002. CD.

ANTHOLOGY

2036 ★*Musiques du Kirghizstan = Music of Kyrgyzstan.*
Musique du Monde. Buda: 92631-2. 1995,
1996. CD.

2037 ★*Tengir-Too: Mountain Music of Kyrgyzstan.* Music
of Central Asia, Vol. 1. Smithsonian Folkways:
SFW CD 40520. 2005. CD, DVD.

MONGOLIA

INDIVIDUAL ARTISTS AND GROUPS

2038 Mandukhai Ensemble. *Mongolie = Mongolia.*
Sunset-France: SA 141006. 1993, 1998. CD.

2039 Tserendavaa and Tsogtgerel. *Chants diphoniques
de l'Altai Mongol = Xöömij Overtone Singing from
Mongolia.* Musique du Monde. Buda. 2008. CD.

2040 Uragsha. *Instrumental and Vocal Music from
Buryatia and Mongolia.* Global Village: CD 2501.
1999. CD.

ANTHOLOGIES

2041 *Mongolia: Living Music of the Steppes: Instrumental
Music and Song of Mongolia* (Haruo Hasumi,
compiler). Music of the Earth. Multicultural
Media: MCM 3001. 1992, 1997. CD.

2042 *Mongolian Instrumental Music.* World Music
Library, 34. King: KICC 5134. 1988. CD.

RUSSIA, SIBERIA

Russia (European)

See chapter 6, Eastern Europe.

Siberia

INDIVIDUAL ARTISTS AND GROUPS

2043 Alekseyev, Ivan, and Spiridon Shishigin. *Sing, My
Khomus: Jew's Harp of the Sakha (Yakut) People,
Eastern Siberia.* Japan Jew's Harp Association:
NKK001. 1996. CD.

2044 Gogleva, Fedora, Albina Degtyaryova, and Olga
Podluzhnaya. *Summer Is Coming: The Art of the
Jew's Harp and the Vocal Techniques of the Sakha
(Yakut) People, Eastern Siberia.* Japan Jew's Harp
Association: NKK002. 2000. CD.

2045 National Dance Theatre of the Republic of
Sakha. *Songs and Dances from Yakutia.* ARC
Music: EUCD 1584. 1997, 2000. CD.

2046 ★Shishigin, Spiridon. *Soul of Yakutia.* Welt
Musik. Wergo: SM 1620 2. 2000. CD.

2047 Sverev, S. A (Kyyl Uola). *Olonkho Doidutun
Toiyuga = Song of the Land of Olonkho.* Studio
NVK "Sakha." 2000. CD.

VIDEO

2048 *Siberia at the Centre of the World: Music, Dance,
and Ritual in Sakha-Yakutia and Buryatia* (Misha
Maltsev and Keith Howard, prods.). SOASIS,
University of London: SOASIS DVD-06, DVD-07.
2008. 2 DVDs.

Siberia, Tuva

INDIVIDUAL ARTISTS AND GROUPS

2049 Alash Ensemble. *Alash* (Sean Quirk, prod.). Alash
Ensemble: MRD5545, 20-36563. 2008. CD.

2050 Huun-Huur-Tu. *60 Horses in My Herd: Old Songs
and Tunes of Tuva.* Shanachie: 64050. 1993. CD.

2051 Shu-De. *Voices from a Distant Steppe.* Realworld:
7243 8 39469 2 1. 1992, 1994. CD.

ANTHOLOGIES

2052 *Chöömej: Throat-Singing from the Center of Asia.*
World Network, 21. Network Medien: WDR
55.838. 1993. CD.

2053   ★*Tuva: Voices from the Center of Asia* (Eduard Alekseyev, Zoya Kirgiz, and Ted Levin, compilers). Smithsonian Folkways: SFW 40017. 1990. CD.

Siberia, Tuva, Sakha

ANTHOLOGY

2054   ★*Tuva, among the Spirits: Sound, Music, and Nature in Sakha and Tuva* (Joel Gordon, Theodore Levin, compiler). Smithsonian Folkways: SFW 40452. 1999. CD.

TAJIKISTAN

INDIVIDUAL ARTISTS AND GROUPS

2055   Badakhshan Ensemble. *Song and Dance from the Pamir Mountains*. Music of Central Asia, Vol. 5. Smithsonian Folkways: SFW CD 40524. 2007. CD, DVD.

2056   Ergashova, Mastâneh, and Jurabeg Nabiev. *Tadjikistan-Ouzbekistan: Tradition savante Shash Maqam = Tajikistan-Uzbekistan: Erudite Shash Maqam Tradition*. Musique du Monde. Buda: 92639-2. 1996. CD.

2057   Kholov, Davlatmand, and Abdoussattar Abdoullaev. *Davlatmand: Musiques savantes et populaire du Tadjikstan*. Inédit. Maison des Cultures du Monde: W 260038. 1992. CD.

ANTHOLOGIES

2058   *Falak: The Voice of Destiny: Traditional, Popular and Symphonic Music of Tajikistan* (Federico Spinetti, compiler). Topic World Series. Topic: TSCD 932 D. 2006. 2 CDs.

2059   *Tadjikistan: Chants des bardes = Songs of the Bards* (Jean During, compiler). Archives Internationales de Musique Populaire, 56. VDE-Gallo: AIMP CD-973. 1990, 1998. CD.

TURKMENISTAN

INDIVIDUAL ARTISTS AND GROUPS

2060   ★Ashkhabad. *City of Love*. Caroline: 2329 2. 1992, 1993. CD.

2061   Djamala, Saparova, Shadurdieva Leila, and Hodjaeva Shemshat. *Turkmenistan: Chants des femmes Bakhshi* (Akhmurad Chariev). Inédit. Inédit: W 260064. 1995. CD.

2062   Dzhumaev, Charyyar, Allaberdi Ataev, and Annaseiit Annamuradov. *Instrumental Music of Turkmenistan*. World Music Library, 75. King: KICC 5175. 1994. CD.

ANTHOLOGIES

2063   ★*Turkmen Epic Singing: Köroglu = Chant epique Turkmene: Görogly* (Slawomira Zeranska-Kominek, compiler). Anthology of Traditional Music. Unesco Auvidis: D 8213. 1994. CD.

2064   ★*Turkmenistan: La musique des Bakhshy = The Music of the Bakhshy*. Archives Internationales de Musique Populaire, 22. VDE-Gallo: VDE 651. 1988, 1991. CD.

UZBEKISTAN

INDIVIDUAL ARTISTS AND GROUPS

2065   Abdorahim, Hamidov, Shohrat Razzakov, and Soltân-Ali Khodâverdiev. *Ouzbékistan: L'art du Dotâr: Hamidov, Khodâverdiev, Razzaqov*. Ocora: C 560111. 1997. CD.

2066   Abdurashidov, Abduvali. *Invisible Face of the Beloved: Classical Music of the Tajiks and Uzbeks* (Academy of Maqam). Music of Central Asia, Vol. 2. Smithsonian Folkways: SFW CD 40521. 2005. CD, DVD.

2067   Alimatov, Turgun, and Alisher. *Ouzbekistan: Turgun Alimatov*. Ocora: C 560086. 1995. CD.

2068   Ergashova, Mastâneh, and Jurabeg Nabiev. *Tadjikistan-Ouzbekistan: Tradition savante Shash Maqam = Tajikistan-Uzbekistan: Erudite Shash Maqam Tradition*. Musique du Monde. Buda: 92639-2. 1996. CD.

2069   Hamidov, Abdurahim, and Abduhâshim Isma'ilov. *Ouzbékistan Maqâm Dugâh: Le Shash-Maqâm Ouzbek-Tadjik = Uzbekistan Maqâm Dugâh* (Nâdira Pirmatova, Shohrat Razzakov, Qudrat Samadov, and Mariam Sattarova). Maison des Cultures du Monde: Inédit W 260111. 2002. CD.

2070   Nazarkhan, Sevara. *Yol Bolsin*. Real World: 72435 43206 2 0. 2003. CD.

2071   Subhânov, Akmâl-khân, Bâbâ-khân, and Jurâ-khân. *Ouzbékistan: Les grandes voix du passé, 1940–1965*. Ouzbekistan. Ocora: C 560142. 1999. CD.

2072 Usmanova, Yulduz. *The Best of Yulduz*. Blue Flame: 398 50372. 2000. CD.

2073 Yalla. *Beard of the Camel*. Imagina: 11010-2. 1995. CD.

ANTHOLOGIES

2074 ★*Asie Centrale: Traditions classiques* (Jean During and Theodore Levin, compilers). Ocora Radio France: C 560035-36. 1993. 2 CDs.

2075 *Bukhara: Musical Crossroads of Asia*. Smithsonian Folkways: SFW CD 40050. 1991. CD.

2076 ★*From Samarkand to Bukhara: A Musical Journey through Uzbekistan*. Long Distance: 7122038. 1996. CD.

2077 *Ouzbékistan: Monâjât Yultchieva* (Yultchieva, Monâjât, Shawqat Mirzâev; Jean During, compiler). Maqâm d'Asie Central, 1. France: C 560060. 1994. CD.

2078 *Ouzbékistan: Musique classique instrumentale = Uzbekistan: Instrumental Art*. Archives Internationales de Musique Populaire, 57. VDE-Gallo: AIMP CD-974. 1998. CD.

2079 *Traditions orales d'Ouzbekistan = Oral Traditions of Uzbekistan*. PlayaSound: PS 65196. 1997. CD.

2080 *Uzbekistan: Music of Khorezm = Ouzbékistan: Musique du Khorezm*. Unesco Collection. Unesco: D 8269. 1996. CD.

TRANSNATIONAL

ANTHOLOGIES

2081 *Asie centrale: Les maitres du Dotar*. VDE-Gallo: VDE CD-735. 1993. CD.

2082 ★*Bardic Divas: Women's Voices in Central Asia*. Music of Central Asia, Vol. 4. Smithsonian Folkways: SFW CD 40523. 2007. CD, DVD.

2083 ★*Central Asia: Music Rough Guide*. Rough Guide. World Music Network: RGNET 1129. 2005. CD.

2084 ★*Chants épiques et diphoniques, Vol. 1: Asie centrale et Sibérie*. Inédit. Maison des Cultures du Monde: W 260067. 1996. CD.

2085 *The Secret Museum of Mankind: Ethnic Music Classics, 1925–1948: Central Asia*. Yazoo: 7007. 1996. CD.

2086 *The Silk Road: A Musical Caravan*. Smithsonian Folkways: SFW CD 40438. 1980, 2002. 2 CDs.

VIDEO

2087 *The JVC Video Anthology of World Music and Dance, Vols. 5, 25–26*. JVC, Victor Co. of Japan; dist. by Multicultural Media. 1990, 2005. 30 DVDs, 9 booklets.

TRANSNATIONAL, KURDISTAN

INDIVIDUAL ARTISTS AND GROUPS

2088 Ghowsi, Mirza Âghe, and Safvati Safvati. *Kurdistan: Zikr et chants Soufis*. Ocora Radio France. 1996. 2 CDs. *See also* Arab World, Middle East (Iran).

2089 ★Rashid, Xalid. *Musiques du Kurdistan*. Musique du Monde. Buda: 92668-2. 1996. CD.

5

Traditional and Popular Music of Sub-Saharan Africa

Compiled by GREGORY F. BARZ, JOE C. CLARK,
SUZANNE FLANDREAU, BETH ISEMINGER, RICHARD McRAE,
HOLLING SMITH-BORNE, *and* LIZA VICK

Sub-Saharan Africa is a rich and diverse musical area. Although traditional and popular forms are difficult to separate, an attempt has been made to divide listings here for organizational purposes. These should not be taken as rigid divisions since many titles could easily fall in both categories. Anthologies are included at the end of the chapter, and the listing includes a sampling of reggae, which had its own section in the third edition (artists included Lucky Dube, Majek Fashek, and Sonny Okosun, on the Shanachie label). Reggae citations and diaspora (Afro-Portugese, Afro-Latin, etc.) also appear in the Caribbean and Afro-Caribbean sections of chapter 2, "Traditional and Popular Music of the Americas and the Caribbean," and in chapter 7, "International Anthologies." Their inclusion here reflects the permeable nature of world music today. The anthology listing is very much a sampling and should not be used as the sole basis for collection building; Afropop (or Afrobeat) is too abundant and widespread to cover fully. Cameroon, although geographically western, is listed here in Central Africa.

It is important to note that some areas list out-of-print items. Smithsonian Folkways, as noted elsewhere, keeps its catalog in print through its Custom Compact Disc Series (CD on demand) and MP3 downloads. Artists and genres listed here may be used as a starting point for collection building. The JVC Video Anthology of World Music and Dance series covers Africa in several of its volumes.

Afropop has become a major market force in world music, with incredible popularity worldwide, and it reflects globalizing popular trends, stylistic fusion, and transnational influences (very prevalent in Africa). Artists such as Paul Simon, Peter Gabriel, and others have, for better or worse, influenced the global profile of artists like Youssou N'Dour and Ladysmith Black Mambazo.

A few general acquisitions sources include Stern's Music (www.sternsmusic.com), Mondomix and Calabash MP3 downloads, and Soundways Records (www.soundwayrecords.com).

WESTERN AFRICA

WESTERN AFRICA TRADITIONAL

Compiled by Joe C. Clark

West Africa consists of many ethnic groups rich in traditional music. Some of these ethnic groups include the Fula, Yoruba, Ewe, Akan, Kon, Dagbani, Mandinka, Vai, and Baoulé. Much of the traditional music focuses on social life, frequently in a village context, with songs that celebrate births, planting songs, funeral songs, and other life events. Dance is virtually synonymous with music and the two usually occur together. Prominent musical instruments in Western African traditional music include the kora, flute, balafon, bowed lute, and drums. Examples of drum types include the *djembe, bata, dundun, gangan,* and *igbin.* Voice is also a featured instrument.

A number of recordings are available on European labels as imports and are available through acquisitions channels, including the online vendors CD Universe (www.cduniverse.com) and Amazon (www.amazon.com). Recording labels include Stern's (United Kingdom), Musique du Monde/Buda (France), Le Chant du Monde (France), Playasound (France), and Celluloid (France). U.S. labels for Western African titles include Rounder and Smithsonian Folkways Records, which recently made many of their older recordings of Western African music available on custom CDs and digital downloads. As in many areas, musical affinities are not always as clear-cut as geographic ones.

Benin

ANTHOLOGIES

2090 *Benin: Bariba and Somba Music = Musiques Bariba et Somba* (Simha Arom, compiler). Unesco Collection. Auvidis: D 8057. 1976, 1994. CD.

2091 *Fula Flute.* Blue Monster Records: BM 002. 2002. CD.

2092 *Yoruba Drums from Benin, West Africa* (Marcos Branda-Lacerda, compiler). World's Musical Traditions, 8. Smithsonian Folkways: CD SF 40440. 1996. CD.

Burkina Faso

INDIVIDUAL ARTISTS

2093 Dramé, Adama. *Djembe Solo.* Air Mail Music. Sunset-France: SA 141196. 1980, 2010. CD.

2094 Farafina. *Bolomakoté.* Intuition: INT 2026 2. 1992. CD.

ANTHOLOGIES

2095 *Burkina Faso: Rhythms of the Grasslands* (Kathleen Johnson, compiler). Explorer Series: Africa. Nonesuch: 79713-2. 1983, 2002. CD.

2096 *Burkina Faso: Savannah Rhythms* (Kathleen Johnson, compiler). Explorer Series: Africa. Nonesuch: 79712-2. 1981, 2002. CD.

VIDEO

2097 *Drums and Djembes of Burkino Faso (Horizons)*. Playasound: PS 69001. 2004. DVD.

Cape Verde

ANTHOLOGIES

2098 *Cape Verde*. Rough Guide. World Music Network: RGNET 1065 CD. 2001. CD.

2099 *Putumayo Presents Cape Verde*. Putumayo World Music: PUTU 156-2. 1996, 1999. CD.

Chad

ANTHOLOGY

2100 *Music of Chad* (Elizabeth Dyer and W. Gurnee Dyer, compilers). Custom Compact Disc Series. Smithsonian Folkways: FE 4337. 1966, 2000s. CD.

Gambia

ANTHOLOGIES

2101 *African Flutes Recorded in the Gambia by Samuel Charters* (Samuel Barclay Charters, compiler). Custom Compact Disc Series. Smithsonian Folkways: FE 4230. 1978, 1999. CD.

2102 *Kora Music from the Gambia* (Foday Musa Suso; Verna Gillis, compiler). Custom Compact Disc Series. Smithsonian Folkways: FW 8510. 1978, 1999. CD.

2103 *Music from Gambia, Vol. 1* (Susan Gunn Pevar and Marc D. Pevar, compilers). Smithsonian Folkways: FE 4521 AB–4521 CD. 1971, 1999. 2 CDs.

Ghana

ANTHOLOGIES

2104 *Ghana: Ancient Ceremonies, Songs and Dance Music* (Stephen Jay, compiler). Explorer Series: Africa. Elektra Nonesuch: 9 72082-2. 1979, 1991. CD.

2105 *The Guitar and Gun*. Stern's Music: STEW 50 CD. 1983, 2003. CD.

2106 ★*Master Drummers of Dagbon, Vol. 1* (Abhaji Ibrahim Abdulai; John Miller Chernoff, compiler). Rounder: CD 5016. 1981, 1992. CD.

2107 *Master Drummers of Dagbon, Vol. 2: Drumming from Northern Ghana* (Abhaji Ibrahim Abdulai; John Miller Chernoff, compiler). Rounder: CD 5046. 1981, 1990. CD.

2108 *Music of the Dagomba from Ghana* (Verna Gillis, Pérez Martínez, and David Moisés, compilers). Custom Compact Disc Series. Smithsonian Folkways: FE 4324. 1978, 2000. CD.

2109 *Music of the Ewe of Ghana* (Seth Kobla Ladzekpo, compiler). Custom Compact Disc Series. Smithsonian Folkways: AHM 4222. 1969, 2001. CD.

2110 *Rhythms of Life, Songs of Wisdom: Akan Music from Ghana, West Africa* (Roger R. Vetter, compiler). Smithsonian Folkways: SF 40463. 1996. CD.

2111 ★*The Rough Guide to Highlife*. World Music Network: RGNET 1102. 2003. CD.

VIDEO

2112 *Dagomba Beats: Lessons with Inusah Hamidu Jawula: Bamaaya and Damba Takai*. Vijay Rakhra Productions. 2006. DVD.

Guinea

INDIVIDUAL ARTISTS AND GROUPS

2113 Amazones de Guinée. *Wamato*. Stern's Music: STCD 1106. 2008. CD.

2114 Ensemble National des Percussions de Guinée = *The Percussionists of Guinea. Percussions de Guinée*. Musique du Monde. Buda: 82501-2. [1989–1990]. CD.

2115 Konaté, Famoudou. *Guinée: Percussions et chants Malinké, Vol. 2 = Guinea: Malinké Rhythms and Songs, Vol. 2* (Ensemble Hamana Dan Ba). Musique du Monde. Buda: 1977832. 1998. CD.

ANTHOLOGY

2116 *African Pearls: Cultural Revolution 2, Guinée*. Syllart Productions: 6129872. 2006. 2 CDs.

Guinea-Bissau

INDIVIDUAL ARTIST

2117 Manel, Zé. *Maron Di Mar*. Cobiana Records: COB-01. 2001. CD.

Ivory Coast

GROUP

2118 ★Ivory Coast National Company. *Indigenous Music of the Ivory Coast National Company, Recorded at the F.E.S.T.A.C., 1977, Lagos, Nigeria.* Custom Compact Disc Series. Smithsonian Folkways: FW 8464. 1977, 1990s. CD.

ANTHOLOGY

2119 *The Baoule of the Ivory Coast* (Donald Ralph Thurow, compiler). Custom Compact Disc Series. Smithsonian Folkways: FE 4476. 1956, 1999. CD.

Liberia

ANTHOLOGIES

2120 *Folk Music of Liberia* (Packard L. Okie, compiler). Custom Compact Disc Series. Smithsonian Folkways: FE 4465. 1954, 1990s. CD.

2121 *Music of the Kpelle of Liberia (Verlon Stone and Ruth Stone, compilers).* Custom Compact Disc Series. Smithsonian Folkways: FE 4385. 1972, 2001. CD.

2122 *Music of the Vai of Liberia* (Jeanne Monts and Lester P. Monts, compilers). Custom Compact Disc Series. Smithsonian Folkways: FE 4388. 1982, 2001. CD.

Mali

INDIVIDUAL ARTISTS AND GROUPS

2123 Sarré, Toka Abagouro, Dinda Hamma Sarré, Nassourou Sarré, and others. *Le Hoddu Peul: The Fulani Hoddu.* Ocora Radio France: C 560198. 2002, 2006. CD.

2124 Sidibe, Sali, and others. *The Wassoulou Sound: Women of Mali.* Stern's Africa: STCD 1035. [1990–1993]. CD.

ANTHOLOGIES

2125 ★*In Griot Time: String Music from Mali.* Stern's Africa: STCD 1089. 1992, 2000. CD.

2126 *Mali.* Putumayo World Music: PUT 236-2. 2005. CD.

2127 *Music of Mali* (Charles Hofmann, ed.; Elizabeth Dyer and W. Gurnee Dyer, compilers). Custom Compact Disc Series. Smithsonian Folkways: FE 4338. 1966, 1999. CD.

2128 ★*Rough Guide to the Music of Mali.* Rough Guide. World Music Network: RGNET 1208 CD. 2008. CD.

VIDEO

2129 *Salif Keita citoyen ambassadeur = Salif Keita Citizen and Ambassador.* World Music Portraits. Shanachie: 115. 1996, 2004. DVD.

Mauritania

INDIVIDUAL ARTISTS AND GROUPS

2130 Ensemble El Moukhadrami. *Chants de Griots = Songs of the Griots.* Institut du Monde Arabe: 321004. [1994–2000]. CD.

2131 Warakane, Coumbane Mint Ely. *Mauritanie: Coumbane Mint Ely Warakane.* Inédit. Maison des Cultures du Monde: W 260139. 2009, 2010. CD.

ANTHOLOGY

2132 *The Sounds of the West Sahara: Mauritania* (Deben Bhattacharya, compiler). ARC Music: EUCD 1870. 2004. CD.

Niger

ANTHOLOGY

2133 ★*Tuareg Music of the Southern Sahara* (Finola and Geoffrey Holiday, compilers). Custom Compact Disc Series. Smithsonian Folkways: FE 4470. 1960, 2000. CD.

Nigeria

INDIVIDUAL ARTIST

2134 Lea, Alhaji Garba. *Alhaji Garba Leo and His Goge Music.* Custom Compact Disc Series. Smithsonian Folkways: FW 8860. 1976, 2000s. CD.

ANTHOLOGIES

2135 ★*Drums of the Yoruba of Nigeria* (William Russell Bascom, compiler). Custom Compact Disc Series. Smithsonian Folkways: FE 4441. 1953, 1990s. CD.

2136 *Music from the Villages of Northeastern Nigeria.* Custom Compact Disc Series. Smithsonian Folkways: F-4532. 1971, 2001. 2 CDs.

2137 *Music of the Idoma of Nigeria* (Ediigwu; Jim Antanavich, compiler). Custom Compact Disc

Series. Smithsonian Folkways: AHM 4221. 1969, 2001. CD.

2138 *Music of the Jos Plateau and Other Regions of Nigeria* (Stanley Diamond, compiler). Smithsonian Folkways: FE 4321. 1965, 1999. CD.

2139 *Yoruba Bata Drums—Elewe Music and Dance* (G. Odukwe Sackeyfio, compiler). Custom Compact Disc Series. Smithsonian Folkways: FE 4294. 1980, 2001. CD.

VIDEO

2140 *Konkombe: Nigerian Music.* Beats of the Heart. Shanachie: 1201. 1980, 2000. DVD.

Senegal

INDIVIDUAL ARTIST

2141 M'Baye, Ousmane. *Songs of Senegal.* Custom Compact Disc Series. Smithsonian Folkways: FW 8505. 1975, 2001. CD.

ANTHOLOGIES

2142 *Music of the Diola-Fogny of the Casamance, Senegal.* Custom Compact Disc Series. Smithsonian Folkways: FE 4323. 1965, 2001. CD.

2143 *Wolof Music of Senegal and the Gambia* (David W. Ames, compiler). Smithsonian Folkways: FE 4462. 1955, 1999. CD.

VIDEO

2144 *Youssou N'Dour et Le Super Étoile de Dakar, Live at Montreux, 1989.* Eagle Eye Media: EE 39112-9. 1989, 2005. DVD.

Sierra Leone

ANTHOLOGIES

2145 *Music of Sierra Leone: Kono Mende Farmers' Songs* (Stuart Leigh, compiler). Custom Compact Disc Series. Smithsonian Folkways: FE 4330. 1981, 2001. CD.

2146 *Music of the Mende of Sierra Leone* (Gary Schulze, compiler). Custom Compact Disc Series.Smithsonian Folkways: FE 4322. 1962, 1999. CD.

Togo

ANTHOLOGY

2147 *Togo: Music from West Africa.* Rounder: CD 5004. 1992. CD.

WESTERN AFRICA TRADITIONAL VIDEO

2148 *The JVC Video Anthology of World Music and Dance, Vol. 17.* JVC, Victor Co. of Japan; dist. by Multicultural Media. 1990, 2005. 30 DVDs, 9 booklets.

WESTERN AFRICA POPULAR

Compiled by Richard McRae

This section comprises popular music from Western Africa. The countries covered include Benin, Cape Verde, Chad, Gambia, Ghana, Guinea, Guinea-Bissau, Ivory Coast (Côte d'Ivoire), Liberia, Mali, Mauritania, Niger, Nigeria, Senegal, Sierra Leone, and Togo. Distributors and sources include Stern's Music (www.sternsmusic .com), Afrison, Universal Music Group (www.universal-music.com), Allmusic (www.allmusic.com), and *World Music: The Rough Guide, Vol. 1: Africa, Europe, and the Middle East,* edited by Simon Broughton and Mark Ellingham (Rough Guides, 1999).

Western Africa is a vibrant contributor to world musical culture—the Afrobeat phenomenon and traditional forms. There are too many to name in a brief introduction but Ghanaian highlife (urban music with rural roots in the colonial era through independence) is one example that comes in many shapes (for example, palm-wine music) influenced by traditionalism and by dance-band (and guitar-band) forms and various African and European influences (Broughton and Ellingham, 488). Highlife is in no way restricted to Ghana; its diaspora reaches other parts of Africa (particularly Nigeria) as well as Europe and North America. Nigeria is also a major musical center, featuring well-known forms that span tradition and pop, such as *juju* (sung) and Yoruba instrumentals, Hausa and highlife. Two famous Yoruban musicians who have garnered worldwide attention are Sunny Ade (*juju*) and Fela Kuti (who combined elements of soul, jazz, traditional, and highlife) (ibid., 594). Senegal and Gambia share *griot* traditions (influences of Mali and Guinea), instruments (kora, balafon), dance music, and pop star Youssou N'Dour (Senegalese). Many other styles flourish and, as in so many areas, there is much fluidity and cross-pollination among these forms and many evolved from each other.

Benin

INDIVIDUAL ARTISTS AND GROUPS

2149 Adé Oyé, Prince. *Juju Music.* Voix d'Afrique: B 00008 FYXO. 1995. CD.

2150 Dougbé, Pedro, Gnonnas Dougbé, Rego Dougbé, and Antoine Dougbé. *Legends of Benin* (Honoré Avolonto and Samy Ben Redjeb). Analog Africa, No. 5. Analog Africa Records: AACD 065. 2009. CD.

2151 Gangbé Brass Band. *Whendo*. Contre Jour; dist. by World Village: 468050. 2004. CD.

2152 Kidjo, Angelique
    2152.1 ★*Keep on Moving: The Best of Angelique Kidjo*. Wrasse: CK 85758. 2001. CD.
    2152.2 *Logozo*. Mango: 162 539918-2. 1991. CD.
    2152.3 ★*Ōÿö*. Razor and Tie: 7930183062-2. 2010. CD.

2153 Oliver, Nel. *Baby Girl*. ACRC Music: SPNO 10012. 2000. CD.

2154 Orchestre Poly-Rythmo and Melome Clement. *Cotonou Club*. Strut: STRUT 077 CD. 2011. CD.

2155 Tohon, Stan, and the Tchink System. *Tchink Attack*. Dona Wana: 50434-2. 1995. CD.

2156 T. P. Orchestre Polyrhythmo. *Kings of Benin Urban Groove, 1972–80*. Soundway: SNDWCD 004. 2004. CD.

ANTHOLOGIES

2157 *African Scream Contest: Raw and Psychedelic Afro Sounds from Benin and Togo 70s*. Analog Africa, No. 3. Analog Africa Records: AACD 063. 2008. CD.

2158 *Bénin: Musiques Yoruba, les voix de la mémoire = Benin: Yoruba Music, Voices of Memory*. Ocora Radio France: C 560237. 2011. 2 CDs.

Burkina Faso

INDIVIDUAL ARTISTS AND GROUPS

2159 Burkina Electric. *Paspanga*. Cantaloupe: CA 21057. 2010. CD.

2160 Dabiré, Gabin
    2160.1 *Afriki Djamana*. Secret World Series. Amiata: ARNR 0494. 1994. CD.
    2160.2 *Kontôme*. Amiata: ARNR 1966. 1998. CD.

2161 Farafina. *Faso Denou*. Real World: CAROL 2328-2. 1993. CD.

2162 Saaba. *Koudougou*. Daquí: 332 002. 1998. CD.

ANTHOLOGIES

2163 *Bambara Mystic Soul: The Raw Sound of Burkina Faso, 1974–1979*. Analog Africa, No. 10. Analog Africa Records: AACD 070. 2011. CD.

2164 *Ouga Affair: Hard Won Sound of the Upper Volta, 1974–1978*. Savannahphone: AFCD 012. 2009. CD.

Cape Verde

INDIVIDUAL ARTISTS AND GROUPS

2165 Bana
    2165.1 *Chante la magie du Cap-Vert*. Lusafrica: 08630-2. 1993. CD.
    2165.2 *Gira sol*. Arco Iris: 3001 803. 1998. CD.

2166 De Barros, Maria. *Morabeza*. Sheer Sound: SLCD 167. 2009. CD.

2167 Evora, Cesaria
    2167.1 ★*Essential Cesaria Evora*. Sony Music Entertainment: 88697 75488 2. 2010. 2 CDs.
    2167.2 *Miss Perfumado*. Nonesuch: 19509-2. 1992. CD.

2168 Tavares, Sara. *Xinti*. Four Quarters Entertainment: FQT-CD-1818. 2009. CD.

ANTHOLOGIES

2169 ★*Cape Verde: Music Rough Guide*. Rough Guide. World Music Network: RGNET 1065 CD. 2001. CD.

2170 *Cape Verde Anthology, 1959–1992*. Musique du Monde. Buda: 92614-2. 1992. 2 CDs.

2171 ★*Music from Cape Verde*. Caprice: CAP 21451. 1994. CD.

2172 ★*Putumayo Presents Cape Verde*. Putumayo World Music: PUTU 156-2. 1999. CD.

2173 *Soul of Cape Verde*. Tinder Production, Lusafrica: 42831732. 1996. CD.

VIDEO

2174 *Cabo Verde in Clips: 1*. IEFE Discos-Unipessoal; dist. by Globe Music Productions: 79558-2. 2005. DVD.

Gambia

INDIVIDUAL ARTISTS AND GROUPS

2175 Ifang Bondi. *Gis Gis*. World Roots Collection, No. 8. MW Records: MWCD 3019. 1998. CD.

2176 Mandingo Griot Society. *Mandingo Griot Society*. Flying Fish: FF 77076. 1978. CD.

2177 Jobarteh, Amadu Bansang. *Tabara*. Music of the World: CDT-129. 1993. CD.

2178 Konte, Dembo. *Kairaba Jabi* (Kausu Kuyateh). Rogue Productions: WEBE 9032. 1996. CD.

2179 ★Suso, Foday Musa. *Two Worlds*. Orange Mountain Music: 53. 2006. CD.

2180 Suso, Salieu. *Griot*. Lyrichord: LYRCH 7418. 1993. CD.

ANTHOLOGIES

2181 ★*Music of West Africa: The Mandinka and Their Neighbors*. Lyrichord: LYRCD 2010. 2010. CD, DVD.

2182 ★*Senegal and Gambia: Rough Guide*. Rough Guide. World Music Network: RGNET 1060 CD. 2000. CD.

Ghana

INDIVIDUAL ARTISTS AND GROUPS

2183 Annan, Nii Otoo. *Ghana Sea Blues* (Steven Feld, prod. and arr.). VoxLox: 112. 2012. CD.

2184 Annan, Nii Otoo, and Steven Feld. *Bufo Variations*. VoxLox: 408. 2008. CD.

2185 Mensah, E. T., and Tempos Dance Band. *Day by Day*. RetroAfric: Retro 3 CD. 1991. CD.

2186 Osibisa. *Osibisa: Woyaya*. BGO Records: BGOCD 646. 2004. CD.

2187 Taylor, Ebo. *Life Stories: Highlife and Afrobeat Classics, 1973–1980*. Strut: STRUT 072 CD. 2011. 2 CDs.

ANTHOLOGIES

2188 *Afro-Beat Airways*. Analog Africa, No. 8. Analog Africa Records: AACD 068. 2010. CD.

2189 ★*Classic Highlife: The Best of Ghanaian Highlife Music*. AIM: AIM 1053. 1995. CD.

2190 *Ghana: Voices of Africa: High-Life and Other Popular Music*. Explorer Series; Africa. Nonesuch: 79701-2. 2002. CD.

2191 ★*Ghana, 1931–1957: From Palm Wine Music to Dance Band Highlife*. Arion: ARN 64564. 2001. CD.

2192 ★*Ghana Special: Modern Highlife, Afro-Sounds, and Ghanaian Blues, 1968–1981* Soundway: SNDWCD016. 2009. 2 CDs.

2193 *Guitar and Gun: Highlife Music from Ghana*. Stern's Music, Earthworks: STEW 50 CD. 2003. CD.

2194 ★*Highlife: The Rough Guide*. Rough Guide. World Music Network: RGNET 1102 CD. 2003. CD.

2195 *Jazz Cosmopolitanism in Accra* (Steven Feld, compiler). VoxLox: 212. 1957, 2012. CD.

2196 ★*Nigeria and Ghana*. Rough Guide. World Music Network: RGNET 1075 CD. 2002. CD.

2197 ★*Vintage Palmwine: Highlife*. Otrabanda: OTB 02. 1983, 2003. CD.

VIDEOS

2198 *Jazz Cosmopolitanism in Accra, Ghana* (Kofi Ghanaba and others; Steven Feld, prod. and dir.). VoxLox. 2009. 3 DVDs.

2199 *Koo Nimo: Palm Wine Guitar*. Banyan Archives. 2001. VHS.

2200 *Living the Hiplife* (Reggie Ossei Rockstone and the Mobile Boys). Third World Newsreel. 2007. DVD.

2201 ★*Traditional Music and Dance of Ghana* (Obo Addy). Resonance Media: RM 209. 2011. DVD.

Guinea

INDIVIDUAL ARTISTS AND GROUPS

2202 Amazones de Guinée. *Wamato*. Stern's Music: STCD 1106. 2008. CD.

2203 ★Balla et ses Balladins. *Sylliphone Years*. Stern's Music: STCD 3035-36. 2008. 2 CDs.

2204 Barry, Mamadou. *Niyo*. World Village France; Harmonia Mundi: WVF 479033. 2009. CD.

2205 Bembeye Jazz National. *Syliphone Years*. Authenticite. Stern's Africa: STCD 3029-30. 2007. 2 CDs.

2206   Cissoko, Ba. *Sabolan.* Marabi: 468082. 2003. CD.

2207   Diabaté, Sékouba. *Kassa.* Stern's Africa: STCD 1074. 1997. CD.

2208   Diabaté, Sona. *Girls of Guinea.* Shanachie: SH 65007. 1990. CD.

2209   Jawara, Jali Musa. *Yasimika.* Carthage, Hannibal: HNCD 1355. 1990. CD.

2210   Kante, Mory. *Sabou.* Riverboat: TUGCD 1034. 2004. CD.

2211   Kouyate, Ousmane. *Domba.* Mango: 539 886-2. 1990. CD.

ANTHOLOGY

2212   ★*Mali and Guinea: Music Rough Guide.* Rough Guide. World Music Network: RGNET 1048 CD. 2000. CD.

VIDEO

2213   *M'bemba Fakoli: A Musical Journey through Guinea, West Africa* (Bolokada Conde). Abaraka Music. 2008. DVD.

Guinea-Bissau

INDIVIDUAL ARTISTS AND GROUPS

2214   Costa, Manecas. *Paraiso Di Gumbe.* BBC Music: BBCLJ 3007-2. 2003. CD.

2215   Djabaté, Kimi. *Karam.* Cumbancha: CMB-CD-12. 2009. CD.

2216   Naka, Ramiro. *Salvador.* Mango: 162-539 921-2. 1990. CD.

2217   Super Mama Djombo. *Super Mama Djombo.* Cobiana: COB-02. 2003. CD.

ANTHOLOGY

2218   ★*Popular Music from Guinea-Bissau.* Intermusic. 2000. CD.

Ivory Coast

INDIVIDUAL ARTISTS AND GROUPS

2219   Kanza, Lokua. *Nkolo.* World Village France: WVF 479043. 2010. CD.

2220   Meiway. *Génies vous parlent.* Lusafrica: 262.30-2. 1997. CD.

ANTHOLOGIES

2221   ★*Côte d'Ivoire, 50 ans indépendance musicale.* Obouo Music: OB 10.013. 2010. 3 CDs. Limited edition.

2222   *Côte d'Ivoire: West African Crossroads.* African Pearls, 5. Syllart Productions: 6145482. 2009. 2 CDs.

VIDEOS

2223   *Masters of the Balafon* (Hugo Zemp, dir.). Documentary Educational Resources. 2009. 4 DVDs.

2224   *Siaka, an African Musician* (Siaka Diabaté; Hugo Zemp, dir.). Documentary Educational Resources. 2009. DVD.

Liberia

ANTHOLOGY

2225   ★*Songs of the African Coast: Cafe Music of Liberia.* Yamgo Music: 389. 2007. CD.

Mali

INDIVIDUAL ARTISTS AND GROUPS

2226   AfroCubism. *AfroCubism* (Eliades Ochoa, Toumani Diabaté, Kassé Mady, Lasana Diabate, Bassekou Kouyate, and Djélimady Tounkara). World Circuit; Nonesuch: 525993-2. 2010. CD.

2227   Amadou and Mariam. *Welcome to Mali.* Because Music; Nonesuch: 517673-2. 2009. CD.

2228   Cline, Nels, Tunde Adebimpe, and Kyp Malone. *Tassili.* Anti: ANTI-87148-2. 2011. CD.

2229   Diabaté, Toumani. *The Mandé Variations.* Nonesuch, World Circuit: 433724-2, WCD079. 2008. CD.

2230   Keïta, Salif
    2230.1   ★*Best of Salif Keita.* Wrasse: GWVCD 40. 2002. CD.
    2230.2   *La différence.* Universal Music France / EmArcy: B0014386-02. 2009. CD.

2231   Mady, Kassé. *Kassi Kasse: Music from the Heart of Mali's Griot Tradition.* Narada World: 72435-80775-2-0. 2002. CD.

2232   Sangare, Oumou
    2232.1   *Moussolou.* World Circuit, Nonesuch: 79575-2. 1999. CD.

2232.2 *Oumou*. World Circuit, Nonesuch: 79827-2. 2004. CD.

2233 Toure, Ali Farka
  2233.1 ★*Ali Farka Toure: Radio Mali*. World Circuit, Nonesuch: 79569-2. 1996. CD.
  2233.2 *Savane*. World Circuit, Nonesuch: 79965-2. 2006. CD.

2234 Touré, Ali Farka, and Toumani Diabaté. *Ali and Toumani* (Orlando "Cachaito" López). World Circuit; Nonesuch: 522937-2. 2010. CD.

2235 Touré, Vieux Farka. *Fondo*. Six Degrees: 657036 1158-2. 2009. CD.

ANTHOLOGIES

2236 *Mali Lolo!: Stars of Mali*. Smithsonian Folkways: SFW CD 40508. 2003. CD.

2237 ★*Rough Guide to the Music of Mali*. Rough Guide. World Music Network: RGNET 1208 CD. 2008. CD.

2238 *Wassoullou Sound: Women of Mali, Vols.1 and 2*. Stern's Africa: STCD 1035, STCD 1048. [1990–1993]. 2 CDs.

VIDEO

2239 *Ali Farka Touré: Springing from the Roots*. Planet Group Entertainment. 2012. DVD.

Mauritania

INDIVIDUAL ARTISTS

2240 Amartichitt, Ooleya Mint. *Louanges: Praise Songs*. Long Distance: 3060572 WAG 331. 2000. CD.

2241 Seck, Mansour. *N'der Fouta Tooro, Vols. 1 and 2* (Ousmane Hamady Diop and Maal Baaba). Stern's Africa: STCD 1061, STCD 1073. 1996. 2 CDs.

ANTHOLOGY

2242 *Wallahi Le Zein!: Wezin, Jakwar and Guitar Boogie from the Islamic Republic of Mauritania*. Latitude Disc. 2010. 2 CDs.

Niger

GROUPS

2243 Etran Finatawa. *Introducing Etran Finatawa*. Introducing, World Music Network: INTRO 105 CD. 2006. CD.

2244 Poussy, Moussa, and Saadou Bori. *Niamey Twice*. Stern's Africa: STCD 1057. 1994. CD.

2245 Tinariwen. *Amassakoul*. World Village; dist. Harmonia Mundi: 468026. 2003. CD.

Nigeria

INDIVIDUAL ARTISTS AND GROUPS

2246 Adé, King Sunny
  2246.1 ★*Bábá Mo Túndé*. Mesa; Bluemoon; IndigeDisc: 2147. 2010. 2 CDs.
  2246.2 ★*Best of the Classic Years*. Shanachie: SH 66034. 2003. CD.

2247 Allen, Tony. *Secret Agent*. Nonesuch: 521074-2. 2010. CD.

2248 Anikulapo-Kuti, Seun
  2248.1 *From Africa with Fury, Rise*. Knitting Factory Records: KFR 1110 CD. 2011. CD.
  2248.2 *Seun Kuti + Fela's Egypt 80*. Disorient: SUSHI CD056. 2008. CD.

2249 ★Kuti, Fela. *Best of the Black President*. Wrasse: WRASS 158. 2002. 2 CDs.

2250 Kuti, Femi. *Definitive Collection*. Wrasse: WRASS 186. 2007. 2 CDs.

2251 Lágbájá. *We before Me*. IndigeDisc: 495003. 2001. CD.

2252 Osadebe, Chief Stephen Osita. *Classic Hits, Vol. 1*. Leader Records. 2000. CD.

2253 Twins Seven Seven. *Nigerian Beat*. World Music Library, 49. Seven Seas: KICC 5149. 1991. CD.

ANTHOLOGIES

2254 *Black Man's Cry: The Inspiration of Fela Kuti*. Now-Again Records: NA 5056. 2009. CD.

2255 ★*Juju Roots: 1930s–1950s*. Rounder: CD 5017. 1993. CD.

2256 ★*Nigeria 70: The Definitive Story of 1970's Funky Lagos*. AfroStrut: STRUTCD 013. 2002. 3 CDs.

2257 ★*Nigeria Special: Modern Highlife, Afro-Sounds, and Nigerian Blues, 1970–76*. Soundway: SNDWCD 009. 2007. 2 CDs.

2258 *The World Ends: Afro Rock and Psychedelia in 1970s Nigeria*. Soundway: SNDWCD023. 2010. 2 CDs.

VIDEO

2259 *Juju Music.* Rhapsody Films: 9016. 1991. VHS.

2260 *Music Is the Weapon: Musique au Poing* (Fela Kuti). Knitting Factory: KNF-DVD-53. 2009. DVD.

Senegal

INDIVIDUAL ARTISTS AND GROUPS

2261 Lô, Cheikh. *Jamm.* Nonesuch: 527269-2. 2010. CD.

2262 Maal, Baaba. *Missing You: Mi Yeewnii.* Palm Pictures: PALMCD 2067-2. 2001. CD.

2263 N'Dour, Youssou

    2263.1 *Once upon a Time in Senegal: Birth of Mbalax, 1979–1981* (Étoile de Dakar). Stern's Music: STCD 3054-55. 2010. 2 CDs.

    2263.2 ★*Rough Guide to Youssou N'Dour and Étoile De Dakar* (Étoile de Dakar). Rough Guide. World Music Network: RGNET 1109 CD. 2002. CD.

2264 ★Orchestra Baobab. *Pirates Choice.* World Circuit, Nonesuch: 79643-2. 2001. 2 CDs.

2265 Seck, Thione. *Orientation.* Stern's Africa: STCD 1100. 2005. CD.

2266 ★Touré Kunda. *Touré Kunda Collection.* Putumayo World Music: PUTU121-2. 1996. CD.

ANTHOLOGIES

2267 *Sénégal 70: Musical Effervescence.* Syllart Productions: 6142032. 2009. 2 CDs.

2268 *Streets of Dakar: Generation Boul Falé.* Stern's Africa: STCD 1084. 1999. CD.

VIDEO

2269 ★*Compilation Senegal* (Various artists). African Music Productions. 2003. 4 DVDs.

2270 *Baaba Maal.* Palm Pictures. 2005. DVD.

2271 *Djabote: Senegalese Drumming and Song from Master Drummer Doudou N'diaye Rose.* Multicultural Media: MCM 1006. 2008. DVD.

2272 *Youssou N'Dour.* Sonic Edge: SEDVD 9162. 2001. DVD.

2273 ★*Youssou N'Dour: I Bring What I Love.* Oscilloscope Pictures: OSC-20. 2010. DVD.

Sierra Leone

INDIVIDUAL ARTISTS AND GROUPS

2274 Refugee All Stars. *Rise and Shine.* Cumbancha: CMB-CD-18. 2010. CD.

2275 Rogie, Sulaman E. *Palm Wine Guitar Music: The 60's Sound.* Cooking Vinyl: COOKCD 010. 2002. CD.

2276 Tee-Jay, Abdul. *Palm Wine a Go-Go.* Far Side Music: FSCD 1001. 2003. CD.

VIDEO

2277 *Sierra Leone's Refugee All Stars.* SodaSoap Productions. 2006. DVD.

Togo

INDIVIDUAL ARTIST

2278 Mensah, King. *Madjo.* Bolibana Productions: BIP 148. 1990. CD.

**WESTERN AFRICA POPULAR
GENERAL ANTHOLOGIES**

2279 *Africa Boogaloo: The Latinization of West Africa.* Honest Jon's Records: HJRCD 41. 2009. CD.

2280 ★*Arthur S. Alberts Collection: More Tribal, Folk, and Café Music of West Africa.* Smithsonian Folkways Archival. Smithsonian Folkways: HRT 15016. 2010. CD.

EASTERN AFRICA

*Compiled by Holling Smith-Borne
and Gregory F. Barz*

This section focuses on geographic borders as well as on representing a broad spectrum of ethnic groups and communities. Within these traditions, historical recording efforts have focused on a select group of musical traditions. The goal here is to represent a broader collection of recordings that encompass a more complete spectrum of the cultures in East Africa. This discography is a balanced collection of both popular and traditional musicians who are respected both in their home countries and abroad. The journal *Ethnomusicology* maintained an online list of new CD titles (African section) in "Current Discographies," which is helpful for developing collections on this topic (www.ethnomusicology.org/?0G_CurrentDisco).

Well-known genres in Eastern Africa include gospel, *benga* style and Kikuyu pop bands, and Congolese and Swahili sounds in Kenya (to name only a few). Tanzanian popular music ranges from Cuban jazz to hip-hop and rap; the Tanzanian/Kenyan Swahili coastal style, *taarab,* uses elements of poetry, drumming rhythms, and Arabic and Asian instruments, with Islamic influences. As in many areas, musical affinities are not always as clear-cut as geographic ones. Madagascar can be considered southern or southeastern and Sudan is often grouped with central Africa and has Middle Eastern influences. For more information about Eastern African (and African music in general), please consult the *Garland Handbook of African Music,* 2nd ed. (Routledge, 2008).

EASTERN AFRICA TRADITIONAL

Burundi

INDIVIDUAL ARTISTS AND GROUPS

2281 ★Drummers of Burundi. *The Drummers of Burundi = Les Tambourinaires du Burundi.* Real World: RWMCD 1, CAROL 2338-2. 1987, 1992. CD.

2282 Ensemble Folklorique Batimbo. *Drums of Burundi.* ARC: EUCD 2053. 2006, 2007. CD.

2283 Michiels, Frank. *Musiques du Burundi.* Traditions du Monde. Fonti Musicali: fmd 213. 1990, 1997. CD.

2284 Nin, Khadja. *Ya . . .* Mondo Melodia: 186 810 062 2. 2000. CD.

ANTHOLOGIES

2285 ★*Africa: Music from Rwanda* (Denyse Hiernaux-L'Hoëst, compiler). Anthology of World Music. Rounder: CD 5106. 1954, 1999. CD.

2286 *Batimbo: Musiques et chants: Tambours du Burundi = Burundi Drums.* Playasound: PS 65089. 1991, 1992. CD.

2287 ★*Burundi: Music from the Heart of Africa* (Giuseppe Corter, compiler). Explorer Series: Africa. Nonesuch: 79706-2. 1974, 2002. CD.

2288 ★*Burundi: Musiques traditionnelles* (Michel Vuylsteke, ed.). Ocora: C559003. 1967, 1988. CD.

Comoros

INDIVIDUAL ARTIST

2289 Hassan, Mohamed. *Duniya.* Dizim Records: 4507-2. 1998, 2000. CD.

ANTHOLOGY

2290 *Musiques traditionnelles des Comores.* Musique du Monde. Buda: 92732-2. 1990s. CD.

Eritrea

INDIVIDUAL ARTIST

2291 Faytinga, Dehab. *Numey.* Cobalt Music France: 09294-2. 2006. CD.

ANTHOLOGY

2292 *Folk Music of Ethiopia* (Harold Courlander, ed.). Smithsonian Folkways: F-04405. 1951, 1991. CD

Ethiopia

ANTHOLOGIES

2293 *Ethiopia: The Falasha and the Adjuran Tribe* (Lin Lerner and Chad Wollner, compilers and eds.). Custom Compact Disc Series. Smithsonian Folkways: FE 4355. 1975, 1999. CD.

2294 *Ethiopia: The Harp of Apollo: Songs Accompanied by the Kirar.* JVC World Sounds: VICG-5013. 1989, 1990. CD.

2295 *Ethiopia: Three Chordophone Traditions.* Unesco Collection; An Anthology of African Music. Auvidis Unesco: D 8074. 1972, 1996. CD.

2296 *Ethiopian Urban and Tribal Music*
    2296.1 *Vol. 1: Mindanoo Mistiru* (Ragnar Johnson and Ralph Harrisson, compilers). Rounder: CD 5152. 1999. CD.
    2296.2 *Vol. 2: Gold from Wax* (Ragnar Johnson and Ralph Harrisson, compilers). Rounder: CD 5153. 1972, 1999. CD.

2297 *Éthiopie: Musiques des Hauts-Plateaux.* PlayaSound: PS 65219. 1999. CD.

2298 *Folk Music and Ceremonies of Ethiopia* (Lin Lerner and Chad Wollner, compilers and eds.). Smithsonian Folkways: FE 4354. 1974, 2001. CD.

2299 *Folk Music of Ethiopia* (Harold Courlander, ed.). Smithsonian Folkways: F-04405. 1951, 2003. CD.

2300 *Liturgies juives d'Ethiopie.* Maison des Cultures du Monde: W 260013. 1990. CD.

2301 *Nyabole, Hamar, Southern Ethiopia.* Museum Collection Berlin. Wergo: SM 1707 2. 1978, 2003. CD, book.

2302 *Religious Music of the Falashas* (Wolf Leslau, compiler). Custom Compact Disc Series. Smithsonian Folkways: FE 4442. 1950, 1999. CD.

2303 *Ritual Music of Ethiopia* (Lin Lerner and Chad Wollner, compilers and eds.). Custom Compact Disc Series. Smithsonian Folkways: FE 4353. 1973, 2001. CD.

Kenya

INDIVIDUAL ARTISTS AND GROUPS

2304 Bobo, Oguta. *Rujina Kalando.* Equator Heritage Sounds. 1998. CD.

2305 Kenge Kenge. *Introducing Kenge Kenge.* World Music Network: IDR 107 CD. 2007. CD.

2306 Nzomo, David
  2306.1 *African Rhythms: Songs from Kenya.* Smithsonian Folkways: AH 8503. 1970, 1999. CD.
  2306.2 *Gospel Songs from Kenya: Kikamba Hymns.* Custom Compact Disc Series. Smithsonian Folkways: FR 8911. 1976, 2001. CD.

2307 Okoth, Ogwang Lelo, and Paddy J. Onono. *Luo Roots: Musical Currents from Western Kenya.* Globestyle: CRORBD 061. 1990. CD.

2308 Zein Musical Party. *Mtindo Wa Mombasa: The Style of Mombasa.* GlobeStyle: CDORBD 066. 1989, 1990. CD.

ANTHOLOGIES

2309 *Before Benga: Kenya Dry, Vol. 1.* Original Music: OMCD 021. 1988. CD.

2310 *Kenya: L'obokano, lyre des Gusii = The Obokano, Lyre of the Gusii.* Archives Internationales de Musique Populaire, 107. VDE Gallo: VDE CD-1414. 2012, 2014. CD.

2311 *Kenyan Songs and Strings, 1950 and 1952, Kenya: Luo, Luhya, Hipsigis, Kikuyu, Nandi, Swahili,*

Wanga, Giriama (Hugh Tracey, compiler). Historical Recordings by Hugh Tracey. Stichting Sharp Wood Productions: SWP 030/HT 019. 1950, 2006. CD.

2312 ★*Missa Luba: An African Mass; Kenyan Folk Melodies* (Muungano National Choir; Boniface Mganga, cond.; Guido Haazen, arr.). Philips: 426 836-2. 1990. CD.

2313 *Music of the Kuria and the Gusii of Western Kenya* (John P. Varnum, compiler). Custom Compact Disc Series. Smithsonian Folkways: FH 4223. 1972, 1990. CD.

2314 *Music of the Waswahili of Lamu, Kenya: Maulidi, Vol. 1* (Alan W. Boyd, compiler). Custom Compact Disc Series. Smithsonian Folkways: FE 4093. 1985, 2001. CD.

2315 *Music of the Waswahili of Lamu, Kenya: Other Sacred Music, Vol. 2* (Alan W. Boyd, compiler). Custom Compact Disc Series. Smithsonian Folkways: FE 4094. 1985, 2001. CD.

2316 *Music of the Waswahili of Lamu, Kenya: Secular Music, Vol. 3* (Alan W. Boyd, compiler). Custom Compact Disc Series. Smithsonian Folkways: FE 4095. 1985, 2001. CD.

2317 *Musiques du Nyanza.* Ocora Radio France: C 560022/23. 1993. 2 CDs.

2318 ★*Rough Guide to the Music of Kenya: Roots Benga, Coastal Taarab, Urban Rap.* Rough Guide. World Music Network: RGNET 1137 CD. 2004. CD.

Madagascar

GROUPS

2319 Pana and D'Gary. *Malagasy Guitar: Music from Madagascar.* Shanachie: 65009. 1991, 1992. CD.

2320 Mèllèssè, Muluqèn, and Mahmoud Ahmed. *Madagascar: Accordéons et esprits ancestraux = Accordions and Ancestral Spirits.* Archives Internationales de Musique Populaire, 65. VDE: VDE CD-1065. 1993, 2001. CD.

ANTHOLOGIES

2321 ★*Madagascar.* Rough Guide. World Music Network: RGNET 1163 CD. 2005. CD.

2322 *Madagascar: Anthologie des voix* (Victor Randrianary, compiler). Maison des Cultures du Monde: W 260076. 1995, 1997. CD.

2323 ★*Madagascar: Awakening the Spirits: Music in Tromba and Bilo Trance Rituals* (August Schmidhofer, compiler). Music of the Earth. Multicultural Media: MCM 3011. 1986, 1997. CD.

2324 *Madagascar: Pays Antandroy, côte sud-ouest = Madagascar: Antandroy Country, South-West Coast* (Alain Desjacques, compiler). Ocora: C 560077. 1994, 1995. CD.

2325 *Madagasikara 1: Current Traditional Music of Madagascar.* GlobeStyle: CDORBD 012. 1986, 1990. CD.

2326 *Pays Bara = Bara Country* (Alain Desjacques, compiler). Ocora: C 560089. 1994, 1996. CD.

Mauritius

GROUP

2327 Fanfan. *Séga Ravanne.* Ocora: C 560137. 1998, 1999. CD.

Réunion

INDIVIDUAL ARTIST

2328 *Réunion, Rodrigues, Maurice/Mauritius: Les Îles Créoles de l'Océan Indien = Creole Islands of the Indian Ocean.* Auvidis: 225716. 1998. CD.

Rwanda

INDIVIDUAL ARTIST

2329 Kayirebwa, Cécile. *Rwanda.* GlobeStyle Records: CDORBD 083. 1994. CD.

ANTHOLOGIES

2330 ★*Africa: Music from Rwanda* (Denyse Hiernaux-L'Hoëst, compiler). Anthology of World Music. Rounder: CD 5106. 1954, 1999. CD.

2331 ★*At the Court of the Mwami, Ruanda, 1952, Rwanda: Tutsi, Hutu, Twa* (Hugh Tracey, compiler). Historical Recordings by Hugh Tracey. Stichting Sharp Wood Productions: SWP 007/HT 01. 1952, 1998. CD.

2332 *Inanga: A Song of Survival in a Daughter's Rwanda* (Gregory Barz, dir. and prod.). Lime Pulp Records. 2009, 2010. CD, DVD.

2333 *Musiques du Rwanda* (Jos Gansemans, compiler). Fonti musicali: fmd 206. 1973, 1995. CD.

2334 *Polyphonie des Twa du Rwanda: Musée Royal de l'Afrique Centrale.* Traditions du Monde. Fonti musicali: fmd 196. 1993. CD.

2335 *Rwanda* (Hugh Tracey, compiler). Sound of Africa Series, 34. International Library of African Music: CDTR 34. 2000s. CD.

2336 *Rwanda: Rwanda/Hutu* (Hugh Tracey, compiler). Sound of Africa Series, 181. International Library of African Music: CDTR 181. 2000s. CD.

2337 *Songs of the Watutsi* (Leo A. Verwilghen, compiler). Smithsonian Folkways: F-4428, FE 4428. 1952, 1999. CD.

Seychelles

GROUP

2338 Compères Grat'fils. *Danses folk de l'Ocean Indien.* PlayaSound: PS 65029. 1988. CD.

Somalia

INDIVIDUAL ARTISTS AND GROUPS

2339 Kershi, Abdullah. *The Freedom Songs of the Somali Republic* (Ahmed Sherif). Custom Compact Disc Series. Smithsonian Folkways: F-5443. 1962, 2000. CD.

2340 Shiekh, Haussein, Chet Williams, and Hassan Hussein. *Baijun Ballads: Somali Songs in Swahili* (Radio Mogadiscio Swahili Singers). Custom Compact Disc Series. Smithsonian Folkways: AH 8504. 1970, 2003. CD.

ANTHOLOGY

2341 *Jamiila: Songs from a Somali City* (John Low, compiler). Contemporary African Music Series. Original Music: OMCD 007. 1987. CD.

Sudan

INDIVIDUAL ARTISTS AND GROUPS

2342 Awlad al-Bura'I and Awlad al-Mahi. *Chants sacrés de Nubie et de Kordofan = Sacred Songs from Nubia and Kordofan.* Institut du Monde Arabe: 321039. 2002. CD.

2343 Din, Hamza el-
   2343.1 ★*Escalay, the Water Wheel: Oud Music.* Explorer Series: Africa. Nonesuch: 79702-2. 1971, 2002. CD.
   2343.2 *Music of Nubia.* Vanguard: VMD 79164. 1980–1989. CD.

2344 Sunni, Mustafa al-. *Songs of the Sudan.* Nimbus: NI 5583. 1999. CD.

ANTHOLOGIES

2345 *Music of the Sudan, Songs of the Dinka, Vol. 1: War Songs and Hymns.* Smithsonian Folkways: F-4301. 1976, 1990s. CD.

2346 *Music of the Sudan, the Role of Song and Dance in Dinka Society, Vol. 2: Women.* Custom Compact Disc Series. Smithsonian Folkways: F-4302. 1976, 1990s. CD.

2347 *Music of the Nile* (David Fanshawe, compiler). ARC Music: EUCD 1793. 2003. CD.

2348 ★*Rough Guide to the Music of Sudan: Desert Rhythms and Savannah Harmonies.* Rough Guide. World Music Network: RGNET 1152 CD. 2005. CD.

2349 *Au royaume de la lyre = In the Kingdom of the Lyre.* Institut du Monde Arabe: 321036.037. 2001. 2 CDs.

2350 *Sudan: Music of the Blue Nile Province*
  2350.1 *The Gumuz Tribe.* Unesco Collection; An Anthology of African Music. Auvidis: D 8072. 1985, 1996. CD.
  2350.2 *The Ingessana and Berta Tribes.* Unesco Collection; An Anthology of African Music. Auvidis: D 8073. 1985, 1996. CD.

2351 *Waza: Blue Nile, Sudan* (Artur Simon, compiler). Museum Collection Berlin. Wergo: SM 1708 2. 1982, 2003. CD.

Tanzania

INDIVIDUAL ARTISTS AND GROUPS

2352 Abdullah, Rashid, Islim Ali, and Masud Hussein Mfaome. *Music from Tanzania and Zanzibar 3.* Caprice Records: CAP 21577. 1996, 1997. CD.

2353 Kidude, Bi. *The Diva of Zanzibari Music = Zanzibara: La mémoire de la musique Zanzibaraise 4: Bi Kidude.* Buda: 860141. 1988, 2007. CD.

ANTHOLOGIES

2354 *Hadzas, Bushmen de Tanzanie = The Hadza Bushmen of Tanzania.* Musique du Monde. Buda: 3015942. 1999, 2003. 2 CDs.

2355 *Maisha: Musiques de Tanzanie.* Musique du Monde. Buda: 92546-2. 1995. CD.

2356 *Music from Tanzania and Zanzibar, Vols. 1 and 2.* Caprice Records: CAP 21554, CAP 21553. 1997. CD.

2357 *Tanzania Instruments: Tanganyika, 1950* (Hugh Tracey, compiler). Historical Recordings by Hugh Tracey. Stichting Sharp Wood Productions: SWP 022. 1950, 2003. CD.

2358 ★*Tanzania: Music of the Farmer Composers of Sukumaland: We Never Sleep, We Dream of Farming.* Multicultural Media: MCM 3013. 1994, 1997. CD.

2359 *Tanzanie: Chants des Wagogo et des Kuria* (Hukwe U. Zawose, Ndahani Bwanik, Kalenda Mweleto Muhawi, Daniel Chidiza Lubasho, and Werema Masiaga Chacha). Maison des Cultures du Monde: W 260041. 1992. CD.

2360 *Zanzibar: Music of Celebration* (Janet Topp Fargion, compiler). Topic World Series. Topic Records: TSCD 917. 1989, 2000. CD.

2361 *Zanzibara: Le son des années 60 en Tanzanie = The 1960s Sound of Tanzania, Vol. 3: Ujamaa* (Jamhuri Jazz Band, NUTA Jazz Band, Atomic Jazz Band, Morogoro Jazz Band, and Dar Es Salaam Jazz Band). Buda: BUD 860142. 2007. CD.

Uganda

INDIVIDUAL ARTISTS AND GROUPS

2362 Muyinde, Evaristo. *Traditional Music of the Baganda.* Ethnic Series. Pan Records: PAN 2003. 1991. CD.

2363 Nannyonga-Tamusuza, Sylvia. *Ouganda: Musique des Baganda = Uganda: Music of the Baganda People* (Sulayiti Kalungi Ensemble and Kanyanya Muyinda Ensemble). Ocora: C 560161. 1996, 2002. CD.

2364 Ndere Troupe. *Ngoma: Music from Uganda.* Music of the World: CDT-142. 1997. CD.

ANTHOLOGIES

2365 ★*Abayudaya: Music from the Jewish People of Uganda* (Jeffrey A. Summit, compiler). Smithsonian Folkways: SFW CD 40504. 2003. CD.

2366 *Delicious Peace: Coffee, Music and Interfaith Harmony in Uganda* (Jeffrey A. Summit, compiler). Smithsonian Folkways: SFW CD 50417. 2006, 2012. CD.

2367 *Exile* (David Bottrill, Brian Eno, Richard Evans, Peter Gabriel, David Rhodes, Michelle Newbury, and Richard Blair; Geoffrey Oryema, compiler). Real World: Carol 2313-2. 1990. CD.

2368 *The King's Musicians: Royalist Music of Buganda-Uganda* (Peter Cooke and Klaus Wachsmann, compilers). Topic World Series. Topic Records: TSCD 925. 1949, 2003 CD.

2369 *Music from Uganda*
    2369.1 *Vol. 1: Tradition.* Caprice: CAP 21495. 1996. CD.
    2369.2 *Vol. 2: Modern Traditional.* Caprice: CAP 21553. 1996. CD.

2370 *Music of the Nile* (David Fanshawe, compiler). ARC Music: EUCD 1793. 2003. CD.

2371 ★*Ouganda, aux sources du Nil* (Groupe N'Gali, Groupe Aboluganda Kwagalana, Groupe Aleka Jazz Band, Groupe Lukeme, Groupe Gulu United Arts, and Groupe Pawidi). Ocora: C 560032. 1992. CD.

2372 *Ouganda: Musique des Acholi* (Pierre Bois, ed.). Maison des Cultures du Monde: W 260130. 2007. CD.

2373 ★*Royal Court Music from Uganda, 1950 and 1952, Uganda: Ganda, Nyoro, Ankole* (Hugh Tracey, compiler). Historical Recordings by Hugh Tracey. Stichting Sharp Wood Productions: SWP 008/HT 02. 1950, 1998. CD.

2374 *Secular Music from Uganda, 1950 and 1952* (Hugh Tracey, compiler). Historical Recordings by Hugh Tracey. Stichting Sharp Wood Productions: SWP 024. 1950, 2003. CD.

2375 *Singing for Life: Songs of Hope, Healing, and HIV/AIDS in Uganda* (Gregory Barz, compiler). Smithsonian Folkways: SFW CD 40537. 2007. CD.

2376 *Tipu pa Acholi = The Spirit of Acholi: Songs and Dances of the Acholi in Uganda* (Joop Veuger, compiler). Ethnic Series. Pan Records: PAN 2029 CD. 1996. CD.

EASTERN AFRICA TRADITIONAL
GENERAL ANTHOLOGIES

2377 *African Acoustic Sounds Eastern and Southern* (John Storm Roberts and Hugh Tracey, compilers). Original Music: OMCD 001. 1950, 1988. CD.

2378 ★*East Africa: Ceremonial and Folk Music* (David Fanshawe, compiler). Explorer Series: Africa. Nonesuch: 79707-2. 1975, 2002. CD.

2379 ★*East Africa: Witchcraft and Ritual Music* (David Fanshawe, compiler). Explorer Series: Africa. Elektra Nonesuch: 79708-2. 1975, 2002. CD.

2380 *Echoes of Africa: Early Recordings, 1930s–1950s.* Wergo: SM 1624 2. 2002. CD.

2381 ★*Music of East Africa: Ethnic Music Classics, 1925–48* (Major Contay, compiler; Richard Nevins, ed.). Secret Museum of Mankind. Yazoo: 7015. 1998. CD.

EASTERN AFRICA POPULAR
Burundi
INDIVIDUAL ARTIST

2382 Nin, Khadja. *Ya . . .* Mondo Melodia: 186 810 062 2. 2000. CD.

Comoros
GROUP

2383 Mikidache. *Kauli (Words).* Long Distance: 3040172 WAG 331, ARC 329. 1998. CD.

Eritrea
INDIVIDUAL ARTIST

2384 Ahmed, Mahmoud. *Almaz.* Ethiopiques, 6. Buda: 82979-2. 1971, 1999. CD.

ANTHOLOGIES

2385 *L'age d'or de la musique Éthiopienne, Vol. 1 = Golden Years of Ethiopian Music, Vol. 1* (Amha Eshèté, prod.). Buda: 82951-2. 1999, 2000. CD.

2386 *Tigrigna Music, Tigray/Eritrea, 1970–1975* (Amha Eshèté, prod.) Ethiopiques, 5. Buda: 82965-2. 1990s. CD.

Ethiopia
INDIVIDUAL ARTISTS AND GROUPS

2387 Admas Band. *Indigo Sun.* C-Side Entertainment. 2000. CD.

2388 Aweke, Aster
    2388.1 *Aster.* Columbia: CK 46848. 1990. CD.
    2388.2 *Fikir.* Kabu Records. 2008. CD.

2389   Eshete, Alemayehu. *Addis Ababa: New Beat Music from Ethiopia.* Shanachie: 64045. 1993. CD.

2390   ★Eshete, Alemayehu, and Girma Beyene. *Ethiopia.* Rough Guide. World Music Network: RGNET 1124 CD. 2004. CD.

2391   Mèllèssè, Muluqèn, and Mahmoud Ahmed. *L'âge d'or de la musique Éthiopienne moderne, 1969–75 = Golden Years of Modern Ethiopian Music, 1969–75.* Ethiopiques, 1. Buda: 82951-2. 1969, 1990s. CD.

2392   Shibabaw, Ejigayehu
      2392.1   ★*Gigi.* Palm Records: PALMCD 2068-2. 2001. CD.
      2392.2   ★*Gold and Wax.* Palm Pictures: PALMCD2128. 2006. CD.

ANTHOLOGY

2393   *Ethiopian Groove: The Golden Seventies.* Buda: 82255-2. 1976, 1994. CD.

Kenya

INDIVIDUAL ARTISTS AND GROUPS

2394   Abdullah, Shabani, Ally K. Sykes, and Henri Bembele. *Colonial Dance Bands, 1950 and 1952: Dar-Es-Salaam, Mombasa, Nairobi, Lourenço Marques, Elisabethville, Hihue: Kenya, Tanganyika, Portuguese East Africa, Northern Rhodesia, Belgian Congo.* Stichting Sharp Wood Productions: SWP 031. 1950, 2006. CD.

2395   Gidi Gidi Maji Maji. *Unbwogable.* A&M. 2002. CD.

2396   Golden Sounds Band. *Swahili Rumba.* Naxos World: 76055-2. 2003. CD.

2397   Ingosi Stars. *Langoni.* Daquí. 2007. CD.

2398   Kilonzo, Kakai. *Best of Kakai, Vol. 1* (Les Kilimambogo Brothers). Shava Musik. 2002. CD.

2399   Konde, Fundi. *Retrospective, Vol. 1.* RetroAfric: 8 CD. 1947, 1994. CD.

2400   Makunguru, Ally. *Nakupenda Bibi.* Equator Heritage Sounds. 1999, 2006. CD.

2401   Malika. *Tarabu: Music from the Swahili of Kenia.* Haus der Kulturen der Welt: SM 1520-2. 1993, 1996. CD.

2402   Mapangala, Samba. *Virunga Volcano.* Earthworks Virgin Records: 2-91408. 1990. CD.

2403   Maulidi and Musical Party. *Mombasa Wedding Special.* GlobeStyle: CDORBD 058. 1989, 1990. CD.

2404   Misiani, D. O. *Benga Blast!* (D. O. Misiani and Shirati Jazz). Virgin Records America: 91314-2. 1989. CD.

2405   Misiani, D. O., and Shirati Jazz. *The King of History: Classic 1970s Benga Beats from Kenya.* Stern's Africa: STCD3051. 1970s, 2010. CD.

2406   Nasery, Abana ba. *Nursery Boys Go Ahead!* Xenophile. Green Linnet: GLCD 4002. 1991, 1992. CD.

2407   Orchestra Makassy. *Legends of East Africa: The Original Recordings.* ARC Music: EUCD 1909. 1982, 2005. CD.

2408   Samba Mapangala and Orchestre Virunga. *Maisha ni matamu = Life Is Sweet.* Virunga Records. 2011. CD.

ANTHOLOGIES

2409   *Before Benga: The Nairobi Sound, Vol. 2.* Original Music: OMCD 022. 1988. CD.

2410   *Kenya Dance Mania.* Earthworks Virgin Records: 3-1024-2. 1991. CD.

2411   ★*The Nairobi Beat: Kenyan Pop Music Today.* Rounder: CD 5030. 1989. CD.

2412   *Zanzibar: Golden Years of Mombasa Taarab, 1965–1975 = L'âge d'or du Taarab de Mombasa, 1965–1975.* Buda: 860119. 2005. CD.

Madagascar

INDIVIDUAL ARTIST

2413   Tarika, Sammy. *Fanafody.* Green Linnet: GLCD 4003. 1992. CD.

ANTHOLOGIES

2414   ★*Madagascar.* Rough Guide. World Music Network: RGNET 1163 CD. 2005. CD.

2415   *The Moon and the Banana Tree: New Guitar Music from Madagascar.* Shanachie: 64074. 1995, 1996. CD.

2416   ★*The Music of Madagascar: Classic Traditional Recordings from the 1930s.* Yazoo: 7003. 1995. CD.

Réunion

INDIVIDUAL ARTISTS AND GROUPS

2417 Farreyrol, Jacqueline. *L'île de la Réunion.* Colibri: COL C.D 21.21. 2001. CD.

2418 Lélé, Groove, and Ernst Reijseger. *Zembrocal Musical.* Winter and Winter. 2010. CD.

2419 Ziskakan. *Ziskakan.* Mango Records: 162-539 938-2. 1993. CD.

ANTHOLOGY

2420 *Musiques Métisses: Océan Indien.* Harmonia Mundi: 46816-2. 2006. CD.

Rwanda

GROUP

2421 Samputu. *Testimony from Rwanda.* Multicultural Media: MCM 4003. 2004. CD.

Seychelles

INDIVIDUAL ARTISTS AND GROUPS

2422 *Les Îles Creoles de l'Océan Indien: Creole Islands of the Indian Ocean: Seychelles, Maurice, Reunion.* PlayaSound: PS 65010. 1987. CD.

2423 *Musiques populaires de Îles Seychelles = Music from the Seychelles.* Musique du Monde. Buda: 1984862. 1965, 2002. CD.

2424 *Splendeur des Îles de l'Océan Indien.* PlayaSound: PS 65171. 1996. CD.

Somalia

INDIVIDUAL ARTISTS

2425 K'naan. *Troubadour.* A&M; Octone: B0012479-02. 2009. CD.

2426 Mursal, Maryam. *The Journey.* Caroline: CAR 2370-2. 1998. CD.

Sudan

INDIVIDUAL ARTISTS AND GROUPS

2427 Jal, Emanuel. *Warchild.* Universal; Fontana; Sonic 360. 2008. CD.

2428 Jal, Emmanuel, and 'Abd al-Qadir Salim. *Ceasefire.* Riverboat Records: TUGCD 1038. 2005. CD.

2429 Kembe, Emanuel. *Shen Shen = Cry for South Sudan.* Simple Sussurations. 2010, 1999. CD.

2430 Salim, 'Abd al-Qadir. *Le Blues de Khartoum = Khartoum Blues.* Institut du Monde Arabe: 321027. 1999. CD.

2431 Salim, 'Abd al-Qadir, 'Abd al-'Aziz Mubarak, and Muhammad Jabarah. *Sounds of Sudan.* World Circuit: WCD 018. 1986, 1990. CD.

2432 Sunni, Mustafa al-. *Songs of the Sudan.* Nimbus: NI 5583. 1999. CD.

2433 Wardi, Mohammed. *Mohammed Wardi: Live in Addis Ababa, 1994.* Rags Productions: RPM 001-2CD.

ANTHOLOGY

2434 ★*Rough Guide to the Music of Sudan: Desert Rhythms and Savannah Harmonies.* Rough Guide. World Music Network: RGNET 1152 CD. 2005. CD.

Tanzania

INDIVIDUAL ARTISTS AND GROUPS

2435 Abdallah, Salum, Suwedi Athmani, and Juma Kilaza. *Ngoma Iko Huku: Vintage Tanzanian Dance Music, 1955–1965* (Cuban Marimba Band). Dizim Records: GEMA 4701-2. 1965, 2000. CD.

2436 Black Star Musical Club and Lucky Star Musical Club. *Nyota.* GlobeStyle. 1969, 1989. CD.

2437 Bongo Flava. *Swahili Rap from Tanzania.* Out Here: OH 003. 2004. CD.

2438 Culture Musical Club. *The Music of Zanzibar.* Taarab, 4. GlobeStyle: CDORBD 041. 1988, 1989. CD.

2439 Ikhwani Safaa Musical Club
   2439.1 *Music of Zanzibar.* GlobeStyle: CDORB 033. 1988. CD.
   2439.2 *Zanzibara, 1905–2005: Cent ans de Taarab à Zanzibar, Vol. 1 = Zanzibara, 1905–2005: A Hundred Years of Taarab in Zanzibar, Vol. 1.* Buda: 860118. 2005. CD.

2440 Mlimani Park Orchestra
   2440.1 *Onyo.* GMC Wasanii Promoers Ltd. 2003. CD.
   2440.2 *Sikinde.* Africassette: AC 9402. 1994. CD.

2441 Ongala, Remmy
    2441.1 *Mambo* (Orchestra Super Matimila). Real World Records: 92129-2. 1992. CD.
    2441.2 *Songs for the Poor Man* (Orchestre Super Matimila). Real World Records: 2-91315. 1989. CD.

2442 Orchestra Makassy. *Legends of East Africa: The Original Recordings.* ARC Music: EUCD 1909. 1982, 2005. CD.

2443 Tatunane. *Tanzanian Beat.* King Record: KICC 5221. 1992, 1997. CD.

2444 X Plastaz. *Maasai Hip Hop.* Out Here: OH 002. 2001, 2004. CD.

ANTHOLOGIES

2445 *Musiki wa dansi* (International Orchestra Safari School, Orchestra Maquis Original, Mimani Park Orchestra, and Juwata Jazz Band). Africassette Music: AC 9403. 1995. CD.

2446 ★*The Rough Guide to the Music of Tanzania* (Werner Graebner, compiler). Rough Guide. World Music Network: RGNET 1158 CD. 2006. CD.

2447 *Yellow Card* (Ndala Kasheba, perf. and compiler). Limitless Sky Records. 2002. CD.

2448 *Zanzibara: Le son des années 60 en Tanzanie, vol. 3: Ujamaa = The 1960s Sound of Tanzania, Vol. 3: Ujamaa* (Jamhuri Jazz Band, NUTA Jazz Band, Atomic Jazz Band, Morogoro Jazz Band, and Dar Es Salaam Jazz Band). Buda: BUD 860142. 2007. CD.

Uganda

INDIVIDUAL ARTISTS AND GROUPS

2449 Magoola, Rachel. *Songs from the Source of the Nile.* ARC Music: EUCD 1973. 2006. CD.

2450 Okello, Omega Bugembe. *Kiwomera Emmeeme* Omega World Music. 2008. CD.

2451 Samite. *Embalasasa.* Triloka: TRI-CD-82071. 2006. CD.

ANTHOLOGIES

2452 *Exile* (David Bottrill, Brian Eno, Richard Evans, Peter Gabriel, David Rhodes, Michelle Newbury, and Richard Blair; Geoffrey Oryema, compiler). Real World: Carol 2313-2. 1990. CD.

2453 *Kampala Flow: East Africa Hip Hop from Uganda* (Gregory Barz and Gerald Liu, prods.). Lime Pulp Records. 2010. CD.

EASTERN AFRICA POPULAR GENERAL ANTHOLOGIES

2454 *African Acoustic Sounds Eastern and Southern* (John Storm Roberts and Hugh Tracey, compilers). Original Music: OMCD 001. 1950, 1988. CD.

2455 *Guitar Paradise of East Africa.* Virgin Records: CDEWV 21. 1990. CD.

2456 ★*Rough Guide to the Music of Kenya and Tanzania.* World Music Network; Kenyan and Tanzanian Music. World Music Network: RGNET 1007. 1996. CD.

CENTRAL AND SOUTHERN AFRICA
CENTRAL AFRICA TRADITIONAL
Compiled by Suzanne Flandreau

The discographies for Central and Southern Africa attempt to focus on field recordings, with only a few reissues of early commercial recordings and a very few studio recordings or recordings made at festivals when field recordings of the music in question were not available.

There are tremendous gaps in the documentation of African music. One reason may be the existence of political repression or civil war in some areas, which leads to dispersal of peoples and cultures, and magnifies the difficulties of fieldwork. The result is that some areas that have been volatile for decades (Angola, Congo) are hardly documented at all. In many cases, social and economic changes have also altered traditional cultures. This may be especially true for the fragile cultures of the Bushmen in southern Africa and the Pygmies in central Africa. In these cases, it is just as important to document change as to document tradition.

It is necessary to note the importance of individual ethnomusicologists, especially Hugh Tracey (1903–77). In his heroic efforts to record African music, he covered most of Southern, Southeastern, and Central Africa, championing indigenous music at a time when the colonial system was not sympathetic to African cultures. Tracey himself issued selections from his field recordings in the Sound of Africa series of 210 LPs. Some of his recordings are now commercially available on the Sharp Wood label, but more significantly, the International

Library of African Music, which he founded at Rhodes University in Grahamstown, South Africa, has made the entire series available on CD. David Dargie's self-issued productions on the Xhosa are also becoming encyclopedic. In Central Africa, Simha Arom's recordings of Pygmy music are similarly outstanding, although many were issued on the Ocora label and are now out-of-print. Pygmy is an admittedly problematic term but is used here to encompass several groups (Mbuti, Baka, and others).

The availability of ethnographic field recordings is market driven. A number of recordings were issued in the 1990s, at the height of "world beat" popularity. Some of the specialist labels especially active in the late twentieth century are now defunct (Ocora, Auvidis), while others, notably Lyrichord, have scaled back their offerings such that important recordings are now out-of-print (although Lyrichord is reissuing some LPs through Multicultural Media). Recordings from Smithsonian Folkways are available on demand, but the documentation is not updated and many were made over half a century ago. These lists include a number of titles that are available via secondhand vendors.

Fortunately, there is at least one recent effort to issue a comprehensive series of field recordings, the Anthologie de la musique Congolaise from the Musée Royal de l'Afrique Centrale in Tervuren, Belgium. Since 2000, twelve CDs have been issued, covering the music of the former Belgian Congo. Chad is included in the Western Africa section, and general African anthologies (including Central and Southern) are also listed in chapter 7, "International Anthologies."

Cameroon

ANTHOLOGIES

2457 *Bulu Songs from the Cameroons* (Edwin Cozzens, compiler). Custom Compact Disc Series. Smithsonian Folkways: FE 4451. 1954, 1999. CD.

2458 *Cameroun: Flutes des Monts Mandara* [1994–1996]. Ocora: C 560110. 1996. CD.

2459 *Flutes et rythmes du Cameroun* [1983–1990?] (Claude Fonfrede, compiler). Musique du Monde. Buda: 82460-2. 1990. CD.

2460 *Music of the Cameroons* [1959] (Robert E. Ritzenthaler and Pat Ritzenthaler, compilers). Custom Compact Disc Series. Smithsonian Folkways: F-4372. 1961. CD.

2461 *Mvet ai mendzang, Beti Cameroon: Musik der Beti in Kamerun = Music of the Beti in Cameroon* [1984, 1989]. Museum Collection Berlin. Wergo: SM 1711 2. 2005. CD.

Central African Republic

ANTHOLOGIES

2462 *Centrafrique, Musique Gbaya: Chants a penser* [1977] (Vincent Dehoux, compiler). Ocora: C 580008. 1992. CD.

2463 ★*Centrafrique: Musique pour Sanza en Pays Gbaya = Central Africa: Sanza Music in the Land of the Gbaya* [1977] (Vincent Dehoux, compiler). Archives Internationales de Musique Populaire, 27. VDE: CD-755. 1993. CD.

2464 ★*Central African Republic: Music of the Dendi, Nzakara, Banda Linda, Gbaya, Banda-Dakpa, Ngbaka, Aka Pygmies* (Republique Centrafricaine) (Simha Arom, compiler). Unesco Collection, Musics and Musicians of the World. Auvidis: D 8020. 1989. CD.

2465 ★*Republique Centafricaine: Musique de xylophones = Music for Xylophones* [1971] (Vincent Dehoux, compiler). Collection du Centre National de la Recherche Scientifique et du Musée de l'Homme. Le Chant du Monde: LDX 274932. 1991. CD.

2466 *Xylophones de l'Ouham-Pende = Xylophones of the Ouham-Pende* [1992–1995] (Sylvie Le Bomin, compiler). Ocora: C 580008. 1996. CD.

Congo, Democratic Republic of the (Zaire)

ANTHOLOGIES

2467 *Anthologie de la musique Congolaise*

2467.1 *Vol. 1: Lunda du Katanga* [1972] (Jos Gansemans, compiler). Fonti Musicali; Musée Royal de l'Afrique Centrale: fmd 401. 2004. CD.

2467.2 *Vol. 2: Songs of the Okapi Forest* [1973–2004]. Musée Royal de l'Afrique Centrale: fmd 402. 2004. CD.

2467.3 *Vol. 3: Musiques du Pays des Mangbetu* [1984–1990] (Didier Demolin, compiler). Fonti Musicali; Musée Royal de l'Afrique Centrale: fmd 403. 2004. CD.

2467.4 *Vol. 4: Musique des Salampasu* [1973] (Jos Gansemans, compiler). Fonti Musicali; Musée Royal de l'Afrique Centrale: fmd 404. 2005. CD.

2467.5 *Vol. 5: Musique des Tshokwe du Bandundu* [1981] (Rene Menard and Benoit Quersin, compilers). Fonti Musicali; Musée Royal de l'Afrique Centrale: fmd 405. 2005. CD.

2467.6 *Vol. 6: Musique des Kwese* [1984–1985] (Rene Menard, compiler). Musée Royal de l'Afrique Centrale: fmd 406. 2006. CD.

2467.7 *Vol. 7: Musique des Kongo—Mbata* (Benoit Quersin, Jos Gansemans, and Ludiongo, compilers). Fonti Musicali; Musée Royal de l'Afrique Centrale: fmd 407. 2006. CD.

2467.8 *Vol. 8: Musique des Tetela* [1975] (Benoit Quersin and Esole Eki Likote, compilers). Fonti Musicali; Musée Royal de l'Afrique Centrale: fmd 408. 2006. CD.

2467.9 *Vol. 9: Musique des Leele* [1985] (Rene Menard, compiler). Fonti Musicali; Musee Royal de l'Afrique Centrale: fmd 409. 2007. CD.

2467.10 *Vol. 10: Musique de l'Ubangi* [1975] (Benoit Quersin and Esole Eki Likote, compilers). Fonti Musicali; Musée Royal de l'Afrique Centrale: fmd 410. 2007. CD.

2467.11 *Vol. 11: Musique des Nkundo* [1971–1972] (Benoit Quersin, compiler). Fonti Musicali; Musée Royal de l'Afrique Centrale: fmd 411. 2007. CD.

2467.12 *Vol. 12: Musique des Azande* [1984–1986] (Didier Demolin, Simon Mondo Mumbanza, and Frank Michiels, compilers). Fonti Musicali; Musée Royal de l'Afrique Centrale: fmd 412. 2010. CD.

2468 *Folk Music of the Western Congo* [1951] (Leo A. Verwilghen, compiler). Custom Compact Disc Series. Smithsonian Folkways: F-4427. 1951, 1999. CD.

2469 *Forest Music: Congo: Northern Belgian Congo, 1952* (Hugh Tracey, compiler). Stichting Sharp Wood Productions: SWP 016. 2000. CD.

2470 ★*Kanyok and Luba: Southern Belgian Congo, 1952 and 1957: Kanyok, Luba-Hasai, Luluwa, Songye, Luba-Hatanga, Hemba* (Hugh Tracey, compiler). Historical Recordings by Hugh Tracey. Stichting Sharp Wood Productions: SWP 011. 1998. CD.

2471 *Mangebetu Haut-Uele* [1984–1988] (Didier Demolin, compiler). Traditions du Monde. Fonti Musicali: fmd 193. 1992. CD.

2472 *Music of the Shi People.* Alula Origins: ALU-5008. 2005. CD.

2473 *Music of Zaire* [1970] (Jacques Jangoux, compiler). Custom Compact Disc Series. Smithsonian Folkways: FE 4241-FE 4242. 1973, 1999. 2 CDs.

2474 ★*On the Edge of the Ituri Forest, 1952, Congo: Budu, Mbuti, Mangbele, Nande, Bira* (Hugh Tracey, compiler). Historical Recordings by Hugh Tracey. Stichting Sharp Wood Productions, International Library of African Music: SWP 009, ILAM 03. 1998. CD.

2475 *The Topoke People of the Congo* (J. Camps, compiler). Custom Compact Disc Series. Smithsonian Folkways: FE 4477. 1959, 1999. CD.

2476 *Zaire: La musique des Nande = The Music of the Nande* [1986, 1988] (Serena Facci, compiler). Archives Internationales de Musique Populaire, 23. VDE-Gallo: CD-652. 1991. CD.

2477 *Zaire: Musiques Urbaines a Kinshasa* [1978] (Bernard Treton and Guy Level, compilers). Ocora: C 559007. 1987. CD.

2478 *Zaire: Polyphonies Mongo* [1970–1972] (Benoit Quersin, compiler). Ocora: C 580050. 1993. CD.

Gabon

ANTHOLOGIES

2479 *Chants des Atege = Songs of the Atege* [1946, 1965, 2003–2004]. Ocora: C 560199. 2004. CD.

2480 *Chants Myene = Myene Songs* [1961, 2005] (Sylvie Le Bomin, Florence Bikoma, and Herbert Pepper, compilers). Ocora: C 56024. 2005. CD.

2481 *Music from an Equatorial Microcosm: Fang Bwiti Music from Gabon Republic, Africa* (James W. Fernandez, compiler). Custom Compact Disc Series. Smithsonian Folkways: F 4214. 1973, 2003. CD.

São Tomé and Príncipe

ANTHOLOGY

2482 *São Tomé and Príncipe: Musiques de l'île du Milieu = Music from São Tomé* (Manuel Gomes, compiler). Musique du Monde. Buda: 3016896. 2004. CD.

Transnational: Pygmies

ANTHOLOGIES

2483 *Africa: The Ba-Benzele Pygmies* [pre-1965] (Simha Arom and Genevieve Taurelle, compilers).

Anthology of World Music. Rounder: CD 5107. 1998. CD.

2484   *Aka Pygmy Music = Musique des Pygmees Aka* [1971] (Simha Arom, compiler). Unesco Collection. Auvidis: D 8054. 1994. CD.

2485   *Cameroon: Baka Pygmy Music = La Musique des Pygmees Baka* [1975] (Simha Arom and Patrick Renaud, compilers). Unesco Collection; Musics and Musicians of the World. Auvidis: D 8029. 1990. CD.

2486   *Centrafrique: Anthologie de la musique des Pygmees Aka* (Simha Arom and Pierre Toureille, compilers). Ocora: C 559012-C 559013. 1978, 1987. 2 CDs.

2487   *Centrafrique: Pygmees Aka: Chants de chasse, d'amour et de moquerie* [1990, 1994, 1997] (Susanne Furniss, compiler). Ocora: C 560139. 1998. CD.

2488   *Congo polyphonies Pygmees du Nord-Congo = Pygmy Polyphonies from North Congo* [2005–2008] (Nathalie Fernando, compiler). Archives Internationales de Musique Populaire, 50. VDE-Gallo: VDE CD-1339. 2011. CD.

2489   *Echoes of the Forest* [1950s–1980s?] (Colin M. Turnbull, Jean Pierre Hallet, and Louis Sarno, compilers). Ellipsis Arts: CD 4020. 1995. CD.

2490   *Heart of the Forest: The Music of the Baka Forest People of Southwest Cameroon* (Martin Cradick and Jeremy Avis, compilers). Hannibal: HNCD 1378. 1990, 1993. CD.

2491   *★Mbuti Pygmies of the Ituri Rainforest* [1950s] (Colin M. Turnbull and Francis S. Chapman, compilers). Smithsonian Folkways: SF CD 4041. 1992. CD.

2492   *Music of the Rainforest Pygmies* [1950s] (Colin M. Turnbull, compiler). Lyrichord: LYRCD 7157. 1990. CD.

2493   *Musique des Pygmies Bibayak: Chantres de l'epopee* [1966, 1973] (Pierre Sallee, compiler). Ocora: C 559053. 1989. CD.

2494   *Polyphonies vocales des Pygmees Mbenzele, Republique Centafricaine* [1986] (Simha Arom, compiler). Inédit Variations. Maison des Cultures du Monde: W 260 042. 1992. CD.

See also Congo (Democratic Republic).

CENTRAL AFRICA TRADITIONAL
VIDEO

2495   *★African Guitar: Solo Fingerstyle Guitar Music from Uganda, Congo/Zaire, Malawi, Namibia, Central African Republic, and Zambia: Audio Visual Field Recordings, 1966–1993, by Gerhard Kubik* (Gerhard Kubik, compiler). Vestapol: 13017. 2003. DVD.

See also Congo, Democratic Republic

SOUTHERN AFRICA TRADITIONAL
Angola
ANTHOLOGIES

2496   *Music and Musicians of the Angolan Border: The Tshokwe* [1973–1976] (Barbara Schmidt-Wrenger, compiler). Lyrichord: LLCT 7311. 1977. LP.

2497   *Sanza and Guitar: Music of the Bena Luluwa of Angola and Zaire* [1973–1976] (Barbara Schmidt-Wrenger, compiler). Lyrichord: LLST 7313. [1980–1987]. LP.

Botswana
ANTHOLOGIES

2498   *Ancient Civilizations of Southern Africa: The Tswana People.* ARC Music: EUCD 2132. 2008. CD. Reissue of Music of the Tswana people, 2000.

2499   *Traditional Music of Botswana, Africa* [1975–1978] (Elizabeth Nelbach Wood, compiler). Custom Compact Disc Series. Smithsonian Folkways: FE 4371. 1983, 1999. CD.

Lesotho
ANTHOLOGIES

2500   *Lesotho Calling: Lesiba and Sekhankula Music* (Michael Baird, compiler). Stichting Sharp Wood Records: SWP 033. 2006. CD.

2501   *Music of Lesotho: Circumcision Songs* (Bill Wood, compiler). Custom Compact Disc Series. Smithsonian Folkways: FE 4224. 1976, 1990s. CD.

2502   *Voices of Africa: Mbube and Sotho a Cappella Choirs.* ARC Music: EUCD 1509. 1999. CD.

VIDEO

2503   *Songs of the Adventurers* [1987] (David B. Coplan, compiler). Media Sales Pennsylvania State University: 51519 DVD. 2008. DVD.

See also South Africa (Republic of).

Malawi

ANTHOLOGIES

2504   ★*From Lake Malawi to the Zambezi: Aspects of Music and Oral Literature in South-East Africa in the 1990s* [1990–1995] (Moya Aliya, Malamusi, and Gerhard Kubik, compilers). Popular African Music: pamap 602. 1990, 2000. CD.

2505   *Northern and Central Malawi 1950, '57, '58, Nyasaland: Tonga, Tumbuka, Cewa* (Hugh Tracey, compiler). Historical Recordings by Hugh Tracey. Stichting Sharp Wood Productions: SWP 014. 1950, 2000. CD.

2506   *Southern and Central Malawi 1950, '57, '58 Nyasaland: Mang'anja, Cewa, Yao* (Hugh Tracey, compiler). Historical Recordings by Hugh Tracey. Stichting Sharp Wood Productions: SWP 013. 1950, 2000. CD.

See also Southern Africa Traditional General Anthologies.

Mozambique

INDIVIDUAL ARTIST

2507   Mbande, Venancio. *Timbila Ta Venancio* [2000] (Venancio Mbande Orchestra). Naxos World: 76016-2. 2000, 2001. CD.

See also Zimbabwe.

ANTHOLOGIES

2508   *Forgotten Guitars from Mozambique: Portuguese East Africa: 1955, '56, '57* (Hugh Tracey, compiler). Historical Recordings by Hugh Tracey. Stichting Sharp Wood Productions: SWP 025. 1955, 2003. CD.

2509   *Music from Mozambique* [1978–1979] (Ron Hallis and Ophera Hallis, compilers). Custom Compact Disc Series. Smithsonian Folkways: FE 4310. 1980, 1999. CD.

2510   *Music from Mozambique, Vol. 3* (Ron Hallis and Ophera Hallis, compilers). Custom Compact Disc Series. Smithsonian Folkways: FE 4319. 1983, 1999. CD.

2511   *Music from Mozambique: Chopi Timbila* [1981] (Ron Hallis and Ophera Hallis, compilers). Custom Compact Disc Series. Smithsonian Folkways: FE 4318. 1982, 1999. CD.

2512   *Southern Mozambique: Portuguese East Africa, 1943, '49, '54, '55, '57, '63: Chopi, Gitonga, Ronga, Tswa, Tsonga, Sena Nyungwe, Ndau* (Hugh Tracey, compiler). Historical Recordings by Hugh Tracey. SWP Records: SWP 021. 1943, 2003. CD.

Namibia

ANTHOLOGIES

2513   *Musical Bows of Namibia* [1981–1988] (Various artists; David Dargie, compiler). Dave Dargie. 1981, 2003. CD.

2514   *Namibie: Bushmen et Himba = Namibia: Bushmen and Himba* [1994–1995]. Musique du Monde. Buda: 92632-2. 1995. CD.

See also Transnational: Bushmen.

South Africa (Republic of)

GROUP

2515   Tulips. *Afrique du Sud: Les ménestrals du Cap = South Africa: The Cape Town Minstrels* [1999]. Musique du Monde. Buda: 1986102. 1999. CD.

ANTHOLOGIES

2516   *African Renaissance: Music from the South African Broadcasting Corporation Archives.* Eagle Records: SABC 001-010. [2000]. 10 CDs.

2517   *Afrique du Sud: Le chant des femmes Xhosa = South Africa: Xhosa Women's Songs* [1995] (David Dargie, compiler). Archives Internationales de Musique Populaire, 44. VDE Gallo: VDE CD-879. 1995, 1996. CD.

2518   *Ancient Civilizations of Southern Africa 2: Tribal Drums of the Venda People.* ARC Music: EUCD 2026. 2006. CD.

2519   *Gumboot Guitar: Zulu Street Guitar Music from South Africa* [1988–1996] (Janet Topp Fargion, compiler). Topic World Series. Topic: TSCD 923. 2003. CD.

2520   *Mbube Roots: Zulu Choral Music from South Africa, 1930s–1960s* [1932–1967]. Rounder: CD 5025. 1976, 1990. CD.

2521 *Music of the Indigenous Christian Churches* [1995–1996] (David Dargie, compiler). Dave Dargie. 2006. 7 CDs. Available from the producer, University of Fort Hare, South Africa.

2522 *The Nguni Sound: South Africa and Swaziland: 1955, '57, '58: Xhosa, Zulu, Swati* (Hugh Tracey, compiler). Historical Recordings by Hugh Tracey. SWP Records: SWP 020. 1900s, 2003. CD.

2523 ★*Nguwe Lo! An Introduction to the Music of the Thembu Xhosa of South Africa, with More Songs, More Instruments Than Before* (David Dargie, compiler). Dave Dargie. 2010. CD.

2524 *Singing in an Open Space: Zulu Rhythm and Harmony 1962–1982*. Rounder: CD 5027. 1990. CD.

2525 *South Africa: Swati; Zulu; Sotho/Pedi; English* (Hugh Tracey, compiler). Sound of Africa Series, 75. International Library of African Music: CDTR75. 2014. CD.

2526 *South Africa: Xhosa/Ngqika; Xhosa/Gaika; Xhosa/Mpondo* (Hugh Tracey, compiler). Sound of Africa Series, 61. International Library of African Music: CDTR61. 2014. CD.

2527 *Southern Sotho* (Hugh Tracey, compiler). Sound of Africa Series, 18. International Library of African Music: CDTR18. 2014. CD. Numerous 2014 releases in this series are available.

2528 *Squashbox: Le Concertina Zoulou et Sotho en Afrique du Sud*. Memoire. Silex: Y 225107. 1993. CD.

2529 *Traditional Zulu Music: Songs of King Shaka* (Amagugu Akwazulu and Abalendeli Bengoma). ARC Music: EUCD 2340. 2011. CD.

2530 *Tsonga Xitende, Swati Makhoyane* [1980–1988] (David Dargie, compiler). Dave Dargie. 2003. CD. Available from the producer, University of Fort Hare, South Africa.

2531 *Zulu Bow Songs* [1981–1982] (David Dargie, compiler). Dave Dargie. 2003. 3 CDs. Available from the producer, University of Fort Hare, South Africa.

VIDEOS

2532 *Mk Die Derde DVD* (Victor Edward and Johan Drotskie, prods.). Next Music: NEXTDV 009. 2006. DVD.

2533 ★*Umngokolo the DVD* [1995] (David Dargie, compiler). Dave Dargie. 2007. DVD. Available from the producer, University of Fort Hare, South Africa.

2534 *Xhosa Music, Parts 1 and 2* (David Dargie, compiler). Dave Dargie. 2005. 2 DVDs. Available from the producer, University of Fort Hare, South Africa.

Swaziland

See also South Africa (Republic of).

Zambia

ANTHOLOGIES

2535 *Batonga across the Waters: Music of the Batonga of Zambia and Zimbabwe* [1996–1997] (Michael Baird, compiler). Stichting Sharp Wood Productions: SWP 005. 1997. CD.

2536 *Kalimba and Kalumbu Songs, Northern Rhodesia, Zambia, 1952 and 1957: Lala, Tonga, Lozi, Mbunda, Bemba, Lunda* (Hugh Tracey, compiler). Historical Recordings by Hugh Tracey. Stichting Sharp Wood Productions: SWP 010. 1952, 1998. CD.

2537 *Music from Petauke, Northern Rhodesia, Vols. 1 and 2* [1961] (John Blacking and Raymond J. Apthorpe, compilers). Custom Compact Disc Series. Smithsonian Folkways: F-4201; F 4202. 1962, 1990s; 1965, 2001. 2 CDs.

2538 *Zambia Roadside: Music from Southern Province* [1996] (Michael Baird, compiler). Stichting Sharp Wood Productions: SWP 019. 2003. CD.

See also Zimbabwe and General Anthologies.

Zimbabwe

ANTHOLOGIES

2539 *The Kankobela of the Batonga, Vols. 1 and 2* [2008; 1996, 2008] (Michael Baird, compiler). Sharp Wood Productions: SWP 036; SWP 039. 2009; 2011. 2 CDs. Recorded 2008.

2540 *Other Musics from Zimbabwe 1948, '49, '51, '58, '63, Southern Rhodesia: Ndau, Sena, Tonga, Shona* (Hugh Tracey, compiler). Historical Recordings by Hugh Tracey. Stichting Sharp Wood Productions: SWP 012. 1948, 2000. CD.

2541 *Zimbabwe: Shona Mbira Music* [1977] (Paul Berliner, compiler). Explorer Series. Nonesuch: 79710-2. 1977, 2002. CD.

2542 *Zimbabwe: The Ndebele People* [1989] (Laade, Wolfgang, compiler). Music of Man Archive. Jecklin: JD 654-2. 1991. CD.

2543 ★*Zimbabwe: The Soul of Mbira: Traditions of the Shona People* [1973] (Paul Berliner, compiler). Explorer Series. Nonesuch: 79704-2. 1971, 2002. CD.

See also Southern Africa Traditional General Anthologies.

Transnational: San (Bushmen)

ANTHOLOGIES

2544 *Bushmen Ju'hoansi musique instrumentale = Ju'hoansi Bushmen Instrumental Music* [1995, 1998, 2001] (Emmanuelle Olivier, compiler). Collection Ocora Radio France. Ocora Radio France: C 560179. 1995, 2003. CD.

2545 *Bushmen of the Kalahari.* ARC Music: EUCD 1995. 2006. CD.

2546 *Chants des Bushmen Ju'hoansi* [1995]. Namibie. Ocora: C 560117. 1997. CD.

2547 *Healing Dance Music of the Kalahari San* [1968–1972] (Richard Katz, Marjorie Shostak, and Megan Biesele, compilers). Custom Compact Disc Series. Smithsonian Folkways: FE 4316. 1982, 1999. CD.

2548 *Instrumental Music of the Kalahari San* [1951–1955, 1969–1972] (Nicholas M. England, Marjorie Shostak, and Megan Biesele, compilers). Custom Compact Disc Series. Smithsonian Folkways: FE 4315. 1982, 1999. CD.

See also Namibia.

SOUTHERN AFRICA TRADITIONAL GENERAL ANTHOLOGIES

See also Central African Traditional for African Guitar DVD.

2549 *Ancient Civilizations of Southern Africa: Bushman, Zulu, Venda, Xhosa, Tswana.* ARC Music: EUCD 1917. 2005. CD.

2550 *Origins of Guitar Music in Southern Congo and Northern Zambia: 1950, '51, '52, '57, '58* (Hugh Tracey, compiler). Historical Recordings by Hugh Tracey. SWP Records: SWP 015. 1950, 2000. CD.

2551 *South Africa: Tswana/Tlharo* (Hugh Tracey, compiler). Sound of Africa Series, 110. International Library of African Music: CDTR110. 2014. CD.

2552 *Tswana and Sotho Voices: Botswana, South Africa, Lesotho: 1951, '57, '59* (Hugh Tracey, compiler). Historical Recordings by Hugh Tracey. Stichting Sharp Wood Records: SWP 017. 1952, 2000. CD.

CENTRAL AFRICA POPULAR

Compiled by Beth Iseminger and Liza Vick

Central African popular music is largely dominated by Congolese forms, one of the most popular of which is *soukous*, a rumba dance style. Popular *soukous* artists include Zaiko Langa Langa, Pepe Kalle, Koffi Olomide, Franco, Tabu Ley Rochereau, Papa Wemba, and Tshala Muana. Although several of the listed Sonodisc releases are out-of-print, Syllart has reissued selected titles, so check regularly for availability (Stern's Music). Lyrichord is also reissuing some LPs through Multicultural Media. Readers may also wish to consult the third edition if interested in older titles not listed here.

The music industry in South Africa grew rapidly in the 1950s with development of labels such as Trutone, EMI/Mavuthela, Teal, and Gramophone Record Company. Dominant genres range from jazz (artists like Miriam Makeba, Hugh Masekela), to gospel (Rebecca Malope), to popular forms like jive and *mbaqanga* (township vocals, artists such as Mahlathini, Mahotella Queens), Zulu a capella vocals (Ladysmith Black Mambazo, Joseph Shabalala), soul, reggae, township (jive, bubblegum). Johnny Clegg is a Manchester transplant who performed traditional Zulu music and went electronic with the band Juluka and later Savuka. These are only a few examples and not enough to do the area justice. For more information please see the *Garland Handbook of African Music* or the *World Music: The Rough Guide, Vol. 1: Africa, Europe and the Middle East* (Rough Guides, 2000).

Cameroon

INDIVIDUAL ARTISTS AND GROUPS

2553 Aliana, Erik. *Songs from Badissa.* Buda: 2768557. 2011. CD.

2554 Baka Beyond. *Call of the Forest: Favorites of the Baka and Beyond.* White Swan: WS 0082. 2008. CD.

2555   Bona, Richard. *Reverence*. Columbia: CK 85270. 2001. CD.

2556   Dibango, Manu. *The Very Best of Manu Dibango: Afrosouljazz from the Original Makossa Man.* Manteca: MANTCD 016. 2000. CD.

2557   Dikongué, Henri. *Biso Nawa*. Buda: 823052. 2004. CD.

2558   Mbassi, Coco. *Sepia*. Tinder Records: 861102. 2003. CD.

2559   Nyolo, Sally. *Zaïone*. Lusafrica: 362782. 2002. CD.

2560   Sitson, Gino. *Song Zin'*. Piranha: CD-PIR1682. 2002. CD.

Congo, Democratic Republic of the (Zaire)

INDIVIDUAL ARTISTS AND GROUPS

2561   Ainley, Mark. *The World Is Shaking: Cubanismo from the Congo, 1954–1955.* Honest Jon's Records: HJRCD 40. 1954, 2009. CD.

2562   Bana OK. *Touchez jouer: Kilo y Kinshasa*. Jacko Production: JP 001. 2000. CD.

2563   Bel, M'Bilia
    2563.1   *Bameli Soy*. Shanachie: 43025. 1991. CD.
    2563.2   *Keyna: Contre ma volonté* (Orchestre Afrisa International). Syllart Productions: SYL 203. 2005. CD.

2564   Bel, M'Bilia, and Tabu Ley. *Boya yé: Ba gerants ya mabala* (Orchestre Afrisa International). Syllart Productions: SYL 201. 2005. CD.

2565   Franco
    2565.1   *Franco et l'OK Jazz* (OK Jazz). Merveilles du Passé. Sonodisc: CD 36505. [1990–1999]. CD.
    2565.2   ★*Francophonic: Africa's Greatest: A Retrospective, Vol. 1, 1953–1980* (OK Jazz). Stern's Africa: STCD3041; 3042. 1953, 2008. 2 CDs.
    2565.3   ★*Francophonic: Africa's Greatest: A Retrospective, Vol. 2, 1980–1989* (OK Jazz). Stern's Africa: STCD3046; 3047. 1980, 2009. 2 CDs.
    2565.4   *Originalite: The First Recordings of This Legendary Band, 1956–57* (OK Jazz). RetroAfric. 1999. CD.
    2565.5   *The Rough Guide to Franco: Africa's Legendary Guitar Maestro* (OK Jazz).

Rough Guide. World Music Network: RGNET 1071 CD. 1956, 2001. CD.

2566   Kanza, Lokua. *Nkolo*. World Village; dist.by Harmonia Mundi: WVF 479043. 2010. CD.

2567   Kasai Allstars. *In the 7th Moon, the Chief Turned into a Swimming Fish and Ate the Head of His Enemy by Magic.* Congotronics, 3. Crammed Discs: Craw 44. 2008. CD.

2568   Kékélé
    2568.1   *Congo Life*. Stern's Africa: STCD 1097. 2003. CD.
    2568.2   *Rumba Congo*. Stern's Africa: STCD 1093. 2001. CD.

2569   Kenis, Vincent. *The Karindula Sessions: Tradi-Modern Sounds from Southeast Congo.* Crammed Discs: Craw 70. 2011. CD, DVD.

2570   Ley, Tabu
    2570.1   ★*Rochereau et l'African Fiesta, 1964/1965/1966* (African Fiesta). Syllart Productions: 823426. 1964, 2006. CD.
    2570.2   ★*Tabu Ley Rochereau, 1971/1972/1973*. Syllart Productions: 823433. 1971, 2006. CD.
    2570.3   *The Voice of Lightness: Congo Classics, Vol. 2.* Stern's Africa: STCD3056; 3057, 1977, 2010. 2 CDs.
    2570.4   ★*The Voice of Lightness, 1961–1977*. Stern's Africa: STCD3027-28. 1961, 2007. 2 CDs.

2571   Ley, Tabu, and Nico. *African Fiesta, Nico/Rochereau.* Syllart Productions: 823417. 2006. CD.

2572   Mangwana, Sam. *Maria Tebbo*. Stern's Africa: STCD 3011. 1978, 1995. CD. Originally released as Maria Tebbo (SAM002) in 1979 and Waka Waka (SAM001) in 1978.

2573   Muana, Tshala. *Mutuashi*. Stern's Africa: STCD 1069. 1996. CD.

2574   Noel, Papa. *Bel Ami*. Stern's Africa: STCD 3016. 1984, 2000. CD.

2575   Simaro
    2575.1   *Faute ya commerçant: Very Best of Poète Simaro Massiya Lutumba: Okozela Trop.* Serie Single Fetish, Vol. 2. Ngoyarto: NG 0102. 2003. CD.
    2575.2   *Very Best of Poète Simaro Massiya Lutumba: Mabele.* Serie Single Fetish, Vol. 1. Ngoyarto: NG 0101. 2003. CD.

2576 Staff Benda Bilili. *Très très fort.* Crammed Discs: Craw 51. 2009. CD.

2577 Tout Puissant Likembe Konono No 1 de Mingiedi. *Konono No 1.* Congotronics, 1. Crammed Discs: Craw 27. 2004. CD.

2578 ★Tshamala, Kabasele. *Merveilles du passé, Vol. 1* (Grand Kallé and l'African Jazz). Syllart World: 823406. 1957, 2006. CD.

2579 Vangu, Dino. *Kin nostalgie* (Yenga-Yenga). Air B.MAS Production: BMP 000 171-2. 2002. CD.

2580 Wemba, Papa
    2580.1 *Le voyageur.* EarthBeat!: 9 42516-2. 1992. CD.
    2580.2 *Molokai.* Real World: CAR 2373-2. 1998, 2008. CD.

2581 Zaiko Langa Langa. *Zaïre-Ghana.* RetroAfric: RETRO 5CD. 1993, 2006. CD.

ANTHOLOGIES

2582 *Compilation Musique Congolo-Zairoise, 1972/ 1973.* Merveilles du Passé. Sonodisc: CD3651. 1993. CD.

2583 *Congo 70: Rumba Rock.* African Pearls. Syllart Productions: 6139342. 2008, 1970s. 2 CDs.

2584 *Congolese Soukous (Rough Guide)* (Mangwana Franco, Koffi Olomidé, Kanda Bongo Man, Tabu Ley, Deyess Mukangi, Pépé Kallé, Rigo Star, Papa Wemba, and Yondo Sister). World Music Network: RGNET 1050 CD. 2000. CD.

2585 *Franco, Simaro, Sam Mangwana, 1982–1985* (Franco, Simaro, Sam Mangwana, and TPOK Jazz). Sonodisc: CD 6854. 1982, 1994. CD.

2586 *Pont sur le Congo.* African Pearls. Syllart Productions: 6147472. 1960s, 2009. 2 CDs.

2587 *Roots of OK Jazz, Vol. 3: Zaïre Classics, 1955– 1956.* Crammed Discs: Craw 7. 1993. CD.

2588 *The Rough Guide to Congo Gold.* Rough Guide. World Music Network: RGNET 1200 CD. 2008. CD.

Equatorial Guinea
GROUPS

2589 Hijas del Sol
    2589.1 *Kchaba.* Intuition: INT 3271 2. 2000. CD.
    2589.2 *Kottó.* Intuition: INT 3229 2. 1998. CD.

2590 Malabo Strit Band. *MSB.* Nubenegra: MNN6116. 2002. CD.

Gabon
INDIVIDUALS ARTISTS

2591 Akendengué, Pierre-Claver
    2591.1 *Afrika Obota: Nandipo.* Omagatoki: OMCX-1011. 1991. CD.
    2591.2 *Silence.* Phantasm Imports. 2010. CD.
    2591.3 *Vérité d'Afrique.* Lusafrica: 56725 562252. 2008. CD.

2592 N'Goma, Oliver
    2592.1 *Bané.* Noli: CD 53 171. 1900s. CD.
    2592.2 *Saga.* Lusafrica: 56725 462612. 2006. CD.

São Tomé and Príncipe
ANTHOLOGY

2593 *1975–1995, Independencia!* Lusafrica: 08736-2. 1995. CD.

CENTRAL AFRICA POPULAR GENERAL ANTHOLOGIES

2594 *Heartbeat Soukous.* Earthworks, Virgin: CDEWV 3. 1987. CD.

2595 Zap Mama. *Supermoon.* Heads Up International: HUCD 3132. 2007. CD.

SOUTH AFRICA POPULAR
Angola
INDIVIDUAL ARTISTS AND GROUPS

2596 Bastos, Waldemar. *Pretaluz: Blacklight.* Luaka Bop: 68089-90020-2. 1998. CD.

2597 Bonga. *Bonga Live* (Barceló de Carvalho and Semba Master). Lusafrica: 462242. 2004. CD.

2598 Lulendo. *Angola.* Buda: 3017263. 2005. CD.

ANTHOLOGIES

2599 *Angola Soundtrack: The Unique Sound of Luanda 1968–1976* (Samy Ben Redjeb, compiler). Analog Africa, No. 9. Analog Africa Records: AACD 069. 1968, 2010. CD.

Botswana

GROUP

2600 Segwana. *Mmasepoto*. Abrams Graphics Center. 2006. CD.

Lesotho

ANTHOLOGIES

2601 *Music of Lesotho*. Smithsonian Folkways: FW04224. 2010. CD.

2602 *Voices of Africa: Mbube and Sotho A Capella Choirs*. ARC Music: EUCD 1509. 1999. CD.

Mozambique

GROUPS

2603 Mabulu
  2603.1 *African Classics*. Sheer Sound: SLCD 171. 2009. CD.
  2603.2 *Soul Marrabenta*. Riverboat Records: TUGCD1024. 2002. CD.

2604 Eyuphuro. *Yellela*. World Music Network: TUG CD 1022. 2001. CD.

Namibia

GROUP

2605 Unathi. *My First Time*. Ghetto Ruff. [2005]. CD.

South Africa (Republic of)

INDIVIDUAL ARTISTS AND GROUPS

2606 Clegg, Johnny
  2606.1 ★*The Best of Juluka/Savuka, Featuring Johnny Clegg* (Juluka and Savuka). Quality Sounds; dist. by Electronicmode Music. 2002. CD.
  2606.2 *Human* (Soweto Gospel Choir). Appleseed: APR CD 1124. 2010. CD.
  2606.3 *Third World Child* (Savuka). Capitol: CDP 7 46778 2. 1987. CD.

2607 Dark City Sisters and Flying Jazz Queens. *Dark City Sisters and Flying Jazz Queens*. Earthworks: CDEWV 31 7243 8 39182 2 5. 1993. CD.

2608 Ladysmith Black Mambazo. *Long Walk to Freedom* (Joseph Shabalala). Heads Up Africa. Heads Up International: HUCD 3109. 2006. CD.

2609 Mahlasela, Vusi. *The Voice*. ATO Records: ATO 0011. 2003. CD.

2610 Mahlathini
  2610.1 *The Lion of Soweto*. Virgin: 2-90867. 1987. CD.
  2610.2 *The Lion Roars* (Mahotella Queens and Makgona Tsohle Band). Shanachie: 43081. 1991. CD.
  2610.3 *Paris-Soweto* (Mahotella Queens and Makgona Tsohle Band). Polydor: 839 676-2. 1988. CD.
  2610.4 *Thokozile* (Mahotella Queens and Makgona Tsohle Band). Virgin, Earthworks: CDEWV6. 1986, 1988. CD.

2611 Mahotella Queens. *Sebai Bai*. Indigo: LBLC 2571. 2000. CD.

2612 Makeba, Miriam
  2612.1 *The Best of Miriam Makeba and the Skylarks*. Camden; BMG Entertainment International: CND 1001, 74321 592862. 1998. CD.
  2612.2 ★*Reflections*. Heads Up International; Gallo Records: HUCD 3087. 2004. CD.
  2612.3 *Welela*. Mercury: 838 208-2. 1989. CD.

2613 Makeba, Miriam, and Lorraine Klaasen. *A Tribute to Miriam Makeba*. Justin Time: 246. 2012. CD.

2614 Malope, Rebecca. *Free at Last*. EMI Hemisphere: 7243 8 57127 22. 1997. CD.

2615 Masekela, Hugh
  2615.1 ★*Hope*. Triloka: 7930185215-2. 1993, 2002. CD.
  2615.2 *Still Grazing: The Musical Journey of Hugh Masekela*. Blue Thumb Records: B0002442-02. 2004. CD.

2616 Shabalala, Joseph
  2616.1 *Classic Tracks* (Ladysmith Black Mambazo). Shanachie: SH 43074. 1990. CD.
  2616.2 *Raise Your Spirit Higher* (Ladysmith Black Mambazo). Heads Up Africa. Heads Up International: HUCD 3083. 2003, 2004. CD.

ANTHOLOGIES

2617 ★*Freedom Fire: The Indestructible Beat of Soweto, Vol. 3* (Mahlathini, Mahotella Queens, and others). Virgin: 91409-2. 1990. CD.

2618 *From Marabi to Disco: 42 Years of Township Music*. Gallo: CDZAC 61. 1994. CD.

2619 *Homeland 2: A Collection of Black South African Music*. Rounder: CD 5028. 1990. CD.

2620 *The Indestructible Beat of Soweto, Vol. 1.* The Earthworks Collection: 20 Years of All-Time Classics. Stern's Africa: STEW 14 CD. 2002. CD.

2621 *Next Stop—Soweto: Jazz in South Africa, 1963–1978, Vol. 3: Giants, Ministers and Makers.* Strut: STRUT 063 CD. 1963, 2010. 2 CDs.

2622 *Next Stop—Soweto: R&B, Funk, and Psych Sounds from the Townships, 1969–1976, Vol. 2: Soultown.* Strut: STRUT 057 CD. 1969, 2010. CD.

2623 *Next Stop—Soweto: Township Sounds from the Golden Age of Mbaqanga.* Strut: STRUT 054 CD. 1968, 2010. CD.

2624 *South Africa.* Putumayo World Music: PUT 301-2. 2010. CD.

2625 *South African Legends* (Mahlathini, Vusi Mahlasela, West Nkosi, Hugh Masekela, Lucky Dube, Johnny Clegg, Miriam Makeba). Putumayo World Music: PUTU 163-2. 2000. CD.

2626 *Urban Africa: Jive Hits of the Townships.* Polydor: 841 470-2. 1990. CD.

Zambia

GROUPS

2627 Amanaz. *Africa.* QDK Media: CD 051. 1975, 2010. CD. Anthology

2628 *Zambush*
   2628.1 *Vol. 1: Zambian Hits from the '80s.* SWP Records: SWP 027. 1983, 2004. CD.
   2628.2 *Vol. 2: Zambian Hits from the '60s and '70s.* SWP Records: SWP 028. 1960s, 2004. CD.

Zimbabwe

INDIVIDUAL ARTISTS AND GROUPS

2629 Chiweshe, Stella. *Talking Mbira.* Piranha: C-PIR1681. 1998, 2002. CD.

2630 Mapfumo, Thomas
   2630.1 *The Chimurenga Singles 1976–1980* (Blacks Unlimited). Shanachie: SH 43066. 1989. CD.
   2630.2 *Gwindingwi Rine Shumba* (Blacks Unlimited). Water: 237. 1970s, 2009. CD.
   2630.3 *Shumba: Vital Hits of Zimbabwe* (Blacks Unlimited). Virgin Records: 3-1022-2. 1990. CD.

2631 Mtukudzi, Oliver. *Tuku Music* (Mwendi Chibindi and Mary Bell). Putumayo World Music: PUTU 152-2. 1999. CD.

ANTHOLOGY

2632 *Zimbabwe Frontline: Spirit of the Eagle, Vol. 2.* Earthworks, Virgin: 2 91410. 1990. CD.

SOUTHERN AFRICAN POPULAR GENERAL ANTHOLOGY

2633 ★*Rough Guide to the Music of South Africa* (Izingqungqulu Zomhlaba, Mahlathini, Noise Khanyile, Lucky Dube, and others). World Music Network: RGNET 1020 CD. 1997. CD.

2634 *The Rough Guide to South African Jazz.* Rough Guide. World Music Network: RGNET 1341 CD. 2016. CD. Second edition of a 2000 release.

AFRICAN DIASPORA

Compiled by Suzanne Flandreau

The African diaspora has resulted from the displacement of African people—usually as workers or slaves—over the past five hundred years. Because displaced peoples take their culture with them and then change or refine it in keeping with local conditions, the music of the African diaspora is widely varied and at the same time clearly African. The recordings listed here range from broadly comparative anthologies of examples from many locations (including the United States) to recordings that focus on the African populations in particular countries or regions. Most are field recordings, but a few studio recordings of traditional artists are included.

The most-documented diasporic group appears to be the Garifuna, people of mixed Caribbean Indian and African heritage who were forcibly removed from their home on the Caribbean Island of St. Vincent in the eighteenth century. Today, Garifuna settlements can be found along the coast of Central America. Also well documented are the Gnawa of Morocco, whose religious music and drumming have inspired a number of studio recordings of traditional musicians. Other African diasporic peoples who have maintained their ethnic and musical identities include the Saramacca Maroons of the northern coast of South America and the Siddis of India. A revival of Afro-Peruvian culture took place in the 1960s and 1970s, resulting in a commercialized revival of Afro-Peruvian folk music. The recordings listed here are anthologies of selections from these commercial recordings. This is also true of the *son jarocho* of Veracruz in Mexico—a studio recording by a representative traditional artist is included.

Sadly, no recordings of otherwise documented African diasporic peoples in Pakistan, Oman, and Iran are currently available. Related citations may be found in chapter 2, "Traditional and Popular Music of the Americas and the Caribbean," and chapter 7, "International Anthologies" (for example, Garifuna are also represented in the Central America list). For Afro-Caribbean music, see chapter 2.

CIRCUM-CARIBBEAN AND LATIN AMERICA

Belize

GROUP

2635 Mr. Peters Boom and Chime. *Haul Up Your Foot You Fool!* [1992]. Fire Ant: FACD 1006. 1992, 1994. CD.

ANTHOLOGY

2636 *Shine Eye Gal: Brukdon!* [1978, 1985]. Corasón: COCD 118. 1978, 1994. CD.

Belize (Garifuna)

GROUPS

2637 Original Turtle Shell Band. *The Original Turtle Shell Band*. Hipi: 79617.2. 2000. CD.

2638 Lambey, Jose, Lady Lard, and Isabel Flores. *Garifuna Punta Anthology* [1973]. Turtle Shell Music: BZE CD 2006. 1973, 2006. CD.

ANTHOLOGIES

2639 *Dabuyabarugu: Inside the Temple, Sacred Music of the Garifuna of Belize* [1981] (Carol Lynn Jenkins and Travis Jenkins, compilers and prods.). Custom Compact Disc Series. Smithsonian Folkways: FE 4032. 1982. CD.

2640 ★*Garifuna Music: Field Recordings from Belize* [2002–2004]. ARC Music: EUCD 1913. 2002, 2005. CD.

2641 *Traditional Music of the Garifuna (Black Carib) of Belize* (Carol Lynn Jenkins and Travis Jenkins, compilers and prods.). Custom Compact Disc Series. Smithsonian Folkways: FE 4031. 1982, 2003. CD.

VIDEO

2642 *Play, Jankunu, Play: The Garifuna Wanaragua Ritual in Belize* [2006] (Oliver Greene, prod. and dir.). Documentary Educational Resources. 2006, 2007. DVD.

Bolivia

ANTHOLOGY

2643 *El tambor mayor: Musica y cantos de las comunidades negras de Bolivia*. Serie Documentation Etnomusicologica, 6. Fundacion Simon I. Patino. 1998. CD.

Colombia

ANTHOLOGIES

2644 *Colombie: Musique funeraire de palenque = Afro-Colombian Funeral Music)*. Musique du Monde. Buda: 3016782. 2000. CD.

2645 *Son de negro: La musica del Canal del Dique* (Manuel Antonio, perf.; Perez Herrera, prod.). Corporacion para la Investigacion Etnomusical. 1999. CD.

Costa Rica

ANTHOLOGY

2646 *Calypsos: Afro-Limonese Music of Costa Rica*. Lyrichord: LYRCD 7412. 1988, 1991. CD.

French Guiana

See also Suriname.

Guatemala (Garifuna)

ANTHOLOGY

2647 *Garifuna Traditional Music from Guatemala* (Grupo Ibimeni; Alphonso Arivillaga Cortés, compiler). Sub Rosa: SR273. 2008. CD.

Guyana

ANTHOLOGY

2648 *Traditional African Ritual Music of Guyana: "Queh Queh," "Cumfa," and "Come Tru"* (David Blair Stiffler, compiler). Custom Compact Disc Series. Smithsonian Folkways: FE 4238. 1982, 2003. CD.

Honduras (Garifuna)

GROUP

2649 Ensemble Wabaruagun. *Honduras: Chants des Caribs noirs = Songs of the Black Caribs; Honduras* [2000]. Ocora: C 560162. 2000, 2002. CD.

Mexico

INDIVIDUAL ARTIST

2650 Silva, Graciana. *La Negra Graciana: Sones Jarochos.* Corasón: COCD 109. 1994. CD.

Peru

ANTHOLOGIES

2651 *Lo Mejor del Ritmo Negro Peruano.* Virrey: CD-VIR 1355. [2000]. CD.

2652 *The Soul of Black Peru: Afro-Peruvian Classics* (David Byrne and Yale Evelev, compilers). Luaka Bop; Warner Brothers: 9 45878-2. 1971, 1995. CD.

Suriname

ANTHOLOGIES

2653 *From Slavery to Freedom: Music of the Saramaka Maroons, Suriname* [1977] (Verna Gillis and Richard Price, compilers). Lyrichord: LLST 7354. 1981. LP.

2654 ★*Music from Aluku: Maroon Sounds of Struggle, Solace, and Survival* [1984–1987, 1995] (Kenneth Bilby, compiler). Smithsonian Folkways: SFW CD 50412. 2010. CD.

2655 *Music from Saramaka: A Dynamic Afro-American Tradition* [Recorded 1967–1968, 1976] (Richard Price and Sally Price, compilers). Custom Compact Disc Series. Smithsonian Folkways: FE 4225. 1977, 2003. CD.

Uruguay

ANTHOLOGY

2656 *Uruguay: Tambores del Candombe.* Musique du Monde. Buda Musique: 92745-2. 1999. CD.

Venezuela

ANTHOLOGIES

2657 *Tierra del Cacao: Afro-Venezuelan Music and Dance* [1986–1995]. Ethnic Series. Pan: 2063 CD. 1986, 1999. CD.

2658 *Venezuela: Chants et tambours des confreries noires = Chants and Drums of the Black Brotherhoods* [1993–1994]. Ocora Radio France: C 560085. 1995. CD.

2659 *Venezuela: Chants et tambours diablos = Songs and Diablos Durms.* Collection Ocora Radio France. Ocora Radio France: C 560163. 2002. CD.

Transnational

ANTHOLOGIES

2660 *Afro-Hispanic Music from Western Colombia and Ecuador* (Norman E. Whitten, compiler). Custom Compact Disc Series. Smithsonian Folkways: F-4376. 1967, 2000. CD.

2661 *Paranda: Africa in Central America.* Detour: 3984-27303-2. 1999. CD. Garifuna

NORTH AFRICA AND ASIA

India

ANTHOLOGY

2662 *Sidi Sufis: African Indian Mystics of Gujarat* [1999-2002] (Amy Catlin-Jairazbhoy and Nazir Ali Jairazbhoy, compilers). Apsara Media for Intercultural Education: 80 PG1221. 2002. CD.

VIDEO

2663 ★*From Africa–to India: Sidi Music in the Indian Ocean Diaspora* (Amy Catlin-Jairazbhoy and Nazir ali Jairazbhoy, compilers). Apsara Media for Intercultural Education. 2003, 2006. DVD.

Morocco

ANTHOLOGIES

2664 *Gnawa Music of Marrakesh: Night Spirit Masters.* Axiom: 314-510-147-2. 1990. CD.

2665 *The Music of Islam, Vol. 6: al-Maghrib, Gnawa Music* (David Parsons, prod.). Celestial Harmonies: 13146-2. 1997. CD.

2666 ★*World of Gnawa* [1990–1995]. Rounder: 8261-5080-2. 1990, 2001. CD.

GROUP

2667 Altaf Gnawa Group. *Gnawa Music from Morocco.* ARC Music: EUCD 1922. 2005. CD.

AFRICAN DIASPORA
GENERAL ANTHOLOGIES

2668   ★*Africa en America: Musica de 19 paises = Africa in America: Music from 19 Countries.* Corasón: MTCD 115/7. 1976, 1992. 3 CDs.

2669   *African and Afro-American Drums* (Harold Courlander, ed.). Custom Compact Disc Series. Smithsonian Folkways: F-4502. 1954, 2000. CD.

2670   ★*Black Music of Two Worlds* (John Storm Roberts, compiler). Custom Compact Disc Series. Smithsonian Folkways: FE 4602 AB. 2001. 2 CDs.

2671   *Negro Folk Music of Africa and America* (Harold Courlander, ed.). Custom Compact Disc Series. Smithsonian Folkways: FE 4500. 1951, 2003. CD.

2672   ★*Roots of Black Music in America* (Samuel Barclay Charters, compiler). Custom Compact Disc Series. Smithsonian Folkways: FA 2694. 1972, 2003. 2 CDs.

2673   *South America: Black Music in Praise of Oxala and Other Gods* [1968] (David Lewiston, compiler). Explorer Series. Nonesuch: 79729-2. 1970, 2003. CD.

2674   ★*The Yoruba/Dahomean Collection* [1939–1957]. Endangered Music Project; Smithsonian Folkways Archival. Smithsonian Folkways: HRT 15020. 2010. CD.

SUB-SAHARAN AFRICA
Compiled by Liza Vick

General Anthologies

2675   *Africa, South of the Sahara.* (Harold Courlander, compiler). Custom Compact Disc Series. Folkways Records: FE 4503. 1957, 1999.CD.

2676   *African Beat.* Putumayo World Music: PUT 311-2. 2011. CD.

2677   *African Groove.* Putumayo World Music: PUT 210-2. 1994, 2003. CD.

2678   *African Moves, Vols. 1 and 2.* Rounder; Stern's Africa: CD 11513; STCD 1029. 1983–1989. 2 CDs.

2679   ★*African Music, Vol. 8, No. 2, 2008.* International Library of African Music. 2008. CD.

2680   *African Odyssey.* Putumayo World Music: PUT- 191-2. 2001. CD.

2681   *African Party.* Putumayo World Music: PUT-276-2. 2008. CD.

2682   *African Rap.* World Music Network: RGNET 1126. 2004. CD.

2683   *African Rhythms and Instruments, Vol. 1.* Lyrichord: LYRCD 7328. 1969, 2005.CD.

2684   ★*Afrique: 50 ans de musique: 50 ans d'indépendances = Africa: 50 Years of Music: 50 Years of Independence.* Discograph: 3218462. 1944, 2010.18 CDs.

2685   *Afrique en or.* Lusafrica: 262962; 262972; 262982; 262992. 1994. 4 CDs.

2686   *Afro-Latin Party.* Putumayo World Music: PUT 235-2. 1997, 2005.CD.

2687   *Badenya: Manden jaliya in New York City.* Smithsonian Folkways: SFW CD 40494. 2002. CD.

2688   *The Best of Alpha Blondy.* World Pacific: CDP 7243 8 37041 2 5. 1995. CD.

2689   *Djin Djin* (Angélique Kidjo). Razor & Tie: 7930182967-2. 2007. CD.

2690   *Dublin to Dakar: A Celtic Odyssey.* Putumayo World Music: PUTU 147-2. 1999. CD.

2691   *East to West* (Baka Beyond). Narada: 72435-43725-2-0. 2002. CD.

2692   ★*Golden Afrique, Vols. 1–3.* Network: 27.677; 29.076; 495115. 1971, 2005; 1950s, 2005; 1900s, 2006. 6 CDs.

2693   *Indian Ocean.* Rough Guide. World Music Network: RGNET 1086 CD. 2002. CD.

2694   *Journey Between* (Baka Beyond). Hannibal: HNCD 1415. 1998. CD.

2695   *Marabi Africa 1.* Marabi; dist. by Harmonia Mundi: 46829-2. 2007. CD.

2696   *Marabi Africa 2.* Marabi; dist. by Harmonia Mundi: 46829-2. 2008. CD.

2697   *Mondo Africa.* Mondo Series. Ark 21: 186 850 036 2. 2001. CD.

2698   *Out of Africa.* World Beat, Africa. Rykodisc: RCD 20059. 1988. CD.

2699   *Putumayo Presents Africa.*Putumayo World Music: PUTU 151-2. 1999. CD.

2700 *Putumayo Presents African Reggae.* Putumayo World Music: PUT-CD-287. 2009. CD.

2701 *Putumayo Presents an Afro-Portuguese Odyssey.* Putumayo World Music: PUT 204-2. 2002. CD.

2702 *Putumayo Presents Congo to Cuba.* Putumayo World Music: PUT 200-2. 1990, 2002.CD.

2703 *Red Hot + Riot* (Fela Kuti). MCA: 088 113 075-2. 2002. CD.

2704 *The Rough Guide to African Guitar Legends.* Rough Guide. World Music Network: RGNET 1259 CD. 2011. 2 CDs. Special edition.

2705 *The Rough Guide to African Street Party.* Rough Guide. World Music Network: RGNET 1201 CD. 2008. CD.

2706 *The Rough Guide to Afrobeat Revival.* Rough Guide. World Music Network: RGNET 1218 CD. 2009. 2 CDs.

2707 *The Rough Guide to the Music of Africa.* Rough Guide. World Music Network: RGNET 1041 CD. 1999. CD.

2708 *Super Guitar Soukous.* Hemisphere: 7243 8 28188 2 3. 1993. CD.

2709 *30 ans de musique Africaine: Les chansons des années d'indépendance, 1960–1990.* Africa No. 1: CD 52910. 1991. CD.

2710 *This Is Reggae Music.* Trojan; Sanctuary: 06076-80470-2. 1960, 2004. 4 CDs.

2711 *Throw Down Your Heart, African Sessions* [2005] (Béla Fleck and others). Tales from the Acoustic Planet, Vol. 3. Rounder: 11661-0634-2. 2005, 2009. CD.

VIDEO

2712 *The JVC Video Anthology of World Music and Dance.* JVC, Victor Co. of Japan, Ltd.; dist. by Multicultural Media. 1990, 2005. 30 DVDs + 9 booklets.

6

Traditional and Popular Music of Europe

Compiled by AARON BITTEL, DEBORAH GRIFFITH DAVIS,
SPIRO SHETUNI, *and* LIZA VICK

Materials listed here are representative of collecting areas and should be used in conjunction with other sources as a guide to artists, series, styles, and genres. These sources include the *World Music: The Rough Guide* series and *Garland Encyclopedia of World Music* as well as vendors such as Harmonia Mundi (among others), which distribute many labels that showcase European music. General anthologies are located in chapter 7, "International Anthologies," and at the end of this chapter. Regional anthologies appear at ends of their respective sections.

European classical music is handled in volume 3. World popular music is touched on but covered more comprehensively in other sources, such as Allmusic (www.allmusic.com) and National Geographic Music (www.nationalgeographic.com). Out-of-print rates are higher in some areas than others, but the artist and genre information provided offers a grounding for further research. Selected items are available though vendors handling out-of-print materials (e.g., Amazon, eBay). Smithsonian Folkways regularly reissues back catalog items in emerging formats, and of course many are available on the Internet as digital downloads or streaming audio.

The geographical arrangement used in this chapter is intended only as an organizational framework, not to imply musical divisions or boundaries. Diaspora music is represented mainly in chapter 7 but is also sprinkled throughout regional lists. This organization reflects the difficulties inherent in the attempt to "organize" world music amid globalization, fusion, and transnational and diasporic movements. Here again, lists are not intended to be taken literally or to be comprehensive. The goal is to provide a starting point for exploration and collecting.

UNITED KINGDOM AND IRELAND

Compiled by Deborah Griffith Davis

The most difficult aspect of selecting traditional folk music recordings from England, Scotland, Wales, and Ireland is the vast range of material from which to choose. The selections below represent a number of genres and performances. Some recordings are remasters from earlier LP recordings. When selecting material for your collection, you may want to consider your focus in determining whether to select only traditional music and performances, to incorporate more progressive performances, or to include recently composed works performed in a traditional manner.

When considering recordings of performances to include in your collection, you may come across the family connections that populate the field and notice the movement of musicians from group to group. For example, Martin Carthy, a well-respected figure in English folk music circles since the 1960s, has performed with Steeleye Span and the Albion Country Band. His wife, Norma Waterson, sang for many years with the Watersons. Their daughter, Eliza Carthy, has had a solo career that leans toward the progressive side of folk music. Yet the three currently perform together as Waterson:Carthy. Robin Huw Bowen, the

Welsh triple harpist, has had a substantial worldwide solo career performing traditional tunes discovered in manuscripts while conducting research at the National Library of Wales. Bowen has also performed traditional music with Mabsant and original works with Cusan Tân, and he currently performs and records both traditional and original works with Crasdant.

The 1960s and 1970s brought the folk music revival, represented in Ireland by popular groups like the Chieftains, the Dubliners, and the Clancy Brothers. In the 1970s and 1980s in Scotland, groups like Runrig and Capercaillie were performing in Scottish Gaelic, while the Whistlebinkies and Boys of the Lough were developing their particular sounds with their choices of bagpipes. In Wales, the revival was directly connected to concerns about the loss of the Welsh language. Dafydd Iwan used his influence as a folksinger; a politician with Plaid Cymru, the nationalist party of Wales; and a founder of Sain Records to promote the Welsh language and devolution for Wales. In England, the roots revival developed in tandem with the spread of the folk music clubs originally begun by A. L. Lloyd and Ewan MacColl and the later electric performance of traditional music by groups like Fairport Convention.

Celtic music has developed great popularity in recent decades, fusing and overlapping with other genres such as pop and folk-rock. A few samplers are included in chapter 7, "International Anthologies." The Celtic diaspora extends throughout many regions of Europe, North America, and elsewhere (notably Cape Breton, Nova Scotia). A few examples include Natalie MacMaster, Buddy MacMaster, and Mary Jane Lamond, and various Smithsonian Folkways releases (Thomas Pease, "Gaelic Music of Cape Breton Island: The Last Fifteen Years," *Notes* 63, no. 2 [2006]: 401–417). Many of the citations listed are available via iTunes (see, for example, the Sain, Deutsche Grammophon, My Kung Fu, Sbme Castle Us, and Marquis labels) and in MP3 format on the web (see, for example, Topic, Compass, Shanachie, Rounder, Empire Musicworks, Culburnie, Survival, Green Linnet, and Rubyworks).

ENGLAND

INDIVIDUAL ARTISTS OR GROUPS

2713 Albion Country Band. *Battle of the Field* (Martin Carthy, Sue Harris, Ashley Hutchings, John Kirkpatrick, Simon Nicol, and Roger Swallow). BGO: BGOCD 354. 1976, 1997. CD.

2714 Anderson, Alistair. *Concertina Workshop* (Graham Pirt, Geoff Harris, Tich Richardson, and Dave Richardson). Free Reed: FRRR 15. 1974, 2008. CD.

2715 Bellowhead. *Hedonism*. Navigator Records: NAVIGATOR0 42. 2010. CD.

2716 Briggs, Anne. *Anne Briggs: A Collection*. Topic: TSCD 504. 1999. CD.

2717 Carthy, Eliza, and Norma Waterson. *Gift*. Topic: TSCD 579. 2010. CD.

2718 ★Carthy, Eliza, and Waterson: Carthy. *The Definitive Collection*. Highpoint Recordings: HPO 6005. 2003. CD.

2719 Carthy, Martin, and Dave Swarbrick. *Martin Carthy*. Topic: TSCD 340. 1965, 1993. CD.

2720 Collins, Shirley, Dolly Collins, and Christopher Hogwood. *Love, Death and the Lady* (Alan Lumsden, Adam Skeaping, Roderick Skeaping, Eleanor Sloan, John Fordham, Terry Cox, and Peter Wood). Fledg'ling: FLED 3039. 2003. CD.

2721 Copper Family. *Come Write Me Down: Early Recordings of the Copper Family of Rottingdean*. Topic: TSCD 534. 1951, 2001. CD.

2722 Cox, Harry. *Harry Cox the Bonnie Labouring Boy: Traditional Songs and Tunes from a Norfolk Farm Worker*. Topic: TSCD 512 D. 1999. CD.

2723 Denny, Sandy. *The Best of Sandy Denny. Millennium Collection; 20th Century Masters*. A&M: 440 063 314-2. 2002. CD.

2724 ★Fairport Convention. *Liege and Lief* (Sandy Denny, Ashley Hutchings, Dave Mattacks, Simon Nicol, Dave Swarbrick, and Richard Thompson). Island Remasters. Universal: 530 111-1. 1969, 2007. 2 CDs.

2725 *The Full English*. Topic Records: TSCD 823. 2013. CD.

2726 Graham, Davey. *Folk, Blues, and Beyond*. Les Cousins: LC 001. 2008. CD.

2727 Home Service. *Alright Jack*. Fledg'ling: FLED 3015. 1986, 1997. CD.

2728 Jones, Nic. *Penguin Eggs*. Topic: TSCD 411. 1991. CD.

2729 ★Kirkpatrick, John, Sue Harris, and Martin Carthy. *Plain Capers: Morris Dance Tunes from the Cotswolds* (Martin Brinsford and Fi Fraser). Free Reed: FRRR 01. 1976, 2007. CD.

2730 MacColl, Ewan, A. L. Lloyd, and Alf Edwards. *Blow, Boys, Blow* (Ralph Rinzler and Steve Benbow). Tradition Years. Tradition; Empire Musicworks: 545 450 849-2. 1950s, 2006. CD.

2731   Pentangle. *Basket of Light*. Castle Music: CMRCD207. 2001. CD.

2732   Prior, Maddy, and Tim Hart. *Folk Songs of Olde England, Vol. 1*. Mooncrest Records UK: CrestCD 006. 1991. CD.

2733   Simpson, Martin. *Purpose + Grace* (Andy Cutting, June Tabor, Richard Thompson, and others). Topic: TSCD 584. 2011. CD.

2734   Steeleye Span. *Please to See the King* (Maddy Prior, Martin Carthy, Tim Hart, Ashley Hutchings, and Peter Knight). Shanachie: 79075. 1990. CD.

2735   Tabor, June, and Oysterband. *Ragged Kingdom*. Topic: TSCD 585. 2011. CD.

2736   Tabor, June. *Airs and Graces*. Shanachie: 79055. 1991. CD.

2737   Tawney, Cyril. *Navy Cuts*. Phantom Sound & Vision: 1300371. 2002. CD.

2738   Thompson, Richard, Linda Thompson, and Simon Nicol. *I Want to See the Bright Lights Tonight* (Timi Donald, Pat Donaldson, John Kirkpatrick, Brian Gulland, Richard Harvey, Royston Wood, and Trevor Lucas). Island Remasters: 981 790-7. 1974, 2004. CD.

2739   Tickell, Kathryn. *The Northumberland Collection* (Terry Conway, Carolyn Robson, Julian Sutton, Willie Taylor, Sean Barry, Ian Carr, Neil Harland, Paul Flush, Matt Scattle, and Paul Handyside). Park: PRKcd42. 1998. CD.

2740   Watersons. *Frost and Fire: A Calendar of Ritual and Magical Songs*. Topic: TSCD 563. 1965, 2007. CD.

2741   Young Tradition. *So Cheerfully Round*. Castle Music: 409. 1999. CD.

IRELAND

INDIVIDUAL ARTISTS OR GROUPS

2742   Black, Mary. *Twenty-Five Years, Twenty-Five Songs*. 3ú Records: TUCD 8. 2008. 2CDs.

2743   Bothy Band. *The Bothy Band, 1975: The First Album*. Green Linnet, Mulligan Music: GLCD 3011, LUN 002. 1975, 1993, 2008. CD.

2744   Boys of the Lough. *To Welcome Paddy Home*. Shanachie: 79061. 1989, 1996. CD.

2745   Burke, Joe, Michael Coleman, and Andy McGann. *A Tribute to Michael Coleman (Felix Dolan)*. Green Linnet, Shaskeen Records: GLCD 3097, OS-360. 1994. CD.

2746   ★Chieftains. *The Best of the Chieftains*. Columbia: CK 86017. 1977, 2002. CD.

2747   Clancy Brothers and Tommy Makem. *The Very Best of the Clancy Brothers and Tommy Makem*. Legacy: 88697 61492 2. 2010. CD.

2748   Coleman, Michael. *Michael Coleman*. Gael-Linn, Viva Voce: CEFCD 161. 1992. 2 CDs.

2749   De Danann. *The De Danann Collection*. Erin, Celtic Collections, BCI: ER 15095, CCCD 160, 40940-2. 1999, 2005. CD.

2750   Déanta. *Whisper of a Secret*. Green Linnet: GLCD 1173. 1997. CD.

2751   Dillon, Cara. *Hill of Thieves* (Sam Lakeman and others). Charcoal Records: PRPACD009. 2009. CD.

2752   ★Dubliners. *The Best of the Dubliners*. Sounds of Ireland. Sony: EK 86021. 2002. CD.

2753   Ennis, Séamus. *Forty Years of Irish Piping*. Green Linnet: GLCD 1000. 1977, 2000. CD.

2754   Four Men and a Dog. *Barking Mad*. Green Linnet: GLCD 3085. 1991, 1993. CD.

2755   Glackin, Paddy, Paddy Keenan, and Donal Lunny. *Doublin'* (Noel Kenny). Tara: TARACD 2007. 1978, 2000. CD.

2756   Hayes, Martin, and Dennis Cahill. *Welcome Here Again*. Green Linnet: GLCD 1233. 2008. CD.

2757   Heaney, Joe. *From My Tradition: The Best of Joe Heaney*. Shanachie: 34019. 1997. CD.

2758   Johnstons. *The Johnstons: The Barley Corn*. Castle Music: CMAR 643. 1969, 2000. CD.

2759   Moore, Christy. *Christy Moore at the Point Live*. Grapevine: GRACD 203. 1994. CD.

2760   Moving Hearts. *Moving Hearts: Live in Dublin*. Rubyworks: RWXCD 60. 2007. CD.

2761   Ní Dhomhnaill, Mairéad. *No Dowry*. Shanachie: 78020. 1991, 1999. CD.

2762   Ó Riada, Seán. *Ó Riada›s Farewell*. Claddagh: 83289-2. 1971, 2000, 2006. CD.

2763   Patrick Street. *Compendium: The Best of Patrick Street*. Green Linnet: GLCD 1207. 2001. CD.

2764 Planxty. *Planxty.* Shanachie: 79009. 1973, 1990. CD.

2765 Pogues. *The Ultimate Collection.* Warner Music UK: 2 56462254 2. 2005. 2 CDs.

2766 Woods, Gay, and Terry Woods. *Lake Songs from Red Waters: The Best of Gay and Terry Woods.* Hux: HUX 040. 2003. CD.

ANTHOLOGIES

2767 *ICTM Ireland: Fieldwork* (Desi Wilkinson and Tony Langlois, ed.). ICTM-Ireland. 2013. CD.

2768 *Ireland: Crossroads of Art and Design, 1690–1840: The Music* (Liz Carroll, et al.). O'Brien International. 2015. CD.

2769 ★*Irish Voices: The Best in Traditional Singing.* Topic: TSCD 702. 1997. CD.

SCOTLAND

INDIVIDUAL ARTISTS OR GROUPS

2770 Bain, Aly, and Phil Cunningham. *The Best of Aly and Phil.* Compass: 7 4403 2. 2005. CD.

2771 Battlefield Band. *The Best of Battlefield Band.* Temple: COMD 2091. 2003. 2 CDs.

2772 Burgess, John. *King of the Highland Pipers.* Topic: TSCD 466. 1969, 1993. CD.

2773 Capercaillie. *Grace and Pride: The Anthology 2004–1984.* Survival: SURCD 030. 2004. 2 CDs.

2774 Dransfield, Robin, and Barry Dransfield. *Even More . . . Popular to Contrary Belief.* Revival Re: Masters Series. Free Reed: FRRR 07. 2008. CD.

2775 Fisher, Archie. *The Man with a Rhyme* (Wendy Grossman, Wendy Westra, Lani Herrmann, Ann Mayo Muir, and Lorraine Lee). Folk-Legacy: CD 61. 1976, 1997. CD.

2776 Fraser, Alasdair, and Paul Machlis. *Legacy of the Scottish Fiddle, Vol. 1.* Culburnie: CUL118D. 2000. CD.

2777 Gaughan, Dick. *The Definitive Collection.* Highpoint Recordings: HPO 6014. 2006. CD.

2778 Incredible String Band. *The Hangman's Beautiful Daughter* (Robin Williamson and Mike Heron). Fledg'ling Records: FRCX 307826. 1968, 2010. CD.

2779 Kinnaird, Alison. *The Harp Key = Crann nan teud: Alison Kinnaird Plays the Scottish Harp.* Temple: COMD 1001. 1978, 1996. CD.

2780 MacColl, Ewan, and Peggy Seeger. *Classic Scots Ballads.* Empire Musicworks: 545 450 764-2. 1959, 2005. CD.

2781 McCusker, John. *Yella Hoose.* Temple: COMD 2083. 2000. CD.

2782 Ossian. *The Best of Ossian.* Iona: IRCD 023. 1994. CD.

2783 ★*Robertson, Jeannie. *The Queen among the Heather* (Alan Lomax, compiler). Alan Lomax Collection. Rounder: 11661-1720-2. 1953, 1998. CD.

2784 Runrig. *Day of Days: The 30th Anniversary Concert.* Ridge: RR 025. 2003, 2004. CD.

2785 St. Clair, Isla. *Tatties and Herrin': The Land.* Greentrax: CDTRAX 145. 1997. CD.

2786 Silly Wizard. *Caledonia's Hardy Sons.* Shanachie: 79015. 1989. CD.

2787 Stewarts of Blair. *The Stewarts of Blair: Alex, Belle, Cathie, and Sheila.* Ossian Publications: OSS CD 96. 1955, 1994. CD.

2788 ★*Tannahill Weavers. *Live and in Session.* Compass: 7 4454 2. 2007. CD.

2789 Whistlebinkies. *Albannach.* Greentrax: CDTRAX 288. 2006. CD.

ANTHOLOGIES

2790 *Clo Dubh Clo Donn.* Greentrax: CDTRAX 9018. 1950, 2001. CD.

2791 *The Best of Scottish Music, Vol. 2* (Greentrax Recordings 15th Anniversary). Greentrax: CDTRAX 215. 2001. CD.

WALES

INDIVIDUAL ARTISTS OR GROUPS

2792 Aberjaber. *Y Bwced Perffaith = The Perfect Bucket.* Sain: SCD 2157. 2006. CD.

2793 Ar Log. *Goreuon Ar Log.* Sain: SCD 2547. 2007. 2 CDs.

2794 Bob Delyn a'r Ebillion. *Sgwarnogod Bach Bob.* Sain: SCD 2429. 2004. CD.

2795 Bowen, Robin Huw. *Hen Aelwyd = Old Hearth.* Sain: SCD 2232. 1999. CD.

2796 Calennig. *Trade Winds = Gwyntoedd Môr Hafren* (Mick Tems, Patricia Carron-Smith, and Peter Davies). Sain: SCD 2091. 1994. CD.

2797 Carreg Lafar. *Hyn: Traditional Celtic Music of Wales* (Linda Owen Jones, Rhian Jones, James Rourke, and Antwn Owen Hicks). Marquis: 81259 2. 1998, 2000. CD.

2798 Crasdant. *Welsh Traditional Music* (Robin Huw Bowen, Andy McLauchlin, Stephen Rees, and Huw Williams). Marquis: 81261. 1999, 2000. CD.

2799 Cusan Tân and Ann Morgan Jones. *Esgair = The Ridge.* Sain: SCD 2115. 1994. CD.

2800 Evans, Meredydd
    2800.1 ★*Merêd: Caneuon Gwerin.* Sain: SCD 2414. 2005. 2 CDs.
    2800.2 *Welsh Folk Songs.* Custom Compact Disc Series. Smithsonian Folkways: FW 6835. 1954, 2001. CD.

2801 Fernhill. *Na Prádle.* Beautiful Jo: BEJOCD-51. 2007. CD.

2802 Fflur, Elin. *Dim Gair.* Sain: SCD 2403. 2006. CD.

2803 ★Iwan, Dafydd, and Ar Log. *Yma O Hyd.* Sain: SCD 2063. 1995. 2 CDs.

2804 Jac-y-Do. *Bant â'r Cart.* Sain: SCD 2179. 1998. CD.

2805 James, Sian. *Gweini Tymor.* Sain: SCD 2145. 1996. CD.

2806 Jenkins, Delyth. *Ar y Ffin.* Sain: SCD 2206. 2006. CD.

2807 Mabsant. *Y Goreuon ar Sain = The Best on Sain.* Sain: SCD 2302. 2002. CD.

2808 Matthews, Cerys. *Awyren = Aeroplane.* My Kung Fu: MYKUNGFU 30. 2007. CD.

2809 Plethyn. *Popeth arall ar CD = Best of the Rest on CD.* Sain: SCD 2437. 2004. 2 CDs.

2810 Stevens, Meic. *Disgwyl Rhywbeth Gwell I Ddod.* Sain: SCD 2345. 2002. 3 CDs.

2811 Super Furry Animals. *Rings around the World.* XL Recordings: BXL 026 CD. 2002. 2 CDs.

2812 Terfel, Bryn, Bryan Davies, and Meinir Heulyn. *We'll Keep a Welcome: The Welsh Album* (Gareth Jones, cond.). Deutsche Grammophon: 463 593-2. 2000. CD.

2813 Thomas, John, and Elinor Bennett. *Alawon Cymreig = Welsh Melodies.* Sain: SCD 2195. 1998. 2 CDs.

ANTHOLOGY

2814 *Corau Meibion Cymru = Take Me Home.* Sain: SCD 2353. 2002. CD.

WESTERN EUROPE

Compiled by Liza Vick

Traditional, folk, popular, and classical music have rich legacies in Western Europe, and the first three are represented in these lists. As stated previously, geographical layout here is intended only to organize, not to convey rigid musical boundaries. Musical and cultural associations include the low countries, Central European, Slavic areas, and Southeastern Europe, to name a few (*Garland Encyclopedia of World Music, Vol. 8* [Garland, 1998–2002], 645). Transnationalism is also represented in these lists, in recordings ranging from Alpine to the Basques of Spain and France to Celtic peoples of Europe to Jewish music and that of the Roma Gypsies (*See also* "Eastern Europe" and in chapter 7, "International Anthologies").

Folk and traditional selections are most numerous here and the out-of-print rate is high in some areas, but as noted in general introduction, many are or will be available. From the bal-musette in France to the Austrian *stimmhorn* to the *bandonion* orchestras of Germany, this is an interesting soundscape to explore. Popular artists are represented in a sampling, but information is widely available in other sources, including those listed above. Labels represented in this list include Trikont, Auvidis, Smithsonian, Ocora, Chant du Monde, and others. The Society for Ethnomusicology maintained a discographies list, which should also be consulted (www.ethnomusicology.org/?OG_CurrentDisco).

AUSTRIA

INDIVIDUAL ARTISTS OR GROUPS

2815 ★Kubat, Karl and Karl Zaruba. *Folk Dances of Austria* (Brass Folk Dance Band and Schuhplattler Dance Band). Custom Compact Disc Series. Smithsonian Folkways: FW 8837, FW 8838, FW 8839. 1959. 2003. 3 CDs.

2816 Rossecker, Trachtenverein. *Music of the Alps: Traditional Music and Yodeling from Austria.* ARC Music: MRM-CD-EUCD 1992. 2006. CD.

2817 Schrammeln. *Music from Old Vienna.* Naxos: 8.550228. 1988, 1989. CD.

2818 Taconnet, Aline, Christian Vistorky, and Jean-Claude Ollier Urfer. *Danses Tyroliennes = Tyrolean Dances.* Air Mail Music. Sunset-France; PlayaSound: SA 141177; PS 65257. 2002, 2009. CD.

ANTHOLOGIES

2819 *Die Besten Schrammeln Instrumental* (Roland Neuwirth, compiler). Trikont. 1997. CD.

2820 *Greetings from Austria.* Custom Compact Disc Series. Smithsonian Folkways: MFS 381, M 00381. 1963, 2001. CD.

2821 *Une mosaïque de musiques Autriche = A Mosaic of Music: Austria.* Ocora Radio France: 600011. 2001, 1997. CD.

2822 *Uncensored Folk Music of Austria* (Chris Strachwitz and Johnny Parth, compilers). Arhoolie: CD 454. 2009. 2 CDs.

2823 *Wien: Volksmusic: Rare Schellacks 1906–1937.* Trikont: US-0198. 1900s, 1994. CD.

BELGIUM

INDIVIDUAL ARTISTS OR GROUPS

2824 Ambrozijn. *Kabonka.* Wild Boar. 2002. CD.

2825 Ialma. *Palabras Darei.* Zoku-EMI: 724382635628. 2000. CD.

2826 Kadril. *All the Best.* Wild Boar: WBM 21029. 2001. 2 CDs.

2827 Laïs. *Laïs.* Wild Boar: WBM 21005. 1998. CD.

2828 Schmitz, Henry, and Elisabeth Melchior. *Airs de fête en Wallonie: Chansons et musiques traditionnelles.* Traditions du Monde. Fonti Musicali: fmd 188. 1974, 1991. CD.

2829 Zap Mama. *Zap Mama.* Adventures in Afropea, 1. Luaka Bop: 9 45183-2. 1993. CD.

ANTHOLOGIES

2830 *Belgique: Ballades, danses, et chansons: Flandre, Wallonie = Belgium: Ballads, Songs, and Dances: Flanders, Wallonia.* Ocora Radio France: C 583061, HM 79. 1952, 2002. CD.

2831 *Belgique, le carnival de Binche = Belgium, the Carnival of Binche.* Musique du Monde. Buda: 82516-2. 1990. CD.

2832 *Flemish Folk Music, 1997.* MAP: 97003. 1997. 2 CDs.

2833 *Greetings from Belgium.* Disky Communications: DC 859412. 1999. CD.

2834 *Musique populaire de la Belgique = Folk Music from Belgium.* Auvidis Ethnic: B 6844, B 6844-1, B 6844-2. 1997. 2 CDs.

FRANCE

INDIVIDUAL ARTISTS OR GROUPS

2835 Aznavour, Charles, and Yvan Cassar. *Aznavour 2000.* EMI Music France: 7243 5290562 1. 2000. CD.

2836 Bratsch. *Rien dans les Poches.* Network: 29.667. 1996, 1998. CD.

2837 Brel, Jacques. *Les plus grandes chansons de Jacques Brel.* Intersong: MF 902. 2005. Score.

2838 Chambaud, Aurélien, and Patrick Vasori. *France: Musiques des provinces: Folk Music.* Air Mail Music. Sunset-France: SA 360713. 2008. 3 CDs.

2839 Gainsbourg, Serge. *Comic Strip.* Philips, Mercury: 314 528 951-2. 1966, 1996. CD.

2840 Malicorne. *Almanach.* Hexagone: GRI 191272. 1976, 2009. CD.

2841 Nubians. *Princesses Nubiennes.* Omtown: OMCD 45997. 1998. CD.

2842 Piaf, Edith. *La vie en rose.* Great French Stars; Living Era. ASV: ASV: CD AJA 5307. 1935, 1999. CD.

ANTHOLOGIES

2843 *Anthologie de la chanson Française Enregistrée.* EPM Musique: 90 VC 98. 1994. 90 CDs.

2844 *Celtic Folk from Brittany.* ARC Music: EUCD 2230. 2009. CD.

2845 *Discovering France = Musiques en France.* Auvidis Ethnic: B 6852, B 6845, B 6849, B 6851, B 6848. 1983, 1997. 4 CDs.

2846 ★*France (Alan Lomax and others, compilers).* World Library of Folk and Primitive Music, Vol. 19; Alan Lomax Collection. Rounder Select: 1836. 1913, 2002. CD.

2847   *France: Une anthologie des musiques traditionnelles* (Veillet, Guillaume, compiler). Frémeaux & associés: FA 5260--FA 5270. 1900, 2009. 10 CDs.

2848   *Les nuits Manouches* (Django Reinhardt and others). Chant du Monde: 274 1381, 274 1382. 2005. 2 CDs.

2849   *Putumayo Presents French Café*. Putumayo World Music: PUT 219-2. 1900s, 2003. CD.

2850   *The Rough Guide to the Music of France*. Rough Guide. World Music Network: RGNET 1111. 2003. CD.

2851   *The Rough Guide to Paris Café, Special Ed.* Rough Guide. World Music Network: RGNET 1240 CD. 2010. 2 CDs.

GERMANY

INDIVIDUAL ARTISTS OR GROUPS

2852   Dietrich, Marlene. *The Cosmopolitan Marlene Dietrich*. Art Deco. Columbia, Legacy: CK-53209. 1951, 1993. CD.

2853   Dissidenten. *Instinctive Traveler*. Blue Jackel Entertainment: BJAC 5015-2. 1997. CD.

2854   Hölderlin Express. *Hölderlin Express*. Akku Disk: ADCD 3028. 1996. CD.

2855   Junker, August, and Jakob Geis. *München: Volkssanger*. Rare Schellacks. Trikont: LC 4270. 1994. CD.

2856   Lemper, Ute, Jeff Cohen, and Robert Ziegler. *Berlin Cabaret Songs*. London: 452 601-2. 1997. CD.

2857   ★Schlamme, Martha, and Pete Seeger. *German Folk Songs*. Custom Compact Disc Series. Smithsonian Folkways: FW 6843. 1954, 2000s. CD.

2858   Taconnet, Aline, Christian Vistorky, and Jean-Claude Ollier Urfer. *Danses Tyroliennes = Tyrolean Dances*. Air Mail Music. Sunset-France; PlayaSound: SA 141177; PS 65257. 2002, 2009. CD.

2859   Well-Buam. *Sautanz*. Indigo: 231822. 1993. CD.

ANTHOLOGIES

2860   *Bayern: Volksmusik: Rare Schellacks, 1906–1941*. Trikont: US-0196. 1900s, 1994. CD.

2861   *The Best of Germany*. Madacy: CLUC 2 65. 2001. CD.

2862   *German Drinking Songs*. Legacy International: CD 304. 1988. CD.

2863   *Mit Zither und Hackbrett*. Koch International: CD 322 442. 1990. CD.

2864   *Music and Song from Germany*. Travel Series. Empire Music, Universal: 545 450 852-2. 2006. CD.

2865   *Music from Bavaria*. Collection Ocora Radio France. Ocora Records; dist. by Harmonia Mundi: C 600020. 2008. CD.

THE NETHERLANDS

INDIVIDUAL ARTISTS OR GROUPS

2866   Kross, Rolinha. *Amsterdam (Mazzeltov)*. Fréa Records; dist. by Music & Words: MWCD 4058. 2008. CD.

2867   ★Kunst, Jaap, and Ernst Wolff. *Living Folksongs and Dance-Tunes from the Netherlands*. Custom Compact Disc Series. Smithsonian Folkways: FP 3576, F-3576. 1956, 2000s. CD.

2868   Mirando, Tata, and Nello Mirando. *World Music in the Netherlands: Tata and Nello Mirando* (Royal Gipsy Orchestra and Hungarian Gipsy Ensemble). RNDiscs: WM 012. 1999, 2001. CD.

2869   Schot, Willem, Floor Van der Vliet, and Ruud Van den Berg. *Het daghet in den oosten = It's Dawning in the East: Bagpipes of the Low Countries*. Ethnic Series. PAN Records: PAN 2025 CD. 1993, 1995. CD.

ANTHOLOGIES

2870   *Achterhoekse Harmonikamuziek*. Musik & Wort. 2000. CD.

2871   *Café Amsterdam*. IMC Music: CAF 800164. 2005. 2 CDs.

2872   ★*Folksongs and Dances of the Netherlands* (Will D. Scheepers, compiler). Custom Compact Disc Series. Smithsonian Folkways: FE 4036. 1963, 2003. CD.

2873   *Jouster Boerebrulloft: Farmer's Wedding in Joure*. Ethnic Series. PAN Records: PAN 2004 CD. 1994. CD.

2874 *Pays-Bas: Chansons Oubliées.* Ocora: C 600003. 1996. CD.

2875 *World Music from the Netherlands: Migrants, Travellers, and Natives.* Pan: PAN 043. 2008. CD.

2876 *World Music in the Netherlands.* Radio Netherlands International: CD 1–CD 2. 1998. 2 CDs.

SWITZERLAND

INDIVIDUAL ARTISTS OR GROUPS

2877 Alpbarock. *Simelibärg.* Chants de la Terre. Alpha: ALPHA 525. 2008. CD.

2878 ★Liechti, Fritz. *Mountain Songs and Yodeling of the Alps.* Custom Compact Disc Series. Smithsonian Folkways: FW 8807. 1958, 2001. CD.

2879 Mytha. *Mythahorns #2.* Hat Jazz Series. Hat: ART CD 6151. 1993, 1995. CD.

2880 Stimmhorn. *Schnee.* Röhrender Hirsch; EMI: 417701. 1997. CD.

ANTHOLOGIES

2881 *Jüüzli: Jodel du Muotatal* (Hugo Zemp, compiler). Collection du Centre National de la Recherche Scientifique et du Musée de l'Homme. Chant du Monde: LDX 274 716. 1979, 1990. CD.

2882 *Musique traditionnelle de la Suisse Romande = Traditional Music from French-Speaking Switzerland.* Musica Helvetica. Swiss Radio International: MH CD 81.2. 1997. CD.

2883 *Musique traditionnelle du Chablais = Traditional Music from the Chablais Region.* Musica Helvetica. Swiss Radio International: MH CD 81.2. 1997. CD.

2884 *Musiques de Suisse Romande.* VDE: CD-1124, CD-1125. 2003. 2 CDs.

2885 *Paysages musicaux = Musical Landscapes.* Suisse. Ocora Radio France: C 600017. 1965, 2004. CD.

2886 *Suisse: Archives de musique populaire = Switzerland: Archive of Folk Music: Constantin Brailoiu Collection [1927–1951].* Archives Internationales de Musique Populaire, 89. VDE-Gallo: VDE CD-1265. 1986, 2009. CD.

2887 *Suisse: Les instruments traditionnels = Switzerland: Traditional Instruments.* Air Mail Music. Sunset-France: SA 141041. 1999. CD.

2888 *Switzerland: Zäuerli: Yodels of Appenzell = Suisse: Yodel d'Appenzell.* Musics and Musicians of the World. Unesco: D 8026. 1990. CD.

2889 *Ticino: Genuine Folk Music from Southern Switzerland.* Musica Helvetica. Swiss Radio International: MH CD 71.2. 1988, 1989. CD.

WESTERN EUROPE
VIDEO

2890 ★*The JVC Video Anthology of World Music and Dance: Europe, Vol. 20.* JVC, Victor Co. of Japan; dist. by Multicultural Media. 1990, 2005. 30 DVDs, 9 booklets.

SOUTHERN EUROPE

Compiled by Liza Vick

Genres such as Spanish flamenco, Portuguese fado, Greek *rembetika*, song dueling, and ballads coexist with Mediterranean and Arabic influences in the diverse cornucopia of Southern European music. Listed selections are abundant in the folk and traditional area, including many from the following series: Musique du Monde, the Alan Lomax Collection, Grands Cantaores du Flamenco, Arquivos do Fado, and Greek Archives. Popular offerings are merely sampled here, and as in many regions, boundaries between traditional and popular are constantly being crossed. Artists, such as Amalia Rodrigues and Mariza (Portugese fado artists), have risen to popularity interpreting traditional forms and bands like Tilak fuse Indian, Greek, Assyrian, and Italian folk music. Recording labels include Chant du Monde, Smithsonian, Rounder, Lyrichord, World Music Network, and many more.

GREECE

INDIVIDUAL ARTISTS OR GROUPS

2891 Athenians. *Canto General: Music of Greece.* ARC Music: EUCD 2342. 2011. CD.

2892 Baka, Theodora. *Myrtate: Traditionelle lieder aus Griechenland = Traditional Songs from Greece* (Pantelis Pavlidis). Raumklang: RK 2303. 2003, 2007. CD.

2893 Bellou, Sōtēria. *The Rebetico of Sotiria Bellou.* Greatest Greek Singers. Lyra: ML 0142. 1966, 1995. CD.

2894 Chalkias, Petros. *Epirus* (Kompania). World Network, 46. World Network: 32.376. 1998, 1999. CD.

2895 Daly, Ross. Eurasia: *Miltos* (Labyrinth). World Network, 8. WDR: 54.035. 1991, 1992. CD.

2896 Eskenazē, Roza. *Rembétissa, 1933–1936.* Heritage: HT CD 35. 1933, 1997. CD.

2897 Parolympioi. *Traditional Music and Songs from Greece.* ARC Music: EUCD 2256. 2009. CD.

2898 Takoutsia. *Grèce: Epire.* Inédit. Maison des Cultures du Monde: W 260020. 1984, 1990. CD.

2899 Tsitsánes, Vassilis. *Vassilis Tsitsánis, 1936–1946.* Rounder: CD 1124. 1936, 1997. CD.

2900 Vamvakarēs, Markos. *Bouzouki Pioneer, 1932–1940.* Rounder: CD 1139. 1998. CD.

ANTHOLOGIES

2901 *Anthologia Dēmotikou Tragoudiou = Anthology of Greek Folk Songs*
  2901.1 *Vol. 1: 1929–1940.* Greek Archives. Greek Archives; dist. by FM Records: 666. 1993. CD.
  2901.2 *Vol. 2: 1928–1940.* Greek Archives. FM Records: 668. [1990–1996]. CD.
  2901.3 *Vol. 3: 1929–1939.* Greek Archives. Hellados Archeion, FM Records: 669. 1928, 1998. CD.

2902 *Folk Music of Greece and Cyprus.* Lyrichord Discs: LYR CD 7435. 1999. CD.

2903 *Greece, a Musical Odyssey.* Putumayo World Music: PUT 225-2. 2004. CD.

2904 *Lost Homelands: The Smyrnaic Song in Greece.* Heritage: HT CD 27. 1994. CD.

2905 *Rembetika: More of the Secret History of Greece's Underground Music 2.* JSP: JSP 77105. 2008. 4 CDs.

2906 *Rembetika, 1936–1940: All the Pre-War Recordings of the Most Important Figure in Greek Popular Music 3.* JSP: JSP 77111. 1936, 2008. 5 CDs.

2907 *Rembetika: The Postwar Years, 1946–1954 4.* JSP: JSP 77123. 2009. 4 CDs.

2908 *The Rough Guide to Greek Café.* Rough Guide. World Music Network: WMN 1197 CD. 2010. 2 CDs.

2909 *The Rough Guide to the Music of Greece.* Rough Guide. World Music Network: RGNET 1066 CD. 2001. CD.

2910 *The Rough Guide to Rebétika.* Rough Guide. World Music Network: RGNET 1142 CD. 2004. CD.

2911 ★*Vocal Music in Crete* (Tullia Magrini and Roberto Leydi, compilers). World's Musical Traditions, 11. Smithsonian Folkways: SFW 40437. 1977, 2000. CD.

2912 *Women of Rembetica.* Rounder: 1121. 1928, 2000. CD.

ITALY

INDIVIDUAL ARTISTS OR GROUPS

2913 Banda Ionica. *Matria Mia.* Dunya: Fy 8050. 2002. CD.

2914 E Zézi. *Pummarola Black.* Lyrichord Discs: LYR CD 7426. 1994. CD.

2915 Esposito, Flavio. *Napoli e Dintorni.* Musique du Monde. Buda: 3018166. 2010. CD.

2916 Sepe, Daniele. *Viaggi Fuori Dai Paraggi.* II Manifesto-Officina: TM 002. 1996. CD.

2917 Squadra
  2917.1 *La Squadra: Cansons Génoises.* Musique du Monde. Buda: 92571-2. 1990. CD.
  2917.2 *La Squadra: Compagnia del Trallalero: Polyphonie Génoise.* Musique du Monde. Buda: 92514-2. 1995. CD.

2918 Tenores di Bitti. *S'amore 'e Mama.* Real World: CAR 2362-2. 1996. CD.

2919 Tesi, Riccardo. *Un ballo liscio: Le bal musette Italien = The Italian "Musette" Dance.* Auvidis Tempo. Auvidis: A 6242. 1997. CD.

2920 Valla, Stefano, and Daniele Scurati. *Italie: Musiques de l'apennin, Vol. 3: Piffero and fisarmonica: Per dove?* Musique du Monde. Buda: 3017926. 2009. CD.

ANTHOLOGIES

2921 ★*Abruzzo* (Alan Lomax and Diego Carpitella, compilers). Alan Lomax Collection; Italian Treasury. Rounder Select: 1811. 1954, 2001. CD.

2922 *The Bagpipe in Italy: Traditional Musicians of Italy.* Lyrichord Archive Series. Lyrichord: LAS-7343.

2010. CD. Originally released on LP, Albatros, in 1978.

2923 *Ballos Sardos: Antologia Di Balli Sardi, Vol. 1.* Ethnica, 15. Taranta: TA 015. 1997. CD.

2924 ★*Calabria* (Alan Lomax and Diego Carpitella, compilers). Alan Lomax Collection; Italian Treasury. Rounder Select: 1803. 1954, 1999. CD.

2925 ★*Emilia-Romagna* (Alan Lomax and Diego Carpitella, compilers). Alan Lomax Collection; Italian Treasury. Rounder Select: 1804. 1954, 2001. CD.

2926 ★*Folk Music and Song of Italy* (Alan Lomax and Diego Carpitella, compilers). Alan Lomax Collection; Italian Treasury. Rounder Select: 1801. 1958, 1999. CD.

2927 *Folk Music and Songs of Italy: Work Songs of Sicilian Peasants and Workers.* Lyrichord Archive Series. Lyrichord: LAS-7333. 2010. CD. Originally released on LP, Albatros, in 1975.

2928 *Italia.* Putumayo World Music: PUT 290-2. 1999, 2009. CD.

2929 *Italian Café.* Putumayo World Music: PUT 238-2. 2005. CD.

2930 *Italian Musical Odyssey.* Putumayo World Music: PUT 159-2. 2000. CD.

2931 *Italie: Musique des Albanais de Calabre = Italy: Music of the Albanians of Calabria* (Fabrice Contri, compiler). Archives Internationales de Musique Populaire, 101. VDE Gallo: VDE CD-1340. 2009, 2011. CD.

2932 *Italie, musiques populaires d'aujourd'hui = Italy, Popular Music Forms Today.* Musique du Monde. Buda: 92702-2. 2000. CD.

2933 *Italy: Music Rough Guide.* Rough Guide. World Music Network: RGNET 1042 CD. 2000. CD.

2934 *La Saltarella dell'Alta Sabina* (Giuseppe Michele Gala, compiler). Ethnica, 5. Taranta; Sudnord: TA 05; SNCD 0031. 1993. CD.

2935 ★*Liguria: Baiardo and Imperia* (Alan Lomax and Diego Carpitella, compilers). Alan Lomax Collection; Italian Treasury. Rounder Select: 1816. 1954, 2002. CD.

2936 ★*Liguria: Polyphony of Ceriana* (Alan Lomax and Diego Carpitella, compilers). Alan Lomax

Collection; Italian Treasury. Rounder Select: 1817. 2002, 1954. CD.

2937 *Musiques de fêtes en Calabre* (Goffredo Plastino, compiler). Inédit: W 260051. 1993. CD.

2938 *Organetto e tarantelle* (Giuseppe Michele Gala, compiler). Ethnica, 2; Le Tradizioni Musicali in Lucania, Vol. 2. Sudnord: SNCD 0028. 1991. CD.

2939 ★*Piemonte and Valle d'Aosta* (Alan Lomax and Diego Carpitella, compilers). Alan Lomax Collection; Italian Treasury. Rounder Select: 1807. 1954, 2004. CD.

2940 ★*Puglia: The Salento* (Alan Lomax and Diego Carpitella, compilers). Alan Lomax Collection; Italian Treasury. Rounder: 1805. 1954, 2002. CD.

2941 *Sardaigne: Les maîtres de la musique instrumentale.* Al Sur: ALCD 157. 1995. CD.

2942 ★*Sicily* (Alan Lomax and Diego Carpitella, compilers). Alan Lomax Collection; Italian Treasury. Rounder Select: 1808. 2000. CD.

2943 *Sicily: Music of the Holy Week = Sicile: Musique de la Semaine Sainte.* Anthologie Des Musiques Traditionnelles; Unesco Collection. Auvidis: D 8210. 1993. CD.

2944 ★*The Trallaleri of Genoa* (Alan Lomax, compiler). Alan Lomax Collection; Italian Treasury. Rounder: 11661-1802-2. 1954, 1999. CD.

MALTA

INDIVIDUAL ARTISTS OR GROUPS

2945 Baldachino, Frans, and Karmenu Bonnici. *Malte: Ballades et joutes chantées.* Inédit. Maison des Cultures du Monde: W 260040. 1992. CD.

2946 Etnika. *Zifna.* Etnika. 2003. CD.

ANTHOLOGIES

2947 ★*Folk Songs and Music from Malta.* Custom Compact Disc Series. Smithsonian Folkways: FM 4047. 1964, 2003. CD.

2948 *Malta's Musical Legacy* (Gukulari Ensemble; Anna Borg Cardona, Jean d'Estrée, Edward Jones, and Augustus Voigt, compilers). Gukulari Ensemble. 2003. CD.

PORTUGAL

INDIVIDUAL ARTISTS OR GROUPS

2949 Amendoeira, Joana. *Sétimo Fado.* Chant du Monde: 274 2020. 2009, 2011. CD.

2950 Brigada Victor Jara. *Anthologie de 15 ans de musique Portugaise traditionnelle.* Playasound: PS 65111. 1992, 1993. CD.

2951 Cabral, Pedro, Perez Caldeira, and Francisco. *Portugal.* World Network, 11. World Network: 54.038. 1988, 1992. CD.

2952 Castelo, Custódio. *The Art of the Portuguese Fado Guitar: Tempus.* ARC Music: EUCD 2315. 2011. CD.

2953 Do Carmo, Carlos. *Portugal: Fado.* Sunset-France: SA 141171. 2008. CD. Originally released in 1978 as Dez fados vividos.

2954 Lusitano. *Portugal: Folklore de minho: Folk Songs.* Sunset-France: SA 141162. 2008. CD.

2955 Madredeus. *Ainda: Original Motion Picture Soundtrack from the Film* Lisbon Story. EMI: 8 32636 2. 1995. CD.

2956 Mariza
    2956.1 *Concerto em Lisboa.* Times Square Records: TSQ-CD-9060. 2006, 2007. CD.
    2956.2 *Fado curvo.* Times Square Records: TSQ-CD-9033. 2003. CD.
    2956.3 *Fado tradicional.* Four Quarters Entertainment: FQT-CD-1828. 2010, 2011. CD.
    2956.4 *Terra* (Ivan Lins). Four Quarters Entertainment: FQT-CD-1814. 2008. CD.

2957 Mísia. *Ritual.* Erato: 8573-85818-2. 2001. CD.

2958 Rodrigues, Amália. *The Art of Amália.* Hemisphere: 7243 4 95771 2 1. 1952, 1998. CD.

2959 Soares, Fernando Machado. *Portugal: Le Fado de Coimbra.* Ocora: C 559041. 1988. CD.

ANTHOLOGIES

2960 *As Fadistas de Lisboa: 1928–1931.* Arquivos Do Fado, Vol. 3. Heritage: HTCD 24. 1994. CD.

2961 *Danças Tradicionais do Portugal: Minho-Douro* (Lou Flagel and Claude Flagel, compilers). Fonti Musicali: fmd 199. 1994. CD.

2962 *Fado.* Rough Guide. World Music Network: RGNET 1117 CD. 2004. CD.

2963 *Fado de Coimbra, 1926–1930.* Fados from Portugal, Vol. 2. Heritage: HT CD 15. 1992. CD.

2964 *Fado de Lisboa, 1928–1936.* Fados from Portugal, Vol. 1. Heritage: HT CD 14. 1992. CD.

2965 ★*Musical Traditions of Portugal.* Traditional Music of the World, Vol. 9. Smithsonian Folkways: CD SF 40435. 1988, 1994. CD.

2966 *Portugal: Chants et tambours de Beira-Baixa* (Manuel Gomes, compiler). Musique du Monde. Buda: 92542-2. 1993. CD.

2967 *Portugal: Musique d'Entre Doure e Vouga.* Ocora Radio France: C 600021. 2010. CD. Field recordings made in 2005.

2968 *Portugal: Portuguese Traditional Music = Musique traditionnelle du Portugal* (Hubert de Fraysseix, compiler). Unesco Collection; Musiques Et Musiciens du Monde. Auvidis: D 8008. 1972, 1988. CD.

2969 *The Rough Guide to the Music of Portugal.* Rough Guide. World Music Network: RGNET 1025 CD. 1998. CD.

VIDEO

2970 Saura, Carlos. *Fados.* Zeitgeist Films: Z 1120. 2009. DVD.

SPAIN

INDIVIDUAL ARTISTS OR GROUPS

2971 Amaya, Carmen. *Carmen Amaya* (José Amaya, Paco Amaya, and Sabicas). Grands Cantaores du Flamenco, Vol. 6. Le Chant du Monde: LDX 274880. 1950s, 1983. CD.

2972 Bonet, Maria Del Mar. *El Cor del temps.* Picap. 1999. 2 CDs.

2973 Budino, Xose Manuel. *Paralaia.* Resistencia. 1998. CD.

2974 Camarón de la Isla. *Camarón de la Isla* (Paco de Lucía and Ramon de Algeciras). Grands Cantaores du Flamenco, Vol. 15. Chant du Monde: LDX 274 957. 1990s, 1997. CD.

2975 Cortés, Montse. *Gypsy Flamenco: Leyenda Andaluza* (Danza Fuego). ARC Music: EUCD 2124. 2008. CD.

2976 Ferrero, José. *Endechar: Sephardic Romances and Songs* (Capilla Antigua de Chinchilla). Naxos: 8.572443. 2009, 2010. CD.

2977 Junkera, Kepa. *Bilbao 00:00h.* Alula: ALU-1017. 1999. 2 CDs.

2978 Lagun Arteak and Ibai Gorri. *Chants du pays Basque.* Arion: ARN 64223. 1993. CD.

2979 Leilía. *Madama.* DiscMedi Blau: DM 796 02. 2000s. CD.

2980 Linares, Carmen. *Cantaora.* Women of the World. Riverboat: TUGCD 1004. 1992. CD.

2981 Llach, Lluís. *Torna aviat.* CBS; Sony: 468163 2. 1991. CD.

2982 Lucía, Paco de
2982.1 *Entre Dos aguas.* Philips: 814 106-2. 1973, 1988. CD.
2982.2 *Siroco.* Verve: 830 913-2. 1987. CD.

2983 Núñez, Carlos, Luz Casal, and Ry Cooder. *Brotherhood of Stars.* RCA Victor: 74321-45375-2. 1996. CD.

2984 Ojos de Brujo. *Techari Live.* Travel Series. Six Degrees Records: 657036 1144-2. 2006, 2008. CD.

2985 Orquestra Àrab de Barcelona. *Maktub.* World Village: WV 498030. 2008. CD.

2986 Pastora, Pavón. *La Niña de los Peines.* Grands Cantaores du Flamenco. Chant du Monde: LDX 274859. 1980, 1987. CD.

2987 Seivane, Susana. *Alma de buxo.* Green Linnet: GLCD 3141. 2002. CD.

ANTHOLOGIES

2988 *Cante Gitano = Gypsy Flamenco* (José de la Tomasa, Burra la María, María Soleá, Paco del Gastor and Juan del Gastor). Nimbus: NI 5168. 1989. CD.

2989 *Early Cante Flamenco* (Paco Aguilera, Melchor de Marchena, Niño Ricardo, and Niño Perez). Arhoolie: CD 326. 1990. CD.

2990 *Flamenco: Disque catalogue.* Le Chant du Monde: LDX 274944. 1992. CD.

2991 *Masters of Flamenco Guitar* (Sabicas, Niño Ricardo, Huelva de Manolo, Marchena de Melchor, and Manuel Vallejo). Hemisphere: 7243 8 59273 2 4. 1959, 1996. CD.

2992 *Sefarad.* Marquis: 7.74718138927. 2008. CD.

2993 ★*Spain* (Alan Lomax and others, compilers). Alan Lomax Collection. Rounder Select: 11661-1744-2. 1955, 1999. CD.

2994 *Spain.* Rough Guide. World Music Network: RGNET 1082 CD. 2002. CD.

2995 *The Rough Guide to Flamenco.* Rough Guide. World Music Network: RGNET 1189 CD. 1900s, 2007. CD.

2996 *The Spanish Recordings*
2996.1 ★*Basque Country, Biscay and Guipuzcoa* (Alan Lomax and Jeanette Bell, compilers). Alan Lomax Collection. Rounder Select: 82161-1772-2. 1952, 2004. CD.
2996.2 ★*Basque Country, Navarre* (Alan Lomax and Jeanette Bell, compilers). Alan Lomax Collection. Rounder Select: 82161-1773-2. 1952, 2004. CD.
2996.3 ★*Extremadura* (Alan Lomax, compiler). Alan Lomax Collection. Rounder Select: 82161-1763-2. 1952, 2002. CD.

2997 *The Story of Flamenco.* Hemisphere. Hemisphere, Metro Blue: 7243 8 55680 2 2. 1997. CD.

2998 *Viva Flamenco!* Narada World: 70876-15252-2-9. 2000. CD.

VIDEOS

2999 *Carlos Saura's Flamenco Trilogy* (Antonio Gades, Cristina Hoyos, Juan Antonio Jiménez, Laura del Sol, Paco de Lucia, Sebastian Moreno, Emma Panella, La Polaca, and Enrique Ortega; Carlos Saura, dir. and chor.). Eclipse, Series 6. Criterion: ECL 026, ECL 027, ECL 028, ECL 029. 2007. 3 DVDs.

3000 *Flamenco.* New Yorker Video: DVD 62203. 2003. DVD.

SOUTHERN EUROPE
VIDEO

3001 ★*The JVC Video Anthology of World Music and Dance: Europe, Vol. 20.* JVC, Victor Co. of Japan; dist. by Multicultural Media. 1990, 2005. 30 DVDs, 9 booklets.

NORTHERN EUROPE, SCANDINAVIA

Compiled by Liza Vick

Cultural influences in Northern Europe include Scandinavian, Baltic, Finno-Ugric, and Russian, among others. Prevalent sounds range from Icelandic epic poems (historical ballads) to an instrument found in traditional and popular (folk-influenced) music in many countries in this region, the hardanger fiddle (or hardingfele). Popular artists have emerged in the traditional realm (for example, Norwegian fiddler Annbjørg Lien) and a striking number in more mainstream pop and rock scenes on the international stage. Familiar examples include the Icelandic artists Björk and Sigur Rós, the Swedish group ABBA, and many more. The Nordic roots revival movement is strong, and here are just a few sources of information and acquisitions: Rootsworld Nordic (www.rootsworld.com/rw/), Finnish Music Information Center (FIMIC, www.fimic.fi), and NorthSide (www.noside.com).

Examples of fusion and diasporic influence abound: Ale Möller and Aly Bain of the Shetland Islands in the North Sea (between Scotland and Norway) blend Celtic (Scottish) and Nordic folk. Gjallarhorn is a group of Swedes in Finland who play modern Nordic folk. Frigg combines folk music of Finland and Norway with Appalachian, country, and western influences. There are many more such examples. For more information about Northern and Southern European music, consult sources like *World Music: The Rough Guide, Vol. 1: Africa, Europe and the Middle East*, edited by Simon Broughton and Mark Ellingham (Rough Guides, 1999).

DENMARK

INDIVIDUAL ARTISTS OR GROUPS

3002 ★Haugaard, Dan. *Danish Folk Songs.* Custom Compact Disc Series. Smithsonian Folkways: FW 6857. 2000s, 1957. CD.

3003 Haugaard and Høirup. *Omsommeren: Traditional and Contemporary Danish Music.* Danish Folk Music Production: GO 0203. 2004. CD.

3004 Lilholt, Lars. *Next Stop Svabonius.* Danish Folk Council: FFS 9801. 1998. CD.

3005 Sorten Muld. *III.* NorthSide: NSD 6055. 2000, 2001. CD.

ANTHOLOGIES

3006 *Danemark: Chanteurs et ménétriers.* Ocora: C 600002. 1930, 1996. CD.

3007 *Songs and Tunes from Denmark, 1993.* Danish Music Export & Promotion: MXPCD 0193. 1993. CD.

3008 *Traditionals Arranged by Dronningens Livstykke, 1976–1984.* Pan: PAN 136 CD. 1990. CD.

3009 *World Music under Northern Lights.* World Music Denmark: WMDCD 09. 2008, 2009. CD.

FAROE ISLANDS

INDIVIDUAL ARTISTS OR GROUPS

3010 Pálsdóttir, Eivør. *Eivør Pálsdóttir.* SHD: SHD 50. 2000. CD.

3011 Spælimenninir. *Flóð og fjøra.* Tutl: SHD 18. 1996. CD.

ANTHOLOGIES

3012 *Traditional Music in the Faroe Islands, 1950–1999.* Frémeaux & Assoc.: FA 5036. 2003. 2 CDs.

3013 *Tutl 2000.* Tutl: HJF66. 2000. CD.

FINLAND

INDIVIDUAL ARTISTS OR GROUPS

3014 ★Hedningarna. *Karelia visa.* NorthSide: NSD 6025. 1998, 1999. CD.

3015 Jamalpur Priority Project. *Kaustinen Rhapsody.* Xenophile. Green Linnet: 4019. 1994. CD.

3016 Järvelän Pikkupelimannit
    3016.1 *JPP.* Olarin Musiikki: OMCD 15. 1988. CD.
    3016.2 *String Tease.* NorthSide: NSD 6020. 1998. CD.

3017 Kalaniemi, Maria. *Iho.* Hannibal: HNCD 1396. 1995, 1997. CD.

3018 Kaustisen Purppuripelimannit. *Finlande: Musiques d'Ostrobotnie: Kaustinen et alentours* (Ostrobothnia). Musique du Monde. Buda: BUD 92756. 2000. CD.

3019 Kurki-Suonio, Sanna. *Musta.* NorthSide: NSD 6021. 1998. CD.

3020   Lepisto, Markku. *Helsinki* (Pekka Lehti). Alto: AICD012. 2008. CD.

3021   Sibelius Academy. *Kuulas hetki* (ensembles and soloists of the Folk Music Dept.) Sibelius-Akatemian Kansanmusiikin Osaston Äänitteitä. Olarin Musiikki: OMCD 46. 1992, 1993. CD.

3022   Troka. *Smash.* NorthSide: NSD 6029. 1999. CD.

3023   Värttinä
   3023.1   *Live in Helsinki.* NorthSide: NSD 6066. 2000, 2002. CD.
   3023.2   *Vihma.* BMG Music: 090266326-2. 1998. CD.

ANTHOLOGIES

3024   *Echos de Finlande.* Musique du Monde. Buda: 1984932. 1998. CD.

3025   *Finlande: Musique traditionnelle = Finland: Traditional Music.* Ocora: C 600004. 1941, 1996. CD.

3026   ★*The Kalevala Heritage: Archive Recordings of Ancient Finnish Songs.* Ondine: ODE 849-2. 1995. CD.

3027   *Tulikulkku.* Kansanmusiiki-instituutti: KICD 30. 1993. CD.

GREENLAND

INDIVIDUAL ARTISTS OR GROUPS

3028   Nuuk Posse. *Kaataq.* Sub Rosa: SR 108 CD. 1996. CD.

3029   Zikaza. *Miki Goes to Nuussuaq.* ULO: CD 45. 1988. CD.

ANTHOLOGY

3030   *Traditional Greenlandic Music: 55 Recordings from 1905–1984.* ULO: CD 75. 1992. CD.

ICELAND

INDIVIDUAL ARTISTS OR GROUPS

3031   Baggalútur. *Sólskinið í Dakota: og fleiri lög við kvæði vestur-íslenskra skálda.* Borgin: BORG 001 CD. 2009. CD.

3032   Björk
   3032.1   *Biophilia.* Nonesuch: 528728-2. 2011. CD.
   3032.2   *Medúlla.* Elektra: 62981-2. 2004. CD.

   3032.3   *Volta.* Wellhart Ltd., One Little Indian Ltd.: tplp16 OCD. 2007. CD.
   3032.4   *Voltaic.* Nonesuch: 519646. 2007, 2009. CD.

3033   Islandica
   3033.1   *Saga Songs = Römm er sú taug: Icelandic Folk Songs.* Fimmund: 4. 1995. CD.
   3033.2   *Songs and Dances from Iceland = Lieder and tänze aus island.* ARC Music: EUCD 1187. 1991. CD.

3034   Sigur Rós
   3034.1   *Ágætis Byrjun.* PIAS America: PIASA 1-2. 2000, 2001. CD.
   3034.2   *Heima.* EMI: 5.09995-1041892. 2008. 2 DVDs.
   3034.3   *Med sud i eyrum vid spilum endalaust.* EMI: 2287282. 2008. CD.

3035   Tómasdóttir, Guðrún. *Íslenzk Þjóðlög = Folk Songs of Iceland* (Ólafur Vignir Albertsson). Islenskrit Tónar: IT 342. 1979, 2009. CD.

ANTHOLOGIES

3036   *Raddir.* Smekkleysa: SMK 7. 2000. CD.

3037   ★*The Icelandic Singers.* Custom Compact Disc Series. Smithsonian Folkways: MPS 585. 1961, 2001. CD.

NORWAY

INDIVIDUAL ARTISTS OR GROUPS

3038   Bjorgum, Hallvard T., and Torleiv H. Bjorgum. *Dolkaren: The Best of Hallvard T. and Torleiv H. Bjorgum.* Genuine Folk Music from Norway. Sylvartun: SYLVCD 3. 1989. CD.

3039   Bråten-Berg, Kirsten. *Songen.* Heilo: HCD 7257. 2010. CD.

3040   Buen, Knut, Kåre Nordstoga, and Erik Stenstadvold. *As Quick as Fire: The Art of the Norwegian Hardanger Fiddle.* Henry Street Records: HSR 0002. 1979, 1996. CD.

3041   Garbarek, Jan. *Twelve Moons.* ECM Records: ECM 1500. 1992, 1993. CD.

3042   Helgeland, Sjur. *Budeiene På Vikafjell* [1910]. Spelarhaugen Folkemusikk: SFCD3. 2008. 2 CDs.

3043   Lien, Annbjørg
   3043.1   *Felefeber: Norwegian Fiddle Fantasia.* Shanachie: 64060. 1995. CD.

3043.2 *Prisme.* Shanachie: 64082. 1997. CD.

3043.3 *Waltz with Me.* Compass: 7 4492 2. 2008. CD.

3044 ★Nyhus, Sven, and Åshild Breie Nyhus. *Traditional Norwegian Fiddle Music.* Shanachie: 21003. 1991. CD.

3045 Reiersrud, Knut, and Iver Kleive. *Footwork.* Shanachie: 64056. 1994. CD.

3046 Slinkombas. *Slinkombas* [1979, 1982]. Heilo: HCD 7230-1. 2008. CD.

3047 Sørbye, Lief. *Springdans: Songs and Dances from Norway.* Musical Heritage Society: 514976 H. 1987, 1998. CD.

ANTHOLOGIES

3048 *Chant et hardingfele = Song and Hardingfele.* Norvège. Ocora: C 560157. 2001. CD.

3049 *Den våre fela = The Delicate Fiddle.* Heilo: HCD 7094. 1994. CD.

3050 *Nordisk Sang: Music of Norway: Selections from the Heilo Catalogue.* New Albion: NA 031 CD. [1991]. CD.

3051 *Norsk folkemusikk = Norwegian Folk Music.* Grappa: GRCD 4099-10. 1934, 1995. 10 CDs.

SAMI LAND

INDIVIDUAL ARTISTS OR GROUPS

3052 Andersen, Johan. *Unnengukká Viezzak.* Idut: ICD 091. 2009. CD.

3053 Boine, Mari. *Idjagiedas: In the Hand of the Night.* Universal: 6024 98554869. 2006. CD.

3054 Frode Fjellheim Jazz Joik Ensemble. *Saajve Dans.* Idut: ICD 943. 1994. CD.

3055 Persen, Mari Boine
  3055.1 *Eallin.* Antilles: 533 799-2. 1996. CD.
  3055.2 *Gula Gula.* Realworld: 2-91631. 1990. CD.

3056 Walkeapää, Nils-Aslak, Seepo Paakkunainen, Johan Anders Baei, and Esa Kotilainen (composers and perfs.). *Dálveleaikkat: Wintergames.* DAT: DATCD-17. 1994. CD.

ANTHOLOGIES

3057 *Bálggis.* Vuelie: VUCD 806. 2011. CD.

3058 ★*Lappish Joik Songs from Northern Norway.* Smithsonian Folkways: FE 4007. 1956, 2000s. CD.

3059 ★*Yoik: A Presentation of Saami Folk Music.* Musica Sveciae. Caprice: CAP 21544. 1953, 1997. 3 CDs.

SWEDEN

INDIVIDUAL ARTISTS OR GROUPS

3060 Frifot. *Järven.* Caprice: CAP 21462. 1996. CD.

3061 Garmarna. *Vengeance.* NorthSide: NSD 6028. 1998, 1999. CD, visual material.

3062 Gjallarhorn. *Sjofn.* NorthSide: NSD 6025. 1999, 2000. CD.

3063 Hedin, Johan. *Låtar: Swedish Folk Tunes II* (Gunnar Idenstam). Caprice: CAP 21807. 2010. CD.

3064 Hedningarna
  3064.1 *The Heathens Fire.* TriStar, Silence: WK 36756. 1992, 1996. CD.
  3064.2 *Trä.* NorthSide: NSD 6008. 1994, 1998. CD.

3065 Hollmer, Lars. *Live, 1992–1993.* Victo: VICTO CD 024. 1993. CD.

3066 Hoven Droven. *Groove.* NorthSide: NSD 6002. 1994, 1997. CD.

3067 Junip. *Fields.* Shock Entertainment: 8CTX592 CD. 2010. CD. Also available on vinyl.

3068 Söderbäck, Nils Olof. *Kvarnresan: Rural Swedish Fiddle Music* (Peter Michaelsen). Soulfelt Music. 2010. CD.

3069 Swåp. *Du da.* NorthSide: NSD 6085. 2005. CD.

3070 Väsen
  3070.1 *Live: At the Nordic Roots Festival.* NorthSide: NSD 6065. 2000, 2001. CD.
  3070.2 *Whirled.* NorthSide: NSD 6006. 1997. CD.

3071 Willemark, Lena, and Groupa. *Månskratt.* Amigo Musik: AMCD 725. 1990. CD.

ANTHOLOGIES

3072 *Agram.* ECM: ECM 1610. 1996. CD.

3073 *Äldre Svenska spelmän = Swedish Fiddlers from the Past.* Musica Sveciae, Nos. 26–28. Caprice: CAP 21604. 1999. 3 CDs.

3074 ★*Arsringar: Svensk folkmusik 1970–1990 = Swedish Folk Music 1970–1990.* MNW: MNW CD 194. 1970, 1990. 2 CDs.

3075 *Koraler and bröllopsmusik från Runö = Chorales and Wedding Music from Runö.* Musica Sveciae, No. 24. Caprice: CAP 21547. 1997. CD.

3076 *Lockrop and vallatar = Ancient Swedish Pastoral Music.* Musica Sveciae, No. 8. Caprice: CAP 21483. 1949, 1995. CD.

3077 *Prillarhorn and knaverharpa: Nordic Folk Instruments.* Musica Sveciae, No. 13. Caprice: CAP 21484. 1996. CD.

3078 *Suède: Entre Triol et Sextondel = Sweden: Between Triol and Sextondel.* Ocora Radio France; dist. by Harmonia Mundi: C 560225. 2009. CD.

3079 *Varjehanda folkmusik = Traditional Folk Music.* Musica Sveciae, No. 3. Caprice: CAP 21474. 1995. CD.

NORTHERN EUROPE, SCANDINAVIA
GENERAL ANTHOLOGIES

3080 ★Clauson, William. *Scandinavia!: Songs and Dances of Denmark, Finland, Norway, and Sweden.* Monitor: MFS 761. 1991. CD. Originally released on LP in 1974.

3081 *Nordic Folksongs and Ballads.* Danacord: DACOCD 686. 2011. CD.

3082 *Scandinavia: Music Rough Guide Enhanced CD.* Rough Guide. World Music Network: RGNET 1051 CD. 2000. CD.

EASTERN AND CENTRAL EUROPE

Compiled by Aaron Bittel and Spiro Shetuni

Historically, recordings of traditional music from Eastern Europe became broadly available to Western audiences in two periods. The first of these waves coincided with the growth of interest in international folk dance and song in the 1960s. Recordings from this period vary in quality of sound, repertoire, and written documentation; still, many are valuable documents for both the scholar and the amateur. These recordings are mostly long out-of-print, with notable exceptions including those released by labels now under the Smithsonian Folkways banner (Folkways, Monitor). Folkways releases were known for their copious, if not always scholarly, notes. Since coming under the Smithsonian umbrella in the late 1980s, liner notes have been written by leading scholars and practitioners of the respective traditions and have become useful secondary sources on their own.

The second wave of recordings to hit Western markets came in the late 1980s and through the 1990s with the introduction and surge of the "world music" commercial genre. These are generally of higher all-around quality, though world-beat fusions of questionable authenticity exist. Two recordings in particular are known for bringing Balkan—and Eastern European generally—music to the consciousness of the wider world music audience: Ivo Papasov's *Orpheus Ascending* and the *Le mystère des voix Bulgares* series. These, of course, are just the tip of the proverbial iceberg, and now, recordings running the gamut of ethnicities, languages, and genres of Balkan traditional and popular music are readily available in the West. Smithsonian Folkways, World Music Network, Traditional Crossroads, Rounder, Sunset-France (Playasound/Air Mail Music), Piranha Musik, and ARC Music are good sources for library acquisitions; many smaller specialty labels also sell online. The relevant JVC Anthology videos are indispensable teaching resources and worth the trouble to acquire. Scores and print anthologies exist but can be difficult to obtain domestically.

In Eastern Europe particularly, it can be misleading to differentiate between national and transnational music. Musical boundaries are blurred by a long history of invading armies, population and territorial shifts, and the tendency for professional folk musicians to come from minority transnational groups. Where, for example, should one classify Esma Redžepova—the Macedonian Romani chanteuse whose songs are known throughout the Balkan region? For one view on these complexities reflected in the region's music, see the documentary *Whose Is This Song?* Romani and Jewish transnational music is represented in this discography, as are Georgia and Armenia (also associated with Middle Eastern and Central Asian music). Romani (or gypsy) musical influence extends into Southern Europe, Asia, and many other areas (*see also* chapter 7, "International Anthologies").

Albanian traditional music exists alongside other traditional music cultures found in the Balkans and the

Mediterranean. An important feature of this region is a large collection of nations and ethnic groups in a relatively small area. Two factors should be emphasized when broadly describing Albanian traditional music. First, as a whole, it contains a collection of unique characteristics that can be thought of as making Albanian traditional music distinctly "Albanian." Second, there is tremendous diversity within it. The field recordings on Albanian traditional music started only during the second half of the twentieth century. Entries represent different musical dialects and styles.

Spiro Shetuni compiled the Albanian citations; Aaron Bittel compiled all other Eastern European regions. Please consult *World Music: The Rough Guide, Vol. 1* (or other sources) for in-depth information about other Eastern European countries. For Jewish music in Europe, see chapter 7.

BALKANS

Albania

ANTHOLOGIES

3083 *Cry You Mountains.* Saydisc: CD-SCD 431. 1999. CD.

3084 *Folk Music of Albania.* Topic: TSCD904. 1994. CD.

3085 *Music from Albania.* Rounder: CD 5151. 1999. CD.

3086 *Mysterious Albania.* ARC Music: EUCD1762. 2002. CD.

3087 *Vocal Traditions of Albania.* Saydisc: CD-SCD 421. 1997. CD.

Bosnia and Herzegovina

GROUP

3088 Mostar Sevdah Reunion
   3088.1 *Café Sevdah.* Snail Records: SR 66009. 2007. CD.
   3088.2 *Saban* (Saban Bajramovic). Snail Records: SR 66008. 2008. 2 CDs.

ANTHOLOGY

3089 ★*Bosnia: Echoes from an Endangered World* (Theodore Levin and Ankica Petrović, compilers). Smithsonian Folkways: SFW40407. 1993. CD.

Bulgaria

INDIVIDUAL ARTISTS OR GROUPS

3090 ★Bulgarian Radio and Television Women's Choir. *Le mystère des voix Bulgares, Vols. 1, 2, and Ritual.* Explorer Series. Elektra, Nonesuch: 79165-2, 79201-2. 1987–1988. 3 CDs.

3091 Karlov, Boris. *Legend of the Bulgarian Accordion = Légende de l'accordéon Bulgare.* Balkan Folk Archives Collection. BMA Productions: BMA-1005. 2003. 2 CDs.

3092 Lolov, Ibro. *Gypsy Music from Bulgaria.* ARC Music: EUCD 1757. 2002. CD.

3093 Papasov, Ivo. *Orpheus Ascending.* Hannibal: HNCD 1346. 1989. CD.

3094 Spasov, Teodosiï. *The Fish Are Praying for Rain.* Traditional Crossroads: 2000. CD.

3095 Yunakov, Yuri
   3095.1 *New Colors in Bulgarian Wedding Music* (Yuri Yunakov Ensemble). Traditional Crossroads: CD 4283. 1997. CD.
   3095.2 *Roma Variations* (Yuri Yunakov Ensemble). Explorer Series. Traditional Crossroads: CD 4306. 2001. CD.

3096 ★Yunakov, Yuri, and Ivo Papasov. *Together Again.* Traditional Crossroads: CD 4330. 2005. CD.

ANTHOLOGIES

3097 *Au déla du mystère: Musique des villages de Bulgarie = Beyond the Mystery: Village Music of Bulgaria, Vols. 1–3* (Yves Moreau, compiler). BMA Productions: BMA-1001, BMA-1002, BMA-1003. 1999–2001. 3 CDs.

3098 *Bulgarian Village Singing: "Two Women Started to Sing"* (Martha Forsyth, compiler). Rounder: CD-1055. 1978, 1990. CD.

3099 *Thracian Rhapsody: The New Wedding Music of Bulgaria, Vol. 1.* Labor Records: LAB 7019-2. 1999. CD.

3100 *Thracian Rhapsody: The Wedding, Vol. 2.* Labor Records. 1994, 2001. CD.

Croatia

INDIVIDUAL ARTISTS OR GROUPS

3101 Klapa Cambi and Klapa Jelsa. *Songs of Croatia: Klapa Singing from the Dalmatian Coast.* ARC Music: EUCD 1899. 2004. CD.

3102 Tamburaski sastav "Veritas." *Folklore from Croatia.* ARC Music: EUCD 2190. 1997, 2008. CD. Reissue of EUCD 1078, Folk Music from Croatia.

3103 Zagreb Folk Dance Ensemble. *Songs and Dances from Croatia.* ARC Music: EUCD 1550. 1999. CD.

ANTHOLOGY

3104 *Music from the Island of Krk, Yugoslavia* (Alt.: *The Diaphonic Music of the Island of Krk, Yugoslavia*). (Wolfgang Laade and Dagmar Laademar, compilers). Ethnic Folkways Library. Folkways: FW04060, FE 4060. 1975, 2000s. CD.

Greece (Northern)

ANTHOLOGIES

3105 *Bright Balkan Morning: Romani Lives and the Power of Music in Greek Macedonia* (Steven Feld and Charles Keil, compilers). Wesleyan University Press. 2002. CD. Accompanies book.

3106 *Bells and Winter Festivals of Greek Macedonia* (Steven Feld and Charles Keil, compilers). Collector's Series. Smithsonian Folkways: SFW 50401. 2000, 2002. CD.

Macedonia

INDIVIDUAL ARTISTS OR GROUPS

3107 Kočani Orkestar
    3107.1 *Alone at My Wedding.* Crammed Discs: Craw 25. 2002, 2006. CD.
    3107.2 *L'Orient est rouge.* Crammed Discs: Craw 19. 2006. CD.

3108 Mustafov, Ferus. *King Ferus: Macedonian Wedding Soul Cooking.* Globestyle: CDORBD 089. 1994, 1995.

ANTHOLOGIES

3109 *Heart of the Balkans: Macedonian Wedding Songs.* ARC Music: EUCD 1894. 2003. CD.

3110 *The Very Best of Macedonia.* ARC Music: EUCD 1822. 2003. CD.

Serbia

INDIVIDUAL ARTISTS OR GROUPS

3111 Boban Markovič Orkestar. *Boban I Marko: Brass Band Fest.* Piranha Musik: CD-PIR1790. 2003. CD.

3112 Branko Krsmanovic Group. *Music of Serbia and Montenegro.* ARC Music: EUCD 1918. 2005. CD.

3113 Folk Dance Ensemble Vila. *Music of Serbia.* ARC Music: EUCD 2121, 2008. CD.

ANTHOLOGIES

3114 *Musiques de Yougoslavie.* Musique du Monde. Buda: 92490-2. [1990–1993]. CD.

3115 *Rough Guide to the Music of the Balkans.* Rough Guide. World Music Network: RGNET 1127 CD. 2003. CD.

3116 *Serbie: Anthologie de la musique populaire Serbe = Serbia: Anthology of Serbian Folk Music.* Archives Internationales de Musique Populaire, 60. VDE-Gallo: CD-993. 1975, 1999. CD.

3117 *Serbie: Danses et melodies pastorales: Musiques traditionelles de la Serbie Orientale.* Ethnic Auvidis: B6759. 1970, 1991. CD.

3118 *Songs and Dances of Yugoslavia* (Laura Boulton, compiler). Folkways: FW 06805, FP 805, 2001. CD.

3119 *Yugoslavia* (Peter Kennedy and Alan Lomax, compilers). World Library of Folk and Primitive Music, Vol. 5. Rounder : 11661-1745-2. 1954, 2001. 2 CDs.

Slovenia

ANTHOLOGY

3120 *Traditional Music of Slovenia.* ARC Music: EUCD 2075. 2007. CD.

EASTERN EUROPE, BALKANS GENERAL ANTHOLOGIES

GROUP

3121 Poza. *Balkans en folie = Crazy Balkans.* Air Mail Music. Sunset-France: SA141082. 2002. CD.

ANTHOLOGIES

3122 *Balkan Blues: Souffles de l'âme.* Network: 33.858. 1999. 2 CDs.

3123 *Brass Noir: On the Trans-Balkan Highway.* Piranha Musik: CD-PIR 2546. 2011. CD.

3124 *Musiques de Yougoslavie.* Musique du Monde. Buda: 92490-2. [1990–1993]. CD.

3125 ★*Rough Guide to the Music of the Balkans.* Rough Guide. World Music Network: RGNET 1127 CD. 2003. CD.

3126 *Songs and Dances of Yugoslavia* (Laura Boulton, compiler). Folkways: FW 06805, FP 805. 2001. CD.

3127 *Village Music of Yugoslavia: Songs and Dances from Bosnia-Herzegovina, Croatia, and Macedonia* (Martin Koenig, compiler). Explorer Series. Nonesuch: 9 72042-2. 1971, 1995. CD.

3128 *Yugoslavia* (Peter Kennedy and Alan Lomax, compilers). World Library of Folk and Primitive Music, Vol. 5. Rounder: 11661-1745-2. 1954, 2001. 2 CDs.

VIDEOS

3129 *The JVC Video Anthology of World Music and Dance: III Europe: Romania/Yugoslavia/Bulgaria/Albania, Vol. 22.* JVC; dist. by Rounder. 1988, 1990. VHS, text.

3130 ★*Whose Is This Song? = Chia e tazi pesen?* Documentary Educational Resources. 2006, 2003. DVD.

BALTICS

Latvia

ANTHOLOGIES

3131 *The Bagpipes of Latvia.* ARC Music: EUCD 1692. 2001. CD.

3132 *Best of Folk Music from Latvia.* ARC Music: EUCD 2128. 2008. CD.

Lithuania

GROUPS

3133 Dainava (music and dance company). *Songs and Dances from Lithuania.* ARC Music: EUCD 1609. 2000. CD.

3134 Ensemble Rasa. *Lettonie: Musiques des rites solaires = Lithuania: Music of the Solar Rites.* Inédit. Maison des Cultures du Monde, Auvidis: W 260062. 1993, 1995. CD.

ANTHOLOGY

3135 *Lithuanian Songs and Dances.* Monitor: MON00305. [1950–1980]. CD.

CAUCASUS

Armenia

INDIVIDUAL ARTISTS OR GROUPS

3136 Azad. *Arménie: Musique traditionelle = Armenia: Traditional Music.* Air Mail Music. Sunset-France: SA141136. 2006. CD.

3137 Gasparian, Djivan
    3137.1 *Apricots from Eden.* Traditional Crossroads: CD 4276. 1996. CD.
    3137.2 *The Soul of Armenia.* Network: 495121. 2007. 2 CDs.

3138 ★Hagopian, Richard, Harold G. Hagopian, and Hagop Jack Zarzatian. *Armenian Music through the Ages.* Smithsonian Folkways: SF 40414. 1993. CD.

3139 Hovhannisyan, Karine. *Classical Music for the Armenian Kanun.* Cbuj Entertainment. 2008. CD.

3140 Kenkulian, Hrant. *Udi Hrant.* Traditional Crossroads: CD 4265. 1950, 1994. CD.

3141 Melkon, Marko. *Marko Melkon.* Traditional Crossroads: CD 4281. 1996. CD.

3142 Shoghaken Ensemble. *Music from Armenia.* Traditional Crossroads: CD 4335. 2008. CD.

Georgia

INDIVIDUAL ARTISTS OR GROUPS

3143 K'art'uli Xmebi. *Les voix de Georgie = The Voices of Georgia.* Musique du Monde. Buda: 92547-2. 1991. CD.

3144 Trio Kavkasia. *The Fox and the Lion.* Traditional Crossroads: CD 4331. 2003, 2006. CD.

ANTHOLOGY

3145 *Georgia: The Resounding Polyphony of the Caucausus* (Minoru Morita, compiler). Music of the Earth. Multicultural Media: MCM 3004. 1992, 1997. CD.

CAUCASUS
GENERAL ANTHOLOGIES

VIDEOS

3146 *The JVC Video Anthology of World Music and Dance: II Europe: Poland/Czechoslovakia/Hungary, Vol. 21.* JVC; dist. by Rounder. 1988, 1990. VHS, text.

3147 *The JVC Video Anthology of World Music and Dance: III Soviet Union: Azerbaijan/Armenia/ Georgia/Dagestan, Vol. 25.* JVC; dist. by Rounder. 1988, 1990. VHS, text.

CENTRAL EUROPE

Czech Republic

INDIVIDUAL ARTISTS OR GROUPS

3148 Druhá Tráva. *Czechmate.* Compass Records: 7 4260 2. 1998, 1999. CD.

3149 Hradistan. *Chants et danses de Moravie = Moravian Songs and Dances.* Sunset-France: PS65190. 1997. CD.

3150 Malina, Lubos. *Piece of Cake.* Compass Records: 7 4263 2. 1999. CD.

3151 Plastic People of the Universe. *Egon Bondy's Happy Hearts Club Banned: PPU III.* Globus Music, Levné knihy: LK 0162-2. 2001, 2005. CD.

ANTHOLOGY

3152 *Folk Songs and Dances from Czechoslovakia.* Monitor: MON00465. 1966. CD.

Hungary

INDIVIDUAL ARTISTS OR GROUPS

3153 Balogh, Kálmán, and Méta. *Gypsy Music from Hungary.* ARC Music: EUCD 2117. 2007. CD.

3154 Csurgó Zenekar. *Folk Music from Hungary.* ARC Music: EUCD 2134. 2008. CD.

3155 Hossu, Ana. *Traditional Music from Transylvania.* ARC Music: EUCD 2017. 2006. CD.

3156 Méta. *Traditional Hungary.* ARC Music: EUCD 1782. 2002. CD.

3157 Muzsikás and Márta Sebestyén. *Live at the Liszt Academy of Music.* Muzsikás: MU005. 2004. CD.

3158 Söndörgo. *Tamburocket: Hungarian Fireworks.* Riverboat Records; World Music Network: TUGCD 1084. 2014. CD.

ANTHOLOGIES

3159 *Hungarian Folk Music* (Sebo Ensemble; Ferenc Sebo, composer). Rounder: CD 5005. 1980, 1993. CD.

3160 ★*Rough Guide to Hungarian Music.* Rough Guide. World Music Network: RGNET 1092 CD. 2002. CD.

3161 ★*Rough Guide to the Music of the Hungarian Gypsies.* Rough Guide. World Music Network: RGNET 1198 CD. 2008. CD.

Poland

INDIVIDUAL ARTISTS OR GROUPS

3162 Karolinka. *Songs and Dances from Poland.* ARC Music: EUCD 1124. 1990s. CD.

3163 Kulisiewicz, Aleksander Tytus
  3163.1 *Sadly Whisper the Leaves of the Willow: Polish Partisan and Folk Songs.* Smithsonian Folkways: FSS 37340. 1980. CD.
  3163.2 *Songs from the Depths of Hell.* Smithsonian Folkways: FSS 37700. 1979, 2003. CD.

3164 Song and Dance Ensemble of Warsaw Polytechnic. *Songs and Dances from Poland.* ARC Music: EUCD 1671. 2001. CD.

3165 Tomasz Stańko Quartet. *Lontano.* ECM Records, Universal Classics: ECM 1980. 2005, 2006. CD.

3166 Tostoki Ensemble and Krosno Song and Dance Ensemble. *Polish Folk Songs and Dances.* International Series. Smithsonian Folkways: FW 6848. 1954, [2003]. CD.

3167 Transkapela. *Klezmer Carpathian Music.* ARC Music: EUCD 2087. 2007. CD.

3168 Ziminska-Sygietynska, Mira, and Mazowsze. *Polish Folk Music.* Polskie Nagrania: PNCD 324. 1995. CD.

ANTHOLOGIES

3169 *Góralska Muzyka: Polish Folk Music (Highlanders' Music).* Polskie Nagrania: PNCD 227. 1993. CD.

3170 *Solidarity! Postulat 22: Songs from the New Polish Labor Movement = Nowe Polskie Piesni Roboticzne.* Smithsonian Folkways: FSS 37251 1. 1981. CD.

Romania

INDIVIDUAL ARTISTS OR GROUPS

3171 Buza, Maria, and Taraful Ciuleandra. *The Gypsies of Walachia.* ARC Music: EUCD 1688. 2001. CD.

3172   Crai Nou Ensemble. *Flûtes Romaines = Romanian Pan-Pipes.* Playasound Collection. Sunset-France: PS65176. 1996. CD.

3173   Doina Timisului. *Romanian Tradition.* ARC Music: EUCD 1835. 2003. CD.

3174   ★Fanfare Ciocărlia. *Baro Biao: World Wide Wedding.* Piranha Musik: CD-PIR 1364. 1999. CD.

3175   Farcas, Dumitru, and Marcel Cellier. *The Art of the Romanian Taragot.* ARC Music: EUCD 1702. 1976, 2002. CD.

3176   Iordache, Toni. *Sounds from a Bygone Age, Vol. 4.* Asphalt Tango Records: CD-ATR 1307. 2007. CD.

3177   Ökrös Ensemble and Sándor Fodor. *Transylvanian Village Music: From Gypsy, Hungarian, and Romanian Traditions.* Rounder: CD 5160. 1999. CD.

3178   Perapaskero, Sapo. *Band of Gypsies* (Kočani Orkestar). Nonesuch: 79641-2. 2001. CD.

3179   Rizea, Gheorghe, composer. *Roumanie: Les Carpats = Romania: The Carpats* (Gheorghe Rizea, compiler). Air Mail Music. Sunset-France: SA141115. 2005. CD.

3180   Rommales. *Les tsiganes de Roumanie = Romanian Gypsies.* Sunset-France: PS65252. 2001. CD.

3181   Taraf de Haïdouks. *Taraf de Haïdouks.* Nonesuch: 79554-2. 1990, 1999. CD.

ANTHOLOGIES

3182   *Hungarian Folk Music from the Kis-Küküllo Region of Central Transylvania, Romania* (László Kürti, compiler). Ethnic Folkways Library. Smithsonian Folkways: FE 4035. 1985. CD.

3183   *Maskarada.* Crammed Discs: Craw 40. 2007. CD.

3184   *Peasant Brass Bands from Moldavia: Zece Prajini = Fanfares paysannes de Moldavie.* Ethnophonie: CD002. 1997, 2000. CD.

3185   *Romania* (Speranţa Radulescu and Alexandru Tiberiu, eds.). World Library of Folk and Primitive Music, Vol. 17. Rounder: 11661-1759-2. 1960, 2001. CD.

3186   *Roumanie = Romania.* Sunset-France: SA141009. 1997. CD.

Slovakia

INDIVIDUAL ARTISTS OR GROUPS

3187   Folklórny Súbor Lipa. *Traditional Music from Slovakia.* ARC Music: EUCD 1750. 2002. CD.

3188   J. Harazin Folk Music Ensemble. *Slovaquie: Musiques de Polana.* Inédit. Maison des Cultures du Monde: W 260097. 2000. CD.

ANTHOLOGIES

3189   *Slovaquie: Musiques Populaires = Slovakia: Folk Musics.* Collection Ocora Radio France. Ocora: C 600014. 2005. CD.

3190   *Slovaquie: Traditions en Slovaquie Centrale = Slovakia: Traditions in Central Slovakia.* Peoples, VDE-Gallo: PEO CD-1094. 1994, 2002. CD.

EASTERN EUROPE
Belarus

INDIVIDUAL ARTISTS OR GROUPS

3191   Mischula, Olga, and Kirmash. *Dulcimer of Belarus.* ARC Music: EUCD 2149. 2008. CD.

3192   Romanskaya, Nataliya, and Kirmash. *Music of Belarus.* ARC Music: EUCD 2067. 1999, [2008]. CD. Reissue of EUCD 1504, *Songs and Dances from Belorussia.*

Moldova

ANTHOLOGY

3193   *Cantemir: Music in Istanbul and Ottoman Empire around 1700* (Ihsan Özgen, Linda Burman-Hall, and Lux Musica; Dimitrie Cantemir, compilers). Golden Horn Records: GHP 019-2. 2004, 2000. CD. Middle East.

Russia (Asian)

See chapter 4, Central Asia.

Russia (European)

INDIVIDUAL ARTISTS OR GROUPS

3194   Balalaika-Ensemble "Wolga."
    3194.1   *Best of Russian Folk Songs.* ARC Music: EUCD 1146. 1995. CD.
    3194.2   *Kalinka.* ARC Music: EUCD 1499. 1999. CD.

3195 Carousel. *The Music of Russia.* ARC Music: EUCD 1784. 2002. CD.

3196 Pit'k Randaane. *Pajod: Lyydiläisiä Lauluja = Ludian Song* (Kari Hakala and Ilpo Saastamoinen, compilers). Global Music Centre: GMCD 0714. 2003, 2007. CD.

3197 Ponomareva, Valentina, and Oleg Ponomareva. *The Very Best of Russia.* ARC Music: EUCD 2031. 2006. CD.

3198 Russian Folk Ensemble Balalaika. *Kamarinskaya.* ARC Music: EUCD 1619. 2000. CD.

3199 Stars of Saint Petersburg. *Balalaika: Russia's Most Beautiful Tunes.* ARC Music: EUCD 1328. 1995. CD.

3200 Talisman. *Russian Gypsy Fire.* ARC Music: EUCD 1789. 2003. CD.

ANTHOLOGIES

3201 *Folk Music of the USSR* (Henry Cowell, compiler). Custom Compact Disc Series. Smithsonian Folkways: FE 4535. 1960, 2001. 2 CDs.

3202 *Invozho: Traditional Songs of Udmurtia* (Kari Hakala, compiler). Global Music Centre: GMCD 0510. 1993, 2005. CD.

3203 ★*Musics of the Soviet Union.* Smithsonian Folkways: SF 40002. 1989. CD.

3204 *The Rough Guide to the Music of Russian Gypsies.* Rough Guide. World Music Network: RGNET 1214 CD. 2010. 2 CDs.

3205 *Russie = Russia.* Air Mail Music. Sunset-France: SA141028. 1999. CD.

3206 *Russie: Choeurs, ballades, and balalaikas = Russia: Choirs, Ballads, and Balalaikas.* Air Mail Music. Sunset-France: SA360710. 2004. 3 CDs.

3207 *Russie: Violons et chants tziganes = Russia: Gypsy Songs and Fiddles.* Air Mail Music. Sunset-France: SA141151. 2007. CD.

3208 *Syulgam: Traditional Songs of Mordovia* (Kari Hakala, compiler). Global Music Centre: GMCD 0512. 1993, 2005. 2 CDs.

VIDEO

3209 *The JVC Video Anthology of World Music and Dance: I Soviet Union: Russia, Vol. 23.* JVC; dist. by Rounder. 1988, 1990. VHS, text.

Ukraine

INDIVIDUAL ARTISTS OR GROUPS

3210 Levtchenko, Hréhory, and Kalena. *Voix Ukrainiennes = Ukrainian Voices, Vols. 1 and 2.* Sunset-France: PS 65114, PS 65145. 1993. 2 CDs.

3211 Liubystok. *Traditions Ukrainiennes = Ukrainian Folk Music.* Air Mail Music. Sunset-France: SA 141078. 2002. CD.

3212 Suzirya. *Songs and Dances of the Ukraine.* ARC Music: EUCD 1604. 1998, 2000. CD.

3213 Ukrainian Bandura Players. *Songs and Dances of Ukraine.* Monitor: MON71301. 1995. CD.

3214 Veseli Muzyky. *From Kiev to the Black Sea: Folk Music from Ukraine.* ARC Music: EUCD 2002. 2006. CD.

ANTHOLOGY

3215 *Music of the Ukraine.* Custom Compact Disc Series. Folkways: FE 4443. 1990. CD.

EASTERN EUROPE
GENERAL ANTHOLOGIES

3216 Fedoriouk, Alexander. *The Art of the Cimbalom.* Traditional Crossroads: CD 4314. 1999, 2003. CD.

3217 Harmonia. *Harmonia: Music of Eastern Europe.* Traditional Crossroads: CD 4313. 2001, 2003. CD.

3218 *Music of East Europe.* ARC Music: EUCD 1955. 2005. CD.

3219 ★*Rough Guide to the Music of Eastern Europe.* World Music Network; Eastern Europe Selection. World Music Network: RGNET 1024 CD. 1998. CD.

3220 *Voix des pays Baltes: Lettonie, Lituanie, Estonie.* Inédit. Maison des Cultures du Monde: W 260055. 1994. CD.

VIDEO

3221 *The JVC Video Anthology of World Music and Dance: II Soviet Union: Latvia/Estonia/Lithuania/Belorussia/Ukraine/Moldavia, Vol. 24.* JVC; dist. by Rounder. 1988, 1990. VHS, text.

TRANSNATIONAL

Jewish

INDIVIDUAL ARTISTS OR GROUPS

3222 ★Khevrisa. *European Klezmer Music.* Smithsonian Folkways: SFW 40486. 2000. CD.

3223 Muzsikás and Márta Sebestyén. *Marmaros: The Lost Jewish Music of Transylvania: Szól a Kakas Már.* Muzsikás: MU002. 1992, 2000. CD.

3224 Nazaroff, Nathan. Jewish "Freilach" Songs. Folkways: FW 6809. 1954, 1961. CD.

3225 Odessa Klezmer Orkestra. *Musique Klezmer = Klezmer Music.* Air Mail Music. Sunset-France: SA141134. 2002, 2006. CD.

3226 Raasche. *Jewish Folksongs of Europe.* Smithsonian Folkways: FW 8712. 1960, 2001. CD.

3227 Rubin, Ruth
    3227.1 *Jewish Life, the Old Country: Ethnic Recordings.* Folkways: FW 3801. 1958, 2001. CD.
    3227.2 *Yiddish Folk Songs.* Custom Compact Disc Series. Smithsonian Folkways: FW 8720. 1978, 2000s. CD.

3228 She'koyokh. *Sandanski's Chicken.* ARC Music: EUCD 2122. 2008, 2005. CD.

3229 Wex, Michael, and Sukke. *Sukke.* World Music Network: INTRO103CD. 2004. CD.

Roma

INDIVIDUAL ARTISTS OR GROUPS

3230 Fanfara din Cozmesti. *Gypsy Brass.* ARC Music: EUCD2001. 2006. CD.

3231 Fanfare Ciocărlia. *Queens and Kings.* Asphalt Tango Records: CD-ATR1207. 2007. CD.

3232 Lolov, Ibro. *Gypsy Music from Bulgaria.* ARC Music: EUCD 1757. 2002. CD.

3233 Redžepova, Esma. *Songs of a Macedonian Gypsy.* Monitor: MCD 71496, 1994. CD.

3234 Redžepova, Esma, and Thierry Robin. *Mon histoire = My Story* (Ansambl Teodosijevski). Accords Croisés: AC 119. 2007. CD.

3235 Schäfer, Martin. *Tzigane = Gipsy.* Air Mail Music. Sunset-France: SA141038. 1999. CD.

3236 Taraful din Baia. *Gypsies of Romania.* ARC Music: EUCD 1618. 2000. CD.

ANTHOLOGIES

3237 *The Gypsy Road: A Musical Migration from India to Spain.* Alula Records: ALU 1013. 1999. CD.

3238 *Latcho Drom.* Caroline: CAROL 1776-2. 1993. CD.

3239 ★*Rough Guide to the Music of Balkan Gypsies.* Rough Guide. World Music Network: RGNET 1159 CD. 2005. CD.

VIDEO

3240 ★*Latcho Drom.* International Cinema. New Yorker Video: NYV 52996. 1993, 1996. VHS.

EUROPE

General Anthologies

3241 *The Alps.* World Network, 24. Network Medien: 56.982. 1973, 1994. CD.

3242 *Clandestino (Manu Chao).* Virgin France, Ark 21: 61868 10036 2 5. 1998. CD.

3243 *Euro Groove.* Putumayo World Music: PUT 275-2. 2008. CD.

3244 *Flammes du coeur: Gypsy Queens.* Network: 32.843. 1999. 2 CDs.

3245 *Gajdy and Bock = Goat and Billygoat: Bagpipes from Central Europe.* Ethnic Series. Pan: PAN 1207. 2010. CD.

3246 *Le monde des musiques traditionnelles = The World of Traditional Music, 6.* Collection Ocora Radio France. Ocora Radio France: C 561066. 1944, 2003. CD.

3247 *Mediterranean Café Music.* Rough Guide. World Music Network: RGNET 1143 CD. 2004. CD.

3248 *Mediterranean Café Songs.* Nascente: NSCD 061. 2000. CD.

3249 *Midnight Sun: Traditional Nordic Melodies* (Tiina Orpana and Sarah Granskou). Dorian: DOR-93195. 1999. CD.

3250 *Musique à la croisée des cultures.* Music at the Crossroads. VDE Gallo: VDE-828-829. 1995. 2 CDs.

3251 *The Mystery of Poliphony (Luigi Lai).* World Network, 31. WDR: 58.393. 1981, 1995. CD.

3252 *Nordic Roots 3.* NorthSide: NSD 6060. 1999, 2001. CD.

3253 *Putumayo Presents Celtic Crossroads.* Putumayo World Music: PUT 243-2. 2005. CD.

3254 *Road of the Gypsies: L'épopée Tzigane.* Network: 24.756. 1996. 2 CDs.

3255 *The Rough Guide to Gypsy Music.* Rough Guide. World Music Network: RGNET 1220 CD. 2009. 2 CDs.

3256 *The Rough Guide to the Music of the Alps.* Rough Guide. World Music Network: RGNET 1103 CD. 2002. CD.

3257 *Scandinavia: Music Rough Guide Enhanced CD.* Rough Guide. World Music Network: RGNET 1051 CD. 2000. CD. *See also* Northern Europe, Scandinavia.

3258 *Unwired: Europe.* World Music Network: RGNET 1101 CD. 2003. CD.

3259 Yannatou, Savina. *Songs of an Other (Primavera en Salonico).* ECM: ECM 2057. 2007, 2008. CD.

VIDEOS

3260 *Eurovision Song Contest, Athens, 2006.* EMI: 94636536927. 2006. 2 CDs.

3261 *The JVC Video Anthology of World Music and Dance: Europe, Vol. 20.* JVC, Victor Co. of Japan; dist. by Multicultural Media. 1990, 2005. 30 DVDs, 9 booklets.

7

International Anthologies

Compiled by **LIZA VICK** *and* **JUDITH S. PINNOLIS**

This chapter is divided into several sections: devotional, ceremonial, and ritual; diaspora; international samplers; and Jewish music. It is crucial to note that these selections are representative only, and not comprehensive in scope or content. They serve to indicate areas of collecting as a starting point in very basic collections. The selections are by nature highly imperfect and should in no way be interpreted as prescriptive. Collecting should be undertaken with a library's local clientele and needs in mind and a variety of sources should be consulted.

Jewish music is included here because it is one of the largest and most widespread diasporas handled in this volume. The list is organized into sections: transnational ethnic groups (European); diaspora in the Middle East, North Africa, Central Asia; and traditional music of North America. More Jewish music selections

appear in various sections of this book (particularly Israel). Other diasporas and anthologies have sections located in regional chapters, particularly African and Afro-Caribbean (in Sub-Saharan Africa) and European (North America, etc.). Islamic music and influence is far-reaching; in this edition you'll find examples in listing in South and Southeast Asia, Africa, the Americas, and elsewhere. Other chapters list general anthologies within regional area lists. There are undoubtedly many areas not addressed in this book (or not addressed adequately), that will be added to future editions and are already covered in other sources (editors welcome expressions of interest and suggestions).

Since it would be impossible to fairly cover all world musical cultures and all strands of diaspora and transnationalism, these lists are only intended as an introductory taste, to be expanded in future editions and in offprints. There are many worthy sources of information including those listed below. The organization of this and other chapters is provided only as a framework, not to convey strict musical categories. In so many areas of world music, the boundaries are blurred, and many recordings are nearly impossible to categorize, due to the modern phenomenon of artists moving around the globe, multiracial artists and groups, and the impact of globalization on the popular music market.

For reasons of space and practicality, multiple performers on samplers are only included where the title doesn't indicate specific content and compilers are not listed for popular samplers (this information is easy enough to find in WorldCat or on the Internet). Labels specializing in compilations include Rounder, Putumayo, World Music Network, Rough Guides, Smithsonian Folkways, and others. *The JVC Video Anthology of World Music and Dance* series is now available on DVD. Insight Media sells entire sets by area; Lyrichord offers them individually, in sets, or the entire series. Please see the general volume introduction for further world music acquisitions and review sources.

DEVOTIONAL, CEREMONIAL, AND RITUAL

Compiled by Liza Vick

INDIVIDUAL ARTISTS AND GROUPS

3262 Association des Chantres Yéménites. *Chants sacrées de Sanaa = Sacred Songs from Sanaa.* Yémen. Institut du Monde Arabe: 321035. 1998, 2001. CD.

3263 Awlad al-Bura'I and Awlad al-Mahi. *Chants sacrés de Nubie et de Kordofan = Sacred Songs from Nubia and Kordofan.* Sudan. Institut du Monde Arabe: 321039. 2002. CD.

3264 Ben-Tzur, Shye. *Shoshan.* White Swan: WS 0019. 2010. CD.

3265 Habboush, Sheikh. *Transe Soufie d'Alep = Aleppian Sufi Transe* (Ensemble Al-Kindî; Julien Jalaleddin Weiss, cond). Chant du Monde: CMT 574 1251. 2002, 2003. 2 CDs.

3266 Hart, Mickey. *The Perfect Jewel: Sacred Chants of Tibet* [1995] (Gyuto Monks Tantric Choir). Smithsonian Folkways Archival. Smithsonian Folkways: HRT 15022. 2002, 2010. CD.

3267 Karaca, Kâni. *Ask Ile: Türk dinî musiki formlari = With Love: Compositional Genres of Turkish Liturgical Music* (R. Hakan Talu, ed.). Pan Yayincilik: 9799758434472. 2002. 2 CDs.

3268 Mailian, Anna. *Arakatz* (Music Masters of Armenia). Musique du Monde. Buda: 3017656. 2008. CD.

3269 Monks of Odessa Seminary. *Russian Orthodox Chant from the Odessa Seminary.* Alto: ALC 1110. 1985, 2010. CD.

3270 Piro, Ahmed, Zia Fariduddin Dagar, and Begonia Olavide. *Hamdulillah: Fes Festival of World Sacred Music, Vol. 2.* Sounds True: STA M 108. 1997, 1998. 2 CDs.

3271 Ron, Youval, and Najwa Gibran. *Under the Olive Tree: Sacred Music of the Middle East* (Yuval Ron Ensemble). Magda: MGD 043. 2004. CD.

ANTHOLOGIES

3272 *Belief: A Collection of World Sacred Music.* Beliefnet: BFT 1001. 2000. CD.

3273 *Festival de Fès des musiques sacrées du monde.* Chant du Monde: 574 1159–574 1160. 2002. 2 CDs.

3274 *Invocations: Sacred Music from World Traditions.* Music of the World: MOW 151. 1998. CD.

3275 *Islamic Liturgy: Song and Dance at a Meeting of Dervishes.* (John Levy, compiler; Martin Lings, ed.). Custom Compact Disc Series. Smithsonian Folkways: FR 8943. 1960, 2003. CD.

3276 *Music of Islam and Sufism in Morocco.* (Philip Schuyler, compiler). Anthology of World Music. Rounder: CD 5145. 1970s, 1999. CD.

3277 *Nusrat Fateh Ali Khan: Sufi Sounds from the Qawwali King* (Nusrat Fateh Ali Khan; Jameela Siddiqi, compiler). Rough Guide. World Music Network: RGNET 1078 CD. 2002. CD.

3278 *Rituals and Celebrations of the World = Rituels et fêtes du monde.* PlayaSound Collection. PlayaSound: PS 66408. 2006. CD.

3279 *The Rough Guide to Sufi Music, 2nd (Special) Ed.* World Music Network: WMN 1262 CD. 1990, 2011. 2 CDs.

3280 *Sacred Music of the World.* ARC Music: EUCD 1560. 1999. 2 CDs.

3281 *Sufi Music [Islamic Mystics Harness the Power of Music].* Rough Guide. World Music Network: RGNET 1064 CD. 1900s, 2001. CD. *See also* diasporas.

3282 *Sufi Soul: Echos du paradis.* Network: 26.982. 1997. 2 CDs. *See also* diasporas.

3283 *Terre sainte: musiques sacrées = Holy Land: Religious Music.* Nordsud music: NSCD 1180. 1957, 2002. CD.

3284 *Under the Moroccan Sky: Fes Festival of World Sacred Music, Fes, Morocco, Vol. 3.* Sounds True: STA MM 00122 D. 2001. CD.

VIDEO

3285 *A Voice from Heaven: Nusrat Fateh Ali Khan, the Most Beautiful Voice in the World* (Giuseppi Asaro, dir.). Fox Lorber CentreStage, Winstar TV & Video: WHE 73145. 2001. DVD.

DIASPORAS

Compiled by Liza Vick

INDIVIDUAL ARTISTS AND GROUPS

3286 Baca, Susana. *Afrodiaspora* (Calle 13 and Quetzal). Luaka Bop: 6 80899 0077-2-6. 2011. CD.

3287 Chao, Manu. *Manu Chao: Radio Bemba Sound System.* Virgin: H 2 7243 8 13242 2 6. 2002. CD.

3288 *Dengue Fever. Cannibal Courtship.* Fantasy: FAN-32622-02. 2011. CD.

3289 Diabaté, Toumani, José Manuel Soto, and Danny Thompson. *Songhai 2* (Ketama). Hannibal: HNCD 1383. 1994. CD. Blending of Spanish flamenco music with traditional music from Mali and Gambia (West Africa)—OCLC.

3290 Din, Hamza el-. *Eclipse.* Smithsonian Folkways Archival. Smithsonian Folkways: HRT 15001. 1988, 2010. CD. Previously released on Rykodisc in 1988.

3291 Gipsy Kings. *Volare! The Very Best of the Gipsy Kings.* Nonesuch: 79541-2. 2000, 1988. 2 CDs.

3292 Hart, Mickey. *The Spirit Cries.* Smithsonian Folkways Archival. Smithsonian Folkways: HRT 15012. 2010, 1993. CD. Previously released on Rykodisc in 1993.

3293 Khan, Shujaat, and Kayhan Kalhor. *Moon Rise over the Silk Road* (Ghazal). Shanachie: 66024. 1999. CD.

3294 M.I.A. *Maya.* Interscope Records: B0014344-02. 2010. CD. World music-influenced.

3295 M.I.A., Afrikan Boy, and Timbaland. *Kala.* Interscope: B 0009659-02. 2007. CD.

3296 Ma, Yo-Yo
3296.1 *New Impossibilities* (Silk Road Ensemble and others). 30 Years Outside the Box. Sony Classical: 88697-10319-2. 2007, 2009. CD. Western-influenced.
3296.2 *Silk Road Journeys: Beyond the Horizon* (Silk Road Ensemble). Sony Classical: SK 93962. 2004. CD.
3296.3 *Silk Road Journeys: When Strangers Meet* (Silk Road Ensemble and others). 30 Years Outside the Box. Sony Classical: SK 89782. 2002, 2009. CD. Western-influenced.

3297 Watcha Clan. *Diaspora Hi-Fi.* Piranha Musik: CD-PIR 2230. 2008. CD.

3298 Zap Mama. *Adventures in Afropea, 1.* Luaka Bop: 9 45183-2. 1993. CD.

ANTHOLOGIES

3299 *Afro Tropical Soundz, Vol. 1.* Soundway: SNDWCD024. 1969, 2010. CD. Selections originally released 1969-1977.

3300 *Afro-Latin Party.* Putumayo World Music: PUT 235-2. 2005, 1997. CD.

3301 *Balkan Beat Box. Balkan Beat Box.* JDub: JD 003. 2005. CD.

3302 *The Music of Islam* (David Parsons, compiler and prod.; Margaret J. Kartomi, compiler). Celestial Harmonies: 13140-2. 1998. 17 CDs.

3303 *Putumayo Presents an Afro-Portuguese Odyssey.* Putumayo World Music: PUT 204-2. 2002. CD.

3304 *Putumayo Presents Gypsy Groove.* Putumayo World Music: PUT 262-2. 2003, 2007. CD.

3305 *Reggae around the World.* Putumayo World Music: PUT 280-2. 2008. CD.

3306 ★*The Silk Road: A Musical Caravan.* Smithsonian Folkways: SFW CD 40438. 1980, 2002. 2 CDs.

3307 *Sufi Music [Islamic Mystics Harness the Power of Music].* Rough Guide. World Music Network: RGNET 1064 CD. 1900s, 2001. CD. *See also* devotional.

3308 *Sufi Soul: Echos du paradis.* Network: 26.982. 1997. 2 CDs. *See also* devotional.

3309 *Tango around the World.* (Ousmane Touré, M. A. Numminen, Sanna Pietiäinen, Bonadeo Melingo, Florencia, Fortuna, Federico Aubele, Alexis Kalofolias, Thanos Amorginos, Liana, Cáceres,

Ariel Prat, and Hugo Díaz). Putumayo World Music: PUT 271-2. 2007. CD.

3310 *Third Planet.* The Third Planet. World Class: 11311-2. 2000. CD.

3311 *To What Strange Place: The Ottoman-American Diaspora, 1916–1929* (Ian Nagoski, compiler). Tompkins Square: TSQ 2608. 2011. 3 CDs.

3312 *Turkish Groove* (Bendeniz, Mustafa Sandal, Sertab Erener, Nilgül, Tarkan, Gülseren, Emrah, Göksel, Tugba Ekinci, Nazan Öncel, and Sezen Aksu). Putumayo World Music: PUT 248-2. 2006, 1999. CD.

3313 *World Reggae* (Apache Indian, Majek, Maria de Barros, Alê Singer Muniz, Chris Combette, Alpha Blondy, Bernard Uedre, and Kaïssa). Putumayo World Music: PUTU 221-2. 2004. CD.

INTERNATIONAL SAMPLERS

Compiled by Liza Vick

INDIVIDUAL ARTISTS AND GROUPS

3314 Afro Celt Sound System. *Release: Further in Time, Vol. 3.* Real World: 7243 10184 0 8. 2001. 2 CDs. Explore other volumes in this set.

3315 Hart, Mickey
    3315.1 *Däfos* (Flora Purim and Airto Moreira). Smithsonian Folkways Archival. Smithsonian Folkways: HRT 15006. 2010, 1989. CD. Previously released on Rykodisc in 1989; explore other titles in series.
    3315.2 *Planet Drum.* Rykodisc: RCD 10206. 1991, 2008. CD.

ANTHOLOGIES

3316 *All Over the Map.* (Astor Piazzolla, Knut Buen, Beau Jocque, Cedella Marley Booker, Fadela, Sahraoui, Stanley Thompson, Clifford Ellis, Tabu Ley, Sisi Chen, Najat Aatabou, Alison Kinnaird, Tish Hinojosa, and others). Rounder: AN 26. 1978, 1996. CD.

3317 *At Home in the World (I Heard It on NPR).* (Bebel Gilberto, Valdes Cachao, Carolo, Lila Downs, Edith Piaf, Paolo Conte, Amália Rodrigues, Ali Farka Toure, Ry Cooder, Youssou N'Dour, Ravi Shankar, Cassandra Wilson, Angelique Kidjo, and others). NPR Classics: NPR CD 0021. 1992, 2003. CD.

3318 *The Best of Both Worlds: The Rykodisc World Music Sampler: The Hannibal World Music Sampler.* Rykodisc: RCD 30298. 1979, 1994. 2 CDs.

3319 ★*The Demonstration Collection of E.M. Von Hornbostel and the Berlin Phonogramm-Archiv.* (Erich Moritz von Hornbostel, compiler). Custom Compact Disc Series; Ethnic Folkways Library; Ethnomusicological Series. Smithsonian Folkways: F-4175. 1962, 2000.2 CDs, MP3.

3320 *Destination Mediterranean: Gifts from the Sea.* National Geographic Music. Sugo Music: SR 0238. 1995, 2002. CD. Consult other titles in series.

3321 *Divine Divas: A World of Women's Voices..* Rounder: CD 5071/2/3. 1997. 3 CDs.

3322 ★*Ecuador and Colombia: Marimba Masters and Sacred Songs: The Afro-Descendent Musicians of the Pacific Coastal Region* (Tierra Caliente, La Voz de Niño Dios, and Groupo Folclórico Alcadia Municipal de Buenaventura; Sacha Mirzoeff, compiler). Music of the Earth. Multicultural Media: MCM 3015. 1998, 1995. CD.

3323 *Emociones: 25 Years Network.* Network: 28.483. 1980s, 2005. 3 CDs.

3324 *Festival in the Desert.* World Village: 468020. 2003. CD.

3325 *Global Divas: Voices from Women of the World.* Rounder: CD 5062/3/4. 1995. 3 CDs.

3326 *Jazz around the World.* Putumayo World Music: PUT 296-2. 2003, 2009. CD.

3327 *Luaka Bop 10th Anniversary: Zero Accidents on the Job.* Luaka Bop: 72438-48922-2-7. 2000. 2 CDs.

3328 *Music from the Chocolate Lands.* Putumayo World Music: PUT 230-2. 2004. CD.

3329 *Music from the Tea Lands.* Putumayo World Music: PUT 180-2. 2000. CD.

3330 *One World.* Rounder: CD AN 15. 1994. CD.

3331 *Putumayo Presents the Best of World Music*
    3331.1 *Vol. 1: World Vocal* (Juan Luis Guerra, Jorge Ben, Miriam Makeba, Gilberto Gil, Majek Fashek, Johnny Clegg, Rossy, Gregory Isaacs, Samite, and others). Rhino: R 2 71203. 1978, 1993. CD. Consult other titles in series.

3331.2 *Vol. 2: Instrumental* (Béla Fleck, Jean Luc Ponty, Ali Akbar Kahn, Loreena McKennitt, Rossy, Govi, Alison Brown, Ottmar Liebert, and others). Rhino: R 2 71204. 1989, 1993. CD. Consult other titles in series.

3332 *Putumayo Presents Women of the World Acoustic* (Sandrine Kiberlain, Marta Topferova, Emiliana Torrini, Luca Mundaca, Lura, Mona, Tamara Obrovac, Anastasia Moutsatsou, Marta Gómez, and Kaïssa Doumbé). Putumayo World Music: PUT 261-2. 1994, 2007. CD.

3333 *Putumayo Presents World Groove.* Putumayo World Music: PUT 227-2. 2004, 1997. CD. Sampler: France, Turkey, Germany, Cuba, Mali, Congo, Algeria, South Africa, Lebanon, and more.

3334 *Putumayo World Party.* Putumayo World Music: PUT 263-2. 2007. CD. Sampler: Italy, Martinique, Denmark, Ghana, Benin, Jamaica, Argentina, Haiti, and more.

3335 ★*The Rough Guide to World Music, Vol. 1: Africa, Europe, and the Middle East.* World Music Network: RGNET 1032 CD. 1999. CD.

3336 ★*The Rough Guide to World Music, Vol. 2: Latin and North America, Caribbean, India, Asia, and Pacific.* (Nava, Yolanda Rayo, Rubén González, and others). World Music Network: RGNET 1044 CD. 1999. CD.

3337 *The Secret Museum of Mankind*
3337.1 *Vols. 1–5: Ethnic Music Classics, 1925–1948.* Yazoo: 7004. 1925, 1995. CD. Explore other volumes in this set.

3338 ★*Smithsonian Folkways World Music Collection.* Smithsonian Folkways: SF CD 40471. 1997. CD.

3339 *Songlines Top of the World Compilation CD.* (Melingo, Camille, Baden Powell, Ry Cooder, Albert Kuvezin, Ko Kan Ko Sata Doumbia, Ali Farka Toure, Toumani Diabaté, and others). Songlines: STWCD 07. 2005. CD. Explore Songlines periodical (CDs accompany issues).

3340 *Songlines Top of the World: The Best New World Music, CD 57.* Songlines: STW CD 33. 2009. CD. Accompanies *Songlines* magazine (no. 57, January-February 2009); explore others in series.

3341 *Travel the World with Putumayo Sampler.* Putumayo World Music: P611-SL. 2011. CD.

3342 *Where in the World Is Rykodisc?* Rykodisc: VRCD 9704. 1988, 1997. CD.

3343 *World Circuit Presents.* Nonesuch: 139132-2. 2007. 2 CDs.

3344 *World Hits.* (Peter Tosh, Youssou N'Dour, Mongo Santamaria, Jimmy Cliff, and others). Putumayo World Music: PUT 267-2. 1960s, 2007. CD.

3345 ★*World Music: A Global Journey.* (Terry E. Miller and Andrew C. Shahriari, compilers). Routledge. 2009. 2 CDs. Accompanies book of same title (2nd edition).

3346 ★*Worlds of Music: An Introduction to the Music of the World's Peoples,* 5th ed. (Jeff Todd Titon, compiler). Schirmer/Cengage Learning. 2008. 4 CDs. Accompanies book of same title.

VIDEO

3347 ★*The JVC Video Anthology of World Music and Dance.* JVC, Victor Co. of Japan; dist. by Multicultural Media: VTMV-31-VTMV-60, JVCVOL01-JVCVOL30. 1990, 2005. 30 DVDs, 9 booklets.

JEWISH DIASPORAS

Compiled by Judith S. Pinnolis

Issues in collecting Jewish folk music include defining and incorporating items representative of a widely divergent community. Jewish folk music varies stylistically across denominational and cultural divides. Both ethnomusicological and historical-religious characteristics must be taken into account in order to build a balanced collection. Major subgroupings of Sephardic, Ashkenazic, and Mizrachi Jewish communities are but one key component in determining the relevance of a selection. Within the United States, religious denominations and heritage communities play a greater role. Jewish folk and synagogue music in America also reflects adoption and assimilation of general American genre types including folk, jazz, pop, and rock.

To find listings of new recordings and occasional reviews, turn to the Klezmershack (www.klezmershack.com) or the Jewish Music WebCenter (www.jmwc.org). The Hebrew University Jewish Music Research Centre offers listings of its publications, as well as a thesaurus of periodical articles and reviews. Use of *RAMBI*, the *Index to Jewish Periodicals* and *Ethnic Newswatch* may prove fruitful in finding music reviews. In addition to standard music journals offering reviews of sound recordings, serials offering reviews of Jewish music include *Association of Jewish Libraries Newsletter, Musica Judaica,* and *Hadassah Magazine.* New York's Jewish *Forward* and *The New York Jewish Week* are newspapers that often carry reviews of Jewish recordings.

A good many Jewish folk albums are self-published, so online sites such as CDBaby (www.cdbaby.com) can be searched with terms such as "Jewish" or "klezmer" or "Ladino" and so forth. Jewish records are sold in specialty shops such as Tara Publications's Jewishmusic.com (www.jewishmusic.com) or Mostly Music (www.mostlymusic.com). Labels that continue to produce albums of Jewish music include Traditional Crossroads, Ergo, Rounder, and Global Village. Other labels such as Flying Fish, Soundswrite, Yiddishland, and Tzadik should also be checked for new titles. Performing artists frequently include clips of their music on their websites or Facebook pages, providing one of the better ways to sample recording artists and hear their style of music. Exploring labels that are organized by linguistic groupings (Ladino, Yiddish, Hebrew), by function (holiday music, synagogue song, lullabies, and the like), or by forces (cantorial, choral, instrumental bands) can lead to finding more Jewish folk music recordings.

Caribbean, Latin American

ANTHOLOGY

3348 *Judeo-Caribbean Currents: Music of the Mikvé Israel-Emanuel Synagogue in Curaçao.* Yuval Music Series.Jewish Music Research Centre, Hebrew University of Jerusalem: AMTI 0901. 2009. CD.

Europe

INDIVIDUAL ARTISTS AND GROUPS

3349 Bloemendal, Hans, Anton Kras, Willy Lindwer, and Yuval Shaked. *Makom: Yerushalayim Shel Ha-Ma'arav: Ha-Masoret Ha-Musikalit Shel Ha-Kehilah Ha-Ashkenazit Shel Amsterdam = Mokum: Jerusalem of the West : The Musical Tradition of the Ashkenazi Community of Amsterdam* (Amsterdam Great Synagogue Choir and various Amsterdam Cantors). Beth Hatefutsoth, Muze'on ha-histori ha-Yehudi: BTR 0401. 2005. 2 CDs.

3350 ★Cohen, Judith R. *Primavera en Salónica* (Jaume Bosser). Technosaga, SA: KPD 10.977. 1991, 1993, 1999. CD.

3351 Cooper, Adrienne, and Zalmen Mlotek. *Ghetto Tango: Wartime Yiddish Theater.* Traditional Crossroads: CD 4297. 2000. CD.

3352 Ensemble Saltiel. *Kantigas de Novia = Sephardic Wedding Songs* (Boda Ensemble Saltiel, Fahrettin Sükrü Yarkin, Aron Saltiel, Flora Saltiel-Vadermouten, Rivka Saltiel, Thomas Bernardini, Yurdal Tokcan, Halil Karaduman, Turay Dinleyen, Sükrü Kabaci, Ugur Isik, Nagme Yarkin, Unal Yürük, and Ferruh Yarkin). Alikobeni Music. 2011. CD.

3353 Gebirtig Mordekhay, *Mayn Fayfele = My Little Flute* (Mariejan van Oort and Jacques Verheijen). I-C-U-B4-T (Music & Words): CUP 8027. 2003. CD.

3354 Goldenshteyn, German. *A Living Tradition* (Aaron Alexander, Josh Horowitz, Alex Kontorovich, Mark "Rubinchik" Rubin, Henry "Hank" Sapoznik, Cookie Segelstein, and Susan Watts). Living Traditions: LTD 1803. 2006. CD.

3355 Jagoda, Flory. *Kantikas Di Mi Nona: Judeo-Spanish Songs from the Bosnian Tradition = Coleção Brasil Em Questão* (Alec Gakner, Sidney Heller, Robert Spracher, Fred Ederer, Elliot Jagoda, Silvana Jagoda, and Andy Jagoda). Global Village: CD 169. 1989. CD.

3356 Kovács, Sándor. *Shome'a Kol Bekhiyot: Liturgy of Dohány Street Synagogue.* Hungaroton: 18134-2, HCD. 1990. CD.

3357 Mazor, Yaakov, ed. *The Hasidic Niggun as Sung by the Hasidim* (Hasidim). Anthology of Music Traditions in Israel, 17. Jewish Music Research Centre, Hebrew University of Jerusalem: AMTI 0402. 1961, 2004. 2 CDs.

3358 Veretski Pass. *Trafik* (Cookie Segelstein, Joshua Horowitz, and Stuart Brotman). Golden Horn: GHP 032-2. 2008. CD.

3359 ★Waletzky, David, et al. *Partisans of Vilna: The Songs of World War II Jewish Resistance* (Michael Alpert, David J. Waletzky, Adrienne Cooper, Josh Waletzky, Irena Klepfisz, and Henry Sapoznik). Flying Fish; New Video Group: FF 70450, NVG-9614. 1989, 2005. CD, DVD, songbook, study guide.

3360 Yannatou, Savina. *Spring in Salonika = Primavera en Salonico* (Lefteris Angouridákis, Yannis Alexandrís, Kostas Vómvolos, Kyriakos Gouvéntas, Yannis Kaimákis, and Michalis Siganídis). Lyra: ML 4765. 1995. CD.

ANTHOLOGIES

3361 *As Dreams Fall Apart: The Golden Age of Jewish Stage and Film Music 1925–1955* (New Budapest Orpheum Society). Cedille Records: CDR 90000 151. 2014. 2 CDs.

3362 ★*Italia!: The Renaissance of Jewish Music* (Zamir Chorale of Boston, Salamone Rossi, Cristiano Giuseppe Lidarti, composers; Joshua R. Jacobson, cond.). Zamir: HZ 919. 2003. CD.

3363 *Italian Jewish Musical Traditions from the Leo Levi Collection, 1954–1961* (Francesco Spagnolo, compiler). Anthology of Music Traditions in Israel, 14. Jewish Music Research Centre, Accademia Nazionale di Santa Cecilia, Roma: AMTI CD 0102. 2001. CD.

3364 *Judeo-Spanish Songs for the Life Cycle in the Eastern Mediterranean* (Susana Weich-Shahak, compiler). Anthology of Music Traditions in Israel, 24. Jewish Music Research Centre, Hebrew University of Jerusalem: AMTI 0114. 2014. 2 CDs.

3365 ★Mlotek, Eleanor Gordon, and Zalmen Mlotek. *Mir Trogn a Gezang: A Collection of Yiddish Folk, Art and Theatre Songs from the Book by Eleanor (Chana) Mlotek* (Yosl Mlotek, Phyllis Berk, Bruce Adler, Michael Alpert, Shura Lipovsky, Robert Abelson, Adrienne Cooper, Batsheva, Joanne Borts, Rosalie Becker, Henry Sapoznik, and Lorin Sklamberg). Workmen's Circle: 658287348225. 1998. CD.

3366 *Or Haganuz: Gems of Ashkenazi Hazzanut and Yiddish Songs Revived.* Contemporary Jewish Music, 4. Jewish Music Research Centre, Hebrew University of Jerusalem: CJM 1501. 2015. CD.

3367 *Pearls of Yiddish Song = Perl Fun Yidishn Lid* (Eleanor Reissa, Rosalie Becker, Michael Alpert, Seymour Rechtzeit, Adrienne Cooper, Hanry Sapoznik, Shoshana Ron, Lorin Sklamberg, Phyllis Berk, and Emil Gorovets; Zalmen, Mlotek, dir.). Workmen's Circle: 658287348324. 1998. CD.

3368 *Two Worlds: The Poetry of Mordechai Gebirtig.* Golden Horn Records. 2014. CD.

3369 *Vemen vestu zingen, vemen? Leibu Levin Performs in Yiddish: Select Archival Recordings from Bukovina, USSR and Israel.* Anthology of Music Traditions in Israel, 25. Jewish Music Research Centre, Hebrew University of Jerusalem: AMTI 0115. 2015. CD.

3370 *Yikhes = Lineage: Early Klezmer Recordings, 1911–1939, from the Collection of Martin Schwartz (Martin Schwartz).* Trikont: US-0179. 1995. CD.

VIDEOS

3371 Haschel, Moshe. *The English Tradition of Jewish Choral Music* (Zemel Choir and Robert Max; Robert Max, cond.). Olympia: OCD 647. 1998. DVD.

3372 *The Key from Spain: The Songs and Stories of Flory Jagoda* (Flory Jagoda; Ankica Petrovic, dir.). National Center for Jewish Film. 2000. DVD.

3373 *A Life of Song: A Portrait of Ruth Rubin.* ERGO Media. 1992, 1986. DVD.

3374 *Vorbei—Beyond Recall* (*Der Judische Kulturbund = The Jewish Kulturbund*; H. J. P. Bergmeier, Jakob Eisler, and Rainer E. Lotz, eds.). Bear Family: BCD 16030 LM. 2001. 11 CDs, DVD, book.

3375 *Yidl Mitn Fidl* (Molly Picon, Simche Fostel, Max Bozyk, Leon Liebgold, Joseph Green, Konrad Tom, Abraham Ellstein, and Jan Nowina-Przybylski; Joseph Green, dir. and prod.). ERGO Media: D 710. 2002, 1936. DVD. Yiddish-language musical-comedy.

Middle East, Africa, and Central Asia Diaspora

INDIVIDUAL ARTISTS AND GROUPS

3376 Benaroya, Samuel. *Ottoman Hebrew Sacred Songs = Zimrat Kodesh 'Ivrit Meha-Kesarut Ha-Ot'manit.* Anthology of Music Traditions in Israel, 12. Jewish Music Research Centre, Hebrew University of Jerusalem: AMTI CD 9803. 1983, 1998. CD.

3377 Bensoussan, Aaron, Gerard Edery, and Alberto Mizrahi. *The Sons of Sepharad* (Rex Benincasa, George Mgrdichian, Francois Houle, and Stuart Rosenberg). Sefarad: 5764. 2002. CD.

3378 Bowles, Paul. *Sacred Music of the Moroccan Jews.* Rounder Select: 5087. 1959, 2000. 2 CDs.

3379 Effendi, Haim. *An Early Twentieth-Century Sephardi Troubadour: The Historical Recordings of Haim Effendi of Turkey = Trubador Yehudi-Sefaradi Mi-Reshit Ha-Meah Ha-'Esrim: Ha-Haklatot Ha-Historiyot Shel Hayim Efendi Mi-Turkiyah* (Rivka Havassy, Edwin Seroussi, and Joel Bressler, eds.). Anthology of Music

Traditions in Israel, Vol. 21. Jewish Music Research Centre, Hebrew University of Jerusalem: AMTI CD 0801. 2008. 4 CDs, booklet.

3380   Haza, Ofra. *Yemenite Songs*. Worldmusic Recordings: AUS 3004-2. 2004. CD.

3381   Kol Oud Tof Trio. *Gazelle*. (Esti Kenan-Ofri, Armand Sabach, and Oren Fried). Magda Music: MGD 037. 2001. CD.

3382   Obadia, Hakki. *Iraqi Jewish and Iraqi Music*. Global Village: CD 147. 1993. CD.

3383   Pal-Yarden, Hadass. *Yahudice Yahudije = Yahudig'eh: Ladino Sehir Müzigi*. Kalan: 272. 2003. CD.

3384   Pezarkar, Pinhas Reuben, Pinhas David Bhalkar, Benjamin Simon Dandekar, and Levi Jacob. *El Eliyahu: Ha-Masoret Ha-Musikalit Shel Kehilat Bene Yisrael, Bombai = Eliyahoo Hanabee: Musical Tradition of the Bene Israel of Bombay*. Beth Hatefutsoth: BTR 0101. 2001. CD.

3385   Shashmaqam. *Central Asia in Forest Hills, NY: Music of the Bukharan Jewish Ensemble Shashmaqam*. Smithsonian Folkways: CD SF 40054. 1991. CD.

3386   Voice of the Turtle. *From the Shores of the Golden Horn*. Paths of Exile: Quincentenary Series, Vol. 1. Titanic: Ti-173. 1989. CD.

ANTHOLOGIES

3387   *Abayudaya: Music from the Jewish People of Uganda*. Smithsonian Folkways Recordings: SFW40504. 2003. CD.

3388   *The Bride's Joys and Sorrows: Songs and Ballads of the Moroccan Jews as Sung by the Women of Tetuan, Morocco* (Women of Tetuan, Morocco; Henrietta Yurchenco, compiler). Global Village: CD 148. 1994. CD.

3389   *Ha-Musikah Shel Ha-Yehudim Ha-Harariyim = The Music of the Mountain Jews* (Pirius Eliyahu, compiler). Anthology of Music Traditions in Israel, 10. Jewish Music Research Centre, Hebrew University of Jerusalem: AMTI CD 9801. 1998. CD. Iranian language (Judeo-Tat); Jews, Caucasus (Europe).

3390   ★*The Hidden Gate: Jewish Music around the World* (Chava Ablerstein, Savina Yannatou, Ofra Haza, Yasmin Levy, Alain Chekroun, Romiel Daniel, Fortuna, Yair Dalal, Maurice El Medioni, Emil

Zrihan, Alicia Svigals, Michael Alpert, and other musical groups). Rounder: 1161-615-083-2. 2003. 2 CDs.

3391   *Judeo-Spanish Moroccan Songs for the Life Cycle = Shire Mahazor Ha-Hayim Shel Ha-Yehudim Ha-Sefaradim Be-Maroko* (Susana Weich-Shahak, compiler; Edwin Seroussi, ed.). Anthology of Music Traditions in Israel, 5. Jewish Music Research Centre, Hebrew University of Jerusalem: AMTI CD 0101. 1989, 2001. CD.

3392   *Liturgies Juives d'Ethiopie* (Simha Arom and Frank Alvarez-Pereyre, compilers). Inédit. Auvidis: CD-W 260013. 1990. CD.

3393   *Out of Babylon: The Music of Baghdadi-Jewish Migrations into Asia and Beyond* (Zaki I Solomon, Natanel Meoded, Charlie Daniel, David Dangoor, Sam Benjamin, Jacob Zion, Ellis Jacobs, Solomon Isaac Solomon, Jacob Baher, Matthew Trush, Nissim Cunio, Ezra Daniel, Baruch Abdallah Ezra, and Nehemia Hudja; Margaret J. Kartomi, compiler; Bronia Kornhauser, ed.). Celestial Harmonies: 13274-2. 2007. CD.

3394   *A Song of Dawn: The Jerusalem Sephardi Baqqashot at the Har Tzyion Synagogue, Vol. 20* (Avraham Caspi; Essica Marks, ed.). Jewish Music Research Centre, Hebrew University of Jerusalem: AMTI CD 0701. 2007. 6 CDs.

3395   *With Songs They Respond: The Diwan of the Jews from Central Yemen* (Naomi Bahat-Ratzon and Avner Bahat, compilers; Edwin Seroussi, ed.). Anthology of Music Traditions in Israel, Vol. 19. Jewish Music Research Centre, Hebrew University of Jerusalem: AMTI CD 0601. 2006. 2 CDs.

VIDEO

3396   *A People and Its Music: Jewish Music Heritage Library* (Asher Tlalim, dir.; Tzipora Jochsberger, prod.). ERGO Media: 790. 1993–1997. 10 DVDs.

See also Israel (Chapter 4).

Folk and Traditional Music of North America

INDIVIDUAL ARTISTS AND GROUPS

3397   Alter, Israel. *Shomeah Tefillah = Prayers of the High Holy Days* (Lois Welber). Temple B'Nai Israel. 2006. CD.

3398 Beckerman, Sid, and Howie Leess. *Klezmer Plus! Old Time Yiddish Dance Music Featuring Sid Beckerman and Howie Leess.* Flying Fish: FF 70488. 1988, 1991. CD.

3399 ★Bikel, Theodore. *Theodore Bikel Sings Jewish Folk Songs* (Fred Hellerman). Bainbridge: BCD 2507. 1992. CD.

3400 Brandwein, Naftule. *King of Klezmer Clarinet.* Rounder: CD 1127. 1922, 1997. CD.

3401 Cardozo, Abraham Lopes, Louis Gerstein, and David de Sola Pool. *Historic Music of the Spanish and Portuguese Synagogue in the City of New York* (Choir of Congregation Sheartih Israel). Shearith Israel League. 2003. 3 CDs.

3402 Carlebach, Shlomo
   3402.1 *At the Village Gate.* Vanguard: 2133-2. 1963, 1990. CD.
   3402.2 ★*The Very Best of Shlomo Carlebach.* Jerusalem Star: CDH 521. 1994. CD.

3403 Contzius, Erik. *Teach My Lips a Blessing* (Johannes Somary, Christopher Creaghan, and Amor Artis Chamber Choir). Contzius Music Publishing. 2008. CD.

3404 Cooper, Adrienne. *Enchanted: A New Generation of Yiddishsong* (Michael Winograd, Marilyn Lerner, and Frank London). Golden Horn Records: GHP 034-2. 2010. CD.

3405 Fried, Abraham. *Chazak!* Noam Productions: 5758; CD-AF. 1997. CD.

3406 ★Friedman, Debbie. *Debbie Friedman at Carnegie Hall.* Sounds Write Productions: SWP 612. 1996. 2 CDs.

3407 Greenman, Steven. *Stempenyu's Dream: New Klezmer Compositions.* Ohio Arts Council & Greenfidl Music. 2004. CD.

3408 Guthrie, Woody, and Klezmatics. *Wonder Wheel* (Susan McKeown, Michael Alpert, Boo Reiners, Kenny Wollesen, Danny Blume, Ron Caswell, Ethan Eubanks, Brian Mitchell, and Adam Widoff). Jewish Music Group: JMG 18033-2. 2006. CD.

3409 Hirschhorn, Linda. *Becoming.* Oyster Albums, Kehila Productions: OA 11110. 2007. CD.

3410 Jacobson, Joshua R. (cond.). *Zamir Chorale of Boston: Greatest Hits* (Zamir Chorale of Boston). Zamir. 2005. CD.

3411 Klezmatics. *Rise Up! = Steyt Oyf!* Rounder: 3197. 2002. CD.

3412 Klezmer Conservatory Band. *Dance Me to the End of Love* (Hankus Netsky, dir.). Rounder: 3169. 2000. CD.

3413 Kol B'Seder. *Snapshots: The Best of Kol B'Seder, Vol. 1.* (Jeff Klepper and Dan Freelander). Empty Chair: KB 800. 2004. CD.

3414 Krakauer, David
   3414.1 *Bubbemeises: Lies My Gramma Told Me* (Socalled and Klezmer Madness). Label bleu: LBLC 6677. 2005. CD.
   3414.2 *Tweet Tweet* (Abraham Inc., Fred Wesley, and DJ Socalled). Table Pounding Records: TPR-001. 2009. CD.

3415 Leverett, Margot. *Margot Leverett and the Klezmer Mountain Boys* (Kenny Kosek, Barry Mitterhoff, Joe Selly, and Marty Confurius). Traditional Crossroads: CD 4318. 2003. CD.

3416 London, Frank, Jacob Ben-Zion Mendelson, Anthony Coleman, David Chevan, and Gerald Cleaver. *Hazonos* (Daniel Mendelson, Simon Spiro, Cookie Segelstein, Dan Rosengard, and Tomas Ulrich). Radical Jewish Culture, 102. Tzadik: TZ 8102. 2005. CD.

3417 Mikveh. *Mikveh.* Traditional Crossroads: CD 80702-4305-2. 2001. CD.

3418 Miller, Benzion, Alberto Mizrahi, Naftali Herstik, Jules van Hessen, and Benedict Weisser. *Cantors: A Faith in Song* (Ne'imah Singers, Netherlands Theater Orchestra). TV Matters: MUM 9040. 2003. CD.

3419 Mizrahi, Alberto, and Roslyn Barak. *A Sho'o in Gan Eyden = An Hour in the Garden of Eden: The Zamir Chorale of Boston Sings Yiddish* (Zamir Chorale of Boston; Joshua R. Jacobson, cond.). Zamir: HZ-913. 1998. CD.

3420 Schechter, Basya. *Songs of Wonder* (Uri Sharlin, Megan Gould, Yoed Nir, Rich Stein, Frank London, and Kyle Sanna). Radical Jewish Culture, 165. Tzadik: TZ 8165. 2011. CD. Settings of poems by Abraham Joshua Heschel.

3421 Shirim Klezmer Orchestra. *Naftule's Dream.* Popular Arts. Northeastern: NR 5014-CD. 1992, 1993. CD.

3422 Shtreiml. *Spicy Paprikash.* Shtreiml. 2003. CD.

3423 Statman, Andy, and David Grisman
  3423.1 *New Shabbos Waltz: A Collection of Timeless Jewish Melodies.* Acoustic Disc: ACD-64. 2006. CD.
  3423.2 *Songs of Our Fathers: Traditional Jewish Melodies.* Acoustic Disc: ACD-14. 1995. CD.

3424 Strauss, Deborah, and Jeff Warschauer (Strauss/ Warschauer Duo). *Rejoicing: Yiddish Songs and Klezmer Music.* Extraplatte Musikproduktions: EX-ED 019. 2005. CD.

3425 Svigals, Alicia. *Fidl': Klezmer Violin.* Traditional Crossroads: CD 4286. 1997. CD.

3426 Werdyger, Mordechai Ben David. *The Hits: Platinum.* MBD Music: MBD 5770. 2009. 2 CDs.

3427 Winograd, Michael. *Bessarabian Hop.* M. Winograd. 2007. CD.

3428 Winograd, Michael. *Storm Game.* Golden Horn Records: GHP 037-2. 2012. CD.

3429 Zorn, John, and Yamatsuka Eye. *Zohar* (Mystic Fugu Orchestra). Radical Jewish Culture, 6. Tzadik: TZ 7106. 1995. CD.

ANTHOLOGIES

3430 *Af Di Gasn Fun Der Shtot = On the Streets of the City* (Michael Alpert, Sharon Bernstein, Adrienne Cooper, Margot Leverett, Frank London, Peter Rushefsky, Binyumen Schaechter, Lorin Sklamberg, Deborah Strauss, and Theresa Tova; Bella Schaechter-Gottesman, composer). Yiddishland: YDL 002. 2003. CD.

3431 *Cantors, Klezmorim, and Crooners, 1905–1953: Classic Yiddish 78s from the Mayrent Collection* (Naftule Brandwein, Nellie Casman, Henri Gerro, Sherry Mayrent, Berele Chagy, and others). JSP: JSP 5201. 2009. 3 CDs.

3432 *Doyres = Generations: Traditional Klezmer Recordings 1979–1994* (Klezmorim, Zev Feldman, Andy Statman, Dave Tarras, Kapelye, Joel Rubin, The Epstein Brothers Orchestra, Klezmer Conservatory Band, Klezmer Plus, Musa Berlin, Josh Horowitz, Muzsikás, Chicago Klezmer Ensemble, New Shtetl Band, and Ukranian Brass Band from Vinnitsa). Trikont's Jewish Music Series. Trikont: US-0206. 1997. CD.

3433 *Eshet Chail: The Singing Jewish Women, Vol. 3* (Sophie Tucker, Shifra Lerrer, Miriam Kressin, Jenya Feirman, Ruth Maymon, Sonya Laizron, Sarah Gorby, Molly Picon, Mary Soriano, and Tova Roni). Israel Music: ICD 5108. 2003. CD.

3434 *Ghettoblaster.* JDub: JDub 105. 2007. CD.

3435 *Katchko: 3 Generations of Cantorial Art* (Theodore Katchko and Adolph Katchko; Deborah Katchko-Gray, compiler and arr.; Velvel Pasternak, ed.). Tara. 2009. CD, book.

3436 *Klezmer! Jewish Music from Old World to Our World* [Recorded 1912–1997] (Abe Elenkrig, Yossele Rosenblatt, Joseph Moskowitz, Gus Goldstein, Naftule Brandwein, Joseph Cherniavsky, Aaron Lebedeff, Sam Medoff, Seymour Rechtzeit, Bagelman Sisters, Sam Musiker, Andy Statman, Zev Feldman, Marty Confurius, Klezmer Conservatory Band, Kapelye, Boiled in Lead, Klezmer Plus, Klezmatics, and Klazkamp Dance Band; Henry Saposnik, ed.). Yazoo: 7017. 2000. CD.

3437 *Kol Nidre Service* (Richard Tucker, Joseph Garnett, and Ben Irving; Sholom Secunda, cond.). Sony Masterworks: MDK 35207. 1959, 1990. CD.

3438 *Music from the Yiddish Radio Project* (Andrew Sisters, Yiddish Swing Orchestra, Dave Tarras Orchestra, Yiddish Swingtet, Abe Ellstein Orchestra, Barry Sisters, Jan Bart, Sam Medoff, Naftule Brandwein Orchestra, Seymour Rechtzeit, and Pincus Sisters; David Saposnik and Henry Saposnik, eds.). Soundtrack to Radio Series. Shanachie: 6057. 1936, 2002. CD.

3439 ★*Mysteries of the Sabbath: Classic Cantorial Recordings, 1907–1947* (Leib Glanz, Samuel Malavsky, Joseph Shapiro, Pierre Pinchik, Pinchos Jassinowsky, Mordechai Hershman, Joseph Shlisky, Moishele Soorkies, Josef Rosenblatt, Gershon Sirota, Zavel Kwartin, David Roitman, Sophie Kurtzer, Alter Yechiel Karniol, Zindel Sapoznik, and Yeshaya Meisels). Yazoo: 7002. 1907, 1994. CD.

3440 ★*The Rough Guide to Klezmer Revival* (German Goldenshteyn, Crepuscule, Chava Alberstein with the Klezmatics, Joel Rubin Ensemble, Brave Old World, di Naye Kapelye, Giora Feidman, Sid Beckerman, Howie Leess, Zmiros Project, Konsonana Retro, Kharkov Klezmer Band, Steven Greenman, Yale Strom with Pastromi and Klassj, Veretski Pass, Budowitz, Klezmer Conservatory Band, Andy Statman, Frank London's Klezmer Brass All-Stars, and Merlin Shepherd Kapelye).

Rough Guide. World Music Network: RGNET 1203 CD. 2008. CD.

3441 *Shomeir Yisrael* (Rabbi Simeon J. Maslin, Richard Allen, and Voces Novae et Antiquae; Ben Steinberg, composer and cond.). Arkay: AR 6126. 1993. CD.

3442 *Shteygers = Ways: New Klezmer Music 1991–1994* (Greta Buck, Don Byron, Matt Darriau, Ted Epstein, Mahmoud Fadl, Mark Feldman, David Harris, David Licht, Frank London, Ray Musiker, Adam Rogers, Marcus Rojas, Josh Roseman, Joel Rubin, Elliott Sharp, Lorin Sklamberg, Sebastian Steinberg, Alicia Svigals, and Jeff Warschauer). Trikont's Jewish Music Series. Trikont: US-0207. 1995. CD.

3443 *Yiddish-American Klezmer Music, 1925–1956* (Dave Tarras, Abe Schwartz Orchestra, Joseph Cherniavsky Yiddish American Jazz Band, Lou Kockett's Orchestra, Russkyj Orkestr "Moskva," Moshe Oysher and Florence Weiss, Michi Michalesco, Alexander Olshanetsky Orchestra, Abe Ellstein Orchestra, Seymour Rechtzeit, Yiddish Swing Orchestra, Bagelman Sisters, Yiddish Swingtette, Boibriker Kapelle, Aaron Lebedeff, and Tantz Orchestra; Henry Saposnik, ed.). Yazoo: 7001. 1925, 1992. CD.

VIDEOS

3444 Brave Old World. *Live in Concert.* Sun-Street Inc.: SU-101. 2006. DVD.

3445 Mendelson, Jacob
   3445.1 *A Cantor's Tale* (Joseph Malovany, Ben-Zion Miller, Alberto Mizrahi, Matthew Lazar, Neil Shicoff, Jackie Mason, and Alan Dershowitz). ERGO Media: D 774. 2007. DVD.
   3445.2 (Introductions) *Legendary Voices: Cantors of Yesteryear* [1931–1950] (Mordechai Hershman, Adolph Katchko, Samuel Malavsky, Moishe Oysher, David Roitman, Yossele Rosenblatt, Joseph Shlisky, and Leibele Waldman). ERGO Media: 765D. 2011. DVD.

3446 Perlman, Itzhak. *In the Fiddler's House* (Brave Old World, The Klezmatics, the Klezmer Conservatory Band, Red Buttons, Fyvush Finkel, Leopold Kozlowski, Kapelye, and Samuel Sanders). EMI Classics: 0946 3 68609 9 2. 2006, 1995. DVD.

CONTRIBUTORS

VOLUME EDITORS

LIZA VICK (Associate Editor, World Music; African Anthologies; Asian Anthologies; Central African Popular; European Anthologies; International Anthologies; Northern Europe; Southeast Asia; Southern African Popular; Southern Europe; Western Europe) is Head of the Otto E. Albrecht Music Library and Eugene Ormandy Music and Media Center at the University of Pennsylvania. Previously she was Music Reference and Research Services Librarian at the Loeb Music Library, Harvard University, where she worked closely with the Archive of World Music and the Ethnomusicology faculty. Prior to that, she was Research Librarian for the Performing Arts at the University of California, Irvine. Her degrees are an M.L.S. and an M.M. in Ethnomusicology from the University of Maryland, College Park and a B.Mus. in Flute Performance from West Chester University. Liza has served as book review editor for *Notes* and has written concert program notes, book reviews for *Music Reference Services Quarterly* and *Ethnomusicology,* among other publications. She is an active member of the Music Library Association (served as member-at-large), served as Chair of the New England Chapter, and is a member

of the Society for Ethnomusicology. Her ethnomusicological interests include Japanese koto and Cambodian classical dance.

DREW BEISSWENGER (Assistant Editor, World Music) is an associate professor and Music and Media Cataloger at Mullins Library at the University Arkansas. He holds a Ph.D. in Musicology, Regional Studies (Ethnomusicology) from the University of Memphis and an M.L.S. from the University of Alabama. His previous positions include Head of the Music Library at Missouri State University, Librarian at Davis & Elkins College, and, in a previous career in arts administration, Folk Arts Coordinator for the Arkansas Arts Council. His research focus has been primarily on fiddle music, and his publications include: *Irish Fiddle Music from Counties Cork and Kerry, North American Fiddle Music: A Research and Information Guide,* and *Fiddling Way Out Yonder: The Life and Music of Melvin Wine.* His honors include a 2009 ethnomusicology Fulbright Scholarship at University College Cork in Ireland, and a 2006 Foundation Award for Research at Missouri State University.

■ ■ ■

GREGORY BARZ (Eastern Africa) is an ethnomusicologist who has engaged in field research in Uganda, Rwanda, Kenya, South Africa, Tanzania, and Israel. He received the Ph.D. from Brown University and the M.A. from the University of Chicago. Barz is professor of ethnomusicology and Associate Dean for Academic Initiatives at Vanderbilt University where he was recently named the Alexander Heard Distinguished Professor. His latest co-edited book, *Queering the Field: Sounding Out Ethnomusicology,* will be published by Oxford University Press. In addition, he co-edited *The Culture of AIDS in Africa: Hope and Healing in Music and the Arts* and two editions of *Shadows in the Field: New Perspectives for Fieldwork in Ethnomusicology,* all with Oxford. His monograph, *Singing for Life: HIV/AIDS and Music in Uganda* applies the central tenets of medical ethnomusicology to a study of HIV prevention in East Africa. He has produced four CDs and a documentary film and received a GRAMMY nomination as producer of the Smithsonian Folkways CD, *Singing for Life: Songs of Hope, Healing, and HIV/AIDS in Uganda.*

AARON M. BITTEL (Eastern Europe; Middle East [Iran, Israel, Turkey]) serves as Archivist-Librarian and Head of Digital Projects for the University of California, Los Angeles Ethnomusicology Archive, one of the largest and oldest ethnographic audiovisual archives in North America, and is also an adjunct faculty member teaching courses on audiovisual archives and oral history at UCLA. He holds Master's degrees in Library and Information Science and Ethnomusicology, and a Bachelor's degree in Music Education. His principal areas of research and professional practice are archives education, digital archives, and the implementation of open standards and open platforms for preservation and access. He served for several years as Co-Chair of the Education and Training Committee of the Association for Recorded Sound Collections (ARSC), and has also held leadership positions in the Music Library Association (MLA) and International Association of Sound and Audiovisual Archives (IASA). Aaron is an active musician with scholarly and performing interests in free-reed instruments, music of the Balkans, and Irish traditional music.

MI-HYE CHYUN (Korea) is Chair of Talbott Library, Westminster Choir College of Rider University (Princeton, NJ). In addition to her role as Chair of the department, she works in the areas of collection development and reference services. Previously she worked for the Institute for Advanced Study in Princeton. She earned her M.L.S. degree from the University of Maryland, College

Park and a B.A. from Sungkyunkwan University, Seoul, Korea. Mi-Hye plays harpsichord and piano, and her interest and involvement with Korean traditional music has given her the opportunity to attend workshops at the National Center for Korean Traditional Performing Arts. Additionally, she has studied *changgo* and *kayagŭm*, and has made presentations and organized concerts on Korean traditional music. She is a member of the Music Library Association, its Greater New York Chapter, and the Association for Korean Music Research.

JOE C. CLARK (Japan; Mexico, Southwestern United States; Western African Popular) is an Associate Professor and Head of the Performing Arts Library at Kent State University. He is active in the American Library Association, Association of College and Research Libraries, and the Music Library Association, and has numerous publications. He holds a B.A. in Music from the University of Utah, an M.A. in Information Resources and Library Science from the University of Arizona, and an M.A. in Ethnomusicology from Arizona State University. Before becoming a librarian, he enjoyed life as a professional guitarist and music educator.

DEBORAH GRIFFITH DAVIS (Ireland, United Kingdom) is an OCLC QuestionPoint 24/7 Reference Librarian. Previously she was central enquiry service manager for Essex County Council Libraries (U.K.) and has held positions at the University of Chicago, Mannes College of Music, New York Public Library at Lincoln Center, and the Juilliard School. She holds a B.Mus. in Music History from American University, an M.A. in Musicology from the Catholic University of America, and an M.S.L.S. (library science) from Columbia University. She also completed doctoral coursework in Ethnomusicology at the City University of New York's Graduate Center. Active in the Music Library Association, Deborah was Coordinator of the World Music Roundtable, served on the Development Committee and the Bibliographic Instruction Subcommittee and was Newsletter Editor and Chair of the Greater New York Chapter. She has contributed a book review to *Notes,* articles to *American National Biography, The New Grove Dictionary of Music and Musicians,* and several North American–Welsh newspapers.

SUZANNE FLANDREAU (African Diaspora; Afro-Caribbean Traditional; Central African Traditional; Southern African Traditional) retired as Head Librarian and Archivist at the Center for Black Music Research, Columbia College Chicago, in 2012. She was a music archivist for over twenty-five years, specializing in music of the African Diaspora. She is a former officer of the Society for Ethnomusicology (SEM), and represented SEM on the National Recording Preservation Board at the Library of Congress. She chairs the Grants Committee of the Association for Recorded Sound Collections and lectures and teaches classes on African-American music.

ROBIN P. HARRIS (Central Asia [Sakha-Yakutia of Russia, Siberia]) lived with her husband and two children in the Russian North for a decade shortly after the fall of the Soviet Union. During this time, she began to study the music of the Sakha, a Siberian minority group, and became intrigued with the virtual disappearance of their epic narrative song genre *olonkho*. Her forthcoming book with University of Illinois Press—*Storytelling in Siberia: The Olonkho Epic in a Changing World*—draws on her research into the revitalization of this genre of intangible cultural heritage. After obtaining her Ph.D. in Ethnomusicology from University of Georgia Athens, she was asked to serve as Director of the Center for Excellence in World Arts (Dallas, TX), which offers undergraduate and graduate programs in applied ethnoarts. She also provides ethnomusicology and arts consulting for SIL International and serves as the President of the International Council of Ethnodoxologists.

BETH ISEMINGER (Central African Popular), music contract cataloger and formerly Senior Music Catalog Librarian at the Eda Kuhn Loeb Music Library of Harvard University, has also cataloged music at Kent State University and at Oberlin College. Iseminger is Past Chair of the Music Library Association Cataloging and Metadata Committee (formerly Bibliographic Control Committee) and of the MLA-CMC Vocabularies Subcommittee (formerly Subject Access Subcommittee). She is also a Past Chair of the MLA Genre/Form Task Force. Iseminger's experience with ethnomusicological materials began with graduate work at the University of Texas at Austin and continued through her professional contributions in support of the ethnomusicology programs at Kent State and at Harvard.

ANDREW JUSTICE (Central America; Folk and Traditional Musics of North America; South America) is Head of the Music Library at the University of Southern California, where he is responsible for collection development and reference/instruction services to support the scholarly and performing activities of the Thornton School of Music. He earned degrees from Oregon State University, the University of Oregon, and Syracuse University, and has worked at the Cornell University and University of North Texas music libraries. In addition to

memberships in the Music Library Association, Association for Recorded Sound Collections, and International Association of Music Libraries, he maintains an active performing career as a violist specializing in historically-informed performance practice of music from the seventeenth through early nineteenth centuries.

ALAN KARASS (Egypt, Northern Africa) is Director of Libraries at the New England Conservatory in Boston, MA. He is a graduate of Clark University (B.A., Music), Simmons College (M.S., Library and Information Science), the University of Connecticut (M.A., Historical Musicology), and the Open University (Ph.D., Ethnomusicology). His current research is focused on connections between festivals, music, and national identity in Tunisia. Alan served as co-editor of the journal *Music Reference Services Quarterly* from 2000 to 2007, and has written articles for *Serials Librarian, American Recorder, Music Reference Services Quarterly, Music Library Association Newsletter,* and *Boston Early Music News*. His chapter "Identity, Music, and Festivity in Southern Tunisia" appears in the *Handbook of Musical Identities* published by Oxford University Press.

CRAIG MACRAE (Central Asia) is an Associate Professor at Berklee College of Music, where he teaches harmony, world music composition, and directs a contemporary Middle Eastern ensemble. Professor Macrae received an M.Mus. in Jazz Studies from Indiana University, and completed coursework at the doctoral level in Ethnomusicology at the University of Illinois at Urbana-Champaign. His research focuses on the music of Central Asia. During the 1990s he spent eighteen months in Uzbekistan, studying the music performed at Uzbek life-cycle ceremonies. While in Central Asia, he established the Tashkent, Uzbekistan office of the International Research and Exchanges Board (IREX). His work has appeared in several edited anthologies and in scholarly journals such as *Asian Music,* and the *Yearbook for Traditional Music*. He has presented papers at meetings of the Society for Ethnomusicology, and in other forums including the U.S. Foreign Service Institute, and the International Conference for Turkic Music in Alma-ti, Kazakhstan.

MARK McKNIGHT (Central America; Folk and Traditional Musics of North America; South America) is the Head of the Music Library and Ozier Sound Recording Archive at the University of North Texas, where he also teaches courses in music history and research in the UNT College of Music. He holds a B.A. in Music from the University of Central Arkansas, an M.A. and

Ph.D. in Music History from Louisiana State University, and an M.S. in Library and Information Science from the University of Illinois. He is active in a number of professional and scholarly organizations, including the American Musicological Society, the Society for American Music, the American Library Association, and the Music Library Association, in which has held a number of offices, including President (2017–2019). He has written and lectured extensively on 19th-century American music criticism, early American sheet music, and the music of Louisiana and New Orleans. Publications include essays, articles, and reviews in *Notes, American Music, Black Music Research Journal, ARSC Journal, Fontes artis musicae, French Baroque Music of New Orleans: Spiritual Songs from the Ursuline Convent (1736), Music Publishing and Collecting: Essays in Honor of Donald W. Krummel, A Basic Music Library,* 3rd ed., *Cambridge History of Music Criticism,* and *Lexikon des Orchesters.* He is also author of *Music Classification Systems* (Lanham, MD: Scarecrow Press, 2002) and a contributor to *The New Grove Dictionary of American Music,* 2nd ed.

ALEC McLANE (China, Taiwan; India [South, Carnatic], Bangladesh, Sri Lanka, Andaman; Southeast Asia [Indonesia]) has been Music Librarian and Director of the World Music Archives at Wesleyan University since 1998. He was educated at the Berklee College of Music and the University of Illinois, receiving from the latter the D.M.A. in composition with a minor in Ethnomusicology, as well as the M.S.L.I.S. from the Graduate School of Library and Information Science. He has taught music at Central Connecticut State University and Youngstown State University, and was Music and Media Librarian at Youngstown State University from 1995 to 1998. He contributed a chapter, "Music as Information," to the 1996 *Annual Review of Information Science and Technology* and was editor of the Digital Media Reviews column in *Notes* from 2002 to 2006. McLane has also been Web Editor and Chair of the New England chapter of the Music Library Association. Pursuing musical interests, he has traveled to both Indonesia and China, most recently presenting at a 2012 music preservation conference at the Central Conservatory of Music in Beijing.

RICHARD McRAE (Caribbean Popular; Western African Popular) is a Catalog Librarian at Sibley Music Library, Eastman School of Music. He holds a B.Mus. degree from the University of Massachusetts (1980) and an M.L.S. (1989) and M.A. in Music History (1993) from the University at Buffalo. He worked as a cataloger for the American Music Center in 1989, and was a faculty member at the University at Buffalo Music Library from 1990 to 2007. He is a member of the Music Library Association and its New York State/Ontario Chapter, and has contributed to *Notes.* As a free-lance trombonist, he has performed in orchestral, chamber, jazz, klezmer, salsa, pop, blues, rock, African/Latin, and Baltic ensembles.

KEVIN C. MILLER (Oceania) holds a Ph.D. in Ethnomusicology and an M.L.I.S. in Library and Information Science, both from the University of California, Los Angeles. His research interests include the musical cultures of the Pacific and the South Asian diaspora, and the ways in which these musical cultures are represented in libraries, archives, and museums. His dissertation, "A Community of Sentiment: Indo-Fijian Music and Identity Discourse in Fiji and its Diaspora," was completed in 2008. Dr. Miller is currently University Archivist at the University of California, Davis.

TOM MOORE (South America [Brazil]) is the Head of the Sound and Image Department, Green Library, Florida International University, Miami, where he also teaches in the area of Brazilian music. He contributes interviews with contemporary composers to *Sonograma* [Barcelona], articles on 19th-century flute music to *Falaut* [Italy], and reviews compact discs for *American Record Guide.* He is active as a translator, with four books translated from Italian, Portuguese and German into English, published by Music Word Media, Pendragon Press, and Lexington Books. He is also active as a flutist, with recordings of baroque chamber music of Telemann and Boismortier for Lyrichord and A Casa Discos.

JUDITH S. PINNOLIS (Jewish Music) is Adjunct Faculty at the School of Jewish Music of Hebrew College, and also currently works as a music librarian at Berklee College of Music and The Boston Conservatory at Berklee. Previously, she served as a Research Librarian at Brandeis University. She has served as Chair of the Jewish Music Roundtable of the Music Library Association, Chair of the Chapters Council of ACRL (Association of College and Research Libraries), President of ACRL New England Chapter, and on the ACRL National Leadership Council. Pinnolis is creator and editor of *The Jewish Music WebCenter* (www.jmwc.org). She has contributed to major reference works such as *Encyclopedia Judaica* and written many book and music reviews. She has published on topics of Jewish music including, "'Cantor Soprano' Julie Rosewald: The Musical Career of a Jewish American 'New Woman'," in the *American Jewish Archives Journal* (2010). Pinnolis received the M.M. at the College-Conservatory of Music of the University of Cincinnati, and the M.S. in Library Science at Simmons College.

MAUREEN RUSSELL (Middle East [Iran, Israel, Turkey]) is an Adjunct Assistant Professor in Ethnomusicology at the UCLA (University of California, Los Angeles) Herb Alpert School of Music, specializing in audiovisual archiving and information literacy and research skills. Russell is also Head of Cataloging and Archivist at the UCLA Ethnomusicology Archive, one of the largest and oldest ethnographic audiovisual archives in North America. She has written two critically-acclaimed books about television and film (*Highlander: The Complete Watcher's Guide*, Warner Books, 1998; and *Days of Our Lives: A Complete History of the Long-Running Soap Opera*, McFarland, 1995). Currently, she is the editor for *Music Reference Services Quarterly*'s "Off the Beaten Path" column and the editor for *Ethnomusicology Review*'s "From the Archives" column.

JEFF SCHWARTZ (Bollywood, Bhangra; Himalayas; India [North, Hindustani]; Middle East [Gulf and Levant]; Pakistan) is a reference librarian at the Santa Monica Public Library. He is a former Chair of the ALA-RUSA Outstanding Reference Sources and Dartmouth Medal committees (Reference and User Services Association, a division of the American Library Association). He holds degrees in English, Popular Culture, and American Studies, as well as the M.L.I.S, has published in cultural studies and library science, and his book *Free Jazz: A Research and Information* Guide is forthcoming from Routledge. Jeff is principal bass of MESTO (the Multi-Ethnic Star Orchestra), a member of the Santa Monica Symphony, and a busy performer of jazz and improvised music.

SPIRO J. SHETUNI (Eastern Europe [Albania]) is a Professor of Library Science and Collections Access Librarian at Winthrop University's Ida Jane Dacus Library (Rock Hill, SC). He received his Ph.D. from Tirana State University (Albania), and a Master's degree in Library and Information Science from Kent State University. Previously Dr. Shetuni chaired the Ethnomusicology Department at the Institute for Traditional Culture in Tirana, Albania (1988-1992). A former visiting scholar at the Austrian Audiovisual Research Archive (1988), at the Institute of Ethnography and Folklore (Rumanian Academy of Sciences, 1992), and a former Fulbright scholar at the University of California, Los Angeles, Department of Ethnomusicology and Systematic Musi-

cology (1992–1993), he has made many contributions to the field of Eastern European ethnomusicology. His academic monograph, *Albanian Traditional Music: An Introduction,* was published by McFarland (2011). Then followed a series of six academic monographs under the main title *Albanian Traditional Music*, published by Outskirts Press (2012–2014). His series of six academic monographs, titled *My People: The Arumanians,* was also published by Outskirts Press (2015).

HOLLING SMITH-BORNE (Eastern Africa) is the Director of the Wilson Music Library at Vanderbilt University where he works closely with Gregory Barz to co-curate the Global Music Archive. Prior to his appointment at Vanderbilt, he was the Coordinator of the Music Library (Associate Professor) at DePauw University in Greencastle, Indiana. His degrees are an M.L.S. from the University of Michigan and a B.Mus. in Piano Performance from Bowling Green State University in Ohio. He is an active member of the Music Library Association where he served as a member-at-large and chaired the Education Committee. He recently contributed a chapter "Staying Current: Keeping Skills and Knowledge Relevant in a Dynamic Professional Landscape" to the book *Careers in Music Librarianship III* (A-R-Editions). Holling is a frequent instructor on the topics of music copyright, education for music librarians, and collection development in music.

■ ■ ■

EDITOR

DANIEL F. BOOMHOWER is director of the library at Dumbarton Oaks, a research center in Washington, DC, affiliated with Harvard University. Previously, he served as the Head of the Reader Services Section of the Music Division at the Library of Congress, as Head of the Performing Arts Library at Kent State University, and as Assistant Music Librarian at Princeton University. He studied music and library science at Case Western Reserve University in Cleveland, Ohio, the University of Illinois at Urbana-Champaign, and Wittenberg University in Springfield, Ohio. His study of music began with the violin and continues with research on the sources and methods used in music scholarship and on the reception of the music of Johann Sebastian Bach.

INDEX

Stars (★) are used to denote high-priority items. Individual artists and groups have artist names, while anthologies and videos do not.

Bangladesh, 1424–1428. *See also* South
    India (Carnatic, Bangladesh, and
    Sri Lanka)
Banjar Tunjuk Klod "Kusma Sari"
    Gong leko: tunjuk-tabanan tabuh-tabuh
        leko, 1615.1
    Gong leko: tunjuk-tabanan tari leko,
        1615.2
Banton, Buju
    Before the Dawn, 666
    Rough Guide to Reggae, 695
Baptiste, Onil Jean, *Rara in Haiti*, 663
Barak, Roslyn, *A Sho'o in Gan Eyden =
    An Hour in the Garden of Eden:
    The Zamir Chorale of Boston Sings
    Yiddish*, 3419
Barbados, 737–754. *See also* Caribbean
    Islands, Other
Barceló de Carvalho and Semba Master,
    Bonga Live, 2597
Barkey, Captain, *Conscious Ragga,
    Vol. 1*, 687
Barradas, Huáscar, *Folk Music from
    Venezuela*, 1055
Barretto, Ray
    Acid, 523.1
    Ancestral Spirits, 523.2
    Boogaloo, 561
    Essential Ray Barretto, 523.3
    Latin Jazz, 563
    ★*Latin Legends*, 564
    ★*Mambo Mania! The Kings and Queens
        of Mambo*, 565
    Rican/Struction, 523.4
    Ritmo en el corazón, 529.7
    ★*Salsa Explosion The New York Salsa
        Revolution, 1968–1985*, 571
    ★*Salsa: Latin Music of New York and
        Puerto Rico*, 578
    ★*Viva Salsa*, 574
Barros, Maria de, *World Reggae*, 3313
Barroso, Ary
    Ary Barroso, 906.1
    Ary Barroso: Songbook, 906.2
    O mais Brasileiro dos Brasileiros,
        906.3
Barry, Mamadou, *Niyo*, 2204
Barry, Sean, *The Northumberland
    Collection*, 2739
Barry Sisters, *Music from the Yiddish
    Radio Project*, 3438
Bart, Jan, *Music from the Yiddish Radio
    Project*, 3438
Basaldúa, Papi, *Tiempo de amar*, 1005
Bashir, Munir
    The Art of the 'Ûd, 1898
    ★*Munir Bashir and the Iraqi Traditional
        Music Group*, 1899
    Taqâsîm: Luth arabe = Arab Lute,
        1900
Bastos, Waldemar, *Pretaluz: Blacklight*,
    2596
Batacumbele, *Con un poco de songo*, 703

★Batsheva, *Mir Trogn a Gezang: A
    Collection of Yiddish Folk, Art and
    Theatre Songs from the Book by
    Eleanor (Chana) Mlotek*, 3365
Battlefield Band, *The Best of Battlefield
    Band*, 2771
Bauls of Bengal and Purna Chandra Das,
    Bauls of Bengal, 1424
Bauzá, Mario
    Mambo, 617
    My Time Is Now, 524.1
    Tanga, 524.2
Bayanihan Philippine Dance Company,
    *Monitor Presents the Bayanihan
    Philippine Dance Company*,
    1508
Beamer, Keola, *Soliloquy: Ka Leo O Loko*,
    277
Bear, Keith, *People of the Willows*, 349
Bear Creek, *XI: Pow-Wow Songs Recorded
    Live at San Manuel*, 332
Beausoleil
    *Allons à Lafayette and More with
        Canray Fontenot*, 241
    *Bayou Deluxe: The Best of Michael
        Doucet & Beausoleil*, 244
Becker, Rosalie
    ★*Mir Trogn a Gezang: A Collection of
        Yiddish Folk, Art and Theatre Songs
        from the Book by Eleanor (Chana)
        Mlotek*, 3365
    *Pearls of Yiddish Song = Perl Fun
        Yidishn Lid*, 3367
Beckerman, Sid
    *Klezmer Plus! Old Time Yiddish Dance
        Music Featuring Sid Beckerman and
        Howie Leess*, 3398
    ★*The Rough Guide to Klezmer Revival*,
        3440
Beken, Munir Nurettin, *Art of the Turkish
    Ud*, 1989
Bel, M'Bilia
    Bameli Soy, 2563.1
    Boya yé: Ba gerants ya mabala, 2564
    Keyna: Contre ma volonté, 2563.2
Belarus, 3191–3192
    Dulcimer of Belarus (Mischula and
        Kirmash), 3191
    Music of Belarus (Romanskaya and
        Kirmash), 3192
Belasco, Lionel, *Calypso Breakaway*, 727
Belasco's Orchestra, *Rough Guide to
    Calypso Gold*, 731
Belgium, 2824–2834
    *Airs de fête en Wallonie: Chansons et
        musiques traditionnelles* (Schmitz
        and Melchior), 2828
    All the Best (Kadril), 2826
    *Belgique, le carnival de Binche =
        Belgium, the Carnival of Binche*,
        2831
    *Belgique: Ballades, danses, et chansons:
        Flandre, Wallonie = Belgium:*

    *Ballads, Songs, and Dances:
        Flanders, Wallonia*, 2830
    Flemish Folk Music, 1997, 2832
    Greetings from Belgium, 2833
    Kabonka (Ambrozijn), 2824
    Laïs (Laïs), 2827
    *Musique populaire de la Belgique =
        Folk Music from Belgium*, 2834
    Palabras Darei (Ialma), 2825
    Zap Mama (Zap Mama), 2829
Belize, 827–833
    Cult Cargo: Belize City Boil Up, 828
    *Dabuyabarugu: Inside the Temple:
        Sacred Music of the Garifuna of
        Belize*, 829
    ★*Garifuna Music: Field Recordings from
        Belize*, 830
    Haul Up Your Foot You Fool! (Mr.
        Peters Boom and Chime), 2635
    Shine Eye Gal: Brukdon! [1978, 1985],
        2636
    *Shine Eye Gal: Brukdon Belizian
        Calypso*, 831
    *Traditional Music of the Garifuna
        (Black Carib) of Belize*, 832
    *Umalali: The Garifuna Women's
        Project*, 833
    Wátina (Palacio), 827
Belize (Garifuna)
    *Dabuyabarugu: Inside the Temple,
        Sacred Music of the Garifuna of
        Belize* [1981], 2639
    ★*Garifuna Music: Field Recordings from
        Belize* [2002–2004], 2640
    Garifuna Punta Anthology [1973]
        (Lambey et al.), 2638
    The Original Turtle Shell Band
        (Original Turtle Shell Band), 2637
    *Play, Jankunu, Play: The Garifuna
        Wanaragua Ritual in Belize* [2006],
        2642
    *Traditional Music of the Garifuna
        (Black Carib) of Belize* 2641
Belkani, Brahim el-, *Wijdan: Mystery of
    Gnawa Trance Music*, 1851
Bell, Mary, *Tuku Music*, 2631
Belleville A Cappella Choir, *Southern
    Journey, Vol. 11: Honor the Lamb*,
    28
Bellou, Sōtēria, *The Rebetico of Sotiria
    Bellou*, 2893
Bellowhead, *Hedonism*, 2715
Bembele, Henri, *Colonial Dance Bands,
    1950 and 1952: Dar-Es-Salaam,
    Mombasa, Nairobi, Lourenço
    Marques, Elisabethville, Hihue:
    Kenya, Tanganyika, Portuguese East
    Africa, Northern Rhodesia, Belgian
    Congo*, 2394
Bembeye Jazz National, *Syliphone Years*,
    2205
Ben, Jorge, *Putumayo Presents the Best of
    World Music Vol. 1*, 3331.1

Evans, Meredydd
   ★*Merêd: Caneuon Gwerin*, 2800.1
   Welsh Folk Songs, 2800.2
Evans, Richard, *Exile*, 2367, 2452
Evarts, Mark, *Music of the Pawnee*, 351
Evora, Cesaria
   ★*Essential Cesaria Evora*, 2167.1
   Miss Perfumado, 2167.2
Express, D. P.
   Haiti, 660
   Haiti chéri, 661
   ★*Konbit: Burning Rhythms of Haiti*, 662
Eye, Yamatsuka, *Zohar*, 3429
Eyuphuro, *Yellela*, 2604
Ezra, Baruch Abdallah, *Out of Babylon: The Music of Baghdadi-Jewish Migrations into Asia and Beyond*, 3393

F
Los Fabulosos Cadillacs, *La luz del ritmo*, 878
Fadela, *All Over the Map*, 3316
Fadl, Mahmoud, *Shteygers = Ways: New Klezmer Music 1991–1994*, 3442
Fadl, Mahmud Ahmad, *Drummers of the Nile in Town: Cairosonic*, 1761
★*Fairport Convention, Liege and Lief*, 2724
Fakhet, Amina, *Sultan Hubbak*, 1858
★*Fakhri, Sabah, Master of Andalusian Folklore*, 1935
★*Familia RMM, Combinación perfecta*, 531
Familia Valera Miranda
   Cuban son, 614
   Oriente de Cuba, 619
Fanfan, *Séga Ravanne*, 2327
Fanfara din Cozmesti, *Gypsy Brass*, 3230
Fanfare Ciocărlia
   ★*Baro Biao: World Wide Wedding*, 3174
   Queens and Kings, 3231
Fania All-Stars
   ★*Best of Fania All-Stars*, 532.1
   Boogaloo, 561
   ★*Latin Legends*, 564
   Live at the Cheetah, Vols.1–2, 532.2
   ★*Viva Salsa*, 574
Farafina
   Bolomakoté, 2094
   Faso Denou, 2161
Farcas, Dumitru, *The Art of the Romanian Taragot*, 3175
Farida, *Mawal and Maqamat Iraqi*, 1901
Faroe Islands, 3010–3013
   Eivør Pálsdóttir (Pálsdóttir), 3010
   Flóð og fjøra (Spælimenninir), 3011
   Traditional Music in the Faroe Islands, 1950–1999, 3012
   Tutl 2000, 3013
Farreyrol, Jacqueline, *L'île de la Réunion*, 2417

Fashek, Majek, *Putumayo Presents the Best of World Music Vol. 1*, 3331.1
Faudel
   Autre soleil, 1789.1
   Baïda, 1789.2
   Samra, 1789.3
Fauve, Ramiro, *Bandera mía: Songs of Argentina*, 883
Fayruz
   B'hebbak Ya Loubnan, 1913.1
   The Lady and the Legend, 1913.2
   ★*Legend: The Best of Fairuz*, 1913.3
   The Legendary Fairuz, 1913.4
   ★*The Life Story of Fairouz*, 1913.5
Faytinga, Dehab, *Numey*, 2291
Fedoriouk, Alexander, *The Art of the Cimbalom*, 3216
Feenjon Group and el Avram Group, *Israeli Popular Hits*, 1969
Fei, Jianrong, *Music of the Ruan Xien, Zhuong Ruan and Da Ruan*, 1081
★*Feidman, Giora, The Rough Guide to Klezmer Revival*, 3440
Feirman, Jenya, *Eshet Chail: The Singing Jewish Women, Vol. 3*, 3433
Feld, Steven, *Bufo Variations*, 2184
Feldman, Mark, *Shteygers = Ways: New Klezmer Music 1991–1994*, 3442
Feldman, Zev
   Doyres = Generations: Traditional Klezmer Recordings 1979–1994, 3432
   Klezmer! Jewish Music from Old World to Our World, 3436
Feliciano, Cheo
   Cheo, 533
   ★*¡Salsa!* 570
Felix and his Krazy Kats, *Calypso Breakaway*, 727
Fella
   La Ma Raayto, 1790.1
   Sahrat Tarab, 1790.2
Fellove, Francisco, *Cuban Gold, Vols. 1–5*, 586
Fender, Freddy, *Canciones de mi barrio*, 481
Fernández, Dioni, *Aquí está el merengue*, 638
Fernhill, *Na Prádle*, 2801
Ferrer, Ibrahim
   ★*Buena Vista Social Club*, 579
   Buenos Hermanos, 587
   ★*Putumayo Presents Cuba*, 620
   A toda Cuba le gusta, 604
Ferrero, José, *Endechar: Sephardic Romances and Songs*, 2976
Fewet, Touareg de, *Touareg de Fewet: Lybie, Musiques du Sahara*, 1812
Fflur, Elin, *Dim Gair*, 2802
Fiesta Filipina Dance Troupe, *Traditional Music from the Philippines*, 1510
Fiji. See Melanesia

Finkel, Fyvush, *In the Fiddler's House*, 3446
Finland, 3014–3027
   Echos de Finlande, 3024
   Finlande: Musique traditionnelle = Finland: Traditional Music, 3025
   Finlande: Musiques d'Ostrobotnie: Kaustinen et alentours (Kaustisen Purppuripelimannit and Ostrobothnia), 3018
   Helsinki (Lepisto and Lehti), 3020
   Iho (Kalaniemi), 3017
   JPP (Järvelän Pikkupelimannit), 3016.1
   ★*The Kalevala Heritage: Archive Recordings of Ancient Finnish Songs*, 3026
   ★*Karelia visa* (Hedningarna), 3014
   Kaustinen Rhapsody (Jamalpur Priority Project), 3015
   Kuulas hetki (Sibelius Academy), 3021
   Live in Helsinki (Värttinä), 3023.1
   Musta (Kurki-Suonio), 3019
   Smash (Troka), 3022
   String Tease (Järvelän Pikkupelimannit), 3016.2
   Tulikulkku, 3027
   Vihma (Värttinä), 3023.2
Fire Crow, Joseph, Jr., *Cheyenne Nation*, 314
Firpo, Roberto, *Instrumental Tangos of the Golden Age*, 876
Fisher, Archie, *The Man with a Rhyme*, 2775
Fitzroy, Eddie, *History of Reggae, Vol.1*, 701
Flames
   Rock Steady, 694
   Rough Guide to Reggae, 695
Flanagan Brothers, *I'm Leaving Tipperary: Classic Irish Traditional Music Recorded in America in the '20s and '30s*, 401
Fleck, Béla
   Putumayo Presents the Best of World Music Vol. 2, 3331.2
   Throw Down Your Heart, African Sessions [2005], 2711
Flex
   La Evolución Romantic Style, 861.1
   Romantic Style: Desde la esencia, Parte 3, 861.2
Floren, Myron, *24 of Polka's Greatest Hits*, 429
Florencia, *Tango around the World*, 3309
Flores, Isabel, *Garifuna Punta Anthology* [1973], 2638
Flush, Paul, *The Northumberland Collection*, 2739
Flying Jazz Queens, *Dark City Sisters and Flying Jazz Queens*, 2607
Fodor, Sándor, *Transylvanian Village Music: From Gypsy, Hungarian, and Romanian Traditions*, 3177

★*Cuban Dance Party*, 612
Cuban son, 614
★*The Rough Guide to the Music of Cuba*, 622
Van Zandt, Townes, *Live at the Old Quarter, Houston, Texas*, 192
Vangu, Dino, *Kin nostalgie*, 2579
Vanuatu. *See* Melanesia
Varela, Carlos
  ★*Cuba Classics 3: Diablo al infierno!* 609
  Monedas al Aire, 603
Vargas, Wilfrido
  Abusadora, 635
  Merengue Dance, 640
Varner, Tom, *The Window up Above: American Songs 1770–1998*, 193
Värttinä
  Live in Helsinki, 3023.1
  Vihma, 3023.2
Väsen
  Live: At the Nordic Roots Festival, 3070.1
  Whirled, 3070.2
Vasori, Patrick, *France: Musiques des provinces: Folk Music*, 2838
Veloso, Caetano
  Caetano Veloso: Songbook, 928.1
  ★*Cantora 1*, 885.1
  Cinema Transcendental, 928.2
  Cores Nomes, 928.3
  Livro, 928.4
  Tropicália 2, 928.4
Venezuala, 1054–1067
  Arpa: Venezuela (Ochoa and Aponte), 1061
  Commercial (Los Amigos Invisibles), 1054
  ★*Dances of Venezuela*, 1064
  Folk Music from Venezuela (Barradas and Maricaibo), 1055
  Fuzionanado (D'León), 1058.2
  La historia de la luz (Orquesta de la Luz), 1062
  Mis canciones (My Songs) (Díaz), 1057
  Music of the Venezuelan Yekuana Indians, 1065
  Music of Venezuela (Granados et al.), 1059
  Nenes con las nenas (Los Melodicos), 1060
  Primera fila (Vita), 1063
  Supremo (Chino & Nacho), 1056
  Tierra del Cacao: Afro-Venezuelan Music and Dance [1986–1995], 2657
  ★*Tranquilamente: Tranquilo* (D'León), 1058.1
  Venezuela: Afro-Venezuelan Music, Vols. 1 and 2, 1066
  Venezuela: Chants et tambours des confreries noires = Chants and Drums of the Black Brotherhoods [1993–1994], 2658
Venezuela: Chants et tambours diablos = Songs and Diablos Durms, 2659
  ★*¡Y que viva Venezuela! Maestros del joropo oriental*, 1067
Venkatesan, T. V., *Shaik Chinna Moula Live in Concert 1973*, 1384
Ventura, Johnny
  20th Anniversary, 1979–1999, 636
  Merengue Dance, 640
Vera, María Teresa
  ★*Cuba Classics 2: Dancing with the Enemy*, 608
  Cuban son, 614
Veretski Pass
  ★*The Rough Guide to Klezmer Revival*, 3440
  Trafik, 3358
Verheijen, Jacques, *Mayn Fayfele = My Little Flute*, 3353
Veseli Muzyky, *From Kiev to the Black Sea: Folk Music from Ukraine*, 3214
Vichules, Ruth, *Mariachi*, 479
Vieja Trova Santiaguera, *Cuban son*, 614
Vietnam, 1544–1569
  Anăk Č' ư' Čhiăng: The Original People of Vietnam's Central Highlands, 1552
  Ethnic Minority Music of North Vietnam, 1553
  ★*Folk Songs of Vietnam*, 1554
  Fragile Beauty (Thanh and Lê), 1550
  Gongs du Vietnam = Vietnamese Gongs, 1555
  Hò! Roady Music from Vietnam 2000, Vol. 1, 1556
  Instrumental Music of Vietnam, 1557
  Moonlight in Vietnam (Khac Chi Ensemble), 1545
  ★*Music from North and South Vietnam: Sung Poetry of the North; Theater Music of the South*, 1558
  Music from Vietnam: Minorities from the Central Highland and Coast, 5, 1559
  The Music of Vietnam, 1560, 1561
  Musique du Théâtre Cai Luong = Cai Luong Theatre Music (Thanh), 1549
  Phạm Duy: Ngày tr'o' ve, Vol. 1 (Duy), 1544
  The Rough Guide to the Music of Vietnam, 1562
  Stilling Time: Ngu' ò'i Ngòi Ru Thò'i Gian: Traditional Musics of Vietnam, 1563
  String Instruments of Vietnam, 1564
  Viet Nam: Traditions of the South, 1569
  Vietnam: Ca tru and quan ho (Traditional Music = Musique Traditionnelle), 1565
  Vietnam: Music from the Lost Kingdom, Huế (Perfume River Traditional Ensemble), 1547
  Vietnam: Musique des Montagnards = Vietnam: Music of the Montagnards, 1566
  Viêt-Nam: musiques et chants des minorités du nord = Northern Vietnam: Music and Songs of the Minorities, 1567
  Vietnam: musiques vocales des plaines du nord = Vocal Music from the Northern Plains: Ca trú, Hát chèo, Quan ho, 1568
  Vietnam: Poésies et chants (Trân and Trân), 1551
  Vietnam: Tradition of the South = Tradition du sud (Nguyên and Trân), 1546
  Vietnamese Folk Theatre: Hát chèo (Quy Bon Family), 1548
Viglietti, Daniel, *Chile: Songs for the Resistance*, 950
Villa, Beto, *Beto Villa, Father of Orquesta Tejana, Vol. 1*, 497
Villarroel, Ligia, *Equateur: Musique des Andes*, 998
Viloria, Angel
  Merengue: Dominican Music and Dominican Identity, 641
  Merengues: 21 éxitos originales, Vol. 1, 637
Vinayakram, T. H., *Eternal Light*, 1398
★*Virgal, Eric, Caribbean Party*, 751
Virgin Islands, U.S., 737–754, 816–820. *See also* Caribbean Islands, Other
  Crucian Scratch Band Music (Blinky and Blinky and the Roadmasters), 816
  Jamesie King of Scratch, 820
  Jamesie King of Scratch (Brewster and Jamesie and the All Stars), 820
  Pumpin' (Stanley and the Ten Sleepless Knights), 818
  Quelbe! Music of the U.S. Virgin Islands (Stanley and the Ten Sleepless Knights), 819
  We Don Skylark [2004] (Brewster), 817
  ★*Zoop Zoop Zoop: Traditional Music and Folklore of St. Croix, St. Thomas, and St. John* [1957–1985], 819
Vistorky, Christian, *Danses Tyroliennes = Tyrolean Dances*, 2818, 2858
Viswanathan, T., *Tribute*, 1404
Vita, Franco de, *Primera fila*, 1063
Vital, Jean, *Rara in Haiti*, 663
Vives, Carlos
  10 de colección, 981.2
  Canta los clásicos del vallenato, 981.1
Vliet, Floor Van der, *Het daghet in den oosten = It's Dawning in the East: Bagpipes of the Low Countries*, 2869
Voces Novae et Antiquae, *Shomeir Yisrael*, 3441

278   INDEX

★Yumurí, *The Rough Guide to Cuban Street Party*, 621
Yun, Chin-ch'ŏl, *Chŏkpyŏkka*, 1240
★Yun, Isang, *Chamber Symphony I*, 1279
Yun, Sŏn-suk, *Two Cycles of the Geomungo Sanjos*, 1241
Yunakov, Yuri
  New Colors in Bulgarian Wedding Music, 3095.1
  Roma Variations, 3095.2
  Together Again, 3096
Yupanqui, Atahualpa, *Mis 30 mejores canciones*, 887
Yurdatapan, Sanar, *Songs of Freedom from Turkey: Behind Prison Bars*, 1995
Yuri Yunakov Ensemble
  New Colors in Bulgarian Wedding Music, 3095.1
  Roma Variations, 3095.2
Yürük, Unal, *Kantigas de Novia = Sephardic Wedding Songs*, 3352
Yuval Ron Ensemble, *Under the Olive Tree: Sacred Music of the Middle East*, 3271

Z

★Los Zafiros, *Cuba Classics 2: Dancing with the Enemy*, 608
Zagreb Folk Dance Ensemble, *Songs and Dances from Croatia*, 3103
Zaiko Langa Langa, *Zaïre-Ghana*, 2581
Zaire. *See* Congo, Democratic Republic of
Zambia, 2535–2538, 2627–2628
  Africa (Amanaz), 2627
  Batonga across the Waters: Music of the Batonga of Zambia and Zimbabwe [1996–1997], 2535
  Kalimba and Kalumbu Songs, Northern Rhodesia, Zambia, 1952 and 1957: Lala, Tonga, Lozi, Mbunda, Bemba, Lunda, 2536
  Music from Petauke, Northern Rhodesia, Vols. 1 and 2 [1961], 2537
  Vol. 1: Zambian Hits from the '80s (Zambush), 2628.1
  Vol. 2: Zambian Hits from the' 60s and '70s (Zambush), 2628.2
  Zambia Roadside: Music from Southern Province [1996], 2538
Zambrano, Jimmy
  De lo nuevo . . . Lo mejor, 963
  Grandes éxitos, 992

Zambush
  Vol. 1: Zambian Hits from the '80s, 2628.1
  Vol. 2: Zambian Hits from the '60s and '70s, 2628.2
Zamir Chorale of Boston
  ★*Italia!: The Renaissance of Jewish Music*, 3362
  A Sho'o in Gan Eyden = An Hour in the Garden of Eden: The Zamir Chorale of Boston Sings Yiddish, 3419
  Zamir Chorale of Boston: Greatest Hits, 3410
Zanes, Dan
  Catch That Train! 199
  Catch That Train! (Zanes), 199
  Parades and Panoramas: 25 Songs Collected by Carl Sandburg for the American Songbag, 200
  Parades and Panoramas: 25 Songs Collected by Carl Sandburg for the American Songbag (Zanes and Sandburg), 200
  Sunny Day, 154
Zap Mama
  Adventures in Afropea, 1, 3298
  Supermoon, 2595
  Zap Mama, 2829
★Zaruba, Karl, *Folk Dances of Austria*, 2815
★Zarzatian, Hagop Jack, *Armenian Music through the Ages*, 3138
Zawose, Hukwe U., *Tanzanie: Chants des Wagogo et des Kuria*, 2359
Zayas, Edwin Colón, *Putumayo Presents Puerto Rico*, 715
Zayas, Edwin Colon and Taller Campesino, *Bien jibaro!* 802
★Zeami, *Noh and Kyogen Plays*, 1178
Zein Musical Party, *Mtindo Wa Mombasa: The Style of Mombasa*, 2308
Zekra
  Wa Tabka Zekra, 1865.1
  Wesh Maseeri, 1865.2
  Youm Liek, 1865.3
Zemel Choir, *The English Tradition of Jewish Choral Music*, 3371
★Zeus, *Cuba Classics 3: Diablo al infierno!* 609
Zhang, Huimei, *Mei li zui jing xuan = A-mei best, 1996–2002*, 1145

Zhang, Qiang, *Music of the Piba*, 1107
Zhou, Jielun, *Initial: Jay Chou Greatest Hits*, 1146
Zhou, Lo, *Tales from the Cave*, 1139
Zhu, Changyao, *Erhu: The Art of Zhu Changyao*, 1108
Ziegler, Robert, *Berlin Cabaret Songs*, 2856
Zikaza, *Miki Goes to Nuussuaq*, 3029
Zimbabwe, 2539–2543, 2629–2632
  The Chimurenga Singles 1976–1980 (Mapfumo and Blacks Unlimited), 2630.1
  Gwindingwi Rine Shumba (Mapfumo and Blacks Unlimited), 2630.2
  The Kankobela of the Batonga, Vols. 1 and 2 [2008; 1996, 2008], 2539
  Other Musics from Zimbabwe 1948, '49, '51, '58, '63, Southern Rhodesia: Ndau, Sena, Tonga, Shona, 2540
  Shumba: Vital Hits of Zimbabwe (Mapfumo and Blacks Unlimited), 2630.3
  Talking Mbira (Chiweshe), 2629
  Tuku Music (Mtukudzi et al.), 2631
  Zimbabwe Frontline: Spirit of the Eagle, Vol. 2, 2632
  Zimbabwe: Shona Mbira Music [1977], 2541
  Zimbabwe: The Ndebele People [1989], 2542
  ★*Zimbabwe: The Soul of Mbira: Traditions of the Shona People* [1973], 2543
Ziminska-Sygietynska, Mira, *Polish Folk Music*, 3168
Zin, *Haiti chéri*, 661
Zion, Jacob, *Out of Babylon: The Music of Baghdadi-Jewish Migrations into Asia and Beyond*, 3393
Ziskakan, *Ziskakan*, 2419
★Zmiros Project, *The Rough Guide to Klezmer Revival*, 3440
★Zomhlaba, Izingqungqulu, *Rough Guide to the Music of South Africa*, 2633
Zorn, John, *Zohar*, 3429
★Zrihan, Emil, *The Hidden Gate: Jewish Music around the World*, 3390
Zumi-Kai Original Instrumental Group, *Koto Music of Japan*, 1169
Zydeco, 261–276
Zydeco Experience, *Live Worldwide*, 274